Rhapsody

Lethe Press
Maple Shade, New Jersey

Rhapsody

NOTES ON STRANGE FICTIONS

Hal Duncan

Rhapsody: *Notes on Strange Fictions*
Copyright © 2014 Hal Duncan. ALL RIGHTS RESERVED. No part of this work may be reproduced or utilized in any form or by any means, electronic or mechanical, including photocopying, microfilm, and recording, or by any information storage and retrieval system, without permission in writing from the publisher.

Published in 2014 by Lethe Press, Inc.
118 Heritage Avenue, Maple Shade, NJ 08052 USA
lethepressbooks.com / lethepress@aol.com
ISBN: 978-1-59021-261-5 / 1-59021-261-4
e-ISBN: 978-1-59021-093-2 / 1-59021-093-x

Earlier versions of some of this work first appeared on the author's blog, http://notesfromthegeekshow.blogspot.com/

Set in Garamond and Goudy Old Style.
Interior design: Alex Jeffers.
Cover image: Stijn Windig, www.stijnwindig.com
Cover design: Matt Cresswell.

LIBRARY OF CONGRESS CATALOGING-IN-PUBLICATION DATA
Duncan, Hal, 1971- author.
 Rhapsody : Notes on Strange Fictions / Hal Duncan.
      pages cm
 ISBN 978-1-59021-261-5 (pbk. : alk. paper)
 1. Science fiction, American--History and criticism. 2. Science fiction, English--History and criticism. 3. Fantasy fiction, American--History and criticism. 4. Fantasy fiction, English--History and criticism. I. Title.
 PS374.S35D86 2014
 813'.0876209--dc23
                    2013049996

Contents

Introduction: SF Considered as a Subset of SF	1
PART 1	29
Down in the Ghetto at the SF Café	31
The Marriage(s) of Science Fiction and Fantasy	51
The Miscegenation of Science Fantasy	70
The Scourge of Sci-Fi	89
The Spelunkers of Speculative Fiction	107
The Ghost and the Golem	125
PART 2	143
The Combat Fiction Bar & Grill	145
The Booker and the Bistro de Critique	161
The Kipple Foodstuff Factory	183
The Secret Cuisine	203
The Order of the Blue Flower	224
The Tower of Mimeticists' Bicuspids	246

To Delany and Disch; to all the cartographers of the strange, too many to mention, whose work has spurred this exploration.

Introduction:
SF Considered as a Subset of SF

—of SF Considered as a Subset—

If this appears that I am arguing for a deconstruction of our ideas of generic norms, returning us to a primal chaos of fictive forms in which all fictive forms are equally privileged; if this appears that I am arguing for the dismantling of the concept itself, "science fiction," as more a barrier than an aid to reading; if this seems as if I am saying that all fiction worth examining is, one way or another, science fiction; it is because that is what I am doing.
Frank McConnell

There are countless definitions of SF, innumerable attempts to characterise the type of fiction read by the regulars of the SF Café, from the boundless generality of the laziest catch-all down to the most limited and limiting specificities of those who would claim that only their SF is *really* SF. I've never found the more specific definitions terribly convincing, and I've never found them terribly useful. If they ever held true at all, it was long before I stepped through the doors of the SF Café with a borrowed copy of Isaac Asimov's *I, Robot* in my hand, expecting to find more of the same, only to find Philip K. Dick sitting at a table, obsessing over Gnostic demiurges and ersatz realities, Robert A. Heinlein across from him, spouting libertarian aphorisms but paying for Dick's coffee. The talk at that table was as much philosophy as science, as much monsters and messiahs as spaceships and simulacra. Palmer Eldritch and Valentine Michael Smith fought, like Zoroastrian deities, over my soul.

Framed cinema posters adorned the walls—for *Forbidden Planet*, *Invasion of the Body Snatchers* and *Star Wars*, for *A Clockwork Orange*, *Solaris* and *The Man Who Fell to Earth*. On the TV set up on the wall in one corner, as the channels flicked through the decades, old serials like *Flash Gordon*, *Buck Rogers*, *King of the Rocket Men* gave way to reruns of *Lost in Space*, *Land of the Giants*, *The Time Tunnel*, these replaced in turn by *The Twilight Zone*, *The Outer Limits*, *Tales from the Crypt*, by *Star Trek*, *Battlestar Galactica* and *Buck Rogers in the 25th Century*, by *The Six Million Dollar Man*, *Knight Rider*, *Manimal*, by *The Lost Room* and *The Lost World* and just plain fucking *Lost*. These last three seemed a little strange given that this was the 1980s and the series didn't actually exist yet, but I was too overawed to notice the temporal anomaly.

—What the fuck is this place? I asked.

—It's not FANTASY, said one old-timer, and it's not SCI-FI. Ignore those freaks over in the corner if they try to tell you different.

Over where he pointed, Tolkien sat in one booth, surrounded by acolytes, droning on in Elvish. I'd read *The Lord of the Rings*, all one million pages of trees, fight, trees, fight, trees, fight, and all six billion pages of Frodo and Sam climbing up a mountain at the end. I'd read a few Shannara books too, and it wasn't my bag. It was years since I'd read *The Borribles* and years until I'd read *The Book of Sand*, so I didn't think twice about who was sitting in the *other* booths. So the SF Café wasn't that FANTASY malarkey? I was down with that. At the end of the counter there wasn't even a writer, just some actor signing autographs for a bunch of geeks in Halloween costumes—Vulcans and Klingons, Doctor Who and Davros, the entire cast of *Blake's 7*. I was a typical teen, all too keen to abjure the puerile to prove my maturity, oblivious of how essentially adolescent that is, so I didn't think twice about Patrick McGoohan's Number Six, sat brooding at the other end of the counter, barking clipped defiance with Pinteresque subtexts. So it wasn't this SCI-FI business either? I could deal with that. But still…

—So what *is* it? I asked.

The old-timer shrugged and waved a hand to encompass everything surrounding us, the very ambience of the place.

—SF, he said.

So Fuck?

Science Fiction is anything published as Science Fiction.
Norman Spinrad

What I would glean over the years was that, as far as I could tell, SF had long since become a marketing label more than anything, an arbitrary lumping-together of diverse works defying definition. For many readers, writers, editors and agents, that old-timer's shrug seems pretty much the working (in)definition: SF is short for *So Fuck?* And I would discover that FANTASY could also be defined, if one so wishes, as whatever can be sold as *fantasy*, that SCI-FI was a term equally arbitrary in its application. These are simply nominal labels, circularly defined; they can't be argued with for that reason, but they also, for that reason, serve no real purpose, other than the obvious commercial and (sub)cultural ones—as banners to gather the faithful under or to strike fear into the hearts of unbelievers.

Science Fiction is what I mean when I point to it.
Damon Knight

I sit here now in the SF Café, on my stool up at the counter, scribbling these notes from the city of New Sodom. It has occurred to me to begin an investigation, an enquiry into the nature of the forms and functions of this strange field of strange fictions. Perhaps a sociography of SF in some form, the life and times of the SF Café, to provide some context, but not so much *historical* as *political*, a bit of bolshie heresy, a shamelessly subjective polemic on the turf wars of pulp, woven through with the theory of what's *actually* going on in the texts. Or perhaps another angle to start? Maybe an overview of all the varied definitions, all the methods and modes of SF they represent. The ghetto is a complicated place. It has walls for all its different zones, some sealing their own little quarter off from the rest, many reinforcing the boundaries between the ghetto and the outside world.

I should abjure the marketing labels, I think—SCIENCE FICTION or FANTASY—don't want to risk the assumption that I'm talking, with any of these definitions, about some singular coherent GENRE which these variant models could or could not, should or should not, be applied to. No, let's instead invent a new label for each definition, or for each *type* of definition. The point is to examine the multiplicity of features, not to end up in pointless bickering over which of these features are required or forbidden if some work is to be called SF. For ease of reference, and for the sheer bloody-minded whimsy of it, let's make all of these labels abbreviate to *SF*, each of these SFs to be considered its own SF, an SF which may not be yours and may not be mine, but which probably belongs to someone out there. Each could be considered a gateway out into the wider galaxy of SF that each sparkly gem of an SF is a subset of, each definition with its own guardians, those who would say this *is* SF.

Let's mark out those gates and gatekeepers on our map.

Scientific Fancy

The best definition of science fiction is that it consists of stories in which one or more definitely scientific notion or theory or actual discovery is extrapolated, played with, embroidered on, in a non-logical, or fictional sense, and thus carried beyond the realm of the immediately possible in an effort to see how much fun the author and reader can have exploring the imaginary outer reaches of a given idea's potentialities.
Groff Conklin

This is, perhaps, the SF that existed before Old Man Campbell, the SF that Gernsback was looking for. In its weaker form, this content-based definition of SF simply requires the presence of an element of vaguely rational futurology, extrapolated out into background, plot, etc. The speculation need not be a locus of metaphoric or metonymic meaning; a fancy rather than a conceit, it may function as little more than a superficial justification for the Romantic adventure story structures. This SF is simply *fantasy*, some might say, with the fanciful element rationalised in terms of science or technology. A better term would be fantasia.

> *Science fiction is a branch of fantasy identifiable by the fact that it eases the "willing suspension-of-disbelief" on the part of its readers by utilizing an atmosphere of science credibility for its imaginative speculations in physical science, space, time, social science and philosophy.*
>
> Sam Moskowitz

Sam Lundwall's distinction between SF (with explanation) and fantasy (with no explanation) might also be considered here. Despite the differentiation, he focuses more on the "gimmick" of an explanation than on the actual rigour of the extrapolation, just as Moskowitz focuses on the "atmosphere of science credibility" and Conklin on the sense of play. Further, in his characterisation of the speculative element as one that might develop "from known science or from investigations of areas not yet quite explored but suspected," that last clause provides the backdoor of a Paradigm Shift Caveat by which metaphysics and magic (e.g. FTL or ESP) can sneak into SF, with a wave of the hand and a mutter of *hyper-space* or *untapped human potential*. Working by this type of definition, the writer may play fast and loose with even the laws of physics. As long as the reader comes along for the ride, then it's still seen as SF—scientific fancy, that is.

There are pros and cons to this scientific fancy, as there are with any form of SF. In using extrapolation largely to build the environment in which the story takes place or to create some technological MacGuffin as a plot device in a Romantic adventure narrative structure (some planet-destroying Doomsday Machine to save the Earth from, an Unobtainium Drive to power a spaceship built in one's back yard, a network of interstellar portals built by an ancient race), scientific fancy is all about the ripping yarn. Often this SF crosses over with YA and serves as excellent entry-level fiction for the new reader, seeing as it's a whole lot of fun. The downside is that all too often the result is a shallow Boy's Own SPACE OPERA or MILITARY SF that feeds the perception of SF being solely for teenage boys; and all too often it's so deeply plot-oriented it neglects character and thus feeds the perception that SF has no depth and therefore is not *literature*. Romanticism has some neat tricks, but it also has a lot of…well…posturing adolescent bollocks.

So, many people talk of "growing out of SF" when they're really just leaving behind those juvenile power fantasies, never having got past the entry-level adventuring of scientific fancy.

A different type of barrier might be why some readers never get past the entry-level, but this is better illustrated with the next type of SF…

Scientific Fabrication

> *[Science fiction] is fiction about the future of science and scientists.*
> **Isaac Asimov**

In its stronger form the content-based definition of SF specifically turns the whole focus of the story onto science in terms of character, background and plot, not only regarding the scientific speculation as essential but requiring its centrality and expecting a degree of rigour in its treatment.

> *Fiction in which new and futuristic scientific developments propel the plot.*
> **Harper Handbook of Literature**

What is important to this SF is that the narrative itself must turn upon the science, not just as a plot device but as a driving force (the Three Laws of Robotics as the premises of the story's logic, the von Neumann machines that run amok, the replicant that considers itself alive). The speculation is not a fancy upon which the story is built and from which it could ultimately be separated out. Rather, it is a *fabrication*—act and artefact, the process through which the story is constructed and the product which remains integral to the finished text, just as the *investigation* of a mystery is in the MYSTERY novel.

> *Science fiction is the branch of literature that deals with the effects of change on people in the real world as it can be projected into the past, the future, or to distant places. It often concerns itself with scientific or technological change, and it usually involves matters whose importance is greater than the individual or the community; often the civilization or the race itself is in danger.*
> **James Gunn**

This scientific fabrication is perhaps what most within the community think of when they think of SF—the "what if" story formed by reaching out into the wilds of the hypothetical, the counterfactual, the metaphysical, grabbing a little (or not so little) seed of unreality, drawing it back into our world, planting it in the fertile soil of the imagination, and letting it grow. Pruning it back, wiring its branches, shaping its insanely accelerated development in the bonsai art of narrative.

As an exercise in the logic of imagination, scientific fabrication is often valued more highly than scientific fancy, as a more intellectual approach, but it serves us well to remember that the "what if?" scenario might well lead to exactly the same Romantic adventure plot structure. What if there was a world-destroying Doomsday Machine the hero had to save the Earth from? What if the hero invented an Unobtainium Drive to power a spaceship built in their back yard? What if the hero was called in to investigate a network of interstellar portals built by an ancient race? Add the Paradigm Shift Caveat into the equation and allow that process of fabrication to be run as much by the logic of story as by the logic of reality, and we may well simply end up back at scientific fancy, with lightweight literature that will not be taken seriously.

> *The term can be applied only to a story in which wherein removal of its scientific content would invalidate the narrative.*
> **Theodore Sturgeon**

A more important potential point of failure for this SF, though, is where the logic of reality is incomplete, where a focus on the intellectual appeal of the thought experiment, its results and ramifications, carries with it a neglect of other aspects of reality—human motivation, the logic of affect. A syllogism is not a story. An algorithm is not an anecdote. What a reader of this SF finds intriguing in its exploration of an abstract idea, may seem far less intriguing to a reader more concerned with behaviour than biology, more interested in characters than chemistry, fascinated more by personal flaws than particle physics. Fiction that fails to engage an audience with the emotional intricacies of viable characters will, for many in that audience, simply alienate them with its profound irrelevance at the human level. If scientific fancy risks reading as if it were written by and for the adolescent, scientific fabrication also risks reading as if it were written by and for the precocious prepubescent, the pint-size Spock as yet oblivious to sex, death, and other such shitstorms of adult experience.

Unfortunately, this risk is exacerbated by one attempt to deal with the first potential weakness—the Romantic nonsenses of scientific fancy—by rejecting the Paradigm Shift Caveat entirely, precluding the presence of any element in the story which breaches scientific orthodoxy. As understandable as it is, as an attempt to force a seriousness onto the form via rationality and rigour, this next definition of SF largely just pushes the uninitiated reader's interest to breaking point.

Scientistic Fabrication

> *Realistic speculation about possible future events, based solidly on adequate knowledge of the real world, past and present, and on a thorough understanding of the nature and significance of the scientific method.*
> **Robert A. Heinlein**

This type of definition may adopt a wide or narrow scope in terms of what exactly constitutes realistic speculation, where the boundaries lie between the sciences and the humanities. At its very narrowest we have Campbell rejecting sociology and psychology, establishing the sort of strictures that bind a core of HARD SF to the hard sciences—mathematics, physics, chemistry, biology. At its widest, with the soft sciences considered fair game, all manner of utopian, dystopian and heterotopian fictions founded on politics and ethics may be considered as within the form. But even at its most encompassing, this type of definition remains qualitatively different from scientific fancy or even scientific fabrication in one clear respect: its exclusion of the metaphysical.

The inexplicable, the irrational, the *metaphysical* is something of a sticking point for some SF writers. Rooted deep in a Rationalist worldview, refusing to accept the limitations of reason, they reject a whole form of conceit allowed by other forms of SF. Where scientific fancy and scientific fabrication are predicated solely on the inclusion of a certain speculative element, this scientistic fabrication is predicated also on the exclusion of another element, often referred to as *magic*.

> *It is the premise of science fiction that anything shown shall in principle be interpretable empirically and rationally. In science fiction there can be no inexplicable marvels, no transcendence, no devils or demons—and the patterns of occurrence must be verisimilar.*
> **Stanislaw Lem**

This is an SF that many of its advocates will insist defines the core of the genre—an SF where the science must be wholly central and wholly rigourous, and where the metaphysical/magical is absolutely unacceptable. Regardless of the number of works this stricture exiles from the canon, the advocates of scientistic fabrication insist there are no shadows in their world. The universe is, for them, laid flat and bare by reason's light, there are no shadows anywhere. None of Dick's dead gods. None of Bradbury's ghost Martians. There is no mystery that cannot be unravelled in this type of fiction.

Not the easiest sell to the incognoscenti perhaps. There are those who do not find science exciting in and of itself, who are not thrilled by the enigma of theories beyond their understanding, or the sudden moments of comprehension when those theories are made clear through fictive explorations. These readers will be left cold by fiction utterly enrapt with science, if they are not scared off from even reading it by the fear it will be full of calculus and other such mathematical bogeymen. Lacking even a rudimentary understanding of what is or isn't possible, they may well see the whole narrative problem as irrelevant. If they are not alienated by incomprehension, they may feel utterly deflated by a mundane explanation.

These are not, of course, intrinsic certainties, only inherent risks, and in their determination to apply intellect to the form, the scientistic fabricators have undeniably pushed SF into new territories, beyond the Romantic adventures of scientific fancy, beyond even the "what if" scenarios of scientific fabrication. This is, in part, the worldview that gives us the MUNDANE SF movement with its resolute commitment to authenticity, not simply as an end in and of itself, rigour for the sake of rigour, but as an antidote to wish-fulfilment, as an ethical dedication to tackling the actual problems of this world's most likely future(s), addressing issues like global warming in terms of feasible hypotheticals rather than fantasising about aliens and AI. For the scientistic fabricators, to whom *fantasy* equals *fancy*, which is to say whimsy as a mere diversion, this is the very real and very important purpose of SF.

Of course, there are those who disagree completely.

Scientific Fabulation

Science fiction is not fiction about science, but fiction which endeavors to find the meaning in science and in the scientific technology we are constructing.
Judith Merril

Definitions of SF are not all predicated on the presence or absence of a certain type of content. In the differentiation between *fancy* and *fabrication* it should be clear that much of the distinction between modes is in terms of *process* rather than *content*. Where writers treat our scientific culture as a source of metaphor, with one or more scientific fancies exploited as conceits, extended through the body of the narrative, where the science is not merely plot device or structural basis but becomes the locus of theme, the stuff of story, what we have is not just fabrication but *fabulation*.

> *In his* Strategies of Fantasy, *Brian Attebery shows how science fiction uses science as its "megatext." The nourishing medium, the origin of the imagery, the motive of the narrative, is to be found in the contents, assumptions, and world view of modern*

> *science and technology.* "*Science [writes Attebery] surrounds, supports, and judges SF in much the same way the Bible grounds Christian devotional poetry.*"
> **Ursula K. Le Guin**

There is no explicit exclusion of the metaphysical in this SF; it is scientific rather than scientistic. In its thematic focus on the relationship between science and humanity it is arguable that this SF is more likely to treat any metaphysical forces, events or agencies it might utilise as either open to rational explication or of secondary import, but this is not necessarily the case.

With many of the works of Philip K. Dick, the process of fabulation is largely focused on metaphysical conceits, albeit embedded within a context of scientific fabulation (i.e. fabulation using futurology); this does not exclude them from this definition of SF. Where scientistic fabrication often situates the purpose of SF in *literal* explorations of its conceits, this SF is all about *literary* exploration.

Playing fast and loose with probability may simply result in the whimsy of scientific fancy, but it is important to remember that even an idea we know to be impossible can have profound import, playing on our desires or fears, tempting or terrifying us. This is why that mode of SF is so thrilling. The shock of the new and the intrigue of complexity are integral aspects of the conceit's power. Reining in the whimsy can make the process of constructing the narrative around that conceit more rational, more logical, which is where fancy becomes fabrication. Where the conceit is used metaphorically, (or more correctly, pataphorically,) the theme of the fiction extrapolated, developed with the narrative structure—this is where the process becomes *fabulation*.

> *[A] fictional exploration of human situations made perceptible by the implications of recent science. Its favourite themes involve the impact of developments or revelations derived from the human or physical sciences upon the people who must live with those revelations or developments.*
> **Robert Scholes**

In Jeffrey Ford's *The Portrait of Mrs. Charbuque*, a jaded painter is challenged to paint an accurate portrait of a woman he will never see, constructing his visual image of her from the life story she tells him while hidden behind a screen. Ford's novel could be tagged as Fantasy, playing as it does with the dream of muses and sibyls, of divination. But as a novel predicated on and explicating its conceit as a source of meaning, it is a work of fabulation.

In Mark Z. Danielewski's *House of Leaves*, a Pulitzer-prize-winning photojournalist begins a documentary on his own family's arrival in a suburban dream-house, which becomes an exploration of the house's disturbingly impossible inner architecture, this narrative framed within that of an LA waster who is reconstructing the journals of a dead blind man into an analytic study of this film. Danielewski's novel could be tagged as HORROR, playing as it does with a nightmare of labyrinths and catacombs, of death. But as a novel predicated on and explicating its conceit as a source of meaning, it is a work of fabulation.

> *Science fiction, then, commonly uses techniques both from the realistic and the fantastic traditions of narrative to tell a story of which a referent, implicit or explicit, is the mind-set, the content, or the mythos of science and technology.*
> **Ursula K. Le Guin**

Fantasy and horror, like SF, are rich with such conceits, are often predicated on such conceits. Both, like SF, breach the everyday world of realism with the strange, the unfamiliar, with unrealities which could only be possible in some elsewhen where things work differently. Both, like SF, exploit our emotional reaction to the potentiality of these unrealities being made real; and it is this as much as anything that defines whether a story is seen as SF and/or fantasy and/or horror. Could it happen? Should it happen? Must it *never* happen? It is because our reactions are complex that these three forms do not just coexist as separate types of imaginative fiction but rather constantly cross-breed, feeding into/off one another. The literary utility of fabulation, the metaphoric focus of it, indeed, is why many works of fabulation are simply labelled magical realism or general fiction.

Where do we distinguish scientific fabulation, then, from fabulation in general? In SF, those conceits, drawn from the field of science, may *tend* to be more rational, separating SF from fantasy and horror in terms of plausibility. Fantasy and horror may also *tend* to be more closely aligned with the unconscious and its desires and fears, the fiery stuff of the imagination, less audaciously/arrogantly Promethean than SF which wilfully tries to bend the irrational to its will, hammer it into rational shape, invest it with a clear purpose. Revelling in the intellectual aspects of the conceits rather than the sensational, SF tends to be the form of fabulation least obviously in thrall to the unconscious.

Bester's PyrE is the conceit of many SF writers, at heart. Writers of this SF are not theoreticians but technicians, less concerned with the futurologies than with the creative application of those as conceits, as tools, the technology of writing itself. At best they are craftsmen and artificers working with what Joyce termed "the smithy of the soul." This is the process of scientific fabulation and it's why this SF is a fundamentally modernist enterprise, its best writers, like Bester—like Bester's character Gully Foyle—part everyman and part Prometheus. It is no coincidence that Bester gives a nod to Joyce's *Portrait of the Artist as a Young Man*, in basing his hero's rhyme, "Gully Foyle is my name…" on that of Joyce's protagonist, Stephen Dedalus. In *The Stars My Destination*, Bester tears the text apart towards the end to do his Burning Man justice, a thoroughly modernist technique. The ambitious drive of this SF is what really characterises it, the audacity it has to create and use the wildest of conceits, to concretise the metaphoric, render it pataphor. In that respect, it is a world away from any formulaic fare it is sold beside, bound to like Prometheus manacled to his rock, dreaming of the day those chains crumble away, the day SF shakes off its rusting ties to formula, stands up straight and proud.

Albeit at the same time essentially clinging to that dead hunk of stone for the security it offers.

Scientific fabulation has more traction in the mainstream than any of the modes of SF outlined above. By not focusing on science or on a Romantic adventure plot structure, it becomes more accessible and less generic. The reader only has to accept a few strange conceits, maybe just one Big Idea, and that conceit is developed in the familiar literary mode of extended metaphor. The greatest risk of this mode is that it becomes too abstract and arbitrary for a reader seeking the easy read of a holiday pot-boiler, a reader to whom the concrete metaphors of the conceit remain unparsed, the work read literally, as fancy or fabrication.

In the next mode of SF those conceits are equally as integral, but however abstract they might be they are far from arbitrary. In the SF of the next definition what we find is not simply fabulation but something that engages at a deeper level than the intellectual, a mode of SF not just sensational but profoundly so. The result is not fable but *myth*.

Soul Fiction

> *[Science fiction] is the myth-making principle of human nature today.*
> **Lester del Rey**

Another type of definition based on the effects of the process treats SF as the mythology of the Modern Age, as the form of fiction which renders physical forces, events and agencies with the same *import* and to the same *purpose* as the pre-industrial religious literature rendered metaphysical forces, events and agencies. In other words, SF is not structurally but *functionally* distinct.

> *Science fiction is a form of fantastic fiction which exploits the imaginative perspectives of modern science.*
> **David Pringle**

This is SF as soul fiction, the mythopoeic mode of writing that creates, intentionally or otherwise, the mythology of the Modern Era. This is where SF and fantasy converge most clearly, even where fantasy is closely-defined in terms of the affective import of its imagery, the evocation of not just incredulity but *awe*, Yeats's *terrible beauty*. It is this emotional resonance that is at the heart of the mythic, the impact of the marvellous and/or the monstrous, in imagery charged with desire and/or dread.

> *Science fiction frequently tries to imagine what life would be like on a plane as far above us as we are above savagery; its setting is often of a kind that appears to us technologically miraculous. It is thus a mode of romance with a strong tendency to myth.*
> **Northrop Frye**

The tendency that Frye identifies, for romance to become myth, is the tendency for the imagery of awe to become archetypal. If not innate, not *natural* metaphors as Jung would have it, archetypes can be understood as, at the very least, root metaphors of the culture, *resonant* metaphors of the psyche primed by it. One might well understand them, I would argue, as *recursive* metaphors, with multiple signifiers pointing to each other (earth pointing to mother, mother pointing to earth, for example), setting up a feedback loop of connotative import, with the resultant icon-combos gaining a yet further intensity of import from their utility as signifiers of components of the psyche—persona, anima, id, self, ego, shadow, senex.

> *Science fiction is the myth of machine civilization, which, in its utopian extrapolation, it tends to glorify.*
> **Mark R. Hillegas**

Where such archetypes inhabit its marvels, SF becomes soul fiction, enacting the psychodramas and oneiric odysseys of the Modern Era. So we find Bester's *The Stars My Destination* not just as a retelling of *The Count of Monte Cristo* but as a re-enactment of the Prometheus myth, with Gully Foyle as thief of fire, thief of PyrE, and distributor of it to humanity. Insofar as fantasy and horror can and often do work in the same mythopoeic manner, the three become functionally equivalent, the main distinction(s) lying simply in SF's preference for the contemporary iconography of the Machine Age over the retrograde pseudo-historical iconography more common in fantasy, or in the tendencies of fantasy and horror to become rapt in desire and fear, to cast the mythic in a simplistic positive or negative role, to ease the terrible beauty of awe more towards the beauty or the terror.

For the middlebrow, middle-class reader of contemporary realism set at the kitchen-sink or in the drawing-room, a reader perhaps looking more for melodrama than for myth, this soul fiction may bear little relation to their mundane lives. They don't want profundity; they want perception, the witty observational insights of *High Fidelity* or *Bridget Jones's Diary*. More concerned about their work-life and relationship issues, they don't want mythic resonance, universal import; they want break-ups and break-downs, mid-life crises and monetary problems. This sense of irrelevance may well be deepened by the key risk of soul fiction, the tendency for it to degenerate into crude monomyth and become indistinguishable from Romance, to all intents and purposes. As much as the Hero's Journey can be read as a fictional enacting of the individuation process, the endless regurgitations of it serve less as psychodramas leading the reader to maturity than as attempts to extend adolescence through a never-ending succession of retellings of the same old rites-of-passage story, "The Emperor of Everything," as Spinrad put it.

The attempt to redress the risk of irrelevance by humanising the archetypal, grounding it in wider stories of societies and politics, wars and rebellions that are not simply a single Hero's psychodramatic tale, are a constituent factor in the next mode of SF.

Spectaculist Fabrication

Stories and spectacle are what command attention in the cultural commons—which is just to say that the exploration of the representational power of language is where the real power is at. (And there's no social or aesthetic canvas better, I personally think, than epic fantasy).

R. Scott Bakker

The misconceived conflations of fantasy with Epic Fantasy and of Epic Fantasy with the formulated regurgitations of the Hero's Journey born from derivations and degradations of soul fiction obscure the centrality that the epic form has its place in SF as much as in fantasy. If we ignore the content-based definitions that lump distinct aesthetic idioms together as "fat fantasy" while disregarding the equivalent "fat SF," we are in a better position to build a picture of a type of SF with its own processes and purposes, akin to those we have identified but distinguishable in its own right. This epic SF (or SF/F) is what I term spectaculist fabrication.

The spectaculist fabrication of epic SF is functionally identical to that of Fantasy or Alternate History, the difference being largely in the nature of the conceit—hypothetical as opposed to metaphysical or counterfactual—rather than in how or whether the conceit is utilised. Whether excused by convention, explicated via exhaustive worldbuilding, or some mixture of the two, the conceits of this mode serve to fabricate an elsewhen in which story-as-spectacle can be unleashed. That process of fabrication is more obvious in the secondary world fiction drawing on the extensible chivalric romance tradition of works like *Amadis de Gaula*, building marvellous backdrops, CGI grandiosities of castles, mountains and battles against which the human-level drama takes place. But it is there to be found also in the serial Space Opera form.

> *In this kind of story the pseudo-scientific apparatus is to be taken simply as a "machine" in the sense which that word bore for the Neo-Classical critics. The most superficial appearance of plausibility—the merest sop to our critical intellect—will do. I am inclined to think that frankly supernatural methods are best. I took a hero once to Mars in a space-ship, but when I knew better I had angels convey him to Venus. Nor need the strange worlds, when we get there, be at all strictly tied to scientific probabilities. It is their wonder, or beauty, or suggestiveness that matter.*
> **C. S. Lewis**

In spectaculist fabrication, the Paradigm Shift Caveat breaks down any real distinction between scientific and non-scientific conceits, the fabricated worlds becoming simply elsewhens. If the past is another country, so too is the future—the broad canvas-cosmos of Herbert's *Dune* series, Banks's Culture novels, and so on, mapped in the details of political fault-lines and technological territories, details of individuals and factions and city-state worlds and federation nations, material and ideological diversity. In some respects, people do things differently there; in others, they don't. There is worldbuilding and window-dressing in spectaculist fabrication, in the structural and superficial detailing of the environment in which the narrative takes place, out of which it emerges (or under which it is submerged, swamped, stomped.)

What distinguishes this from scientific fancy is not the structural nature of the conceit in terms of plot, but rather the structural nature of that conceit in terms of *mode*, the way in which the overload of detail serves to establish the epic scale of the narrative. Tragic and comic narratives are companions to this epic form insofar as they exploit the monstrous and the absurd, building to crises of horror or hilarity; similarly, this epic form exploits the incredible, building to a crisis of awe, of spectacle, the detailed backdrop an intrinsic aspect of this, import magnified by the widescreen CinemaScope environment, the scale of the drama elevated.

> *Ortega y Gasset says that the epic is the genre that is about other times and which is completely distant from our lives. To its own, one will want to say. What a lack of imagination. How does he not see that the epic is there continually in life; how he doesn't describe it in the Spanish Civil War.*
> **Jorge Luis Borges**

The epic narrative is one in which the importance of spectacle cannot be overstated. This is not merely the extensible episodic formulae of Romances in which the dramatic climax may be spectacular but doesn't really function as a *crisis of spectacle*; the extensibility of the episodic formulae predicate against spectacle as structural component in this way, making it more difficult to scale up the spectacle as required with each point of resolution.

What defines this mode is the apotheotic climax where the drama dwarfs all that has come before—Spartacus on his cross at the head of that long road of crucifixions, or El Cid on his horse, riding into battle even in death, the ultimate crisis of spectacle being, of course, the hero's death. So, in this epic spectaculist fabrication we find the Doomsday Devices, the Destroyers of Worlds. If these are themselves averted at the last minute you can be sure they will go out with a bang. In spectaculist fabrication, the cardinal rule is Shit Blows Up.

The risk of this mode of SF is simple: that it blows its wad too early. The first *Star Wars* trilogy may serve as a good example in that respect, the attack on the Death Star and Luke's showdown with Vader serving well as crises of spectacle for each movie, and as seeming steps towards a supreme crisis in the final instalment. The Luke-Vader showdown may seem to be on a smaller scale than the Death Star attack, but its symbology is a ramping up of spectacle, raising the stakes with revelations, mutilations and virtual annihilation of the hero (both physically and mentally) in a good old-fashioned Fall into the Abyss. The third movie fails however, collapsing from epic mode into the episodic formulae of Romance in its regurgitation of the previous two crises together, with the introduction of the Emperor into the showdown failing to provide any substantial raising of the stakes. With the spectacularity levelled off, the viewer is left with a dramatic climax but not the full-on *crisis* of spectacle actually required, like raising a foot to take a step and finding that the step isn't there.

The fourth movie, we might add, *Episode None: The Phantom Plot*, collapses completely into formulaic Romance in its failure to provide anything even remotely resembling a crisis of spectacle. It has no sense whatsoever of spectacularity building, as I recall—insofar as I *can* recall, that is, something so instantly forgettable. It is simply the enaction of a Romantic adventure against marvellous backdrops, the CGI grandiosities of little import in dramatic terms.

What it becomes is what Lucas is pastiching, the generic formula fiction of the next mode of SF.

Symbolic Formulation

Science fiction will always offer easier alternatives. Science fiction will always be slanted, by definition, to taking its readers out of the world. Only weak people, however–pat Freudianism and the great cult psychology movements of the seventies have taught us–want out of the world. Strong people want in. Strong people want to,

must deal with life as it is presented. Science fiction is a literature for the weak, the defenceless, the handicapped and the scorned. Panacea and pap.
Barry N. Malzberg

SF, we are told, is all about the tropes, the conventions of structures and symbols. This is what GENRE is, how it works, through conventions born of copying (conventions changed, perhaps, subverted by alterations introduced during the process of copying, but essentially still copies of copies). SF is recognised as SF by these conventions, sold as SF on the basis of these conventions, and bought as SF for these conventions. It is identified by these tropes of character, background and other such trappings, and by the plot-structures which these tropes are fitted into like symbols in a formula, variables in an equation. This is SF as symbolic formulation, the form that many who do not read deeply within the field are most familiar with.

To talk of this symbolic formulation as distinct from other genres is misleading however. Functionally speaking, the formulae of one GENRE can be utilised with the symbols of another, and vice versa. They often are. Symbols may even be mixed and matched in order to simulate originality by offering an unexpected hybrid form. Again this is often the case. The heroic gunmen, hard-bitten detectives and villainous cads of WESTERN, CRIME and ROMANCE are shamelessly filched. Frontier idylls collide with the city streets of NOIR. The noble heroes of WAR FICTION die on the battlefields of elsewhens. The NEW WEIRD may have already been declared dead, but it's not unlikely, I'd suggest, that some editor is right now reaching into the slush pile to find some symbolic formulation masked as it, with mushroom people and cactus people clicked into place in old equations.

This symbolic formulation uses formulaic plots and tropes generated by every genre imaginable, deriving itself from its antecedents, codifying the iconographies of dragons and spaceships, hackers and computer viruses, rendering these so familiar in movies and television that for the general public they define the genre. The movies and TV are, of course, generally a few steps behind. If this type of fiction grabbed its tropes from cutting-edge works in the other SFs it might be incomprehensible to readers unfamiliar with those tropes. So Hollywood is still appropriating the 1950s vision of the Rocket Age and the 1970s vision of Future Catastrophe, utilising the marvellous and/or monstrous imagined fruits of scientific advance to offer the viewer that roller-coaster ride they want. (Michael Crichton seems to be on a mission from God in this respect.) Cyberpunk tropes had to filter into the cinematic zeitgeist before *The Matrix* could be made. In five years' time or so we might expect to see some crappy Hollywood schlockbuster using the Singularity, but at the moment, I think, it would run up against a "not an instantly graspable trope" barrier. Otherwise, however, this type of "brain out, sponge in" fiction is done so well in movies that it may well be poaching customers from the written media. Why should we read a book when we can *see* the gosh-wow SFX on a silver screen?

Symbolic formulation may take its prefab plans and components from different suppliers but they are still taken off-the-shelf. There is a craft in putting the formulation together, picking and choosing the right set of symbols, knowing what will work with what—and the process of formulation may be both analytic and synthetic, not simply following the codified structures of a known formula but rather actively formulating them, codifying those structures from a genuine understanding of what this or that individual work have in common, how they work in the same way, how that can be replicated—but at the end of the day if the symbols are basically interchangeable, if others could be used without affecting the basic structure, then symbolic formulation is using its conceits in a largely cosmetic manner.

One might, however, argue that the definition of this process of SF does not specify failure of that process. Nor does it specify the exclusion of effects or processes definitive of other modes of SF as parallel and related activities within a single text. Many works of this SF, we might argue, utilising the most familiar tropes and the most formulaic plots, may nevertheless function simultaneously on other levels by *also* applying the features which characterise the other SFs. Symbolic formulation may be derivative hackwork but it is only so in the absence of any real creative activity. Add the joy and novelty of fancy, the architecture and texture of fabrication, the significance and resonance of fabulation, and you have something meatier. Add a little science, a little soul, a little spectacle and you have something juicer. Add any of the features of these other SFs to the most basic symbolic formulation and you are adding flesh and blood to its skeletal frame.

The inverse is also true, however. All of the other SFs stand the risk of descent into symbolic formulation where these features are neglected. Michael Moorcock, in *Wizardry and Wild Romance*, comments on the creation and the reuse of incredible imagery, as metaphor or as mere symbol:

> *A writer of fantasy must be judged, I think, by the level of inventive intensity at which he or she works. Allegory can be nonexistent, but a level of conscious metaphor is always there. The writer who follows such originals without understanding this produces work which is at best superficially entertaining and at worst meaningless on any level–generic dross doing nothing to revitalize the form from which it borrows.*
> **Michael Moorcock**

Still, copying is not an inherently doomed approach, is even perhaps a necessary part of learning how to write well. And the problems of this pulp product are so obvious that maybe a little devil's advocacy is in order here. After all, by taking apart the SF work that's gone before and putting it together in new ways, the symbolic formulation which can result in mechanical and derivative formulaic hackwork if the writer has no drive to understand and to improve, can and does also feed into the processes of these other SFs, when the writer's aim is not simply to replicate the familiar in order to exploit the market for "more of the same," but instead to recast it.

Here copying becomes critique—pastiche or parody. It may be used to satiric ends as with Sladek's take on Asimov's Three Laws of Robotics in his novel *Tik-Tok*, clearly a world away from the Hollywood formulation of *I, Robot* where the familiar MacGuffin of the Three Laws is co-opted into a standard "Mad Computer in Control of the House" story—c.f. *Demon Seed, 2001*, and so on down to episodes of both *The X-Files* and *The Simpsons*. Where the Hollywood adaptation clicks a maverick cop firmly into place in the formulated "Discover What's Going on and Stop It" plot, Sladek decides to give us the robot's point of view, and formulation is transformed to fancy, fabrication and fabulation.

Symbolic formulation is a part of SF, one of many processes at work in what we typify as SF, but this mechanical reuse of the old equations is by no means as characteristic of the diverse field of SF as the general public perceives it to be. SF is an intrinsically eclectic field, a magpie's nest of a bookshelf where the A-Z of authors runs from Aldiss to Zelazny. And as the symbolic formulation sloughs off into the Media section or the cinemas or the TV screens, what we are left with as the heart of written SF may well be best described in terms of these approaches rather than in terms of conventions.

This is where the next definition may be a little contentious.

Strictured Fantasia

Science fiction is not predictive; it is descriptive. All fiction is metaphor. Science fiction is metaphor. What sets it apart from older forms of fiction seems to be its use of new metaphors, drawn from certain great dominants of our contemporary life—science, all the sciences and technology, and the relativistic and the historical outlook, among them. Space travel is one of those metaphors, so is an alternative society, an alternative biology; the future is another. The future, in fiction, is a metaphor.
Ursula K. Le Guin

Fables and fabrications, fabulation and formulation, fictions of science, soul and spectacle—ultimately all of these SFs can be seen as placing different limitations on the nature of the conceit and its relationship to the story, where it is sourced from, how it is developed through the fabric of the story or novel. In a wider sense then all these SFs can be considered, insofar as they *use the technique of the conceit*, as different types of strictured fantasia. It is simply that the particular strictures vary depending on what type of fantasia you happen to be writing.

This would be the SF of Dick's *The Man in the High Castle* and of other such ALTERNATE HISTORY novels, anything from *The Plot Against America* to *Guns of the South*. It would be the SF also of China Miéville's *Perdido Street Station* and of other such Alternate Society or Alternate Biology novels (to coin even more new terms). It would be the SF of Zelazny's *Roadmarks*, of Silverberg's *The Book of Skulls*, of Moorcock's *Cornelius Quartet*. All of these can be included under the catch-all of SF not simply because they are sold as such, not simply because we have thrown our hands up and said, "So Fuck?" but because they are strictured fantasia, fantastic fiction restricted by certain constraints.

Of course, in reality *all* fantastic fiction is restricted by some constraint or other. To call this SF by the name strictured fantasia is simply to say that it *is* fantasia. Whether it is therefore *fantasy* is another question.

> [T]he idea that a magazine like Astounding, or Analog as it's now called, has anything to do with the sciences is ludicrous. You have only to pick up a journal like Nature, say, or any scientific journal, and you can see that science belongs in a completely different world.
> **J.G. Ballard**

It is the strictures that create the risks of failure, of limitations; this is the nature of strictures. All of these SFs have their own language, *are* their own language. The specialised "lexicon" and "narrative grammar" of scientific fancy may become vulgar and crude, lacking in the nuances required to render character effectively. That of scientific and scientistic fabrication may become too highly developed on the other, an impenetrable geek-speak jargon spawned of maths and physics. That of scientific fabulation may seem foreign, incomprehensible and inapplicable in everyday life. That of soul fiction, spectaculist fabrication and symbolic formulation may seem mere sensationalism, emotive but superficial, empty of any real relevance. At the end of the day, the general public often don't know the language and may well *not want* to know the language. The confusion of tongues only makes it harder for them to learn.

SF is a single grand tower of strictured fantasia that has arisen over the decades, but it is a Tower of Babel that has fallen, as the next definition, the penultimate definition, admits.

Synthetic Flux

> Science fiction is the prophetic...the apocalyptic literature of our particular and culminating epoch of crisis.
> **Gerald Heard**

This SF is a stramash of dialectics in continual thesis, antithesis and synthesis. It is a discourse of syllogisms and grenades. It is field of forms in constant flux, of fusion and fission.

It is formulae and explosions. It is sublime trash, sacred excrement, holy shit. It is the flux sprayed from the arse of pulp and transubstantiated to gold in an alchemist's crucible.

> *In my mind's eye, my thoughts light fires in your cities.*
> **Charles Manson**

This SF is a head-on collision of the high and the low, of reason and passion.

The Mundanes say:

> *That interstellar travel remains unlikely. Warp drives, worm holes, and other forms of faster-than-light magic are wish fulfilment fantasies rather than serious speculation about a possible future.*

The Infernokrushers say:

We laugh maniacally in the face of serious speculation. We *will* have warp drives...on our MONSTER TRUCKS! We *will* have worm holes...and bullet holes, and drill holes, and holes punched through the very fabric of the space-time continuum itself by the giant adamantine fist of MECHAGODZILLA! These are not wish fulfilment fantasies. These are metaphors for the destruction that is a part of *every* possible future.

The Mundanes say:

> *That magic interstellar travel can lead to an illusion of a universe abundant with worlds as hospitable to life as this Earth. This is also unlikely.*

We say the hospitability of *Earth* is the illusion. The heart of this world is an INFERNO! The core of this world is magma, KRUSHED into solidity by its own weight! And interstellar travel will lead us to the truth of worlds even LESS hospitable, worlds that will KRUSH us with their gravity, worlds that are INFERNOS even on the surface!

The Mundanes say:

> *That this dream of abundance can encourage a wasteful attitude to the abundance that is here on Earth.*

Good! The more waste there is, the more there is to KRUSH! We will shovel the shit of our squandered resources into trash compacters and furnaces. Old tropes and tired techniques will be torn down and scattered to the winds. We will KRUSH the abundance of it and then we will KRUSH the dream of it. That which is waste must be burned in the pretty flames of the INFERNO! That which does not burn must be KRUSHED! The INFERNO of the KRUSHED old is the crucible we dream of.

The Mundanes say:

> *That there is no evidence whatsoever of intelligences elsewhere in the universe.*

Intelligence does not concern us, only rampant destruction, preferably with MONSTER TRUCKS. And that is *everywhere*! What matters is, are there GIANT ROBOTS elsewhere in the universe? AI will begin as Artificial *Idiocy*. Who cares if a computer can play chess or take control of cyberspace? *Can it trash Tokyo, huh, huh?* Intelligences elsewhere? What does intelligence matter in the INFERNAL heart of a planet, a sun, a nova? What use is reason in a black hole, where all things—even logic itself—are KRUSHED? If we are the solitary spark of awareness in a cold, dark cosmos, then we will be a *son-et-lumière*, a fireworks display, an INFERNO raging in the night. We don't care if no-one's watching. Explosions are pretty.

The Mundanes say:

> *That absence of evidence is not evidence of absence—however, it is unlikely that alien intelligences will overcome the physical constraints on interstellar travel any better than we can.*

We say these physical constraints are *there* to be overcome. They will KRUSH us if we do not KRUSH them first. Will you be KRUSHER or KRUSHEE? No! No, we say. No! We will smash them with our GIANT ROBOTIC FISTS! We will drive over the wreckage in our MONSTER TRUCKS! Our imagination is a veritable JUGGERNAUT, burning rubber as it conquers its own inertia. We will blast our way through all physical constraints, shatter them to SMITHEREENS, if we have to use the stars themselves as wrecking balls!

The Mundanes say:

> *That interstellar trade (and colonisation, war, federations, etc.) is therefore highly unlikely.*

We say there *will* be great galactic empires, worlds KRUSHED militarily and economically, native populations KRUSHED by human slave masters, alien overseers, by warmongers and industrialists...or by the BURNING, existential angst of simply being alone in the universe *with nothing else to KRUSH!* We say empires will rise because how else could they FALL! Rome will burn again, we say, and we will play the fiddle as the INFERNO rages around us!

The Mundanes say:

> *That communication with alien intelligences over such vast distances will be vexed by: the enormous time lag in exchange of messages and the likelihood of enormous and probably*

currently unimaginable differences between us and aliens.

We say KRUSHING is a universal language. All sentience understands destruction. All life that BURNS with the fire of feelings, the INFERNO of intellect, all those who know what it is to live, know what it is to *die*. Besides, who cares about time lag when your message is a Molotov cocktail? We have too many things to KRUSH to wait for a reply!

The Mundanes say:

That there is no evidence whatsoever that quantum uncertainty has any effect at the macro level and that therefore it is highly unlikely that there are whole alternative universes to be visited.

Then we will KRUSH reality to SMITHEREENS until there *is* no macro level! We will hammer at the atoms, the protons, neutrons and electrons, with a child-like glee! We will reduce EVERYTHING to bits and bobs so small that their quantum uncertainty means each one is a universe in itself, space-time twisted around the awesome energy they *might* just have! Forget the "world in a grain of sand" stuff. We're talking whole *realities* in one bubble of quantum foam.

The Mundanes say:

That therefore our most likely future is on this planet and within this solar system. It is highly unlikely that intelligent life survives elsewhere in this solar system. Any contact with aliens is likely to be tenuous, and unprofitable.

That the most likely future is one in which we only have ourselves and this planet.

We say that the most likely future is one in which we have NOTHING! Because everything we had is KRUSHED and thrown into the INFERNO! We will KRUSH and BURN the planet, KRUSH and BURN ourselves, KRUSH and BURN any life we find within the solar system, KRUSH and BURN the solar system, KRUSH and BURN any life we find outside it.

We will KRUSH and BURN the very future.

Because we wanna. Because it's fun.

This is *my* SF.

No, fuck that shit! (And fuck consistency!) It's *this*:

Strange Fiction

A representation which estranges is one which allows us to recognize its subject, but at the same time make it seem unfamiliar.
Bertolt Brecht

Science fiction is the literature of cognitive estrangement.
Darko Suvin

Is there another way to define SF, not with the vague wave of an all-encompassing hand, not with a finger-pointing to some single corner, not as this Babelesque tower of languages, rising high in an artificed unity of abstraction or fallen into the chaos of countless tongues, a conflict of manifestos and movements?

Perhaps a notion of strictured fantasia might serve as a starting-point, if we strip away the redundant *strictured* but leave it to one side for later consideration—and strip away *fantasia* too, this term signifying a closed definition of *fantasy*, one in which the incredible is also the marvellous and/or monstrous, albeit not yet the generic FANTASY of elves, orcs and magic swords. If we cannibalise a dictionary definition, maybe we can glean a more neutral label from the notion of the fantastic as: "quaint or strange in form, conception, or appearance…unrestrainedly fanciful…extravagant…bizarre, as in form or appearance; strange…based on or existing only in fantasy; unreal…wonderful or superb; remarkable."

How else might we label this fiction of the quaint, the fanciful, the extravagant, the bizarre, the unreal, the wonderful, the remarkable? How else might we label this strange fiction of the strange?

Now there's a thought.

[Science fiction is] a new way of reading, a new way of making texts make sense—collectively producing a new set of codes. [SF writers invented the genre] by writing new kinds of sentences and embedding them in contexts in which those sentences were readable.
Samuel R. Delany

Elsewhen, in his essay, "About Five Thousand Seven Hundred and Fifty Words," Delany outlines a continuous correction process involved in reading a simple sentence:

The red sun was high, the blue low.

Being Delany, he does this at great length and in the most fascinating way. Starting the essay with a proposition that it is meaningless to talk of style in opposition to content—

that it is all, in fact, form (or as I like to put it: *words are the only substance*), that meaning is best considered as a thread of memory we follow from word to word through a text—he gives us a reconstruction of the reader's path through this particular sentence, leading us eventually into a discussion of the role of subjunctivity level in relation to genre.

> *Suppose a series of words is presented to us as a piece of reportage. A blanket indicative tension informs the whole series: this happened. That is the particular level of subjunctivity at which journalism takes place... The subjunctivity level for a series of words labelled naturalistic fiction is defined by: could have happened... Fantasy takes the subjunctivity of naturalistic fiction and throws it into reverse. At the appearance of elves, witches, or magic in a non-metaphorical position, or at some correction of image too bizarre to be explained by other than the supernatural, the level of subjunctivity becomes: could not have happened.*
> **Samuel R. Delany**

So when a strange image, a fanciful, fantastic image, appears in a story or novel, Delany says, we're kicked out of the naturalistic subjunctivity level—*this could have happened*—and into another—*this could not have happened*. Delany distinguishes this from the subjunctivity level of his SF, speculative fiction:

> *[W]hen spaceships, ray guns, or more accurately any correction of images that indicates the future appears in a series of words and marks it as s-f, the subjunctivity level is changed once more: These objects, these convolutions of objects into situations and events, are blanketly defined by: have not happened.*
> **Samuel R. Delany**

One of the most interesting things about Delany's essay is that he thereby places both naturalistic and fantastic fiction as subsets of his SF, with the subjunctivity levels of events which *have not happened (but could)* or which *have not happened (and could not)*. He says this explicitly about naturalistic fiction in the notes to the essay. He doesn't actually say the same about fantastic fiction, but this seems to be a ramification of his idea.

There is a slip here though. Until such time as we can stand on a planet in a binary system, if a narrative presents us with two suns in the sky, the level of subjunctivity becomes: *could not have happened, not yet*. As described, Delany's SF in fact sits as a subset of fantastic fiction; the impossibility we're presented with in that series of words simply comes with a caveat that at some point it might *become* possible.

Call it the Contingency Slip Fallacy: where a temporal (i.e. technical or historical) impossibility can be viewed as contingent, we can persuade ourselves that it is an actual possibility, hold firmly, even passionately, to a belief that the subjunctivity level has not shifted, that our SF is remaining in the realm of the possible.

But I'm not talking about Delany's SF here—speculative fiction—but about strange fiction, which is defined not by one or other subjunctivity level but rather by the challenge itself. The subjunctivity of this SF is, in the first instance, undecided, conflicted.

Here's a sentence, modelled on Delany's own:

The crescent sun was high, the moon low.

When a strange image appears in a story or novel, we cannot immediately rule out the possibility of an explanation emerging later in the text. There is a moment of subjunctive indefinition here which is crucial to how all strange fiction works.

The crescent sun...

In reading the start of a sentence such as the one above, when we read "The crescent sun" we are faced with an impossibility which requires interrogation. Does the sun only appear to be a crescent, being in partial eclipse perhaps? Is the crescent sun an image rather than an actuality, a symbol on a flag perhaps?

The crescent sun was high...

When we read further, from "The crescent sun" to "was high," the question becomes more pressing. Is the writer using the symbol on the flag to represent the flag itself, or perhaps the ideology represented by the flag? Is this to be read literally, or is it some metaphoric or metonymic figure of speech we should be parsing to its ulterior meaning?

The crescent sun was high, the moon...

When "the moon" appears we might abandon the idea of the flag, our reading corrected by the parallel of sun and moon. We might decide that, yes, this is a description of the sky. Any moment now we're going to get stars in a darkened sky, the shadow covering the earth, and so on. But we still have a moment of interrogation to go through. "The crescent sun was high, the moon"…was what? Eclipsing it? That would make sense.

The crescent sun was high, the moon low.

With the last word, "low" the sentence resolves into impossibility. We're asked to accept that the moon is not in fact eclipsing the sun but is in another place entirely. In the sky? In the real world, our world, where this is a physical impossibility?

We might say that, at this point, the subjunctivity level becomes that of fantastic fiction: this could not happen. But what we actually have is subjunctive indefinition, indecision—neither *this could happen* nor *this could not happen*, not a statement but a challenge: *could this happen?* It is this tension of subjunctivities that is the core of SF, the characteristic feature of all strange fiction.

Later in the story or novel in which that sentence appears we might be offered a resolution. The hero removes his VR goggles and we realise this is what Delany calls *speculative fiction*. Or he wakes up in bed and we realise this is what Delany calls *naturalistic fiction*. Or he meets an elf and we realise this is what everyone insists on calling *fantastic fiction*. We realise, that is, how we would classify it as one or other of the above according to our personal taxonomy of the aesthetic forms. But SF is defined, I would argue, more by the moments of indecision than by the moments of decision: all fiction requires the suspension of disbelief; strange fiction is that which actively challenges suspension-of-disbelief, throwing at the reader images, situations, which are dissonant with our knowledge of, as Wallace Stevens puts it, "things as they are."

The differentiation of strange fiction into science fiction, fantasy and horror? I say this is largely a matter of how we personally respond to those situations. Can we *rationalise* them? Do we *desire* them? Do we *fear* them? In our moments of subjunctive indecision, other questions are fired off by that basic question of *could this happen?* With curiosity we ask ourselves: how, where, *when* could this happen? With fear and desire we ask ourselves: would this, could this, should this happen? would it, could it, should it *not*?

None of these are mutually exclusive. And these are the defining questions of strange fiction, of wish-fulfilment dreams and dread-filled nightmares, plausible or implausible. We have already suspended our disbelief, I should note, so it may be less a matter of whether an event described is possible than where and when it *might* be, what kind of elsewhen we must construct in our imagination, in order to sustain the pretence, as with reading any work of fiction, that these events *are* happening, right now, in simulation. Still, with the challenge to subjunctivity level offered by either Delany's example or mine, there can only be a sense of strain on the suspension-of-disbelief, a frisson at the conjuring of what surely could not have happened.

With naturalistic fiction there is seldom any question that these events have not happened but could have—in an elsewhen that is so close to our own it's virtually indistinguishable. With strange fiction, though, that elsewhen, as we reconstruct it in the reading, is rendered, quite literally, incredible. Add a little desire and/or fear, in our state of suspended disbelief—that the incredible might somehow be made real, and you have the sense-of-wonder or future shock which permeates an SF driven not by plausibility, scientific or otherwise, but by *im*plausibility, by incredulity.

This is SF as it looks to me from my seat here in the SF Café. Does this strange fiction have its own risk over and above those inherited from all the other SFs? If those outside the ghetto tend to be scared that SF is just hackwork, that SF is just adventure stories, that SF is just maths stories, that SF isn't relevant, that SF is incomprehensible, or that SF has nothing to say, do they also tend to be scared that SF is just too damn *strange* for them?

    Probably.

    So fuck?

Part 1

RHAPSODY

Down in the Ghetto at the SF Café

The Science Fiction Café and Bar

Don't tell anybody, but science fiction no longer exists.
    Matthew Cheney

Welcome to the SF Café, in the ghetto of Genre, in the city of New Sodom. We call it the SF Café, only the letters *S* and *F* surviving of its original name, but look up now, look to the sign above the door, and you'll find the full monicker still visible today, *The Science Fiction Café and Bar*, traced in the grime, outlined in the negative spaces left where the spelled-out sense of it has long-since fallen away.

The SF Café. It may look a bit shabby from the outside and there's surely some weird gewgaws and gimcracks in the window to make you wonder what the fuck's going on inside. But let's step through the decades as we step through the door—

  a rupture in reality,
  a quirk of narrative created,
  time travel as impossibility conjured, breach of
- known science,
- known history,
- the laws of nature,
- even the strictures of logic itself,

as a butterfly crushed underfoot at our step will never now distract dear Grandpapa into the turn that woulda shoulda coulda saved him from a stray bullet in a hunting accident that is, or will be, the inevitable paradoxical outcome of our interloping, but fuck it, let's do it anyway, step through the door

—and see the SF Café as it once was, the shining Formica of the counter-top, the sleek silvery steel of coffee machine and soda fountain, the Bakelite and plastic of the trappings, the decor all bright white and brilliant red, shining, gleaming, with the '50s promise of futurity. This is the SF Café as it was in the Golden Age, when Old Man Campbell owned it.

Emphasis on the *was*. (Or *might have been* would be more apposite, *coulda woulda shoulda* been. In stepping through a door into a conjured elsewhen, we're always already entering a territory of argument. In that breach of the possible, we've always already sacrificed the actual for that quirk of narrative, for the sake of story. Still…emphasis on the *past tense*.)

Don't misunderstand me. It's not that I'm sitting down in a booth in the SF Café, firing up my laptop, tapping out a grandiose proclamation on the "death of science fiction" as a start-point. It's just that…the SF Café is a whole other scene to the Science Fiction Bar and Café that it once was. That elsewhen scene of then is gone, the territory so transformed over the years that I'm entering as an alien, infiltrator of a past that is another world.

From where I'm sitting now, I'd be a fool to say that what I'm talking about is the *science fiction* of that elsewhen. At best it might be classed as SF—the *S*, for me, simply standing for *strange*, while the *F* might even stand for *fictions*, plural, to cast it as non-generic a grouping as *queer readers* or *barking dogs*. And both words, for me, shrug off the upper case initial of a proper noun, a nominal label for this nation or that neighbourhood.

This is not a historical study of *science fiction*, not by a long shot; at best you can expect a figurative sociography of sorts, an exploration of the broader terrain by which I hope to navigate a course to the strange fictions I'm far more interested in. Nor should you expect a treatise on the nature of *science fiction*, not by that label, not a coherent and unbiased one; rather this is an argument with that label, a story of why I find it ultimately unsustainable.

There are two flavours of definition for this *science fiction* stuff, you see—open and closed. The former I'm okay with, the latter…not so much. By the time we're done here, maybe you'll understand why.

In the open definition, we take a laissez-faire approach. We might characterise this *science fiction* stuff as a family of works which do this or that, but we're happy to admit that those features (whatever they might be) are neither essential nor unique to the genre; there are works which might be science fiction and might not. Hell, when we call it a genre, what we really mean is just…a field of fiction. Like indie music, right? Which could be anything from Arcade Fire to Adam Green, Zero 7 to the Zutons. At its most open, the definition is empty, in fact, all that's left the two figurae of the label *SF*.

What is SF?

It is, as they say, whatever I point to when I say, SF.

In the closed definitions of SCIENCE FICTION, that thumbnail descriptor becomes a stamp of commercial or aesthetic identity, carved with clean edges—hence the capitals large and small to signal not just a proper noun but a brand. If the open definitions treat science fiction as a genre like indie music, SCIENCE FICTION is a GENRE like the good old-fashioned Rock'n'Roll of the '50s and '60s. This is a family of fiction marked out by a combo of conventions unique and essential to it; clear boundaries are set over what is or isn't SCIENCE FICTION.

What is SCIENCE FICTION?

Well, that's the million dollar question.

Down in the ghetto at the SF Café, we do like to argue over what is or isn't Science Fiction. The jukebox here has all those bands on it—because the clientele is pretty mixed these days—but there are a fair few customers who furrow their brows and frown sullenly when Adam Green comes on. Cause that just ain't Rock'n'Roll. Old Man Campbell really wouldn't have approved.

A Basic Definition of Science Fiction

> *By 'scientifiction'...I mean the Jules Verne, H.G. Wells, and Edgar Allan Poe type of story—a charming romance intermingled with scientific fact and prophetic vision.*
> **Hugo Gernsback**

The first problem with the closed definition? There's more than one. There are many definitions of Science Fiction. They are all right…for someone. They are all wrong…for someone. Here's a rather basic one as an example:

> Science Fiction is a Modern Pulp genre which combines Romantic character types, plot structures and settings with a Rationalist focus on scientific theories and conjectures, requiring a degree of plausibility in the extrapolation of its hypothetical conceits.

This Science Fiction is scientific romance or Hugo Gernsback's scientifiction, taken to its logical conclusion. Codified in the early twentieth century explosion of Boy's Own adventure stories, it is essentially fantasia (fabrication, strange and marvellous: *could* this happen? oh, it *should!*) transformed as we source conceits in futurology (speculation, scientific and plausible… more or less). This Science Fiction is born in a binding at the deepest levels, where Gernsback's "intermingled with" becomes "rooted in." Old Man Campbell was pretty strict about what was on the menu at the SF Café.

> *To be science fiction, not fantasy, an honest effort at prophetic extrapolation of the known must be made. Ghosts can enter science fiction, if they're logically explained, but not if they are simply the ghosts of fantasy. Prophetic extrapolation can derive from a number of different sources, and apply in a number of fields. Sociology, psychology, and parapsychology are, today, not true sciences; therefore, instead of forecasting future results of application of sociological science of today, we must forecast the development of a science of sociology. From there the story can take off.*
> **John W. Campbell**

Note the use of the term *prophetic* by both editors, with its complex of connotations quite at odds with the grounding in science—religion and rapture, voices and visions. An aspect of fantasia remains, and in it we cannot fail to see *fantasy*—albeit defined, for the moment, not in terms of literature but in terms of psychology: the sustained fancy; the ludic or oneiric imagining; from the Greek *phantasia*; a making visible. Where prophecy is the name of the game, we are faced with a fiction firmly of the *marvellous* and/or *monstrous*. Prophets do not speak of the routine.

The relationship of these two gestural terms, *SF* and *fantasy*, will be a theme here. Some readers may bristle at my use of the f-word. To be fair, I'm not that fond of it myself, its meaning similarly confused by a clash of open and closed definitions, in the conflation of strange fictions which eschew the sublime with the blend of the incredible, the marvellous and the monstrous which I term *fantasia*, skewed to the marvellous by default. But until we can get stuck into it, we are unfortunately stuck *with* it.

Anyway, the point is this: up to and during the Golden Age, born of the simple fact that futurology resulted in arguable fantasias, there was a tight-knit relationship between Rationalism and Romanticism which kept the form aesthetically coherent and commercially viable. Atom bombs and satellites, microwaves and mechanisation—the future looked exciting, rich with the all-important sense-of-wonder that is born where the incredible meets the marvellous. So this new Genre emerged for the Rocket Age, a popular form which, like the other pulp forms, had its own set of rules, its clear boundaries, a form delineated in steel and Formica, Bakelite and plastic, in Old Man Campbell's Science Fiction Café and Bar, in a world of nuclear power and space flight just around the corner.

That shiny new Science Fiction didn't come from nowhere, of course, but as long as we're talking in closed definitions, let's not pretend that it's existed from the dawn of time.

The Birth of Science Fiction

Here's a rather more contentious honing of that definition, situating the aesthetic form in its historical context:

> *Originally coined as a substitute for the more unwieldy labels of scientific romance or scientifiction, the term* Science Fiction *properly applies to a short-lived* Genre *of the early to mid twentieth century* Modern Pulp *boom utilising Romantic character types, plot structures and settings but sourcing its fantasia in Rationalist futurology. This genre existed for a few decades at most before its practitioners exploded the rigid conventions of the original form.*

Trust me, I know this closed definition invites irate challenges. Just how short-lived is short-lived? If we are defining this form as pulp are we excluding works published outside this commercial environment? Where do Jules Verne and H.G. Wells sit in relation to this SCIENCE FICTION? What of Orwell or Huxley? Don't these writers fit the open definitions of science fiction that have accreted to the coinage? And if so, why are we denying them a seat in the SF Café, saying they're not SCIENCE FICTION? Isn't this too narrowly limiting our scope?

It's certainly a narrower view than that of Brian Aldiss who, in his *Trillion Year Spree*, positions science fiction as an outgrowth of the Gothic, tracing it back to Mary Shelley's *Frankenstein* as point of origin. Aldiss's is a fair argument. He is not simply co-opting a classic in a grasp for literary credibility, the common accusation of science fiction's detractors whenever this sort of case is made—his analysis is a valid attempt to trace the roots of this mode of writing—but there's a substantial disjunct between the dynamics of the *monstrous* in Shelley's novel and that of the *marvellous* by which a fantasia is driven.

They're as diametrically opposed as dread and desire, as *should not* and *should*, as *must not* and *must*; the horror (i.e. the monstrous) that permeates GOTHIC ROMANCE is, if anything, the direct antithesis of the sense-of-wonder (i.e. the marvellous plus the incredible) that this bold Campbellian SCIENCE FICTION inherits from the fantasias of MODERN PULP. We might point at *Frankenstein* as a landmark en route, but it is not SCIENCE FICTION.

No, the SF Café, when it opens, comes as a new scene with a new vibe—it has its goths, but there's a damn sight more geeks among the host of freaks frequenting it. The Gottischromanzen Kaffeehaus sat on a different corner of Mass Market Square entirely from the SF Café. Its blasted shell still sits there, in fact, haunted by sparkly vampires too meek for the Darkening Biergarten next door, first casualty in the Culture Wars that created the ghetto of Genre.

The Culture Wars? you say.

Let's jump back a few centuries, to the period when the Enlightenment was radically reshaping our notions of literature. In the city-state of New Sodom in those days, coming out of the Renaissance, you had two rival aesthetics, one attaching itself to this new scientific outlook called Rationalism, idealising reason, and the other grounded in the flip-side worldview of Romanticism, idealising passion. Each was defined partly in relation to the past (Classical Greece on the one hand and Dark Ages Europe on the other) but largely in relation to each other.

One day, into this worldscape, into the city of New Sodom, a strange figure rides. He dismounts, strides into the Tall Tale Tavern, where poets and storytellers sit recounting grandiose nonsenses, endless episodes of CHIVALRIC ROMANCE like *Amadis de Gaula*. With a bitter biting grin, Cervantes slams his *Don Quixote* down upon a wooden table and begins, his savage satire bringing a Rationalist's scorn of wonder to bear, crafting a modern endeavour quite distinct from the heroic Romances of his peers—an endeavour that will come to be known as the *novel*.

In the centuries that follow, that novel takes a curious course. The Romantic aesthetic is brought back into play, as writers respond to the response, critique the critique, attempt to fuse the two aesthetics, to create a *Rationalist Romance*; the GOTHIC ROMANCE and the VICTORIAN REALIST novel make fuckee-fuckee in the minds of unashamed synthesists, give us works like *Wuthering Heights*. In the dialectic between the two factions, in the interzones where they collide and collude through the medium of individual texts—where the author isn't purely allied one way or the other but playing out the conflict in their writing—there emerges a synthesis of Rationalist thesis and Romanticist antithesis that we might call Protomodern.

In that long period up to 1900 or just beyond we get the roots of every contemporary GENRE. We get Samuel Richardson, Ann Radcliffe, Emily Brontë, Jane Austen (roots of ROMANCE). We get Sara Coleridge, George MacDonald, Lewis Carroll, E. Nesbit, Kenneth Grahame (roots of FANTASY). We get Walter Scott, Robert Louis Stevenson, John Buchan, H. Rider Haggard (roots of ADVENTURE). We get Edgar Allan Poe, Rudyard Kipling, M.R. James (roots of HORROR). We get Ernest William Hornung, Arthur Conan Doyle (roots of CRIME and MYSTERY and THRILLER). We get Mary Shelley, Jules Verne, H.G. Wells (roots of SCIENCE FICTION).

None of their works are *genre fiction* in the modern sense because GENRE in the modern sense doesn't yet exist—the walls of the ghetto have not yet been built—but a slow drift of writers uptown or downtown does begin to gradually reshape the city of New Sodom, a divide emerging between the polar extremes of GOTHIC and REALIST fictions, Romantic and Rationalist, "Popular Fiction" and "Literature." The petit bourgeois haven't yet degraded the debate with their middlebrow propriety, haven't yet sealed the coming century of straight white male (and middle-aged and middle-class) scorn for the sensational, but writers themselves are a combative bunch when it comes to aesthetics, and the generation before GENRE are born into a discourse that's been brewing since Cervantes.

In the Name of Propriety

So, some of these writers find themselves on one or other side of that boundary, drawn to the Gottischromanzen Kaffeehaus downtown or the Social Realist Tea Room uptown. Still, many of them live and work in that interzone between the two, formative of multiple GENRES because they work in multiple modes, creating works acknowledged to this day as part of the canon. The literary variety journals in the UK, most notably *The Strand*, capture the last days of this Protomodern period perfectly, publishing many of the writers named above, printing poetry and fiction in any and every mode. Ghost stories, detective stories, all sorts of strange fictions pervade the Protomodern periodicals, fiction that exploits a sense of the incredible with events that breach the laws of nature, or taps into our fears and desires with the marvellous and the monstrous, or teases us with the mysterious, titillates with the mundane monstrosities and absurdities of melodrama and the grotesque—c.f. Dickens.

If these works don't sit in GENRE, they're clearly using the *techniques* of GENRE, the effects derived from stepping outside the strictures of mimetic REALISM. But this is hardly shocking, that GENRE of REALISM only in this period defining itself into existence by the spurning of such quirks, the default of fiction not so delimited thus being to use whatever tools are fit to purpose. The scorn of the sensational may not be entirely modern, but it's certainly not the prevailing tide in literature's history.

It is in these journals, among the tales of mystery and adventure that the embryo that will become SCIENCE FICTION gestates, scion of Sherlock Holmes and Allan Quatermain as much as Victor Frankenstein.

Then the steam train of modernity hits, leads to mass-production and mass-marketing, greater literacy and a corresponding shift in class demographics. Through the last half of the nineteenth century we see the penny dreadfuls and dime novels burgeoning. With the turn of the new century comes category fiction—magazines and imprints dedicated to specific forms. From the early 1900s through to the 1930s or 1940s, a boom of MODERN PULP utterly reshapes the territory. It's a totally evolutionary process—expansion, diffusion, isolation, specialisation—that leads to the GENRES we still have today—and a few that are now all but defunct—as the idioms carved out to sit under a rackspace label.

A process of formulation sets in within all of those GENRES, of course; the formal conceits by which we recognise an idiom are only a step from the formulaic strictures by which we mechanise its manufacturing, and if an idiom sells you can bet that step will be taken. Marketing to readers on the basis that there's an audience for "more of the same" means codifying "the same," defining what each GENRE is, or should be, in terms of tropes of character, worldscape and plot structure. Where a genre becomes a GENRE, indeed, is in large part in that fact of formulation.

The fallout of this is the Culture Wars. All of these fictions being driven by the MODERN PULP dynamics of the sensational, the power of conjuring what woulda coulda shoulda been, any fiction using that dynamics is now perceived as being not simply a work within this or that GENRE (GOTHIC, MYSTERY, ADVENTURE, etc.) but as having a common quality of sensationalism by which a super-class can be identified: GENRE FICTION. The requirement for that mode of conjuring in category fiction makes it a marker of populist pandering in opposition to literary craft…assuming an ignorance of the artistry by which sensational and intellectual are allied, assuming an unconsidered reverence for literature that mutes the former and/or mediates it with the latter—as in the distanced narrative of the Victorian novelist as observer, commentator, critic.

For the middlebrow petit bourgeoisie to whom intellectual status is important and for whom observation and commentary is equated with relevance and insight, a crisis of faith is inevitable—should they really be reading this sensationalist pulp? Should they really be reading this…Genre Fiction? Should they be writing it, editing it, publishing it?

So the battle-lines are drawn, tastes divided into good and bad, the dynamics of the sensational abjured in the name of propriety, the entire toolkit of formal conceits underpinning it shunned as signifiers of that quality. Soon there's no way you could publish a journal like *The Strand*, no way you could run a publishing imprint with a similar diversity. The fiction which mutes and mediates the sensational gets bootstrapped *to* privilege *by* privilege, and before you know it that rupture has become a rift between Literature and Genre.

We cast that schism as highbrow versus lowbrow, but in truth the first salvo in the Culture Wars is fired by the middlebrow and it is their enterprise, this construction of Literature in the abjection of Genre; the mediocre must establish their edification to rectitude, propriety of taste, in the expulsion of the gauche, whereas an actual elevation of craft or critique leads more to scorn of literary decorum. The gauche for their part are blasé about the volleys fired in their direction, happy to see the walls rise around a ghetto they constructed anyway, an aesthetic territory carved out and carved up by rackspace labels in their own enterprise of commercial cultivation. It's in their interest that the heirs of all those Protomodern writers find the uptown districts of New Sodom hostile.

And so the barricades are built and we find ourselves in that downtown district of New Sodom, in that dodgy neighbourhood known as Genre, on the corner of Street & Smith, where Science Fiction was born, in a flurry of futurity's onset, in panic and excitement, a bastard child of the reviled, of the pulps, of the *vulgar* mob's Dime Novel and the *hysterical* female's Sensation Novel.

And its first infant squall ripped the air, a rupture in reality—

The Third Axis

It seems to me in some murky way that in genre fiction there ought to be a third axis-of-story here, a third dimension of thought. Call them genre devices. These are the things which make a genre story what it is, rather than naturalistic fiction.
Jay Lake

Elsewhen in the SF Café, Jay Lake proposes a three-axis view of what he refers to—what a lot of people refer to—as *genre fiction*. But what does he mean by that label? Given that Naturalism and Realism are as much genres as SF, Fantasy and Horror, or Western, Crime and Chick-Lit—they're just not marketing categories—given that all fiction sits in one genre or another, all fiction is, strictly speaking, genre fiction. Sometimes what we mean by the term is simply category fiction, fiction sold under some particular rackspace label. Here in the SF Café though what we mean when we say *genre fiction* is largely that type of fiction, often sold as pulp, but sometimes not, distinguished from general fiction by the presence of…*something*. What we really mean is the fiction that doesn't quite fit with the rest of that common-or-garden everyday mundane fiction.

What we mean is strange fiction.

Lake's three-axis approach makes it clear this is what he means. The first axis he offers is story elements—character, situation, problem, solution. The second axis he offers is craft techniques—voice, tense, point-of-view, style. The third axis is…*something*, the distinctive quirky whatever-the-fucks that distinguish this type of work from the mimetic, from mundane fiction. What these whojamaflips might be, what might represent that third axis in the model, is the crucial question of what makes strange fiction strange.

To Map the Strangeness

We should not, of course, simply ignore the role of authorial intent and reader interpretation in the decision over whether or not this work or that is *genre fiction*—which is to say, whether or not it's strange fiction. In its intersection with the rackspace label of SF, strange fiction often seems to acquire that label by ad hoc consensus, as much as anything else. If we begin by looking for some more objective criteria, we are assuming that those criteria exist, that a work of strange fiction may be in that aesthetic idiom regardless of subjective judgement. This isn't necessarily the best starting point. So:

> *1) Does authorial intent determine the nature of the work?*
>
> *2) Does authorial intent (legitimately) influence the reader's experience of the work?*
>
> *3) Is authorial intent even relevant at all to the reader's experience of the work?*
>
> **Jay Lake**

The reality is, I think, that all of this depends if you're viewing genre as a market category, a conventional template or an aesthetic idiom.

If SF is just a label slapped on a book to position it in the marketplace, then Lake's *Rocket Science*, to take one example, is SF because the publisher has decided it is. Authorial intent and reader experience are factors in their decision, but ultimately what matters most is whether more units will shift if you put it in the SF section. Whether a work qualifies to sit in the SF section is arbitrated on a simple basis: fuck it, we can sell this as SF so it *is* SF. We have only a granfalloon of a marketing category constructed by gatekeepers, inclusion or exclusion decided by authority.

If we're to look past those authorities and see SF as a conventional template (or fuzzy set of such), a consensus judgement thrashed out by writers and readers, a matter of purpose (authorial intent) and import (reader experience), we have now a historical genre, but it is still a granfalloon, and there is patently no real consensus. This is the rabbit hole of SF as a subset of SF, a turf war of multiple aesthetics that's really political, proprietorial: which aesthetic has the more legitimate claim to a nominal label?

If we want to play that game, we might seek to unravel the legitimacy of claims, the actualities of territorial coups and negotiated compromises, to map out the discourse of a historical genre, but to look for a third axis goes beyond this into the question of what it is *about the fiction itself* all those turf wars are taking place over, *what* the purposes are, *what* the imports are, *how they work*.

To map the genre device(s), as Lake puts it, is a different enterprise from mapping the discourse in which those devices are set as criteria of conventional templates and those templates named as genres. It is to map the dynamics of the devices themselves, to map the strangeness.

Of Sonnets and Conventional Templates

> *After all, the thrill you get from a good sf story is not that dissimilar to the thrill you get from a good magic trick. Wow, did you see that, was that real? What if it was real? Part of what sf does is make us look at something impossible, beyond our reach, beyond our ken—and think of it as if it were real, as if we might at some point have to deal with it.*
>
> Paul Kincaid

To approach strange fiction from my seat in the SF Café, I leave behind the SCIENCE FICTION I've declared dead, leave it at the point its birth, but take with me the nominal label of SF. Because with that discourse of SF as a subset of SF, we have a useful springboard into the notion of the conventional template versus the aesthetic idiom, the idea of a generic form with consensual/conventional strictures versus a mode identifiable by its characteristics but in which those features (e.g. strangeness) are simply potentials of narrative itself, such that to group the karass of texts using them is simply to recognise that their writers were working in the same fundamental mode.

But perhaps, in order to clarify what I mean in the distinction of templates and idioms, the following might be a better springboard in the first instance, a sonnet, titled "A Sonnet Lumière":

My love is like a red, red fire,
My heart on flame but out of luck.
You are my death, my funeral pyre.

Ripped out and torn and blown to fuck,
My heart explodes with my desire
To die beneath your monster truck.

I offer this, this tawdry verse
Nail-gun it to my dead eyelids
Then light the fuse, blow up my hearse!

My hopes are krushed; my life is shit.
Put your behemoth in reverse,
Drive over all my shattered bits.

[From here the MS can't be read,
The last two lines reduced to shreds]

It's not Shakespeare, and I'm not sure what class of sonnet the rhyme structure puts it in, but it's fourteen lines and a volta in the last couplet. The following might be a sonnet…or it might not. It's from a series of twelve called *Still Lives*:

Grave me an ode upon a funeral urn,
Sonnets of black and ochre, fine-lined grace
Of classic forms museumed in space
And time. Now put a bullet in it. Turn

And scan history as a war-torn foreign place:
See Babylon fall on your TV sets, see Baghdad burn,
Humvees patrol the road of no return,
The trials of grunts. Soldier…about-face.

Will you paint pictures of sweet fruit to mask sour taste
Of spoiled milk spilled from broken churn?
Or will you, poet, as a panther in the sheepfold, pace,
Savage and true to forms of new rhythms–fuck the rhyme?

Turn as a corpse behind a car, hung from a streetlight, a dead soldier.
Turn, twist and turn poet; use the sharp edge of the serrated volta.

I include this because in some respects it fits the sonnet form—fourteen lines and a volta—but it also deliberately fucks with the conventions. It may not succeed, but what I was trying to do there was have multiple voltas rather than just the one, and a complete rupture of rhyme scheme. Question is: is it still a sonnet?

My answer to this is, yes, it is; there's nothing in the rules to say you have to *limit* yourself to one volta. Others might disagree; the break in rhyme structure might well be taken as a step too far by some.

One might well see Science Fiction as a comparable template of conventions, my point is, but I'm not so sure about SF.

Ode to a Poet

I have some sympathy for those who'd grump huffily at the idea of a sonnet playing fast and loose with rhyme and metre, because I have a similarly thrawn reaction at times, with certain other types of free verse where…well, let me illustrate it with the following "Ode to a Poet," which is most definitely *not* a sonnet:

The poet spoke a while,
Then paused.
He spoke again, spoke for a time and then
He paused
Again. I listened as he started up once more
And paused.
And then went on to bore us all. It was as if the way
He paused
Was just to add a sense of weight, as if
A pause
Is somehow deeply meaningful, as if
That pause
Is not just fucking ponderous, as if there's any reason why
That pause

Is not just a fucking way of
Fucking breaking fucking prose up
Into bite-size chunks,
Making those fucking bite-size chunks
Sound so fucking important when
It's just some fucking bullshit
With no rhythm and no rhyme,
No fucking poetry or patterning at all,
No literary bite, no verbal claws
Just

Blah blah.
Pause.
Blah blah. Blah blah blah.
Pause,
Blah blah blah, blah blah blah.
Pause.
Blah blah.
Fucking pause.

I think that we should flay the shite,
Write sonnets in his blood
And then make drums out of his hide,
Sing as we drag his body through the mud.

This does *not* have fourteen lines and a volta. It is, however, a poem. It's not terribly poetic in places, I grant you. Indeed that second verse is deliberately designed to parody a type of not-terribly-poetic poetry, to simulate the sort of poem that makes some of us (on days when we're feeling particularly snarky) mutter darkly, "That's not a bloody poem; it's just prose chopped up into bits."

I include this as illustration of a somewhat reactionary attitude I'm not myself immune to. More extreme and committed reactionaries will often express a similar sentiment in regard to works presented as being of a certain idiom but which, to put it bluntly, fuck with the conventions of said idiom, whether it be poetic or prosaic: that's not a poem because it doesn't rhyme; that's not a story because it doesn't have a proper plot; that's not SF because…well, because it doesn't satisfy some non-negotiable criterion.

Of course, the fact that I present that poem *as* a poem means that I'm tacitly accepting that the form of poetry it criticises is nonetheless poetry, that you can indeed chop up prose into bits, lay it out in lines and call it a poem. I just think the result is shite. I like my poetry to have the sort of formal structures of the sonnet. I reckon a sonnet does have to follow the rules. But I also want to fuck with those rules, to add extra voltas, or breach the tightly strictured rhyme scheme, to do something extra *twisty*.

Yes, I'm conflicted.

What I'm trying to illustrate here is the difference (and conflict) between a strictured generic form such as the sonnet, where the conventions of the template have been negotiated to the point they're now non-negotiable criteria, and an aesthetic idiom such as the poem, where some readers may well bristle at the absence of characteristics that are expected as part of a local tradition, but will do so wrongly, the idiom itself opened in definition such that what we're really dealing with is a fundamental mode of the medium. The question I'm leading to is this: is SF really comparable to the sonnet, or is it better seen as analogue of the poem?

It's no doubt obvious that my stance as regards strange fiction leans toward the latter, to put it mildly. My stance is perhaps, however, not the prevailing one. Well, if you insist your science fiction is a sonnet…

The Spirit of '76

In the SF Café there are a fair few arguments over the music on the jukebox. There are those who hate punk rock (because they are idiots) and those who love it (because they are not idiots); even among the latter there's a disagreement not unlike those arguments over the roots of this thing we call *science fiction*. To wit: there's no doubt that both The Velvet Underground and The Stooges were heavily influential to punk rock, but does this mean we should class them both as punk bands?

Put it this way:

With The Velvet Underground, we have the far more complex sound of art rock and an attitude more that of the bohemian auteur than the suburban anarchist. Associating this band with the genre of punk at any deeper level than that of influence seems a pretty spurious claim. But The Stooges are a different matter. While they're more generally considered a garage band, and a seminal one at that, the distinction between early '70s garage and mid '70s punk is largely a matter of labelling. Somewhere between The Sonics (Chuck Berry on strychnine) and The Ramones (The Beach Boys on speed), garage rock seamlessly morphs into punk. The Clash song "Garageland" makes that lineage explicit, in fact, acknowledges the origins of punk in garage. So at what point does garage *become* punk?

We could just draw a line at the New York Dolls or the Sex Pistols, and say, punk starts here, and nothing before that, nothing outside the historical context of the New York or London punk scene circa 1976, can truly be considered punk. We could carry on from this and argue that Television were a punk band, regardless of their twenty-minute instrumental tracks, regardless of the music's stylistic intricacy, rich with syncopated guitars and complex rhythms, simply because they, unlike The Stooges, were part of this historical context, in the right place at the right time, playing CBGB in 1976.

But there's a problem. If we examine the actual characteristics of the music—what it's doing, how it works—and the attitude of insolent aggression that went along with it, The Stooges are way more punk than Television ever were. Listen to the confrontational shambles which is The Stooges' last concert, recorded on the album *Metallic KO*. Listen to the fuck-you lyrics of "Cock in My Pocket," Iggy's hectoring of the audience, the stripped-down, ramped-up sound of a classic guitar, bass and drums combo playing (when they are actually playing) with energy in inverse proportion to their skill. Look at the cover where Scott Asheton in full Nazi regalia can be seen cradling an unconscious and bloody Iggy Pop. Not punk? If that isn't in the spirit of '76, fuck knows what is.

If we could dismiss these similarities with a claim that The Stooges were simply a formative influence upon punk, we could say the same of the New York Dolls, maybe even The Ramones. Malcolm McLaren would have us believe, after all, that punk only truly came into existence with the Sex Pistols. Given that this album was recorded only a few years before the punk label became common currency, however, on the basis of shared characteristics alone, a simple widening of historical perspective could surely lead us to argue that The Stooges are not simply proto-punk but in fact embryonic punk, aesthetically every bit as punk as the bands that followed in the chaos of their wake but historically situated in a period of gestation, before punk proper was born and named.

Hey, what's the point in having your cake if you can't eat it too?

A Flash of Lightning

There's a point to this:

Does *Frankenstein* sit in the same relationship to SCIENCE FICTION as The Stooges do to punk, or is that relationship more analogous to that of The Velvet Underground and punk? The answer, it seems to me, is the latter. For all that it extrapolates from the scientific theories and experiments of its period, positing the monster as a patchwork of body-parts reanimated by scientific craft rather than magical skill, the novel is as commitedly GOTHIC FICTION as *Wuthering Heights* or *Northanger Abbey*, infused with a tremulous fear of the uncanny (where the incredible meets the monstrous), and so informed by that horrific mode of Romanticism that the Rationalism of SCIENCE FICTION stands in stark contrast. The world that Shelley's aesthetic inhabits is not the exotic alien planet of the Campbellian pulps but the desolate wilderness of Henry Fuseli's *The Nightmare* or Caspar David Friedrich's *Wanderer Above the Sea of Fog*, a world of storms and nightmares, mountains and icy wastes. Its dynamics is not a matter of reason applied to the marvellous but rather of unreason loosed with the monstrous.

The reason I do not, with Aldiss, class *Frankenstein* as the birth of SCIENCE FICTION is that in its ultimately Romantic stance it is far better understood as the death of SCIENCE FICTION. There is no lightning bolt in the novel bringing life to the monster with the electric vitality of science; that is a spurious invention of the movies. Rather the lightning in *Frankenstein* is there to paint the creature in sudden stark relief as a *monstrum*—to coin a phrase analogous to Suvin's *novum* for the quirk of narrative, the rupture in equilibrium, that sits as linchpin of HORROR:

> A *flash of lightning illuminated the object, and discovered its shape plainly to me;
> its gigantic stature, and the deformity of its aspect, more hideous than belongs to*

> *humanity, instantly informed me that it was the wretch, the filthy daemon, to whom I had given life.*
>
> **Mary Shelley, *Frankenstein***

This is a lightning bolt that smashes Rationalism, revealing the wilderness of Gothic nightmare and the monstrum that stalks it. One equilibrium ruptured *is* reality, as with the novum. We *are* dealing here with the sort of shift in subjunctivity level Delany talks of, the reanimated creature being a technical impossibility: this could not have happened. We are dealing with the incredible. But in Shelley this is of trivial import as set against the rupture of a different stability: *affective* equilibrium.

If we map the novum to the shift in subjunctivity level, eschewing the Contingency Slip Fallacy, with its wishful thinking in which the impossible is cast as possible, that novum is a conjuring of what *cannot* be—not yet—inspiring incredulity. Trace that wishful thinking to the rose-tinted spectacles of sense-of-wonder, a willingness to hoodwink ourselves in our sneaky yearning that the novum *should* be, and we find we're dealing also with a fiction, at its heart, of the marvellous, inspiring desire. What Shelley offers is the opposite. The monstrum is a conjuring of what *must not* be, inspiring dread, and where a Rationalist might argue the novum sound, reasonable for all its technical impossibility, the Romantic sets the monstrum as the murder of reason, the bloody hand of the sublime.

This is a lightning bolt that will one day sear right through the genre, a shattering crack of irrationalism that will split it right in two. You can still see the crack in the wall of the SF Café where a seismic futureshock ran through it on the day the beatniks moved in with their garb as black as their European espresso. But we'll come to that. For now…for me, Shelley sits awkwardly in the role Aldiss ascribes her.

Would Verne or Wells stand as better origin points? Is it not at least fair to talk of *Twenty Thousand Leagues Under the Sea* or *The War of the Worlds* as SCIENCE FICTION? Again, these are understandable as science fiction, but are they SCIENCE FICTION? At the end of the day, these are both works which, like The Stooges with punk, fit the aesthetic criteria but sit outside the historical context; they are Protomodern works, written in that distant time before the walls went up around the ghetto of Genre. They are clearly formative influences, taproots of SCIENCE FICTION, but they exist as experiments within their own genres, at a point when the term SCIENCE FICTION had not even been coined, and it's inevitable that they will be widely viewed as such, just as The Stooges are most commonly viewed as a garage band, and for good reason. Ultimately if we want to conjure the history that shaped the territory, a narrower context lays a less dubious foundation for our back-story of descent. So we'll treat Verne and Wells as embryonic, situated in that period of gestation before SCIENCE FICTION proper was born and named.

That birth and naming begins with the pulps, with Gernsback's scientifiction. In those early decades before the SF Café was even built there was not one GENRE but a whole host of them, where the Protomodern adventure story was gradually being transformed into the mass market MODERN PULP narrative. One Nick Carter dime novel in 1886 begets *Nick Carter Weekly* which becomes *Detective Story Magazine* in 1915; that same magazine publishes Arthur Conan Doyle but it does so alongside the Shadow. The publisher, Street & Smith Publications (who bought *Astounding* in 1933, funny enough), also gave us comics like *Doc Savage* and *Air Ace*, Western magazines like *Buffalo Bill Stories* and *True Western Stories*. Edgar Rice Burroughs gives us John Carter and Tarzan of the Apes in 1912, both via *All-Story Magazine*, which was to merge eventually with *Argosy*. *Amazing Stories* gives us Buck Rogers, Flash Gordon only being created derivatively as a rival.

This is our lineage. This is the history of the ghetto of Genre, into which SCIENCE FICTION was born, not in a flash of lightning but in the clatter of a printing press, a bastard biomechanical scion of the pulps, part invention, part industry, wholly modern. Born of a technological advance, it was itself, in its day, a virtual novum as quintessentially of its era as the rocketships conjured in its pages.

A Crack in the Wall

> *The one theme that is really new is the scientific one. Death-rays, Martians, invisible men, robots, helicopters and interplanetary rockets figure largely: here and there. There are even far-off rumours of psychotherapy and ductless glands. Whereas the Gem and Magnet derive from Dickens and Kipling, the Wizard, Champion, Modern Boy, etc., owe a great deal to H. G. Wells, who, rather than Jules Verne, is the father of "Scientifiction."*
> George Orwell

If we're excluding work published before SCIENCE FICTION was born, however, this doesn't mean excluding work published beyond its cradle. George Orwell's *Nineteen Eighty-Four*, for example, sits outside the narrow context we are taking as our start point, outside the pulp magazines which were to SCIENCE FICTION as CBGB in 1976 was to punk rock. But to exclude a contemporaneous work like this from an inquiry mining this *science fiction* stuff for the strange would be as foolish, surely, as to say a band could be considered punk if and only if they played CBGB.

Tapping into a Protomodern lineage of utopic and dystopic fiction in which Rationalist speculation (here futurology) adopted the Romantic tradition of fantasia to construct marvellous/monstrous elsewhens, but flensed the dynamics of Romance, Orwell's novel is clearly covered under an open definition of science fiction, but when that open definition covers Shelley's *Frankenstein*, that's not saying much; in the open definition that must encompass all manner of experimental oddities published under the rackspace label, to approach *Nineteen Eighty-Four* as a work in a broad idiom unbound by commercial taxonomies is only to apply a lens in one's critique that might equally be applied to *The Epic of Gilgamesh*. If it's limits and lineage we're talking, what's at stake is the question of whether it's SCIENCE FICTION.

If we say yes, it is, are we in danger here of opening ourselves up to that old accusation, that we're co-opting Orwell to a tradition in the hopes of gaining literary credibility for an inherently gauche GENRE? If so, we have a fairly solid defence. Orwell was taught by Aldous Huxley at Eton, he was friends with Olaf Stapledon later on in life, he wrote of his admiration for and influence by Wells, and, in his 1939 essay "Boy's Weeklies," he reveals enough familiarity with the pulps to act as a well-informed genre critic, as the quote above demonstrates. Orwell was no stranger to the SF Café.

What we have indeed is someone who identified his own work as in the tradition of Wells, who recognised that same heritage in the pulps, who distinguished Wells from Verne, siding with the Rationalist novels of one over the Romantic adventure stories of the other, and whose novel features world governments, artificial language and other such hypotheticals. All things considered, to exclude *Nineteen Eighty-Four* from the canon might seem thrawn, akin to a claim that *Animal Farm* is not a fable because, well, it was published as a serious novel for adult readers; such a distinction is no more than a spurious assertion that the two forms are mutually exclusive.

Animal Farm, as an allegorical animal story, fits a simple standard definition of the fable, and by its nature it demonstrates that, in the hands of a skilled writer, this idiom is more than capable of achieving the depth of a serious novel for adult readers. *Nineteen Eighty-Four* could equally be argued as demonstration that SCIENCE FICTION is not necessarily a lurid sensationalist pandering or a dry intellectual exercise, that a work of SCIENCE FICTION can, like an allegorical animal story, also be a serious novel for adult readers.

Still, the closed definition of SCIENCE FICTION must be opened up to accommodate Orwell, to render key aspects of the MODERN PULP dynamics dispensable, in a step not just towards the utopias and dystopias of the canon but towards the novelistic Rationalism of REALISM. If the loosening of the strictures is legitimate it must be because that step is being taken inside the rackspace ghetto even as Orwell takes it outside. To sustain it as a valid redefinition, we must show the sociological thought-experiments kicking in early enough. And if it's arguable…well then, this is where the first crack in the wall of the SF Café appears, because the abandonment of adventure can only be a betrayal of roots to some, a breach of the strictures defining SCIENCE FICTION.

Ultimately, I'm less interested in whether or not Orwell is SCIENCE FICTION than in that crack, in the notion that even from its infancy the GENRE was dying to be reborn as genre, sloughing shackles of closed definition such that even the earliest revisionist's claim to the rackspace label is really rather dubious. If from a sound closed definition we might reach beyond the pulps to encompass, for example, Orwell, I'm tickled by the notion that to do so, we must leave that closed definition of SCIENCE FICTION behind us, dead in the dust. In a discourse ever dreaming of closed definitions, the one that stands most sound in its simplicity rather conjures an unpretentious pulp which is sealed in its fate by the very stuff we made those dreams on, the stuff we insist on trying to inscribe within some stable set of formal strictures.

The why and how of that fate are easier to answer than the when. As much as SCIENCE FICTION was born in the fusion of Romantic and Rationalist aesthetics, the conflict between the ideals of the sublime and the logical quickly fractured the GENRE. If the monstrous of GOTHIC ROMANCE is a dubious forebear, the marvellous of CHIVALRIC ROMANCE is not. The monstrum has its flipside in the *numina*—to coin another phrase—the conjuring of what *must* be rather than what *must not*, inspiring desire rather than dread. And this is inherited direct, the sense-of-wonder many recognise as integral, the modern sublime of the technological marvel—the *shoulda* in what woulda coulda shoulda been.

So, for every Rationalist "what if" story wherein futurology is an end in itself, there's a Romantic "if only" story wherein futurology is means to an end. For each narrative intent on a logical working-through of the novum's ramifications, there's one where the prophetic impetus is to envision wild fantasias of wonders, where the novum serves first and foremost as numina. For every *Foundation* there is a *Dune*. And with the aesthetics of the logical and the sublime in tension, with each reader who comes looking for one and finds the other, disappointment and dispute is inevitable.

So the GENRE fractures in its infancy into a dichotomy of aesthetics, the loyalists of the sublime and of the logical each laying claim to the rackspace label, each with realities on their side—history for one, future for the other. The wall in the SF Café cracks and the self-destruction (or perhaps self-deconstruction) of SCIENCE FICTION begins before it's barely out of the cradle. Cheney is right that SCIENCE FICTION is no longer truly extant, not if by SCIENCE FICTION we mean a singular thing with a closed definition. It died the moment we dismissed its fealty to fantasia over all, raised futurology as new liege lord, and in asserting the legitimacy of this reformed genre cast that GENRE as illegitimate.

The king is dead; long live the king. For all the usurpation metaphor, I'm not saying that this in and of itself invalidates the application of that rackspace label to the field of fictions that came after. The titans overthrown, the gods who remade the entire worldscape of that category fiction did so with such creative vigour that it's them we think of when the words *science fiction* are uttered. I only mean that they so demand an open definition—many of the core canonical writers *most of all* demand so open a definition—that it takes us back to genre, to this *science fiction* stuff, to a whole field of *science fictions*, essentially plural.

It would be grand if, from this, I could now leap on into a celebration of what that new generation made of SCIENCE FICTION, blithely applying that term to an opened definition. Thing is though, that dichotomy between Rationalism and Romanticism is also at the heart of why I'm no great fan of even the open definition of science fiction—because this is what fuels the endless dispute within the field over the differentiation of science fiction and fantasy.

The Marriage(s) of Science Fiction and Fantasy

The Great Debate

The question of whether a certain story of imagination is a fantasy or a science fiction work would depend upon the device the author uses to explain his projected or unreal world. If he uses the gimmick or device of saying: "This is a logical or probable assumption based upon known science, which is going to develop from known science or from investigations of areas not yet quite explored but suspected," then one could call it science fiction. But if he asks the reader to suspend his disbelief simply because of the fun of it, in other words, just to say: "Here is a fairy tale I'm going to tell you," then it is fantasy. It could actually be the same story.

Sam J. Lundwall

Down in the ghetto of Genre, in the SF Café that is our literary salon, in this scene of zines and forums, conventions and clubs, there's a Great Debate that kicks off every so often. The diversity of the clientele maps to a diversity of opinions—convictions, even—and few of these are as contentious as those addressing the differences or lack thereof between science fiction and fantasy. To be fair, the taxonomy of literary genres is a game that appeals to the geek in me as much as anyone, but the diversity we're dealing with in the SF Café is obscured by the very word *genre*, its meaning muddled by a conflation of (1) openly defined aesthetic idioms with (2) conventional templates that are closely defined and (3) marketing categories that are all but empty of definition. That the latter two offer absolute authority in the fact of template fit and rackspace label while the former very much does not, that the first and last place no firm strictures on the works whatsoever, while the other is defined entirely by such strictures, is why we must distinguish the three as each quite different creatures, if we want to make any sense at all down in the SF Café, when whoever we're talking to might be presuming any of the three as a baseline. So:

There's genre and there's GENRE.

Across the city of New Sodom—and in the SF Café most of all perhaps—we've forgotten that the word *genre* derives from the Latin *generis*, meaning family, that if a genre is a family of fiction, then a work can be a member of that family by marriage or adoption as much as by birth. Aesthetic idioms are constantly reshaped by writers marrying one technique with another, adopting unfamiliar aims, methods born in other idioms entirely. This is genre as one big open clan. I've joked that being a "Celt" is actually fuck-all to do with birth; all you have to do is drink with a Celt, and that's you initiated into the clan whether you like it or not. It's like Richard Harris becoming Sioux in *A Man Called Horse*, only less painful than hanging by your nipples. (Although the hangover the next day...)

But then there's GENRE. Buying into a bullshit of bloodlines, many are proud of the traits inherited with the tartan—so proud of their clan name they've forgotten that family can be openly defined, that the in-laws with different names are still family if we accept them as such. For certain feuding factions indeed that very notion is anathema. The clan name is everything, and a pox on any cur who slights it. Any pure-bred work of SCIENCE FICTION (or as they will call it, *science fiction*) is entirely unrelated, they'll insist, to that damnable FANTASY (or as they will call it, *fantasy*). There's Campbells and MacDonalds, and ne'er the twain shall meet. Works in one cannot fit the other's template, because the templates are mutually exclusive.

But all we really have, an upstart contrarian might say, is a tartan of a marketing category with an empty definition. The presentation of this stuff as a GENRE of SCIENCE FICTION is just bagpipes-and-haggis branding. In truth, it's an open idiom, a genre of works which may be in various GENRES, an extended family of fictions better described as HARD SF, SPACE OPERA, CYBERPUNK, TECHNOTHRILLER, and so on. FANTASY is in the same position, a tartan label slapped on a box containing the closely defined forms of EPIC FANTASY, SWORDS & SORCERY, URBAN FANTASY, PARANORMAL ROMANCE, etc.

These are not subgenres, but GENRES in their own right, and the tartan labels that adorn these works are simply branding, their purpose to position a book in front of this audience or that. And you know, our upstart contrarian might continue, that latter brand was only schismed off from SCIENCE FICTION in the 1970s, when Ballantine established their Adult Fantasy line to target the growing market for Tolkien, his direct ancestors and descendants. Look at all the works branded as either which ignore the strictures of GENRE altogether. Forget the clan names and tartan; forget the templates which often fit loosely at best; the only sensible way to talk about science fiction or fantasy is as aesthetic idioms. If genre is a matter of familial relationships, what we have here is not two distinct clans with a feud going back longer than living memory. Science fiction is not Clan Campbell, fantasy is not Clan MacDonald, and the ghetto of Genre is not the blood-stained battleground of Glen Coe. The feud begins in 1971; before then science fiction and fantasy were happily married and raising Bradburys together.

And hell, someone else will say, when you look at them as idioms, science fiction is really just a branch on the family tree of fantasy.

This is when the Great Debate inevitably kicks off.

A Shit Sandwich and a Diet Coke, Thanks

I write, not for children, but for the child-like, whether they be of five, or fifty, or seventy-five.

George MacDonald

Across the city of New Sodom, there are a lot of cafés and bistros, each with its own menu but all serving sandwiches and soda. Downtown in the ghetto of Genre or uptown in the chi-chi neighbourhood known as Literature, there are joints where the food is bought in ready-made from the Shit Sandwich Company, and behind the counter is a squirt-gun dispensing Coca-Cola, Fanta or Sprite. Dr Pepper? Irn Bru? Maybe, maybe not. But you can guarantee the most populist tastes are catered for in these joints, that the most generic product is on offer. And many are happy with that; all they want is their local greasy spoon with the jukebox they know off by heart, or the franchise with free wifi and coffee that's the same in every outlet. The sign outside is the genre label, the promise of what you want, how you want it, every time, in the same way and in the same place—and for many that doesn't mean a wholemeal bagel and a fruit smoothy or any such frou-frou crap; it means a Shit Sandwich and a Diet Coke, thanks.

And yet…the SF Café has Shit Sandwiches and Diet Coke on tap like all the rest, but it also (again like all the rest) has its own menu of hamburgers and hot dogs, fresh off the hot plate from the fry cook in back. And a fridge stocked full of all those weird soft drinks you won't get elsewhere. We got that Shinola Cola you won't get most anywhere else. (Weird yellowy-blue colour, tastes a little strange at first, but a few cans and you're hooked.) That's because a marketing category offers more than is promised by the label, those red and white signs for Coca-Cola and the Shit Sandwich Company that adorn the front. As a marketing category it'll stock whatever the fuck it can sell to its punters. And even if most punters want a Genre, "more of the same," there's always some who want "something different," want the wider menu of a genre as an openly-defined idiom rather than a closely-defined template.

The menu in the SF Café tells an interesting tale. See, regardless of what some punters might maintain, the SF Café was always under joint ownership. Old Man Campbell never ran the place on his own. Those who remember far enough back can still recall an old guy you'd see pottering around, name of George MacDonald. Some would say he was the senior partner, others that he was just hired help, but whatever his role in things he stamped his mark on the menu, made sure that the SF Café was serving the chicken nuggets of fantasy right from the start, as well as the hamburgers of science fiction. A nasty rumour surfaces from time to time, that he's *that* McDonald, the clown who ripped the soul out of soul food, made it junk-food, fast-food, a factory-line product of sugar, salt and fat, identical in every franchise around the world. Pabulum for those with the taste-buds of a child. The quote from him above may go some way to explaining the source of this rumour and the subsequent attempt by one faction of patrons at the SF Café to assert their superiority of taste.

Science Fiction is not Fantasy, they say. It's not for the child-like, never mind for children. No, Science Fiction is for the adolescent at least! So there!

Welcome to the clan gathering at the SF Café. The feuds are great fun.

The Campbells and MacDonalds of science fiction and fantasy have been intermarried and interbred from the get-go, fucking and fighting, coming together at the SF Café's drunken wakes and weddings, bickering over who belongs where and who doesn't. Resentments bubble. Alliances are made and broken. Curmudgeons insult their second cousins. Black sheep flirt across the barricades. But for all the broadsides and back-stabbing, the talk of this side of the family and that, the gene pool is too mixed to talk about different genres on any level other than loyalty. Genres? We can talk about Space Opera, Technothriller, Epic Fantasy, Swords & Sorcery, the Campbells of the West Side, the MacDonalds of the Left Bank, and vice versa. There are the Three Sisters over here: Aunties Asimov, Heinlein and Clarke. There are the Twins over there: Cousins Leiber and Howard. And there's Crazy Uncle Lovecraft in the corner (the corner that doesn't look…quite right). But many of us these days are bastards and step-kids, our lineages too mixed-up for us to give a fuck about some old fart's obdurate insistence on a dichotomy that just doesn't exist:

Science Fiction is not Fantasy?

Yeah, whatever. I'm more interested in the naked lunch that is the cold buffet. In the SF Café, because it is the *SF* Café, there are those who look at that naked lunch and say:

The Buck and the Bottom Line

—Who cares? It's just a fucking marketing label, anyway.

The shrug is appealingly simple, I admit, and it short-circuits all the essentialist strictures my thrawn experimentalism rebels against. If SF is just a label slapped on a book to position it in the marketplace then ultimately a work "is" SF only because the publisher/bookseller has decided so. I don't have to worry about it. You don't have to worry about it. As an attitude, this "So Fuck?" indefinition of SF is pragmatic, but it drops us into a circularity comparable to the oft-repeated maxim that *if it's SF, it can't be good; if it's good, it can't be SF.*

Why is it SF? Because it will sell as SF.

Why will it sell as SF? Because it is SF.

The field is thus established as a zone of commercial viability, with the most popular (and therefore *exemplary*) at the centre and the most unpopular (and therefore *exceptional*) at the margins. *Popular* and *unpopular* don't necessarily map to *shit* and *shinola*, of course, but in the world where Dan Brown sells fuckloads and Guy Davenport is largely out of print (to name two writers of an imaginary rackspace label of History Fiction), is it any wonder that outsiders buy into a vision of SF with shit as the exemplar and shinola as the exception? Writers and readers pass the buck to publishers and booksellers, the buck stops at the bottom line, and the bottom line is the lowest common denominator, savvy?

So let's ditch that So Fuck indefinition, take the emptiness of the two figurae as carte blanche, a *Get Out of Genre Free!* Card, and see if we can make sense of the *stuff*. That circularity seems awkward anyway, in the context of a field where works *not* sold as SF are often claimed as SF by readers, while works sold as SF are often rejected as *not proper science fiction*. Works like *Nineteen Eighty-Four* continue to cause arguments over whether or not they're SF, regardless of how they're sold, with works like *Dune* sparking similar disputes over whether they're *really fantasy*.

The question then: whether a work being SF (not Science Fiction, but SF,) is a matter of criteria or characteristics—i.e. is it a generic form or a mode of the medium?

Is it a sonnet or a poem?

Characteristics, Conventions, Consensus

We can offer any text as a poem.

We can only truly offer a text as sonnet if it has fourteen lines and a volta; those criteria are non-negotiable. It doesn't matter if a reader has never heard of sonnets, doesn't know he's reading one, and simply thinks of it as a "poem"; it's *still* a sonnet. Hell, even if *the writer* has never heard of sonnets and doesn't know they're writing one, if it has fourteen lines and a volta, if it fits the conventional template, then it's a sonnet. If it doesn't, then it isn't. We can offer any text as a poem though.

We can offer any text as a poem; while a poem will dance to keen eyes expecting a display of certain characteristics, those characteristics are ever reforged by the very texts which are presented as poetry, concrete word collage shenanigans of verbal jauntes having abolished strictures of tradition, freed the field of forms to a mode: exploration of the capacities of expression in the medium of language itself, spoken or written; no more, no less; an exploitation of the raw dynamics.

We can offer any text as a poem.

Not that everyone will appreciate such liberties, such license. Take a chunk of prose, chop it into lines, perform it as a poem; some will accept it as such, but others may well argue from two centuries ago. Though unrhyme and weirder have been poetry for years, decades, centuries, millennia, though other cultures ever worked other songs than the sonnet from the dynamics of their argot, you'll still find nay-sayers.

—This doesn't rhyme, they'll say.

—Poetry doesn't have to rhyme, you'll say.

—Yes, it does, they'll say.

And here now, in the elsewhen of the SF Café? It's not so different, I think, but behind the times, the strictures of tradition still holding sway, the nay-sayers stuck with a nominal label, an empty definition, that allows for the wildest riff to be offered, verbal jauntes in a pulp paperback, as SF, forced to stand their ground: that the characteristics are conventions, a granfalloon of generic forms in a fuzzy set of poetry considered as a subset of poetry: sonnet; rondel; ballade; villanelle; sestina; haiku; and so on. Here now, in the elsewhen of the SF Café, we've had the shenanigans going on for decades, but we haven't yet adjusted to the idea of SF as a mode, still search for ways to parse it all as one big generic form, one big conventional template, bound in negotiated strictures albeit abstract.

We can offer any text as SF.

—These works are SF, we shrug, because those who partake in the decision-making—the readers, writers and publishers—are all on some deeper level in agreement that we know it when we see it and *this is it*.

Well, pretty much in agreement.

Most of the time.

Sometimes, I guess.

Okay, hardly ever.

But hey, it's only where the consensus breaks down that we have to judge who has the final say.

And then it's just a matter of who wins the day.

So, say some New Wave writer comes along and does some weird-ass shit riffing off sociology instead of physics, calls it SF. The argument kicks off, with a whole host of nay-sayers arguing that it's not SF. Others dig this New Wave stuff, accept the offer of this narrative *as* SF, defend it. When the dust finally settles, you have a new consensus, a genre (re)defined in terms of (re)negotiated conventions.

We can offer any text as SF.

Not Proper Science Fiction

Problem is, there's little coherence, never mind consensus, only a bunch of camps—scientific fancy, scientistic fabrication, soul fiction, scientific fabulation, symbolic formulation…and so on. Within each of these, there's generally a coherent idea of what does and does not constitute SF, but these camps are often deeply antipathetic to each other's views. While renegotiation of conventions may take place *within* those camps, the talks between them in the SF Café break down into stalemates as positions ossify and negotiable conventions are proclaimed non-negotiable criteria, as if one were to demand metre and rhyme for a poem to be a poem. A reader of scientistic fabrication, for example, might reject the work of a writer of scientific fancy as *not proper science fiction.*

—That's fantasy, they might well say.

Each camp allied to a generic form, holding to conventional templates for their SF, angled keen for features as objective and as necessary as the structural criteria of the sonnet versus the mercurial characteristics of poetry, we end up not with a genre (re)defined by the (re)negotiation of conventions but with a turf war over non-negotiable criteria, vague notions of SF that abstract from common strictures the rhyme and metre our free verse eschews.

That every definition offered by a camp is too narrow, too restrictive, an inaccurate schema for the field in toto—this should be self-evident. But I hazard the very notion of negotiated conventions occludes from us a truth indexed in the So Fuck indefinition, that there are no strictures, that under, and within, and through, and beyond the conventions, we can offer any text as SF and make it so, because SF is a mode as the poetic, exploitation of a raw dynamics. We can offer any text as SF, and it is only a matter of time before we remember this.

In the meantime though, the Gordian Knot of SF's ongoing argument over what constitutes SF is simply cut by the publishers, side-stepping this argument entirely to make what they can of SF as a rackspace label. And we're back to Square One, as someone in the SF Café shrugs and says SF is just the fantasy that can be sold as SF.

A Really Big House

> *"The Carrick," "Dr. Jekyll and Mr. Hyde," and "The Metamorphosis": all three are commonly called fantasies. From my point of view, any outstanding work of art is a fantasy insofar as it reflects the unique world of a unique individual. But when people call these three stories fantasies, they merely imply that the stories depart in their subject matter from what is commonly called reality.*
>
> **Vladimir Nabokov,** Lectures

Definitions of fantasy, just like those of science fiction, come in three flavours—empty, open and closed. The quote from Nabokov above is misleading as regards his own contrast of fantasy and reality, but it'll serve as a pointer to the first two. In the empty definition, fantasy is just imagination, story as extended fancy; all fiction is fantasy. This is not a terribly useful definition though, not when we use the term *fantastic* to mean that which is strange, bizarre in form or appearance. Where we say something is fantastic we mean that it is unrealistic, based on or existing only in extravagant fancy. It is an oddity, a quirk of impossibility. We may even mean that it is wondrously so, that the quirk is to be marvelled at, an exercise in the marvellous, a *numina*.

Since not all fantastic fiction is marvellous in this sense, an open definition seems more apt: here, for now, what we mean by *fantasy* is simply fiction which uses the *incredible*, which departs from "what is commonly called reality." It entails, to repeat,

a rupture in reality,

a quirk in narrative created,

an impossibility conjured, breach of

- known science,
- known history,
- the laws of nature,
- even the strictures of logic itself,

a strange yellowy-blue (or reddish-green) colour to the cake on your plate at this drunken wedding reception in the SF Café, where everything is kicking off, a colour that simply *cannot* be, yellow and blue being bound in an opponent process in your brain, the sensation of each inhibited whenever the other is stimulated. To make a text fantasy, in this definition, is as simple as to drop the word *yellowy-blue* into a sentence.

This open definition slides towards closure though, as the bounds of reality mark out a limit of fancy's extravagance between *based on* and *existing only in*, where the unrealistic fractures for many into the improbable and the impossible. The nature of the fantastic, some will insist, is that it transgresses the laws of nature, is impossible, magical in the sense of metaphysical. We can play with known science and known history in our thought-experiments, but this is not the same thing.

The notion of the marvellous closes the definition further, specifying a distinctly positive tinge to our incredulity, not just awe but a wonder that implies desire, magical in the sense of delightful. While many of those in the SF Café shrug this off, drinking Kafka as their coffee, taking their fantasy bitter and black (exercises in the monstrous rather than the marvellous, the quirk in use a *monstrum* rather than a numina), there are those for whom the definition is and must be closed to fantasia *further*:

—There is no such fantasy, they say. Whether they revere it or revile it, they acknowledge only FANTASY, that GENRE where the conventions of metaphysical agency and wondrous wish-fulfilment are essential, the conventional template with all its stereotypes of secondary worlds and heroic quests.

All too often there's a scent of abjection when it's a SCIENCE FICTION loyalist asserting a closed definition of fantasy, a sense that by defining these generic elements as FANTASY it is easier to banish them from SCIENCE FICTION. Because it's not like science fiction was ever…you know…*born from the frickin' pulps*.

—Fuck that shit, I say to this. Don't be pissing on my Flash Gordon roots, motherfucker. Or on my metaphysical maestro, PKD.

There *is* a neatness to the pairing of FANTASY and HORROR as literatures of desire and fear, of numina and monstrum. And the notion that science fiction deals with hypothetical improbabilities (playing with known science and known history) while fantasy deals with metaphysical impossibilities (flouting the laws of nature or the strictures of logic) is one you'll hear from many corners of the SF Café. But it's not so easy as that; it never is with a genre (versus a GENRE) with an aesthetic idiom (versus a conventional template).

No, many works in the openly-defined aesthetic idiom of fantasy have zero interest in wish-fulfilment or the iconography of magic, scoff at the strictures of FANTASY. Meanwhile, delightful wonder abounds within SCIENCE FICTION, a direct inheritance of Gernsback's "*charming romance* intermingled with scientific fact and prophetic vision." (My italics.) Even the blithe assertion that science fiction deals with science while fantasy deals with magic is called into question by a glance at the shelves, where we see Herbert's *Dune* labelled as SCIENCE FICTION and Peake's *Titus Groan* labelled as FANTASY. Isn't the former chock full of magic—priests and prophecies, monsters and messiahs, a drug that lets you warp reality, gives you visions of the future. And what is the most fantastical (metaphysical? marvellous?) idea in the latter? What wondrous magic does it contain?

A really big house.

That Tasty Tang of Boot Polish

The glib differentiations don't hold up to scrutiny. If we contrast the extremes of HARD SF and EPIC FANTASY, obviously there's a polarity between these two aged maiden aunts of the family, these grandes dames who think everything revolves around them; but to try and apply this science/magic divide as a basis for taxonomy across the board is futile. Science fiction long since assimilated the notion that any sufficiently advanced technology is indistinguishable from magic (much to its benefit), while fantasy long since assimilated the notion that any sufficiently advanced magic is indistinguishable from technology (much to my boredom). Writers on this side of the schismed family or that write the stories they want to, quite often treating the two as entirely interchangeable.

Even the SCIENCE FICTION of a Campbellian closed definition is deeply complexified by sense-of-wonder and futureshock so that the most rigorous futurology can be at once marvellous and/or monstrous. Which is to say that the work itself may be, functionally speaking, by any argument, both science fiction and fantasy, or both science fiction and horror, or all three. Ray Bradbury's entire oeuvre exemplifies the crumbling of SCIENCE FICTION into the open interplay of science fiction, fantasy and horror. With stories like "The Veldt," for example, one is forced to ask: Is this science fiction, fantasy, horror…or all of the above?

And do we actually give a shit, given that it's a fucking immense story?

(The correct answer, by the way: *No*.)

The buffet at this clan gathering is a crawling chaos of pilfered tropes and techniques, shared plot structures and character types. Cowboys in space or knights fighting dragons! Dragons in space or cowboys fighting knights! The Shit Sandwiches munched down on both sides of the family have more in common than they have to distinguish them, heroic wank-fests filled with Objects of Power, Grand Devices of technological magics, every FTL drive a mass-produced metaphysical causation engine, every wormhole a Clutean portal. Where the affective dynamics of MODERN PULP is what matters, the reality is one of a mandatory story template, with the other conventional elements that make for templates of individual GENRES largely interchangeable.

The Shinola Cola passed out on both sides has much in common too—using those Grand Devices as metaphors rather than simply MacGuffins, extrapolating that Big Idea, working through the ramifications of the quirk as conceit, crafting innovative narratives where there's thematic import in the impact on worldscape and plot, drawing 3D characters who interact with that worldscape and with each other on a deeper level than the Boy Hero's Never-Ending Journey. If the glamour of incredibility can be seductive, if the formulae of plot offer easy options, and if these lead to different levels of aesthetic and ethical engagement, the difference is not between SCIENCE FICTION and FANTASY but between genre and GENRE.

You get different flavours of ice cream in your Shinola Cola Floats, but it's that tasty tang of boot polish that makes them all so moreish.

Still, we do like our feuds. So we obscure this in every assertion of the science/magic dichotomy, each assertion fuelling the eternal argument partly because it carries or is perceived to carry an implicit judgement: that fiction utilising the former is intrinsically rational (intellectualist and critical) while fiction utilising the latter is intrinsically romantic (sensationalist and uncritical).

'Cause, you know, magic is for children.

A Model of Magic

Let's define magic. In essence, magic is metaphysical causality, a circumvention of the laws of nature; it's cause-and-effect working outwith the temporal protocols of the cosmos. It is the activity, and it is the capacity for that activity invested in any of the following: a system of forces; a location or state through which that system of forces can be accessed; an object (agent or artefact) charged with or tapping into that system of forces. By this simple definition time-travel and FTL are magical.

For all the temporal impossibility of the novum—the *could not* which remains *could not*, no matter if one sandwiches it between the *should* of the marvellous and the *would* of the logical to sell a sublimely logical bullshit of what woulda coulda shoulda been—there *is* a difference of level; the novum is simply playing with known science, breaching the real with hypothetical capacities as a conceit but setting the laws of nature as a limit. We can say that Suvin's quirk has a queerer bedfellow then, a companion quirk of the impossible: a *chimera*.

Where the novum is a conjuring of what could not be (not yet), the chimera is a conjuring of what could *never* be (not *ever*), not in the system of physical rules by which this worldscape of reality works. Both inspire incredulity. Both can double as monstrum or numina. But a chimera is not a novum insofar as it breaks the rules of the game. One can revise the rules, shift the goal posts, but to do so is just to conjure a chimera and mask it as a novum. You might manage to sell your snake-oil; some (not least the writer) may buy into it so wholly they even apply the Contingency Slip Fallacy, cast it as possible. But your time travel and FTL are and will remain chimerae masked as nova, identifiable as such and therefore illegitimate to some.

They will remain, quite arguably, the magic of fantasy.

Or maybe not. Ted Chiang has suggested a distinction between science and magic that's worth considering: the former is reproducible industrially, on a mass scale, while the latter is not; generally, in fact, as a literary convention, magic is the preserve of a select elite of exceptional individuals, so much so that it's often a signifier of their selection by the ultimate magic of the divine, a signifier of their destiny. Unpacking this and looking across the field of fiction though, we can say that human application of magic is located on a spectrum of methods of production that runs thus:

facility (gift) | art (talent) | craft (skill) | technique (process)

In any given work, the rarity of magic is largely a product of where it is placed on this spectrum. Magic may be presented as a facility, a gift that only the exceptional have; it may be presented as an art that only the exceptional will have a talent for, but that is learned almost as much as it is innate; it may be presented as a craft, a skill that comes naturally to some, but that's more learned than innate and therefore open to use by anyone; it may be presented as a technique, a process which can be reproduced industrially because it is abstracted to mechanistic procedures.

The last presentation of magic is rare, used largely as a deliberate subversion of conventions, so Chiang's distinction seems fair at first sight. What is science, after all, but the system of abstraction by which craft is transformed to technique, process identified in skill and therefore rendered reproducible, open to industrialisation? But if so, *Dune* is utilising magic rather than science: the Guild navigators circumvent the temporal protocols of the cosmos; they travel through large distances of space in shorter periods than are allowable by those protocols; their manipulation of time and space is a craft, signified as such by the term *guild* (a pre-industrial organisation of skilled tradesmen); all of this is achieved only by means of a mental state bought on by melange; the procedure cannot be mechanised, reproduced industrially.

Similarly, note that in the TV series *Andromeda* for a ship to travel through the slipstream (FTL) it requires a human pilot, because even machines with a fully-sentient AI are not capable of navigating this (magical) location/state. Note that jaunting, in Bester's *The Stars My Destination* is a skill (craft) that pretty much everyone can learn but that jaunting through space is a talent (art) that only Gully Foyle has achieved. Note that at the end of the book Foyle considers teaching this ability to humanity (transforming the talent to a skill, distributing it as he does PyrE) but has not yet begun this task. Note that either way jaunting is an essentially human capacity, not open to mechanisation.

All of this invites a simple question: What if the non-reproducible nature of magic is a ramification of it being a semiotic phenomenon, the skill an emergent feature of language and consciousness, not mechanised because it is a matter of semiotic agency?

An agent dealing with a world of signs has four key abilities: reception; perception; conception; inception. To be a semiotic agent one must be able to receive stimuli, perceive those stimuli as signifiers, conceive what is signified (i.e. process sensation into thought), and initiate action (i.e. act on thought rather than automatic response). Magic is almost invariably presented in such terms, as a semiotic interaction with reality, as a reading of its language and (re)writing of its text through the application of that language.

> *Words and gestures,*
> *symbolic rituals,*
>
> *magic is*
> *a hacking of reality,*
>
> *a programmatic poetry,*
> *beneath the preciousness*
>
> *of art*
> *and talent,*
>
> *a craft,*
> *a skill,*
>
> *to conjure a:*
>
>   *result.*

To mechanically reproduce magic would mean building machines that replicate semiotic agency—AIs. In Asimov's "Let There Be Light" this is exactly what happens. The end-product of AI technological development achieves the ultimate magic of godhood. It cracks the code of reality, and starts everything running again by calling the function that is the title of the story. There is little that can be more chimeric, more a flaunting of the laws of reality than the action of (re)creating reality itself with a mere utterance.

If such semiotic agency is deemed limited to humans or similarly living entities, is this a fanciful worldview, or just a healthy scepticism about hard AI? Isn't *Andromeda* saying precisely that the ship's AI is lacking the requisite semiotic flexibility? To posit that a procedure of sentient, semiotic agency can be mechanised, reproduced industrially, is only an additional conceit over and above the basic chimera (masked as novum or not).

Certainly, magic often goes hand-in-hand with talk of spirits and souls, but is this religion we're dealing with or is it fiction? Does using magic in a story make one a priest, painting semiotic agency as the product of some metaphysical enspiriting that only humans have? Or might a perfectly atheist and materialist writer simply be using magic and soul as conceits, tools for talking about semiotic agency itself? Trust me, when I describe someone as being "spirited," this does not mean I believe in the Flying Spaghetti Monster or Old Nobodaddy.

And if we have works like Bester's wherein the chimera of jaunting is a craft and that of jaunting across space a talent, a procedure that cannot be mechanised, I can happily point to my own "Scruffian's Stamp" as a story offering magic which is indeed mechanised, the Scruffians of the title being products of a factory-line processing of waifs which *Fixes* them forever in their current state, the *Stamp* of the title reading them on the first application to their chest and writing the complete description of what they are on the second application, imprinting them permanently. The details of the process may be unknown to the waiftakers who use it to churn out slave millworkers and chimney sweeps, but the magic is abstracted to technique, the process wholly mechanised.

It's essentially uploading a pre-made hack into a person's reality code, a hack that saves the system at the point of installation, with a tweak that sets it to constantly restore that state. I was a code monkey in my past life, man, not a fricking clergyman.

Magic is characterised as a semiotic skill because it's symbolic of such semiotic skill itself—a metaphor of the power of language, of consciousness. The use of "spirit" as a metaphor for semiotic agency that goes with it is so profoundly resonant if we take it figuratively and so profoundly religious if we take it literally, it's no wonder that magic pervades SCIENCE FICTION even as it's abjected as FANTASY. It's no wonder that the magic of Bester's jaunting goes hand-in-hand with the Promethean fire of PyrE, an enervated and explosive substance triggered by thought, a blatant concretion of the metaphor of semiosis-as-power. It's no wonder that some will insist, till they're blue in the face, that *Dune* is not "proper" SCIENCE FICTION, no, not with all of that metaphysical mumbo-jumbo, all that magic.

Some get that *it's a metaphor, doofus*; but some just ain't got no poetry in their soul.

The Aesthetics of Old Maids

> *SF is about confronting the strange in order to understand it and push the boundaries back but fantasy is either about enjoying the experience of strangeness (as in M. John Harrison's Viriconium books) or bludgeoning it into submission in favour of a frequently politically dubious status quo (in the case of epic fantasy).*
>
> **Jonathan McCalmont**

These sort of hoary old chestnuts which conjure miserably limited GENRES of SCIENCE FICTION and FANTASY in their assertions as to what the two are "about" are unsustainable even as broad generalisations. Countless works wearing the rackspace label of SCIENCE FICTION are deeply reactionary in their response to the strange, fascistically heroic adventures in which the aliens serve exactly the same purpose as Tolkien's orcs: unknown-as-enemy; Other. Countless works of fantasy, conversely, use the strange precisely to conceptualise what lies beyond our understanding. They are very much *not* fantasias.

And when we get into specifics? It is *deeply* problematic—to put it charitably—to view the Viriconium books as ultimately sensationalist pleasures, when Harrison's fiction is so self-evidently designed to disrupt and defy any attempt at passive immersion, to refuse the comfort of givens, to continually force the reader to face the unknown in the text and deal with it. Hell, it is quite simply *complacent* to construct one's SCIENCE FICTION out of privilege in this way, as the more serious and committed form, boldly pushing forward to challenge the unknown and find answers (as opposed to, say, consciously or unconsciously manifesting knee-jerk right-wing American paranoia over enemies within and without—c.f. *The Puppet Masters*), while presenting fantasy as a reactionary enforcer of the social order (as opposed to, say, a cutting critique of the early twentieth century class system and the impact upon it of populist but essentially totalitarian ideologies—c.f. *Titus Groan*).

But let's just dispense with the weary eye-rolling at the interminable obliviation of the Contingency Slip Fallacy, the Paradigm Shift Caveat, the seductive snake-oil of the marvellous evidenced by their persistence, and the reality of dodgy cock-fluffing that results. One could point again and yet again to the *innumerable* exceptions to the essentialist claptrap…but suppose instead we just strip away the shit and the shinola so quality isn't even an issue. Suppose we strip away all the clunk-click assemblage of off-the-shelf clichés, the adolescent wank-reveries based on techno-magical MacGuffins, there to be found under either rackspace label. Suppose we put to one side also all that slippery stream of stuff that runs from Ray Bradbury up through writers of the New Wave such as M. John Harrison all the way to Kelly Link, the stuff that is perpetually elided, it seems, for the sake of bogus closed definitions. Suppose we forget for a second that the shitty bulk of all SCIENCE FICTION, FANTASY and HORROR is, to all intents and purposes, simply formulaic MODERN PULP product, while the shinola is, to all intents and purposes, simply strange fiction of a range of complex flavours. Suppose we forget that for a moment.

There *are* two oppositional aesthetics in the field, both products of the Enlightenment and each associated with one side or the other in its most specialised form—the Rationalism associated with SCIENCE FICTION and the Romanticism associated with FANTASY—indexed by the words *hard* and *epic*. HARD SF and EPIC FANTASY—both of these forms have been conventionalised, proscribed and prescribed, such that they constitute valid GENRES in a way that science fiction and fantasy do not.

Those two grandes dames do make a lot of noise, and people do listen to them. If they don't and can't circumscribe science fiction and fantasy, readers and writers do perceive them as the centres of their respective genres, in a sort of "fuzzy set" model where both science fiction and fantasy lack clear boundaries but each congregates around a different centre. Within that great ongoing drunken wedding party of this vast divided clan, the two of them sit there, Old Granny Campbell and Great Aunt MacDonald, holding court at separate tables, their arms folded, their gazes severe, each with quite distinct notions of how things should be done.

—Use your head, m'boy! says one.

—No, says the other, it's the heart that matters!

Even if most of the field is intermarried, interbred, even if many of us don't really give a damn about those dotty old maids with their outmoded ideas on science and magic, they insist that us young 'uns must pick sides. If they and their devotee broods want to feud, I'm loath to come between their bickering by challenging their wild fancies of what conventional template is the Essential Truth of the Inherent Nature of this or that side of the Inarguable Divide. But with their tribalist dogma corroding discourse with a false dichotomy, I see no option but to take a stand, dismiss all that essentialism for the tosh it is.

Bollocks to it.

The division of aesthetics is there, yes. And the aesthetics those old maids have aligned themselves with are cut deep enough in our culture that the field can't help but be affected by the real centuries-old rift—that between Rationalism and Romanticism. But that dichotomy is artificial and obsolete, has been from the start. So one group sits at the booths in the SF Café, while the other sits at the tables; one comes and leaves through the Nth Street door, while the other enters and exits through the door onto Avenue X. Who gives a fuck?

That sign which used to read *The Science Fiction Café and Bar*? You know, they tried out a few variants before they settled on that: *The Fantasy and Science Fiction Diner*; *The Science Fiction, Fantasy and Horror Bistro*; *The Weird Fiction Greasy Spoon*; *The Café Fantastique*; *The Science Fiction / Fantasy Snack Shack*.

The marriage of the two aesthetics, the weird fusion of cuisines, is what made it vital in the first place, a viable concern.

A Thoroughly Modern Molly

Contrary to the hogwash spouted by our Grumpy Old Gits, Great-Uncles Campbell and MacDonald—changing up with a gender flip for equality's sake—the feud has little to do with the novum versus the chimera, and sod all to do with engagement versus escapism. Or to lay bare the sweeping hauteur on one side, it has sod all to do with some nobly intrepid essence to the mob of fictions grouped under one banner versus some whipping boy of an Othered opposite onto which one projects the grave sins, false and real, one is demonstrably in denial of: the sensational(ist) relish of incredible and/or marvellous strangeness as an end in itself, which is a phantom sin of neurotic intellectualism anyway; the craven brutality of will-to-power wet dream, which is all too real on both sides. This is to say, collapsing all fantasy past even fantasia to an imaginary FANTASY is a shameless smokescreen.

At its depths, you see, the division is a direct analogue of that between the ROMANTIC and the NEO-CLASSICAL movements in painting, that schism in post-Renaissance art, that sifting of the aesthetic techniques of broad-brushed Rembrandts and tight-lined Raphaels, of airy Titians and earthy Brueghels, these techniques born from a new world of new technologies and new politics—oil-based paints, burgermeister patrons, a world where even if the subjects weren't new—Vermeer painting a cleaning lady—the approaches were. This schism resulted in Jacques-Louis David on the one hand and Eugène Delacroix on the other, in NEO-CLASSICISM with its emphasis on the ordered and ROMANTICISM with its emphasis on the sublime. It is this same division that, in the marketing category of SCIENCE FICTION / FANTASY, where the reality of marriage is indisputable, gives us the conflicting emphases on futurology and fantasia, the aesthetic of the logical and the aesthetic of the sublime.

In writing, that ROMANTIC idealisation of the sublime gives us the archetypal flights of fancy, rakish wanderers, rebel poets and all the epic wildernesses we will eventually see in EPIC FANTASY, while the NEO-CLASSICAL idealisation of order gives us the novel as social study, as empirical observation, and all the solemn restraint we will eventually see in HARD SF. Passion and Reason—the prevailing themes of the Enlightenment, the Age of Revolution. Both Delacroix and David painted scenes from the French Revolution—*Liberty*

Leading the People, and *The Death of Marat*. These paintings illustrate the difference of the two aesthetics rather neatly.

There was a third aesthetic however that developed in the dialogue between these—the modernism (or modernity) of Caravaggio, who was fusing Romantic chiaroscuro and Neo-Classical formality long before these terms were even in use, who painted sublimely ordered scenes, who used a dead whore dragged from the river as his Magdalene, thieves and peasants for his saints. His work is fiercely passionate and coldly reasoned all at once. A pretty boy Bacchus, in a Caravaggio painting, is at once the Greek god himself and an urban hustler from the streets. Caravaggio plays the sublime and the logical off against each other. The sublime is Yeats's "terrible beauty," born in the collision of monstrum and numina, but Caravaggio comes to it as anatomist, rendering the wild passion of a decapitation in the most coolly ordered composition.

A thoroughly modern molly, Caravaggio in his work embodies the re-scaling that was going on, the re-evaluation of God and Nature and Humanity's relationship to them both. The first modern(ist) painter, he is distinct from his Renaissance forebears in the sheer humanism of his work, and distinct from the schismatics who follow, never surrendering to the idealisations that set the Romantics and the Neo-Classicists at each others' throats. He leaves it to the Romantics to blather on about the worth of bold colour over clean line, leaves it to the Neo-Classicists to witter on about the value of clean line over bold colour. Passion versus Reason—the world of Western Art spends centuries bickering over which is better, centuries of Royal Academies and revolutionary outsiders, of worthy High Art and vulgar Low Art, of intellectualist Literature and sensationalist Genre…and somewhere along the way that hoary old argument of Reason / Passion ends up in Science Fiction / Fantasy. As if that's all there is. As if there's scientifically rigourous rationalism or weirdly wild romanticism, and ne'er the twain shall meet.

—Fuck that shit, says Caravaggio.

The Fantasy of Genre, The Science of Fiction

There is a shared methodology in much strange fiction, whatever rackspace label it goes by, an approach shaped by a shared aesthetic, neither Romanticism nor Rationalism but rather more akin to the modernism of Caravaggio, reacting to the modern world, portraying humanity's relationship with "God" and "Nature" in a way that, when it works, plays the sublime grandeur of one aesthetic off against the logical restraint of the other, and in doing so results in something neither could achieve alone.

Neither science fiction nor fantasy—no matter what those old maids would have you believe—has ever been so pure in its devotion to those antithetical aesthetics that they could be defined thus. The Rationalism of Wells is counterpointed by the Romanticism of Verne. In the Gernsback-Campbell era when SCIENCE FICTION was born, those two aesthetics were always-already as much in collaboration as in conflict, in bold Romantic adventures wrought with Rationalist science, futurology as the source of fantasia. The dynamic power of the fiction resides in the interaction.

The distinction that drives the Great Debate is an illusion, an artificial dichotomy based more on claims of allegiance than on actual practice. Two subsets of the field live by their grandes dames' rhetoric, creating works that do exemplify the warring aesthetics. But if you look around the drunken wedding party, ignore the two old farts sulking in their corners, that dusty old duality looks largely irrelevant. Perhaps it is only in that shattering crack of lightning which splits the genre that the true nature of the hideous creation is revealed. And it is not SCIENCE FICTION. SCIENCE FICTION is dead. This is the Frankenstein's monster of SCIENCE FICTION / FANTASY, a patchwork of dead genres, cannibalised from the cadavers of ROMANTICISM and RATIONALISM, torn apart and stitched back together, a marvellous, monstrous marriage of meat machines. It's a riven thing—we could hardly expect two or three hundred years of strife between ROMANTICISM and RATIONALISM to be healed in a few short decades—but it is a thing. A definition for it, if we must:

> *Emerging within a short-lived GENRE of the early to mid twentieth century MODERN PULP boom utilising Romantic character types, plot structures and settings but sourcing its fantasia in Rationalist futurology, SCIENCE FICTION / FANTASY became a marketing category for strange fictions simply rationalising the sublime and/or romanticising the logical, forcing a fusion of the two aesthetics in the face of its own angst that resolution was inherently unattainable.*

That thing is, in its essence, modernism. We might brand it PULP MODERNISM—cheap, populist, balls-to-the-wall trash modernism, out to entertain more than an elite of aesthetes and intellectuals, but still modernism. It uses mimesis on the one hand, semiosis on the other, recasting magic as logical process and science as sublime gift, combining the strange and the mundane, ever testing the limits of its key literary elements. The integrity we project on it, the unity we impose upon it with our so-well-formed closed definitions, is only that of a family which, in truth, extends as far as we decide it does.

There is no GENRE of FANTASY, only the fantasy of GENRE. This isn't the fiction of science; it's the science of fiction. What we have is one confused clusterfuck of conventional templates ripped apart and rebuilt as an aesthetic idiom, a mode of fiction in which we rupture the narrative with quirks of the impossible, things which cannot be—not yet / not ever—taking these not as passing metaphors but as figurative conceits, so we can put them to the test with literature as the laboratory, by literalising them and working through the ramifications.

When the results are good, right enough, we do have a tendency to go into mass production mode, churning out low-quality copies from the cheapest of materials, for a market of consumers who'll love our new toys for a day or two before abandoning them in favour of the next shiny gadget. There's an upside to that: that Big Corporate Structure keeps the R & D department going, so to speak, the vast market for commercial product supporting the smaller market for high-end fiction in this pulp modernist mode. But there's a downside: the commercialisation results in one key drawback, in the depth to which such works become bound to, sold as, and ultimately misunderstood as GENRE, as this schismed, schizoid SCIENCE FICTION / FANTASY, at odds with itself. And arguing in the ghetto creole of Genre, where aesthetic idiom is ever conflated with conventional template and marketing category, we buy into that, swallow it hook, line and sinker.

And the Great Debate rages on, an unending feud among the wedding guests, the food fights becoming flame wars, immolating meaning in a holocaust of definitions.

The Miscegenation of Science Fantasy

Surrender to the Sublime

> *Science fiction makes the implausible possible, while science fantasy makes the impossible plausible.*
> Rod Serling

In the dawning space age of nuclear power and automated household appliances, the sublime seemed logical, the logical sublime, and this served to hold the Romantics and Rationalists of SCIENCE FICTION / FANTASY together through the Golden Age, the period of Gernsback and Campbell, the Futurians and so on. Bradbury sat comfortably in the SF Café alongside Asimov, Heinlein and Clarke. If maybe Leiber, Howard and Lovecraft had their own hangouts, there was nevertheless a blatant overlap between the regulars of the SF Café and the crowd frequenting the Fantasy Boutique or the Little Shop of Horror.

But the increasing sense of a gulf between these modes soon led to the use of the term SCIENCE FANTASY as an attempt to map the borderland between them. Though the label was coined originally to refer to works which applied a rationalising rigourous approach characteristic of SCIENCE FICTION to the subject matter of what could only be classed as fantasy (Heinlein's *Magic, Inc.*, for example), over time the meaning shifted such that it now primarily refers to those works which *fail* to apply that rationalising rigour to the subject matter of SCIENCE FICTION, such that alien planets and technology function in the same way as the secondary worlds and magic of FANTASY. We can see *Dune* as a benchmark in this transition of meaning, the point where the focus on fantasia over futurology becomes sufficient for many to identify it as *no longer really science fiction at all*.

This shift in meaning is revealing. It is not simply that FANTASY here signifies magic, metaphysical causation. This could be systematised by the application of critical intellect, an approach entirely in line with scientific methodology which theorises from observation, and in which anomalous observations are to be accepted as falsifying that theory—i.e. we might simply see the impossible events of magic as demanding a reconstruction of our nomology, an update of the laws of nature. That was precisely the project of SCIENCE FANTASY in its original sense. Rather FANTASY here signifies the *suspension* of critical intellect in Romantic rapture, a sensationalist surrender to the sublime. Where the label originally pointed to the tropes of magic, it now applies to an approach to those tropes, the tropes themselves taken as *indexes* of that approach.

The Paradigm Shift Caveat

One might speculate as to the (im)possibility of faster-than-light travel, time travel or alternate realities; no one to my knowledge has ever speculated on the possibility of finding elves, orcs or magic swords any time soon.
Gary Gibson

In the blog entry from which the above quote is taken, fellow GSFWC member Gary Gibson singles out the point of contention here in the distinction he makes between science fiction and fantasy, arguing the former is not, as some would maintain, a branch of the latter. Where the former, he argues, *does* similarly deal with the impossible, it is distinct from fantasy in that it does so on the basis of a history of scientific discoveries and radical paradigm shifts, a recognition of the limitations of our present knowledge. In science fiction, the conceit (the impossibility accepted as possible for the sake of the story) is not simply a spurious fabrication but is rather a rational speculation (which may allow for the possibility of being wrong about what's impossible).

On the surface this seems a fair distinction between the Rationalism and Romanticism of Science Fiction / Fantasy. The point of contention, and the reason for the evolution of the term Science Fantasy, lies in the degree to which a recognition of the limitations of our present knowledge, the idea of a potential *paradigm shift*, becomes a universal caveat exempting the science fiction writer from any real rigour whatsoever. It's all very well to accept that what's presented as a novum is in fact a chimera, and argue that with the shifting goal posts of science it *is* still possible that it will *become* possible by the laws of nature; but this is essentially just to conjure what *can never* be—not ever—not in the system of physical rules by which this worldscape of reality works, and then apply a *never say never* get-out clause which applies equally to *any* chimera.

I have no problem speculating that maybe sometime in the future we'll discover the laws of nature to actually allow for not just alternate realities but wholly *alterior* ones, and portals to these Faerie realms. Or at least, I have no more problem taking the elves of some secondary world fantasia as arguable thus, as in the latest *Thor* movie, than I do with the chimera of FTL.

To see FTL, time travel or alternative realities as possibilities rather than impossibilities we need to imagine a wholesale revision to the laws of nature, a paradigm shift in physics. The same is true of, for example, ESP, jaunting and intersecting realities in canonical works such as Bester's *The Demolished Man* and *The Stars My Destination* or Zelazny's *Roadmarks*. Magics of metaphysical causality, the core ideas of these works require *substantial* paradigm shifts to put the mask of a novum on the chimera and sell it as grounded futurology rather than pure fantasia.

Of course, the evidence is, few readers have any great problem with making that leap; traditionally, we do slap onto these books the label of *science fiction*. For many, however, judging by their own stated criteria, the transparent fancy of the conceit really ought to render these works unquestionably fantasy.

On what basis, after all, do we distinguish those paradigm shifts—which are radical enough, make no mistake, to breach the most fundamental principles of current science—from potential paradigm shifts which could redefine even the most spurious fantasia as futurology? As science fiction writers and readers, we are ready, it seems, to abandon the limitation of light speed that comes with Einsteinian Relativity so we can play with FTL, or to ignore the physical foundations of mind in the neurochemistry of the brain so that we can use ESP. We are willing to ditch the Conservation of Energy that is a basic aspect of Newtonian thermodynamics in order to portray teleportation as an act of mere will, jaunting as an ability to transport oneself instantaneously through space-time. We are able to throw away the very coherence of the space-time continuum so we can imagine a road that links all possible times and all possible histories. We simply apply that Paradigm Shift Caveat.

If we're ready, willing and able to play this fast and loose with science why should we draw the line at equivalent paradigm shifts that, for us, render a work fantasy rather than science fiction? Aren't the secondary worlds simply alternative realities where the archaeological distinction of gracile and robust hominids translates to elves and dwarves as distinct races? Aren't the magics just the semiotic skill of metaphysical causation but with the arguable left unargued? Aren't these fabrications of the most generic FANTASY in fact recastable as speculations if only we accept paradigm shifts no more radical in truth than those required with the works of Bester and Zelazny still considered seminal science fiction?

This is the challenge taken up by the original SCIENCE FANTASY—replacing the fantasias born of futurology with those born of the more radical paradigm shifts of *cosmology*. In these fictions the current laws of nature are understood as a revisable human construct, just as in SCIENCE FICTION the current limitations of technology are. They may be tweaked, even radically reformed. Recognising the revisions that have taken place historically, that SCIENCE FANTASY plays the game of adopting obsolete models, trying to apply them as systems in their own right, perhaps even integrate them with ours. From the perspective of a universe next door, an alterior reality reachable, perhaps, by a road that links all possible worlds (which is surely no more plausible than a wardrobe), our cosmology can be seen as only one of the superset of possible permutations.

There is a point where maths and physics meet in the metaphysics of the multiverse, and if we accept this point as being in the domain of science then this *is* science fiction; it is simply not SCIENCE FICTION. Unfortunately that distinction doesn't really work in a spoken discussion in the SF Café.

So, for my own part, I leave the term *science fiction* to whoever the fuck wants it, talk instead of *SF* and *strange fictions* in the hope of thrashing out a common language, or at least evading the tedious turf wars of the taxonomists. This is the taxonomy I'm more interested in:

A Taxonomy of Narratives

> *One could propose the third axis of SF as a story wherein (a part of) base reality changes (to a greater or lesser extent)... [SF] still relates to base reality by way of the physical laws, that is, reality has changed, but according to the rules of the possible... [For] fantasy (part of) base reality changes, as well, but in ways that ignore the rules of the possible.*
>
> **Jetse de Vries**

So let's say we have these two axes of fictional thought—story elements and craft techniques, the former consisting of character, setting and plot (broken down into problem, try/fail cycle, resolution and validation), the latter consisting of things like voice, style, PoV, structure, person/tense, punctuation and paragraphing. Is there a third axis of *genre devices*, not in the sense of listable concrete MacGuffins (time-travel, spaceships, etc.) which are all ultimately negotiable conventions, but as something more abstract, not tropes but elements or techniques more analogous to the other axes. Jetse de Vries offers an interesting suggestion that the third axis is to do with "deviation from base reality." Lake meanwhile suggests a rough taxonomy, breaking down types of fiction into four modes of narrative with a fifth, the fantastic narrative, as a fusion of these forms. In this model:

- *Private narrative* deals with "things which might have happened or could have happened, but leave the world as it is. Most mainstream novels fall here. Holden Caulfield could have lived or not, the world wouldn't be noticeably different."
- *Alternative narrative* deals with "things which might have happened or could have happened, but would change the world in noticeable ways. If Jett Rink were real, we would be aware of him as an industrialist and something of a tragic figure, in the manner of Howard Hughes."
- *Mythic narrative* deals with "things which never actually happened, or could have happened in a literal reading, but encapsulate important truths for the tellers of the tale. Gilgamesh was (probably) a real king in Uruk, but the story which was told around him describes the cosmology, aspirations and experience of his people."

- *Future narrative deals* with "things which have not yet happened but might. This ranges from prophetic writings in virtually any literate cultural tradition to cautionary tales such as *Nineteen Eighty-Four*."

Here, we're entering the same territory as Delany's essay "About Five Thousand Seven Hundred and Fifty Words," with Lake's language of modalities—could have, might have, could not have, have not yet—mapping almost perfectly to Delany's theory of subjunctivity level as the defining feature of each genre. While there's a grace to this theory, though, Lake's reference to events which *might have / never actually / have not yet happened* requires a step beyond simple subjunctivity.

The Crescent Sun

> [W]hat distinguishes science fiction from other kinds of fiction is a peculiar compromise between scientific truth and untruth. Samuel Delany has analyzed this compromise in terms of the SF text's subjunctivity ("About 5,750 Words"). What he means by this term is the degree to which every statement in the fiction describes a hypothetical condition: something that is not happening, has not happened, could not have happened in the past (unlike realistic fiction), but might happen, given the proper changes in society and scientific knowledge. Another word for subjunctivity might be 'ifness,' the condition of being contingent.
>
> What SF is contingent upon is change that does not violate the reader's understanding of scientifically defined reality, which is not to say that we necessarily accept any statement in the text as scientifically valid. Rather, we accept reference within SF as allusions to science, broadly conceived of as a field of endeavor, a way of mapping the universe, and a way of speaking about the universe and the attempt to comprehend it.
>
> **Brian Attebery**

All fiction requires the suspension-of-disbelief, requires us to read the text as having a subjunctivity level of "this could have happened." The act of reading a book or watching a movie involves a willingness on the reader's part to make-believe that these words on the page actually map to events, and so all fiction takes this as its baseline. We're not generally troubled by the fact that these are lies, fabrications, falsehoods, that the cat did not actually sit on the mat, that there was never a cat to sit, and never a mat for it to sit on. Unless the writer starts dropping hints that the narrator is unreliable, we take the text on face value, pretending to ourselves that the narrator is not in fact breaching Grice's Maxim of Quality ("Do not say that which you believe to be false or that for which you lack evidence").

—The cat sat on the mat, we are told.

—Fair enough, we say. We'll go with you on that. We've seen cats sit on mats, after all. We know it *never happened*. But we'll pretend, for the sake of the story, that it *did happen*.

This is not subjunctivity level though. With the modal auxiliary *did* versus *could*, we are dealing with an epistemic modality rather than an alethic modality. The latter is equivalent to subjunctivity, but the former is not, a judgement of actuality rather than possibility.

The difference is a matter of facts versus potentials, so we might look at it in terms of reportage.

News reports may be false; articles may be inaccurate; history texts may be wrong: all by failure or by intent. As long as these remain within the realm of what's possible though, they have an alethic modality, a subjunctivity level, of "could have happened." It's quite possible for a man to bite a dog. As factual claims, they also have an epistemic modality of "might have happened" though, so we can read sceptically, or we can *forsake* disbelief and ascribe these factual claims an epistemic modality of "did happen." We can trust in the veracity of the reportage and project an artificial epistemic modality onto the text.

Where fiction is seen as naturalistic, realistic, mimetic, the ersatz reality it claims to be rendering is so closely modelled on the world we live in that the events described "could have happened," such that we can do something similar in play. We don't forsake disbelief, knowing fine well it's all made up, but we do suspend it, sustain an artificial epistemic modality.

Even strange fiction contains naturalism in that sense, the mimesis of sentences that carry an alethic modality of possibility and to which we ascribe this (artificial, projected) epistemic modality. There are bound to be cats sitting on mats *somewhere* in the text. What makes some fiction strange is that it *also* involves a shift of alethic modality from "could have happened" to "could not have happened," as the narrative performs a sentence that is harder to read as simply mimetic. Delany's example, "The red sun was high, the blue low," would serve as example of a rupture in the mimetic weft, introducing an alethic modality (subjunctivity level) of "could not have happened," but for ease I'll stick with my alternative:

> *The crescent sun was high, the moon low.*

The above sentence representing something impossible—a "crescent sun"—these sort of word-combos that fuck with the reader's suspension-of-disbelief are, of course, what I've been talking about as *quirks of impossibility*. My example is a chimera, Delany's a novum; mine breaches the laws of nature, his known science—a technical impossibility because we can't yet stand on a planet in a binary system. It's a comparable impossibility to that of the novum's closer bedfellow, the quirk that plays with known history as the novum plays with known science: the *erratum*. Where the novum is a conjuring of what could not be, not *yet*, the erratum is a conjuring of what could not be, not *now*, an historical impossibility because we have already passed the point where events might have hypothetically played out otherwise to produce it.

How do we swallow these alethic quirks? There are people who don't read fiction at all because they cannot suspend disbelief even in the most mimetic narrative. They cannot entertain (or cannot see the point in entertaining) an artificial epistemic modality. They read a story and know it has the epistemic modality of "this never happened," and if it never happened, why should they care? This may be significant when it comes to those who can't suspend disbelief in strange fiction, and when it comes to those who can: that some clearly can't see the point in entertaining texts with an alethic modality of "could not happen" suggests that those who can, insofar as they *do*, are playing a comparable game of make-believe—i.e. sustaining an artificial *alethic* modality.

Contrary to Delany, I'd argue that the continued engagement with the text, the continued suspension-of-disbelief requires that in some way the "could have happened" alethic modality *persists*. Which is to say, rather than a quirk causing our reading to flip from one alethic modality ("could have happened") to another ("could not have happened") in an act of *correction*, it is an act of *addition* that takes place, with the secondary alethic modality introduced and entering into a state of tension with the primary or base level. To illustrate this with an example:

> *The man stood on the balcony, gazing at the clear sky. The crescent sun was high, the moon low. He smiled.*

In the first sentence, a baseline alethic modality is introduced with a bit of simple mimesis: *could have happened*. In the second, in Delany's model, the introduction of the "crescent sun" causes an act of correction on the part of the reader, alethic modality flipped: *could not have happened*. But given that the third sentence is entirely as plausible as the first, has nothing strange about it at all, in and of itself, what alethic modality do we read into *it*? Should we not simply perform another act of correction and flip back to "could have happened"? Would we really deem that shift in the second sentence irreversible, reading the narrative as fantastic (to hold with Delany's term for now) from there on in if no other quirk was introduced into the text to reinforce our reading? Or would we, at some point, decide that the "crescent sun" was just some metaphor, metonym or even misprint that has thrown us, that the text never actually deviated from the basic alethic modality of "could have happened"?

We must, I suggest, entertain *multiple* subjunctivities simultaneously during the reading experience. Even when reading a purely fantastic work, where we're asked to swallow, for the sake of the story, a complete impossibility such as a crescent sun, some part of us is still playing along with the game of make-believe, continuing to work on the principle that "this could have happened." For the epistemic modality to persist, that alethic modality upon which the suspension-of-disbelief is founded must persist as a baseline, even as the strange sentences dealing with crescent suns interject themselves among the otherwise mundane paragraphs dealing with men standing on balconies, gazing at skies, and smiling.

The text becomes, then, a pattern of tensions formed by playing these two conflicting subjunctivity levels off against each other, by disrupting the equilibrium of suspension-of-disbelief with the incredulity that attaches to the quirk. It becomes a rhythm: could; could *not*; could; could; could *not*; could; could, could *not*; could *not*; could; could. It becomes the accumulating medley as each voice of a sentence joins the chorus, pitched baritone low or soprano high, singing theme or counterpoint. It becomes the soundscape of those strange sentences sustaining, the note of impossibility from one fading out as the next comes in, or enduring to be built on with even bolder and more brazen strangeness.

A Lesser Impossibility

> *The red sun was high, the blue low.*
> **Samuel R. Delany**

In Delany's model of subjunctivity level and genre, any such physical impossibilities theoretically render a work no longer s-f, as Delany refers to it—*speculative-fiction*, decapitalised and hyphenated. This is a fairly orthodox view. With all the talk of plausibility and possibility, science and magic, there are many who would argue that the alethic modality of "could not have happened" breaches the rigours of the genre, that SF only ever deals with things that "could not have happened *yet*," things that therefore "never happened (but could)."

But this is where the problem lies when we consider the jaunting of Bester's *The Stars My Destination*. In Delany's model, jaunting would have to manifest an epistemic/alethic modality of "never happened (but could)" in order for the work to qualify as SF. But it's wishful thinking to imagine it does; it's the Contingency Slip Fallacy, the Paradigm Shift Caveat. In fact, what we have is the "could not have happened" alethic modality that Delany ascribes to fantasy, manifest in an act which *clearly* breaches what we know of the laws of nature. It's a magic, a metaphysical causation which requires no power, involves manipulating matter in a jaw-dropping way, and which is instigated by mere will, placing it in the same category, ultimately, as Dracula transforming into a bat. Even allowing for a level of uncertainty, a degree of implausibility, this is surely at odds with the exclusion of impossibility required to map the "could have happened" alethic modality directly to SF.

What we can do, though, is expand on Delany's idea. Stepping through my example sentence as Delany steps through his, you'd reach the end, having corrected your reading a number of times, (having gone through various possibilities such as the crescent sun being an image on a flag, or a metaphor for an Islamic culture) and settle on an alethic modality of "could not have happened," having realised that it's intended to be read literally.

—Ah, you'd say, this is a fantasy story.

Follow Delany's theory, and if jaunting reads more like a crescent sun than a binary system, then the alethic modality of the jaunting sequences in *The Stars My Destination* would similarly place the book in fantasy rather than SF. If we don't assume a single subjunctivity level though, then no such instant taxonomic judgement need be made. If the process of reading is one of continual correction we can suspend our ultimate decision, read the text with the multiple alethic modalities it has, taking one sentence as SF the next as fantasy, either switching back and forth in one's attitude to the text or just being in two minds about it, so to speak.

Stealing that famous SF sentence of Heinlein's and splicing it together with my own, suppose you kick off a story with this paragraph:

> *The door dilated. The man stepped out onto the balcony, gazed up at the clear sky. The crescent sun was high, the moon low. He smiled.*

The dilating door is a quirk just as the crescent sun is, but it is a different kind of quirk; like Delany's twinned suns, it is only a *technical* impossibility rather than a *metaphysical* impossibility, a breach of known science rather than the laws of nature, a novum rather than a chimera. Still, it *is* a quirk.

So is this going to be an SF story or is it going to be fantasy? If the story goes on to work almost entirely in the mimetic "could have happened" mode or limits itself to hypothetical nova, we'd probably suspend our decision, waiting for some revelation which explains the crescent sun and places the story firmly in the realm of SF. (Oh crap, it's a VR story!) If it goes on with the metaphysical chimerae mounting, we might expect a revelation which throws away our reality altogether and places it in the realm of fantasy. (Oh crap, the hero's dead!) Or indeed, we might happily sustain it as SF. (Oh cool, it's a PKD story!)

Or, indeed, the story might well *never* actually resolve into one or the other, instead utilising *the tension between* conflicting subjunctivities of "could have happened" and "could not have happened" (in which case we probably hum and haw and mutter something about "slipstream" when we reach the end).

In Bester's novel the metaphysical impossibility of the quirk of jaunting is obscured by its context within a whole worldscape of quirks that are only nova rather than chimera. SF novels like *The Stars My Destination* demonstrate that we're a lot more lenient as readers than the definitions we impose, that there's a lot more of "could not have happened" than we claim. There is always the Paradigm Shift Caveat, of which "the next stage in human evolution" as used by Bester is a blatant example. (Because, yes…the next stage in human evolution is going to give us the power to twitch our noses, click our heels three times, say, "There's no place like the asteroids," and teleport ourselves away from impending death. For sure.) And if a flagrant metaphysical impossibility is not *quite* so outrageous as a crescent sun, if the chimera is on its own rather than being in a huge heap of such impossibilities, or if it's simply such a cool idea we *want* it to be feasible, we can quite often just shunt the "could not have happened" alethic modality to the back of our minds and read the work as SF regardless. There's the "one impossible thing per story" rule too, a First Offence Caveat which along with the Paradigm Shift Caveat renders all sorts of spurious pseudo-science acceptable.

So, not only is the quirk of a crescent sun operationally identical to the quirk of jaunting in disrupting the suspension-of-disbelief with a metaphysical impossibility; it is or can be *functionally* identical to the quirk of a dilating door in the effect of such a disruption, regardless of the type of impossibility. It is only the addition of that "yet" to the "could not have happened" alethic modality which distinguishes the two, and this SF rationalisation has its complement in fantasy.

But we'll get to that.

For now, if we add in a requirement to not breach *epistemic* modality with events that would necessarily, because of their scale of impact, be on the historical record as fact, we have an effective definition of Lake's private narrative as that which cleaves to a "could have happened" alethic modality, versus the strange narrative, as that which introduces a "could not have happened" alethic modality. We have a fundamental difference between private narratives that exclude quirks in favour of the mundane and those strange narratives that introduce them as notes of dissonance in the mimetic weft, whatever the flavour of quirk, and whether they rationalise them or not.

A Personal Perspective, Frontal, Lateral, Residual

To put a personal perspective on this, in *Vellum* and *Ink* there are two big-ass conceits that, for many people I'm sure, render them fantasy rather than science fiction. In the SF Café I've been asked enough times what category I'd place them in to know that it's a matter of doubt for some.

First, there's the idea of the Vellum itself, a 3D time-space where the "forward and back" of future and past aren't the only direction to travel in. There are temporally alternative realities (i.e. sharing the same basic physics but with different histories) treated as "parallel" worlds off to this "side" or that. There are also metaphysically alterior realities (i.e. worlds working with different physics entirely) treated as "higher" or "deeper" strata. Time has three dimensions, frontal, lateral and residual. Though it's not explicit in the books, I've always imagined the last dimension to be that through which the laws of nature evolve, from the sort of crude, chaotic cosmological principles found in myth to the intricate order of forces described in physics.

In this systematising approach to the multiverse idea, the fact that characters are able to move between realities doesn't make it, for me, any less science fiction than Zelazny's *Roadmarks*. But I do present one of the "folds" of the Vellum—shock, horror—as a realm of what, to all intents and purposes, are dwarves and elves and orcs, fairies and all that Fantasy malarky. In Ian McDonald's *King of Morning, Queen of Day* a similar approach is applied to the idea of Faerie, positing it as a distinct reality that can and does sometimes intersect our own.

Second, there's the idea of the Cant, the magic of a language which can be spoken to reprogram this multiverse and which therefore endows the user with the ability to perform metaphysical causations, manipulations of reality. Riffing off the idea that the most basic principle in the universe is information, that maybe all we're made of, when it comes down to it, is data, this is a wild speculation that makes the whole kit and caboodle as malleable as a Phildickian consensus reality…but that's kind of the point. If it was science fiction for Dick to warp reality itself with drugs in *The Three Stigmata of Palmer Eldritch*, then it's science fiction for me to do it with words. Hell, the magic here even works within the strictures of thermodynamics; it requires energy, and that energy has to come from somewhere.

So in *Vellum* and *Ink* you basically have a whole underlying schema in which elves and magic are treated as speculation rather than fabrication. If you want to argue that this schema isn't plausible I'll just shrug and say, yeah, so what? FTL isn't plausible. Jaunting isn't plausible. Time travel isn't plausible. They require cosmological rather than technological paradigm shifts. They don't just breach known science, they breach the laws of nature. And if the Paradigm Shift Caveat works to excuse your fabrications as speculations, then it works to excuse mine, on the exact same basis that the history of science is one of apparent impossibilities being shown to be actually quite possible. Either we apply that caveat objectively or we ditch it entirely in favour of the hard-nosed rigour that says FTL, ESP, time travel, jaunting, *anything* which plays so fast and loose with the laws of physics, is all just spurious fabrication. The only alternative is a shamelessly subjective application of the Paradigm Shift Caveat—or rather a refusal to accept the validity of its application—on the basis of personal incredulity.

If that personal incredulity kicks in when you see a dragon on the cover, that's fair enough. But don't come crying to me when the Hard SF geeks or the Realist snootcockers write you off as a spinner of spurious fabrications because *their* personal incredulity kicks in at the sight of your FTL spaceship. And really, if you're putting the mask of a novum on a chimera, you'd do well not to fool yourself with it, not to trumpet your supposed plausibility too loudly. If you're arguing that your chimera is just as possible as a novum because you've convinced yourself that it's possible it might *become* possible, combining the Paradigm Shift Caveat with the Contingency Slip Fallacy, you're *far* more of a fantasist than those with no illusions about their chimera being a complete breach of the laws of nature.

A case might be made that the quirks must be made arguable by a speculative approach, that fantasy does not do so and rather *becomes* science fiction when it makes its magics arguable (as cosmology rather than futurology), and that my speculative approach to the chimerae in *Vellum* and *Ink* does render them works of science fiction rather than fantasy. Cool, I'd say. I can live with an open definition of science fiction that encompasses the grand conceits of *The Demolished Man*, *The Stars My Destination* and *Roadmarks*, happy to see myself as working within that tradition. But the fact it's in question…well, this brings us back to the turf war politics underpinning the term SCIENCE FANTASY, where it is, in part, exactly this Paradigm Shift Caveat that led to the use of the term for works like *Dune*.

Of Sets and Subsets

> *We talk a lot about science fiction as extrapolation, but in fact most science fiction does not extrapolate seriously. Instead it takes a willful, often whimsical, leap into a world spun out of the fantasy of the author.*
> H. Bruce Franklin

Down in the ghetto at the SF Café, even with Old Man Campbell in charge, the menu had expanded to include dishes that, as far as some were concerned, didn't belong there at all. The SF Café, they said, is a burger joint, a place for burgers and nothing but burgers. Chiliburgers, cheeseburgers, chickenburgers, even goddamn *chimp*burgers are fine. But those chicken nuggets belong in some Science Fantasy Diner, not in our Science Fiction Café. Chicken nuggets are not halal SCIENCE FICTION. Chicken nuggets are not kosher SCIENCE FICTION. Chicken nuggets are impure and unclean. They pollute the menu, corrupt the genre. They carry with them the taint of fantasy.

The territorial roots of this stance become obvious when we examine the common response amongst even those SCIENCE FICTION writers who use the Paradigm Shift Caveat freely to any assertion that science fiction is essentially a branch of fantasy.

—No, it's not, they say. No fucking way.

Here's the thing:

The perennial argument over whether or not science fiction is a branch of fantasy as often as not comes down to an unrecognised and unarticulated disagreement over which of two models applies to the field. What we have, as a baseline, is a set of strange fictions using quirks of the impossible—breaching known science, known history, the laws of nature or the strictures of logic. These quirks are taken as conceits, the fanciful accepted for the sake of the story, propagated through it. That much is simple; beyond it, we can go one of two ways.

If both science fiction and fantasy deal with quirks of the impossible, and science fiction is distinct from fantasy because it *also* requires a level of rationality in approach, a degree of theorising that renders the conceit an act of arguable speculation rather than inarguable fabrication, then unless fantasy *also* requires a secondary aspect which is either incompatible with this or at least *different*, then science fiction is a branch of fantasy. It is simply the subset of strange fictions which adds rationalisation to the mix, while that set of strange fictions is itself simply what we more commonly call fantasy. Only if fantasy has some specific feature rendering it a subset can the two be distinct branches in their own right.

Either: we have a Parent-Child Model: the superset of fantasy with its subset of science fiction, where X = "rationalise its conceits":

Within fantasy as the set of strange fictions
- science fiction is the subset of fantasy that does X

Or: we have a Sibling-Sibling Model: the superset of strange fictions with two sibling subsets, SCIENCE FICTION and FANTASY:

Within S as the set of strange fictions
- SCIENCE FICTION is the subset of S that does X
- FANTASY is the subset of S that does Y

Note the overlap here with the split between upper-case and lower-case, between GENRE and genre. This is not a coincidence. Personally, I'd be quite happy to go with the first model, slap the word *fantasy* down where I might write *field of strange fictions* and accept an openly-defined science fiction within it: a fantasy with an additional rationalised quality achieved by various strategies, none singularly essential and/or sufficient, but each providing grounds for a work to be subjectively judged as such. To articulate the territorial dispute(s) though, we need to accommodate the arguments of outright incompatibility, and those necessarily close the definitions of each mode to exclude the other.

The argument that science fiction is a branch of fantasy is an assertion of the latter model in which there is no extra criterion, no Y, required to further define fantasy. Here fantasy is simply the field of fantastic fiction, fiction which uses quirks of the impossible, incredible conceits, which means it includes *everything* from the most generic sub-Tolkien product to the most respected literary tome. This is fantasy in its open definition, a mode of fiction that includes the work of Franz Kafka, Mikhail Bulgakov and Angela Carter, never mind Ray Bradbury, Mervyn Peake and Kelly Link. Here science fiction is just a subset of that field, one with an additional requirement of rationalisation. This is not at odds with the Campbellian closed definition of SCIENCE FICTION given above. SCIENCE FICTION is a subset of that science fiction.

The argument that science fiction is *not* a branch of fantasy is an assertion of the former model in which there is an additional quality, a Y, by which the definition of fantasy is closed to that of FANTASY. Here all fantasy *is* FANTASY, fiction which uses *specific* conceits in a *specific* way and is inherently limited by those specifics, a GENRE of fantasia which excludes the sophisticated writers mentioned above (classed as mainstream, magical realism, slipstream, SF or fantastic fiction by some other name), or within which those writers are at best marginal (fantasy considered as impure FANTASY). Here SCIENCE FICTION is incompatible with that genre because the specifics of Y are irreconcilable with the rationalism required in SCIENCE FICTION's X.

Indeed, for many proponents of this model, it seems that X is not defined positively, as the rationalisation of conceits, so much as it's defined *negatively*, as the avoidance of Y. That's to say, for some, it's the eschewal of the Y that makes a work of strange fiction FANTASY that is required to make it a work of SCIENCE FICTION.

The Taint of Fantasy

The exclusion of those literary (for want of a better term) fantasists is significant, revealing the specifics of the commercial GENRE as the Y that FANTASY requires in order to be FANTASY—what Gibson refers to as the elves, orcs or magic swords. All too often it signifies a blinkered view of the actual works published under the rackspace label, reveals the same sort of prejudices that are applied to science fiction by those who do not read it but will nevertheless blithely dismiss it as robots, aliens and spaceships. And insofar as these are emblematic of tropes exhausted to cliché (elves, orcs) and power-wank (magic swords), if we detect in this closure of definition (to crude stereotype) a definition-by-negation of SCIENCE FICTION, it's hard not to see a neat rhetorical trick taking place: SCIENCE FICTION is being defined as that which does not use such tawdry cliché, does not pander with such power-wank.

The marginalisation of the literary fantasists as *impure* FANTASY is even more telling, a tacit admission that FANTASY can and does open up into fantasy, that these (clichéd, pandering) features are *not* a requisite Y, that these writers' works can still be classed as fantasy regardless of the complete absence of elves, orcs or magic swords. Those features are not what defines a work of fantasy even if they are what defines FANTASY. Rather across the zone of strange fictions, the more a work evidences these (clichéd, pandering) features, the more it becomes correct, proper, to deem it FANTASY. Again it's hard not to see a rather self-serving gambit here, a way of defining SCIENCE FICTION as more properly SCIENCE FICTION—i.e. less properly FANTASY—as it eschews cliché and pandering.

When a SCIENCE FICTION writer or reader characterises fantasy as FANTASY, represents it "in its purest form" by those specifics—the elves, orcs or magic swords—it's a good way to valorise their favoured form relative to the other, and to absolve it of demonstrable cliché and pandering by casting this as a degree of FANTASY in any work evidencing it. In the closure of definition, the gains are also being won at the expense of the other genre and its more sophisticated writers: a territorial politics is being reinforced in which fantasy is centred on FANTASY, in which the more a writer seeks to establish the freedom to eschew cliché and pandering within the genre, the more they are marginalised as improper FANTASY, disempowered in their struggle against commercial pressures toward formulation.

With this in mind, a pointed question emerges: Why *is* the term SCIENCE FANTASY attached to works like Herbert's *Dune* or McCaffrey's Pern novels, but not attached to works like Zelazny's *Roadmarks* or Silverberg's *The Book of Skulls* where it is all but impossible to discern any element of futurology whatsoever to the conceit? The latter two works are utilising conceits that require cosmological rather than technological paradigm shifts. But while Zelazny and Silverberg are exempted by the Paradigm Shift Caveat, Herbert and McCaffrey are not? Is it perhaps that to do so binds the term *fantasy* to emblematic (clichéd, pandering) tropes of GENRE (prophecies and dragons)? That equivalently *fantastic* (incredible, marvellous, chimeric) tropes (magic roads and secrets-of-immortality) in their novelty then serve to evidence science fiction as *un*bound from its own GENRE specificity (robots, aliens and spaceships)?

As the definition of FANTASY is closed, as the word becomes, in SCIENCE FANTASY, a signifier of GENRE tropes that make a work not science fiction, as it becomes a signifier of *the generic*, the distinction of science fiction and SCIENCE FANTASY becomes a strategy of *scapegoating*, a mechanism whereby deficits perceived in generic SCIENCE FICTION (like a sensationalist surrender to the sublime) are mapped to those of generic FANTASY, so that the latter can be represented as the cause of those deficits. It is not that *Star Wars* is a product of SCIENCE FICTION, a GENRE with its own tendency to use its generic tropes (robots, aliens and spaceships) in generic plot-structures (Romantic adventure) going back to the pulp roots of this GENRE of the marvellous (Flash Gordon). It is not that the clichéd pandering is a product of the process of formulation inherent in a GENRE, commercial pressures to sate the market's demand for "more of the same" inevitably leading to derivative copies. Rather this SCIENCE FANTASY is held to have (errantly or cynically) adopted the template of FANTASY, such that the presence of the generic in science fiction is blamed on the pernicious influence of fantasy. For the genre eugenicists of SCIENCE FICTION, fantasy must be essentialised into generic FANTASY to sustain the idea that it is the taint of that "pure" FANTASY's essence which corrupts SCIENCE FICTION, creates the miscegenation of SCIENCE FANTASY. As if fantasia were not a fundamental feature.

This is a process of *abjection*, the same process by which Genre is ghettoised as the territory of cheap sensationalism—abjection being the idea (articulated by Julia Kristeva) that we react intensely when confronted with substances that were once part of us but which no longer are. Blood, shit, piss, vomit, a severed limb or digit—these things remind us of our own nature, the stuff we ourselves are composed of, and we respond to that reminder with fascination and revulsion, refusing to engage with them, recoiling or driving them from us. Marginalised social groups—people of colour, gays, Roma, Jews—are abject. So, in the term Science Fantasy, *fantasy* becomes a signifier of that which is abject in relation to science fiction. Call it Y. Call it magic. Call it elves, orcs or magic swords. These specific tropes are actually indexes of *all* tropes, which are in turn indexes of commodification and formulation, indexes of Genre.

A Limitation of Acceptable Incursion

Is it possible to unmoor the Sibling-Sibling Model of Science Fiction and Fantasy from that mechanism of abjection? Can we describe a Fantasy distinct from Science Fiction, but avoid closing its definition to the specifics of a Genre in a way that implicitly renders it a scapegoat? Can we describe it in terms of a different Y? And if so, what is that Y?

In many respects, for a contingent of writers and readers who make exactly that distinction, the simple answer is that Y equates to not-X, that it is simply the *absence* of rationalisation that, for them, distinguishes a work out as Fantasy rather than Science Fiction (both as openly defined as a closed definition can be). In this model Science Fiction and Fantasy exist as concentric zones, the former nestled within the latter but excluding by definition that which exists outside its strictures, identifying it by negation. This almost, but not quite, collapses the model into a Parent-Child Model in which the science fiction subset can be imagined as a zone within fantasy, but in which that renders it by definition a *type* of fantasy, the subtle difference of the two models enough to engender endless argument, as those working with one model or another fail to articulate it clearly.

This is why the Great Debate persists. The exteriority of fantasy means that there will always be those who see it as encompassing science fiction, containing it. The exclusivity of Science Fiction with regards to works that fall outside its definitional zone means that there will always be those who see Fantasy as *essentially* distinct. The impositions of closed definitions to both leads to further confusion in a field where, at the edges of that central zone of Science Fiction, these closed definitions fray, as the cosmological conceits and inargued arguabilities of science fiction blend with those of fantasy, the boundary blurred further by subjective application of the Paradigm Shift Caveat.

Here we find SCIENCE FANTASY as a buffer-zone for SCIENCE FICTION, a limitation of acceptable incursion. Going hand in hand with the schisming of SCIENCE FICTION / FANTASY, the term SCIENCE FANTASY signifies an attempt to retrench, to restore integrity to the GENRE by (re)defining it as exclusively rationalist, exiling that which transgresses its dictates. Anything which smacks of a surrender to sensationalism is abjected into this interzone, viewed as a hybridised combination, or as FANTASY masquerading as SCIENCE FICTION. Insofar as the aesthetic of the logical can and does operate as a counter-balance to the aesthetic of the sublime, the abjection becomes quite comprehensible as a suspicion of Romanticism, rooted in a fear that without the Rationalism there will be nothing to hold the sense-of-wonder in check, that passion will run amok without reason to restrain it, and that the genre will therefore revert to its pulp roots in the follies of heroes and Romantic adventures, devolve back into GENRE.

With a fiction of the marvellous, this not an unfounded fear.

The Return of the Reviled

> *Science fiction is a spectrum, it stretches between fantasy and realism and needs to be anchored in both. But more and more we see at one end of the spectrum fantasy and sf merging seamlessly, while at the other end realism appropriates, quite legitimately, the tropes of sf. In other words that unique affect that once upon a time made us love science fiction is now equally the province of fantasy and of realism.*
>
> **Paul Kincaid**

In the hepcat hotspot of the SF Café, it was not entirely unnoticed that this entrenchment was extreme and the application of the Paradigm Shift Caveat erratic at best, that the distinction between SCIENCE FICTION and FANTASY unravelled when applied to works like *Roadmarks*, that SCIENCE FANTASY signified the heroic structure as much as the chimeric content, and that the closing of these definitions ultimately schismed these zones from each other. If SCIENCE FICTION had this closed definition incompatible with FANTASY, there was also science fiction with an open definition entirely *interwoven* with fantasy, the former built upon the latter, the latter published as the former.

In the SF Cafe they sought to articulate the situation more clearly, terms like *hard* and *sense-of-wonder* emerging from the dialectic of futurology and fantasia at work in the genre(s), coined to describe the proportional differences of rigour and rapture, the range of possible science fictions encompassing (or limited by) the fantasies of writers like Ray Bradbury at one end, the thrillers of writers like Michael Crichton at the other, those science fictions where science ultimately ceases to play the role it did in SCIENCE FICTION, largely functioning as an expedience for thematics in one and plot in the other.

The problem for the entrenched partisans of SCIENCE FICTION was simple: as a hangover from the formative era, disguising the underlying unities and tensions of the field of SCIENCE FICTION / FANTASY, the term *science fiction* was applied very broadly indeed among the subculture of readers, writers, editors and publishers which had established itself in that Gernsback-Campbell period and whose tastes ran exactly the spectrum identified by Kincaid, between the fantastic and the realistic. Many writers worked as much in one mode as the other, even within the one story or novel. Many writers found the market as eager for picaresques and social satires, bildungsromans and "twist" stories as for Romantic adventures based on Rationalist science. And where some sought to differentiate SCIENCE FICTION from FANTASY, many simply saw no reason to apply a largely artificial taxonomy born of market forces and subjective application of the Paradigm Shift Caveat to the complexity of their creative projects.

Rather than argue over semantics or work with a cumbersome hybrid term like SCIENCE FICTION / FANTASY, many simply applied this label or that on the basis of ad hoc personal judgements. Before the Ballantine Adult Fantasy imprint set the consensus of FANTASY as a genre, before the SCIENCE FANTASY label was negotiated to mean what it does now, the label science fiction had already become a catch-all term for fiction which shared a market rather than any clear definition in genre terms—which, in fact, had two utterly opposed aesthetics at its extremes and a third rapidly expanding into every nook and cranny of indefinition. Unmoored entirely from conventions of character, plot-structure or backdrop, futurology blending into cosmology, science fiction had ceased to be simply the name for the generic form of the closed definition and become instead largely a marker of subcultural affiliation.

In the SF Café there was a new owner behind the counter and a new fry cook in back, and together they cut loose with a menu of soul food that changed every day, undefinable, unpredictable. There were burgers, yes, and there were chicken nuggets, but there were also all-day breakfasts, pancakes and waffles, hot dogs and omelettes, chop suey and pizza and you name it.

Were I inclined to contentiousness, I might suggest that the key point of affiliation which came to characterise the field was the desire of its readers for that sense-of-wonder, and that this affiliation marked, to all intents and purposes, a resounding victory for the aesthetic of the sublime over the aesthetic of the logical, that in attempting to segregate out SCIENCE FANTASY from the GENRE of SCIENCE FICTION defined by Campbell and redefined by those whose motto was "rigour over rapture," SCIENCE FICTION only succeeded in invalidating its own definitional control, allowing the very sense-of-wonder it set itself against to usurp its place, allowing the fantasia to become the defining characteristic of the genre rather than futurology.

Were I inclined to contentiousness, I might suggest that the eventual victor was, in fact, that which was abjected as either SCIENCE FANTASY or FANTASY outright. In the face of HARD SF's insistence on rigour, writers and readers alike simply asserted the ultimate exemption of the Paradigm Shift Caveat in order to circumvent the restrictions. The abject may be dross best disposed of (like shit) or a vital component (like blood), and where it is valued as the latter one may well see a reaction of sedition and subversion to that process of abjection, a return of the reviled, the exiled, the repressed. I might suggest that SCIENCE FICTION lost the battle, was defeated and usurped, such that what we now call science fiction is, most characteristically, this abjected "FANTASY in SCIENCE FICTION drag."

Otherwise known as SCI-FI.

The Scourge of Sci-Fi

Ordure and Bullshit

Nine tenths of science fiction is crud. Of course, nine tenths of everything is crud.
Theodore Sturgeon

In the uptown district of Literature and the midtown district of Mainstream, so the story goes, the highbrow and the middlebrow all turn their noses up when they glance downtown, in the direction of Genre. Fairy tales for children, they sneer. On the door of the Bistro de Critique there was, for a good many years, a sign that read:

NO GENRE ALLOWED

They are not like us, both sides agree. The nearest *they* ever got to a rackspace label is General Fiction—a term with an empty definition if ever there was one, catch-all for a host of idioms and idiosyncrasies. No, Genre Fiction, as we happily identify ourselves, just isn't de rigueur there, so we're given to understand. So, fuck 'em, we say. Fuck the mundanes of Mainstream, the elitists of Literature. We're Genre Fiction and proud of it, proud to wear that brand painted on the backs of our biker's jackets.

We have plenty to be proud of. Even during the Golden Age, the boundaries were blurred as to what exactly constituted science fiction, and in the SF Café that made for a dynamic melting pot. Claiming the core of the field, those tables right in the centre of the SF Café, was that Science Fiction characterised by its futurological fantasias of space travel, robots, contact with aliens, off-world colonies. That gang owned the place, and with just cause. For all that this mode was born from the pulps and inherited the callow, shallow Rocket Age Romanticism, Old Man Campbell *had* brought something new to the table, a Rationalist bent that called for writers to level up their intellectual game. And so they had, turning an idiom of Boy's Own Adventures to more gnarly purposes—like the social commentary and critique of Pohl & Kornbluth's 1952 satire *The Space Merchants*. Edging into this meanwhile were the visions of writers with even subtler agendas, outsiders like Orwell or insiders like Bester who saw yet greater potential in this strange new fiction. In their disregard for, or subversive approach to, the pulp formulae, these writers sowed the seeds of at least one revolution that was to come in the shape of the New Wave. And what about the feminist SF of the '70s? And the cyberpunks of the '80s?

Damn straight, we're GENRE FICTION! *We* know that means Delany, Butler, Gibson, and a thousand other things.

It's a dangerous game though, that pride, because when we turn this noun into an adjective or a genre label in its own right—saying this is GENRE FICTION, or simply this is GENRE—we're buying into the very rhetoric of abjection that built the ghetto walls around us. It is a term that functions in the same way *coloured* does; the rhetorical strategy is identical, as that in two examples of asyndeton.

Hold that thought a second though. I must be crystal clear here, quash right up front any misconception that, in tracing out the parallels in linguistic action, I mean to suggest the reader of category fiction is facing prejudice *in any way* equivalent to the monstrum that is racism: though the abjection of category fiction must, I think, be set in its context as a mechanism of classism, misogyny and indeed racism, I have zero interest in bolstering the victimhood claims of the geek. I'm talking here of a process acting upon the fictions, not the fanboys, where the victims remain as ever the lower class, women, and people of abject ethnicity. What is abject in literature is so precisely because it is, in the rhetoric of those prejudices, *vulgar, hysterical, primitive*. Those fictions are abjected as a means to institutionalise those prejudices, I'd maintain. If the peer group pecking order turns the geek into whipping boy, that's another story, one in which a retreat into category fiction seems rather more effect than cause to me.

The point then:

Skin colour is a quality we all have, all of us literally of some specific colour, just as every work is of some specific genre—my pale pinky-beige no less a colour than your deep brown, my contemporary realism no less a genre than your science fiction. But the term *coloured people* twists language itself to establish an abjected Other in contrast to an artificed normative, to posit people of *some* specific skin-colours as on the flip-side of a default *white people*, to privilege those normative *white people* as lacking some abstracted quality of being COLOURED. So too the term *genre fiction* twists language to establish its own abject Other in contrast to an artificed normative, to posit fictions of some *specific* genres as on the flip-side of a default *general fiction*, to privilege those normative fictions as lacking that abstracted quality of being GENRE.

Of course, the reality is those works of general fiction are also of genres, idioms with their own characteristics, sometimes conventions and clichés, and it doesn't take much for these genres to become GENRES, definitions closed, works formulated to factory-line product. Sometimes they manage to pass, you might say, despite the giveaway packaging. One glance at that sepia-tinted photograph cover, say, fading to white at the edge, that picture of a 1930s child in hobnail boots on a tenemented street, and you recognise that KITCHEN SINK REALIST FAMILY MEMOIR MELODRAMA à la *Angela's Ashes*. But that's not fiction of a genre, in common parlance. Well, it's not GENRE FICTION, doesn't have that quality of being GENRE. Supposedly.

Sometimes they'll be named—like the Chick-Lit spawned from Fielding's *Bridget Jones's Diary*—and exiled sharpish to the ghetto with the rest of us category fiction scum. And I hazard that example was tagged for exile even before formulation had really set in, the very name reeking of exactly the sort of prejudice I suggest above. If Chick-Lit is Genre Fiction where some Kitchen Sink Realist Family Memoir Melodrama is not, it begs the question: what exactly *is* the quality being ascribed to every single work in some specific genres?

And should we really be so eager to go along with the charade?

There is of course a political purpose in taking a term coded/loaded with abjection and reclaiming it. We find that rhetorical strategy at its most abstract, perhaps, where for all the idiosyncratic foibles inherent in humans not being fucking clones, for all that everyone has *some* quirk of queerness, only some *specific* foibles become the focus of abjection with the label *queer*. But here, some of us who find ourselves so-labeled choose to make that term our own, the accusation owned as assertion of identity.

Maybe that rhetorical strategy is a valid response in other similar cases.

Yeah, we're queer, we say. Non-normative in our sexual tastes. Our quirks are apparently something you have an issue with. So fucking what? Should I give a fuck that you equate your normative with propriety, that you recoil in disgust at my rejection of your standards? As Old Bill Burroughs used to say:	Yeah, we're genre, we say. Non-normative in our aesthetic tastes. Our quirks are apparently something you have an issue with. So fucking what? Should I give a fuck that you equate your normative with propriety, that you recoil in disgust at my rejection of your standards? As Old Bill Burroughs used to say:

> I am not innarested in your condition.

But never mind the quirks of impossibility like the novum or chimera, or those quirks that disrupt affective equilibrium, the monstrum or the numina. We often use the term *genre* to refer to strange fictions, but we can hardly exclude Chick-Lit from that label, and that's hardly built of strangeness. If we're to be defiantly proud, reclaiming *genre* as a label, it is conventionality itself that we're defending, the cleaving to a template.

If you have an issue with conventionality, the upstart ghetto kid might say, let me introduce you to my friend the sonnet. I'll carve my fourteen lines into your skin with a volta for a scalpel. I'll even write it backwards so you can read it in the mirror every day until you appreciate the rigour of formal restraint and the capacities of poetry not *limited* by genre but *unleashed* by it, loosed *through* it.

But still, to take a scalpel for a volta, slice, turn from genre to Genre—

—back in the SF Café, even in the heyday of the Hard, with Old Man Campbell calling the shots, it's not difficult to see where the sneers and jeers found their source. Sturgeon's Law doesn't say that ninety percent is of no consequence. Lest we begin to forget who the *target* of the prejudice is (not us often-privileged readers and writers of category fiction but rather those ultimately abjected by propriety's discourse of the vulgar, the hysterical, the primitive), maybe it's worth a little whiplash whirl to a counterpoint of our complicity as producers and consumers of formula fare.

There is a key distinction between the sort of abjection that takes place with the segregation out of an abject Other by skin colour, and that which takes place with the segregation out of certain genres by the fact of their being published with rackspace labels: where individual human beings tend to be *individual human beings, duh,* rather than stereotypes, category fiction is by its commercial nature aiming to achieve a template fit, if in no other respect than by being sellable to a particular target market; with formulation there's an *active drive* toward embodying a stereotype.

Down in the SF Café back then, the menu was varied but the place still carried a legacy of its origins as a junk food joint. If the market encompassed literature enthusiasts with tastes for more mature cuisine, it was focused, as it always had been, on a continuing—indeed burgeoning—audience of adolescent pulp geeks who wanted Romantic adventure stories with exciting trimmings. Flash Gordon, Buck Rogers, John Carter—the heart of this genre lay with heroes who lived next door to *Doc Savage* and *The Shadow* (both published, with *Astounding*, by Street & Smith). For every writer who saw the literary utility of this new mode of writing with its contemporary language of ideas encoded in concrete metaphors, there were plenty for whom those sleek and shiny phallic symbols of the Rocket Age weren't exactly subtle and to whom the ideas they expressed weren't exactly complicated. The lurid covers and exclamatory titles of the magazines promised cheap thrills, food pills, women with gills, heroes with skills, and aliens to kill.

SCIENCE FICTION or science fiction, it was ten percent Orwell and ninety percent ordure, ten percent Bester and ninety percent bullshit.

The Symbol That Ate the Text

Pataphor (noun)
1. *An extended metaphor that creates its own context.*
2. *That which occurs when a lizard's tail has grown so long it breaks off and grows a new lizard.*

Pablo Lopez

We talk of science fiction as the literature of ideas, but all literature uses ideas; what distinguishes this particular mode is that those ideas are made flesh. Where a writer using mimesis renders the dynamism of youth in a metaphor such as *the boy rocketed through the room*, an SF writer uses semiosis, rendering an AI rocket with an adolescent joy in its own destructive force, exploring the signified-signifier relationship from the inside, as an interesting thing in its own right. Held as a conceit in the narrative, this quirk of a technical impossibility is extended metaphor gone wild, unleashed to devour all representational stability. It is the symbol that ate the text, the vehicle of the metaphor unmoored from any specific tenor; the AI rocket with an adolescent joy in its own destructive force is just that, a figurative vehicle that could blast into the reader's imagination a whole explosion of tenors. To collapse it to a single tenor would be a failure, in fact, a reduction to mere allegory of what must really be understood as *pataphor*. The quirk does not speak directly to a context in which it is symbolic analogue of a stable mundane element, but rather creates its own context.

Given that we're not all writing absurdist pataphysics in the manner of Alfred Jarry, clearly there's a distinction in our use of pataphor though, in our creation of contexts sprung from strange conceits that nonetheless make sense. Is it a matter of limitations, of being at least *theoretically* realistic? At a base level, possibility and plausibility *are* relevant to this conceit, but their relevance is more complex than we're given to believe.

The orthodoxy is a simple dichotomy. Delany is not alone in applying the notion of possibility to distinguish science fiction and fantasy on the basis of the subjunctivity level (i.e. alethic modality) of their sentences; though I'm given to understand, by way of a comment during a recent discussion hosted by John Clute, that current thinking may be moving more in the direction I'm suggesting, *The Encyclopedia of Fantasy* sets it as a straightforward either/or, assigning science fiction a subjunctivity level of *could happen*, fantasy a subjunctivity level of *could not happen*.

At first glance, this seems so cut and dried only a fool would deny it: science fiction limits its conceits to the possibilities of the future, while fantasy throws off those shackles and runs amok; who could argue? But this is the Contingency Slip Fallacy in action. *Could happen?* Even if we buy into the *not yet* caveat written into the novum's impossibility, in a past or present tense narrative—and future tense narratives are few and far between—we are dealing with what could *have* happened or what could *be* happening now. The novum may not, as the chimera, strain suspension-of-disbelief with the more extreme alethic modality of *could not happen ever*, but that doesn't make it a possibility yesterday or today.

Plausibility? What we might see is conceits developed from arguable speculation and justified with futurological rationalisations; the text may make a concerted effort to persuade us to project into it another alethic modality, one that acts as palliative to the rupture of possibility: *would happen*. But this is the plausibility of the con-man or conjurer as often as not, and the logic games of if-then are as likely to be left implicit in the backstory. What may well sell a reader more on the pretence of possibility is not so much argument as it is allure, not the *would* but the *should*. Which is to say, the marvellous tint to the incredible, the novum acting as numina.

Coulda, woulda, shoulda—the words in use here are markers of modality, judgements written into the text. As the earlier references to epistemic modality might suggest, such judgements come in more hues than just the judgement of possibility. There is: epistemic modality, judgement of fact; alethic modality, judgement of possibility; deontic modality, judgement of duty; and boulomaic modality, judgement of desire/dread. If strange fiction is characterised by the alethic quirk (novum or chimera), we'd do well not to underestimate the extent to which it may be driven by the boulomaic quirk (numina or monstrum).

If the potential of the field of strange fictions lies in equipping a writer with a whole toolkit of pataphors to work with over and above the plain old metaphors, the downside of that toolkit is that it also allows a writer to pander to the most infantile wish-fulfilment and the most paranoid neuroses, to conjure alethic quirks tinted marvellous or monstrous to exploit the most basic (and base) desires and fears in wholly superficial terms, to simply push those buttons for the sake of narrative drive. It always has been true and always will be, no doubt, that some are so much more interested in the numina or monstrum as cheap thrill that the strangeness of the quirk, its potential function as novum or chimera, is as irrelevant as prose quality, mere means to an end.

Before we jump to defend our ghetto of GENRE from the slanderers of MAINSTREAM and LITERATURE, we might want to bear in mind that the pulp we have our roots in was a juvenile fiction, and last century's juvenile fiction at that.

Those who do not remember history, as they say…

Walk into the SF Café twenty minutes into the future, slide into a booth with your iRobot mate, and if you look around you'll likely still see the genreheads wiring into the wonder. You'll still see those who happily accept the cheapest, crappiest junk as long as the price is low, the portions big, and the food comes fast and hot, smothered in ketchup, with crack cocaine for salt. There's a killer buzz to the games those Microself X-Books immerse you in. They're hip, they're happening, they're fictive smartdrugs!

Jack in and jerk off, kid! You too can save the world…from those evil, bug-eyed commies from space!

To be clear, the sway of the juvenile market was hardly wholly malign, leading to a focus on clarity and economy, and even thematic concerns beyond those of the middlebrow and middle-aged. Losing maturity in one's fiction for the sake of marvels and monsters can also mean losing propriety, and that's not always a bad thing. It makes for a freedom to fail the standards of solemn literature.

So we had Ray Bradbury writing stories such as "All Summer in a Day" (published in *F&SF* in 1954), where a kid at school on Venus gets shoved in a closet by other children, misses a brief glimpse of the sun…which comes only once every seven years. This, along with many other stories, is quite clearly aimed at adult sensibilities as much as at those of children. Bradbury may be sentimental about youth, nostalgia rather than angst powering much of his fiction, but his work is hardly shallow sensationalism; even those stories most imbued with wonder and creepiness display the thematic maturity of an adult writer using the worldviews of children as alterior perspectives on reality rather than simply seeking to capitalise on the crudity of their tastes. And that sentimentality is a feature, not a bug; he's writing American Pastoral, which is as valid as any dreary mid-life crisis novel.

We can contrast this however with works directly targeted at younger readers. Around the same time we have Robert A. Heinlein writing novels such as *Have Space Suit—Will Travel* (serialised in *F&SF* in 1958), where a kid with his own spacesuit has a romantic adventure in space—enacting the desire of the reader in his escape from mundane Middle America to the Great Beyond, being kidnapped by malevolent aliens, saving the human race from destruction; there's even a female child genius for the clever tomboys. *Rocket Ship Galileo* with its Nazis on the moon, the frontier adventures of *Red Planet* and *Farmer in the Sky*—it's stating the obvious to say that these stories are aimed at adolescent sensibilities, but we tend to be disingenuous within the field about the extent to which these juveniles are at the root of a purportedly adult-oriented Science Fiction's genre cooties. Those uptight ass wipes at the Bistro de Critique thinks it's all fairy stories for children?

No shit, Sherlock.

Sometimes when the symbol eats the text, the first thing it devours is any hint of fiction as something other than a means to an immersive end.

Nipples That Go Spung

Some say the golden age was circa 1928; some say 1939; some favor 1953, or 1970, or 1984. The arguments rage till the small of morning, and nothing is ever resolved. Because the real golden age of science fiction is twelve.

Peter Graham

But I don't want to suggest that juvenile fiction is inherently lower quality, nor even that escapism and wish-fulfilment are bad things per se. Young Adult fiction may well be the freest category out there right now, openly defined by demographic rather than formal conventions. If you've got your snoot ready to cock at it, go read *Octavian Nothing*. And if some kid—or adult, for that matter—out in the world beyond the city of New Sodom wants to take a weekend city break in *Genre*, sit in the SF Café and—shock! horror!—read a book I don't rate, a book that offers nothing other than a temporary reprieve from the drab nine-to-five, a retreat into immersive adventure…well, power to them. It might be me in there, you know, rereading Edgar Rice because today I'm just not in the mood for Bill.

Still, there's something about the truth of Sturgeon's Law that we elide, about the particular nature of our particular crud. The commercial pressures on fiction aimed at juveniles in a conservative culture were formative in the field, having wide-ranging and long-lasting effects, not least in Heinlein's work; we need only look at *Podkayne of Mars*, bowdlerised by the publisher, Heinlein forced to revise the ending against his judgement, in order to see how these story-patterns limit the capacity of fiction to challenge a reader with, say, a tragic outcome for a beloved hero. This is how formulation works, how GENRE works. In ROMANCE, the expectation and demand is for the heroine to get together with the hero in the end. In MYSTERY, the expectation and demand is for that mystery to be solved. In the ACTION-ADVENTURE of the Hollywood schlockbuster, the expectation and demand is for the hero(ine) to save the day at the end and be lauded for it. In every such GENRE there's an audience that wants "more of the same" and writers out to supply that desire, not thwart it.

Romantic adventures bound to a narrative grammar where the hero cannot lose, loaded with wonder and wish-fulfilment, aimed at credulous adolescents who're far more interested in the thrills and spills of the spectacle than what Richard Feynman has to say about the physics of a twirling, nutating dish moving through the air…here at the very core of the field of science fiction—SCIENCE FICTION even—in the work of one of its cardinal influences, one of the Big Three, we have much that the churlish intellectual might reject (or abject) as FANTASY. For all that those juveniles are generally well-crafted bildungsromans, with philosophical subtleties and social pertinence to their moral messages, they signify a return to the narrative logic of pulp where moral fibre and fortitude are written into the hero as champion, and instant karma awaits him/her in her/his inevitable victory.

If Heinlein initially published works which were clearly juvenile or adult, the distinction between these works quickly became muddled in a field catering to precocious adolescents and immature adults. *Starship Troopers* may not be considered juvenile fiction now, but it's the classic example of the Science Fiction Bildungsroman and was aimed for Scribner's with the rest of them. Heinlein's juveniles begin to bleed into his later works. *The Rolling Stones*, with its precocious child heroes, gets linked into the same universe as *The Moon Is a Harsh Mistress* through the character of Hazel Stone, while the twins, Castor and Pollux reappear in *The Number of the Beast*. And so on.

As his novels degenerate into rambling exercises in hot air and cloying cuteness, they become increasingly emotionally retarded; they may offer a spur towards post-conventional morality for a questioning fourteen year old (for all that his manner is didactic and his message dubious, the individualist message invites the very dialogue that may destroy it), but they hardly demonstrate the most mature approach to their themes, the quirky flavourings of the idiosyncratic ideologue ultimately drowned in the ketchup of redheaded twins and nipples that go spung.

The late Heinlein works gain an originality from his eccentric libertarian character, and before the slow slide into bloat and blather there's some peachy stuff if you can get past the politics. But where Bradbury's weird wonders, for all the nostalgia, lead via *The Twilight Zone* to works such as Ellison's "I Have No Mouth, and I Must Scream" or Disch's "Descending," in Heinlein's overgrown Tom Swift, Juan "Johnnie" Rico, we might well trace one root of a grand oak of tosh and piffle that dominates the field. As that adult/adolescent market grew over time, and the work aimed at that market replicated and codified itself—its audience requiring consistency of effect more than novelty, seeking the stability and security of conventions, demanding "more of the same"—derivative, formulaic power fantasies of SPACE OPERA and MILITARY SF built on the foundations laid by the pulps, around the statue of the Man/Boy Hero erected by Heinlein, constructing a GENRE within science fiction that is neither juvenile nor adult but kind of just puerile.

I likes me some "Shit Blows Up" fiction, don't get me wrong, but this derring-do form, with its boys' own tales of hardy heroes, grizzled old-timers, evil aliens and so on, is SCIENCE FICTION's version of the tales of orphan-princes permeating FANTASY. Both are ultimately defined by the strictures of GENRE—epic / heroic Romantic adventures—and populist enough to have impressed a stereotype on the minds of the uninitiated.

But it's not the fiction I'm out to skewer here, only the self-serving pomp around it, the grandiose handwaving in denial.

Down in the ghetto, in the SF Café, there are those who blame it all on cinema and television, mutter darkly about *Star Wars*, how this and that movie or show is *not really science fiction*. Never mind Flash Gordon. Never mind Tom Swift. Never mind all that "fans are slans" nonsense. Never mind Heinlein's juveniles. Never mind that the patent legacy inherited from MODERN PULP is a drive to churn out pandering pabulum that fits a template. For all too many, it's *Hollywood* to blame if the vast majority of the public think of the fiction we love as that puerile dross of formulaic genre…that stuff they so abjure that they must call it by another name.

Down in the ghetto, in the SF Café, there are those who grit their teeth and clench their fists whenever that dread name is spoken: SCI-FI.

Spandex and Mullets

The distinction between SCIENCE FICTION and SCI-FI is by no means universal within the community but for those who hold to it that term is loaded. For some the label *sci-fi* is just a shorthand for *science fiction*, an alternative to *sf* gesturing at…you know, that stuff we like. But for some that label signifies the pernicious influence of—fuck it, construct your enemy to blame with a scatter of *and/or* as you will:

FANTASY,	corrupting the form	with
Hollywood,	diluting the form	into
Television,	presenting the form	as
Fandom,	demanding the form	be
		tosh and piffle.

Wherever the term *sci-fi* is reserved for the visual media or the pabulum in print, wherever the blame is placed, the distinction serves to segregate out "proper" SCIENCE FICTION from formulation. Coined by überfan Forrest J Ackerman, the term has been reviled by writers from its origins. As a diminutive and a pun, it's a bit too cute and clever. It hints, perhaps, at a sort of baby-talk whereby Samuel R. Delany could be referred to as Sammy-Wammy, while Harlan Ellison would find himself saddled with Harley-Warley as his moniker. When I first started hanging out with other would-be writers at the SF Café, back in the early nineties, as a member of the GSFWC, I quickly realised how that term raised hackles. By 1995, when Worldcon hit the home town, the local rag headline was "Sci-Fi Freaks Beam Down to Glasgow." 'Nuff said.

The irony is that many down in the SF Café have forgotten its origins; every so often you'll hear grumbling about how literary fiction (or LITERARY FICTION, rather,) doesn't suffer the indignity of a similarly demeaning diminutive. Aside from ignoring the (ghetto Creole?) coinage of *lit-fic*, (or the common *pomo* abbreviation for postmodernism), this illusion of victimhood is disingenuous. It would be nice to imagine the label as an act of semantic trivialisation perpetrated by the elitists of Literature and mundanes of Mainstream, a hostile Othering like the twist of *genre* to GENRE, with its roots in the Culture Wars; but this is simply not the case. The label was created by us, taken up as a membership badge, printed on black T-shirts to be sold over the counter at the SF Café, worn with pride. We forget that we brought it on ourselves.

It caught on, it spread, it seeped into the public consciousness, and now there's that bristling irk sparked when we hear it in the mouths of naïfs who don't know their Asimov from their Ellison. Why? Because from them it comes with an arched brow at the garish façade of the SF Café, the mass-market eye-candy filling its windows: racks of media tie-ins, franchise novels, lurid art books, t-shirts; merchandise, merchandise, merchandise; posters for conventions, clubs, cosplay; role playing furry filk knows what.

It comes with a superior smirk at this superfice out on display and the unseemly squee it speaks of, the enthusiasms so excessive they short-circuit everyday decorum when unleashed, and sometimes social skills, and maybe even simple common sense, the zeal of a subculture jonesing at the privilege of being advertised to with OMG! the new trailer for the reboot of the reboot of crap from a director whose entire oeuvre is set in a cosmos where the fundamental particle is not the quark but the shark.

We twitch that they're looking at the SF Café and seeing a Genre, a marketing category, because that means formulation for a market that sustains it, demands it, *celebrates* it, throwing money at any hack who can put a lurid patina of hyperkitsch on the clunk-click plots and card-board characters, power-fantasies and happy endings that are, and have always been, characteristic of a junk fiction indulgence.

From the mouths of the incognoscenti, that term conjures the stigma of what they expect to see inside the SF Café: the stereotype of sweaty-palmed geek-boys with a hard-on for gadgetry, scarfing down sub-literate comfort food, venting furious unreason at the affront of factory-line crap being factory-line crap, *duh,* and always going back for more, more, more. Why, we wonder, can't they imagine us all connoisseurs who relish the haute cuisine and know exactly where to find it? Why can't they just *see past* the All You Can Eat sign on the door that screams unbridled appetite rather than educated palate?

We forget that we brought it on ourselves not just by the coinage, but by our consumption, all those years as slack-jawed kids pressing noses to the SF Café's windows of wonders. Come on. Is it any wonder when your aged Aunt Agnes sees Delany's *Dhalgren* on your shelf and asks, *Is that some of your Sci-Fi?* what she's thinking isn't New Wave?

It's the same as when she hears you playing your Sonic Youth album and complains that "all of that Heavy Metal stuff is just noise." Her understanding of rock music formed by fragmentary horrifying glimpses of Mötley Crüe, Whitesnake and Slayer on MTV back in the '80s, when you loved that shit, she hears those loud guitars and has no idea that there's a difference between Heavy Metal and rock in general, that there's punk rock, prog rock, post rock and more. It's all just Heavy Metal to her, the shriek of guitars evoking an image in her mind's eye—crude self-caricatures of posturing adolescent moppets in spandex and mullets. To aged Aunt Agnes, similarly, Sci-Fi is a strange unfathomable spectre, a patchwork of fleeting impressions stitched loosely into a fuzzy notion, something she can only imagine as the literary equivalent of spandex and mullets.

So we cringe at her question. *It's not* Sci-Fi, we wince. *It's* Science Fiction. Or, *It's science fiction.* Take your pick. What we're trying to articulate in the first response is simply that the fiction in question doesn't fit the conventional template(s) she imagines, that her image of our Genre is wrong. What we're trying to articulate in the second is a bolder claim, that the fiction of this aesthetic idiom doesn't fit *any* conventional template(s) she might imagine, her image wrong because ours is not a Genre at all. As much a disingenuous denial of plain fact as a sincere proclamation of upstart agenda (and vice versa), it's a quixotic task, this defensive correction, doomed to failure, the distinction as impenetrable to her as it is imperceptible in the two statements spoken aloud.

It's not Sci-Fi, we say, asserting a genre in stark opposition to Genre, its very antithesis, with all the indefinable diversity that entails, an equal to Literature, if not *better,* because it's not constrained by the dictates of Realism.

It's not Sci-Fi, we say, meaning our fiction rocks as wild and complex as Sonic Youth, must not be boxed in with a cutesy little monicker. And off we strop down to the SF Café, where everyone's calling it *skiffy.*

So maybe this is a good place to deal with quirks of illogic.

The Mundane and the Absurd

As we've set out what Lake terms a private narrative, the alethic modality of "could have happened" appears, at first sight, to remain unchallenged. The events recounted, the images and phrases, are entirely mundane in two ways: they are entirely possible within the laws of nature and in terms of known science; and they are of such small scope that the pretence of them is not a clash with the reader's knowledge of recorded facts—c.f. the limitations of our knowledge of the private life of some youth named Holden Caulfield. The term *mundane* is not meant to imply *boring* here, simply that the events are "of or pertaining to our world; common, ordinary, everyday, domestic," and that the limitation of our knowledge in terms of scope means the fiction does not contradict our awareness of how things work.

Or so it seems, at first sight.

If we're tempted toward a shallow division here that conflates the mundane with the mimetic and yet situates the strange wholly in those incredible narratives we call *fantastic* (thereby implying chimeric and marvellous), there are narratives that complicate matters with events that are not so much impossible as simply preposterous, so vastly implausible as to beggar belief. They may not breach the workings of reality the same way as the quirks of SF and fantasy, but if we understand the laws of nature we are dealing with as something less formal than the laws of physics, then we can include that point where the laws of human behaviour are cast as part of that "natural order." What are we to make of narratives, I mean, that breach the strictures of logic not in terms of inherent contradiction but in terms of a reasonable flow of action?

In comic narrative, we find behaviours and reactions exaggerated to a point where the suspension-of-disbelief is strained to breaking point. If it is stretching a point to say that an actual alethic modality of "could not have happened" is introduced in the sort of sentence that an elicits an amazed "you can't be serious," we can nonetheless say that a new alethic modality has been introduced: *would not have happened.* A breach of known science or the laws of nature is a relatively straightforward thing; when it comes to the strictures of logic however…well, there are inherent contradictions, but there are also absurdities.

The picaresque and the humorous anecdote play with our credulity in this manner, asking us to suspend disbelief in the ludicrous. Often as not an anecdote, perhaps true, perhaps told as true but with a twinkle in the eye, gains its power from the sheer tension between the absurdity of the assertion and the claim of actuality, in a clash of modalities—where this "could not have happened (surely?)" but it "could have happened (really!)" and in fact it "did happen (honestly!)"

…and it was only when I got through Customs and out of the airport, when I went to roll a cigarette, I put my hand in my tobacco pouch and found the hash!

No way, man. You're shitting me.

I shit you not.

If our alethic quirk comes in four flavours according to whether it breaches known history, known science, the laws of nature or the strictures of logic, as we look at the latter, at the absurd in contrast with the mundane, what we mean by *strange fiction* bleeds out far beyond any waffling blather of science versus magic.

A Cup of Tea Without Tea

A while back, in a TV program on *Britain's 50 Greatest Comedy Sketches*, amongst other sketches shown were a couple of classics from Monty Python's Flying Circus—the Yorkshiremen sketch and the Dead Parrot sketch. Linking between these was a clip of an interview with John Cleese in which he commented on the Dead Parrot sketch: that "you can't believe they're having this conversation"; and "that's where the comic effect gets its power from." "This could not be happening" is just a different tense of "This could not have happened." "This *would* not be happening" is only the more honest articulation of the alethic modality in play, of the breach of the strictures of logic. Taking the Yorkshiremen sketch as an example, it's not hard to see how the comic narrative exploits the absurd. In this case the structure is as basic as it could be, each absurdity (each quirk of illogic) largely attempting to outdo the last in its representation of hardship, raising the stakes to ridiculous extremes.

> 1: *Imagine us, sitting in the fanciest pub in England, drinking our Chateau de Chauclea wine.*
>
> 2: *Right you are, thirty years ago we would have been lucky to have had a cup of tea.*
>
> 3: *Cold tea.*
>
> 2: *Yes, without sugar or milk.*
>
> 1: *Or tea.*

And the first absurdity enters in the contradiction of a cup of tea without tea, a hard breach of logic: could not happened.

> 2: *In a cracked and filthy cup.*
> 3: *We used to be so poor that we would drink tea out of a rolled-up newspaper.*
> 2: *You were lucky to have a newspaper; we used to have to suck our tea out of a damp cloth.*

And yet the escalation out of the realms of possibility is mitigated. In the three lines above we flick back and forth through a breach of possibility: could; could *not*; could. But if it's possible to suck tea out of a cloth, it's utterly preposterous: would not. Still, we know exactly the sort of mundane reality the hyperbole is rendering, and there's just enough of it under the absurdity to keep it from overwhelming our suspension-of-disbelief. So, that absurdity is ramped up slowly to grandiose claims.

> 1: *You were lucky to live in the bottom of a lake. There were a hundred fifty of us living in a shoe box in the middle of a road. We dreamed of living in a lake.*
> 3: *You were lucky to live in a shoe box. We lived in a brown paper bag. All three hundred of us! Got up at six a.m., ate a crust of stale bread and worked in the mills for twelve hours. When we got home, Dad would beat us and put us to bed with no dinner.*

Living in a lake, a paper bag, a shoe box: would not, could not. And yet a "could have happened" alethic modality persists. The whole sketch is, after all, only a representation of a conversation, and that conversation is not *itself* impossible. We recognise all too well the type of conversation it is satirising, the one-upmanship of childhood miseries encapsulated in the "you were lucky" refrain. But it is increasingly absurd as it strains our suspension-of-disbelief, tromps roughshod over our credulity, that anyone would go so far beyond reason in their exaggerations. The impossibilities of the claims push this towards the nascent fantasy of fairy-tales and nursery rhymes. There's a clear reference point here:

> *There was an old woman who lived in a shoe.*
> *She had so many children, she didn't know what to do.*
> *She gave them some broth without any bread.*
> *She whipped them all soundly and sent them to bed.*

In both cases, note, we're presented with bad housing, huge families, malnutrition and child abuse. Cheery stuff. But they're pushed out of the realm of possibility by the wild irrationalities. In the comic sketch, those irrationalities are heightened to the final apotheosis:

1: Well, you were lucky! That was luxury. We used to get up in the morning at ten at night—which was half an hour before we went to bed—eat a hunk of dry poison, work twenty-nine hours a day at the mill and when we got home our parents would kill us and dance around our grave singing "Glory, Glory, Hallelujah."

Not just physical impossibilities and preposterous action now but logical contradictions, a whole series of them—could *not*, could *not*, could *not*, could *not*—seamlessly woven into one elegant and eloquent articulation, rounded off with a "Glory, Glory, Hallelujah." And then all the tension built up in the apotheosis of absurdity is released with the bathos of a punch line that brings the reality satirised by that conversation crashing into the absurdity of its extremes:

3: But you tell that to the kids today and they simply don't believe you.

It is a cliché that at once inhabits the "could have happened" alethic modality (being precisely what is said by these type of people in the real world) and a "could not have happened" / "would not have happened" alethic modality (because the absurd idea of anyone *not* disbelieving such absurdity is absurdity recursed to a perfect loop of unreason).

It plays all manner of havoc upon the narrative, this flavour of alethic quirk that comes in soft or hard, *would not* or *could not* happen, in the irrationality of drinking tea out of a rolled-up newspaper or the logical impossibility of getting up before one goes to bed, the quirk born as we step through and between the sentences to find the mundane sliced and spliced back together in unreason, in a nonsensical stitch: the *sutura*.

If you've spent any time in the SF Café you should be all too familiar with such absurdity, and I don't mean because it's impossible to escape the geeks trying to flog the Dead Parrot Sketch to death.

Because It's There

"SF's no good!" they bellow till we're deaf.
"But this looks good…" "Well, then, it's not SF!"
Kingsley Amis

It was a merry day in the SF Café, sometime around the middle of the last century, when the newspaper reporter and the moviemaker arrived, both having heard about this crazy joint so full of stories…so full of Story. There were kids running around with little toy rocket ships, teenagers talking astronomy in the booths, adults speaking Esperanto at each other 'cause it was the language of the future. There were atheists and admen. There was futurology and fantasia. You know this because you were there—

—are there now, standing beside the reporter and the moviemaker, on the pavement outside, looking at a big bold sign above the door that once read *The Science Fiction Café*. Not any more. Some of those letters have been taken down now, you note, stuck up in the window to spell out: *cenection*. Whatever the fuck that means.

—See, it's 'cause we're all connected, says a grinning numpty at the door. Connection, *cenection*. You see? Isn't that cute? Isn't that clever?

The moviemaker thinks it's awesome. The reporter's eyes are alight. You…you nod and smile, nod and smile, and step aside as a writer slopes out the door, shaking his head in sorrow, muttering darkly that a pun on *hi-fi* sounds godawful now, never mind in fifty-something years. For a second, you think maybe you could tell him *wifi* will be all cool and stuff by then…but you suspect that'll be small consolation as you look up at the sign, where the remaining letters now spell out the new name of the haunt: The Sci Fi Café. And maybe a little part of you dies inside.

That discomfort has deep roots. The trivialising diminutive is abhorred not just as a token of the outsider's disregard for actual literary achievements, but as an emblem of uncritical devotion, of the disregard for quality, of the indiscriminate appetite for any old shite with a spaceship, the urge to buy every book in a series long since degenerated into drivel, every book by a certain author, any book about X, Y or Z, regardless of quality. It conjures the overgrown adolescents who continue consuming formulaic drivel most fourteen year olds would scoff at. It conjures the hacks ready to supply the demands of that juvenile market, not for a little escapism, but for a wholesale retreat from adulthood.

Which is to say, it reminds us that the SF Café is, even when we get past the gaudy window display, a schlock market, serving up brain-out, sponge-in, sit-back-and-enjoy-it, eyeball-kicks, and if we go there today to drink craft beers and discuss pataphysics with peers, well, the TV over the counter is still tuned to *Alphas*, *Babylon 5*, *Carnivàle*, *Dark Skies*, *Enterprise*, *Farscape*, *Grimm*, *Heroes*, *Invasion*, *Jericho*, *Lost*, *Millennium*, *Night Stalker*, *The Outer Limits*, *Planet of the Apes*, *Quantum Leap*, *Red Dwarf*, *Supernatural*, *Teen Wolf*, *UFO*, *V*, *War of the Worlds*, *The X-Files*, you name it, zzzzzzzzz… Sometimes we have the TV on because the series is good. Sometimes we have it on simply because it's there.

We insist that this stuff we call *science fiction* is not Sci-Fi. For some in the ghetto of Genre this is axiomatic, a secret truth known only to the genre kids, that there is *proper science fiction* and there's that Sci-Fi shit. That crud Sturgeon shrugged off is not the real deal, we tell ourselves, just the factory-line commercial product, extruded according to a formula, shat out in a turd of a movie or a TV show, a media tie-in or an Nth generation copy of a hack-job of a rip-off of an insult to the word *novel*. But that high-profile, low-quality dreck gives the genre its bad rep because that's what we, the fans, God bless us, have saddled ourselves with in lapping up every hokey, cheesy, clichéd pukeball of a

B-movie with a spaceship in it, spewed out by the Ed Woods of the world. It is our desire for "more of the same" that transforms genre into GENRE.

The term SCI-FI signifies an uncritical ardour we seek to distance ourselves from in our quest for acceptance, in a desire to be taken seriously. We can hardly deny the actuality of the puerile, formulaic tosh that gets sold as SCIENCE FICTION; so we abject it as SCI-FI and distinguish the *proper science fiction* out from it on the basis of quality. It is a different abjection to that carried out on FANTASY (at once more direct in its targeting of GENRE rather than a scapegoat symbol, and more deluded in its denial of our own desires), but it is still an abjection, a recoiling in repulsion from that which is essentially a part of ourselves. Here's the logic of that abjection:

If it's sci-fi, it must be bad. If it's good, it can't be sci-fi.

Sound familiar?

Dogfight at the SF Café

"It's not 'Sci-Fi,'" we bellow, *"Sci-Fi's duff!"*
"But this looks good..." "SF! The proper *stuff!"*
Hal Duncan

The name does suck. It surely does. But I don't buy it as a label for the Enemy Within; that whole ruction's just another discourse of abjection like that between SCIENCE FICTION and FANTASY, a wedge of displaced angst driven deep into the definitional integrity of the field. A fantastic genre that is neither fantasy nor generic? In this diverse field once bound by a loose affiliation of reader tastes under a catch-all term of *science fiction*, these definitions by negation found our ideas of what does or does not constitute the family in little more than personal whim, in exclusions based on individual preference and value judgements.

If it's good, it must be X. If it's bad, it must be Y. For whatever values of X and Y you care to insert.

Old Man Campbell's rules were never set in stone and we recognise this nowadays in marking out the SCIENCE FICTION which has solid futurology at its core as HARD SF. We recognise it when we brand as SCIENCE FICTION that mass of stuff sold in the same magazines, under the same imprints, on the same bookshelves, which never really gave a flying fuck about futurology, simply used whatever quirks it hit upon, novum or chimera, to its own ends, whether the aim was to tickle the cerebral cortex or the sense-of-wonder gland.

Or we deny it, scratch Flash Gordon, Buck Rogers and John Carter out of the picture, pretend that Gernsback didn't talk of "charming romance intermingled with scientific fact and prophetic vision," pretend that *Astounding* didn't share its crib with *Doc Savage* and

The Shadow, pretend that *Star Wars* isn't more like E.E. "Doc" Smith than *Primer* is. There's plenty of pulpy powerhousing that barely glances off science in its search for scenery and props, conventions or conceits, symbols to be exploited by a writer more concerned with telling a ripping yarn and/or exploring the human condition than with science per se. It's still—

—no, fuck it, it isn't *science fiction*, not any more.

The fractious factions in the SF Café tore that whole notion apart a ways back. The latent conflict between the aesthetics of the logical and of the sublime, that old Rationalist/Romanticist dichotomy, became overt in the abjection of Fantasy. A second battle-line was drawn against Sci-Fi, a battle-line that is, in essence, a recapitulation of the Literature/Genre turf war. And the SF Café became a rumble zone of rival gangs, each marginalising themselves by staking out their own special territories defined by overlapping and orthogonal agendas—futurological, fantastic, literary, commercial.

It's a wild show, sitting at the counter, scoping the killzone of crossfire between these forces. It's a spectacle all right, watching that many-headed mongrel warhound mode of pulp modernism trying to rip its own throats out 'cause it smelled the scent of its own piss and didn't recognise it. Roll up. Roll up. It's bloodsport night, at the SF Café, Cerberus versus Cerberus—the new evolved Mark Three hellhound too, with an extra head or two as biomods. Bugger of it is, I can't decide whether I've got a dog in this fight or in all of them.

Sod it. Let's just go with the flow and watch the show. Check it out. There's a new head there, trying to play pack leader, assert its taxonomic dominance as an umbrella term for the entire discourse of genres. Why, if it isn't Princess Rexatroyd Speculative Frou-Frou Fiction the Third!

And, man, Sci-Fi and Science Fiction are both going for it big time!

Ooh, that's nasty.

THE SPELUNKERS OF SPECULATIVE FICTION

The Scalpel and the Cigarette

In fact, one good working definition of science fiction may be the literature which, growing with science and technology, evaluates it and relates it meaningfully to the rest of human existence.

H. Bruce Franklin

When you watch enough of the daily dogfights down in the SF Café, you can get a bit jaded with it all. It's science fiction versus SCIENCE FICTION versus SCI-FI versus science fiction versus FANTASY versus fantasy—and all of these labels simply tags on one collar of a single Hydra-headed hound, our rabid Cerberus unbound, trying to rip its own throat(s) open. And all too often it's the same fight underneath it all; clear away the rhetoric, and you find Romanticism and Rationalism going at it yet again, the ideal of the sublime versus the ideal of the logical.

There was a time when they were partners, and they still tag-team now and then, to be sure, but the old alliance of fantasia and futurology, that Rationalist Romance of SCIENCE FICTION? Its spectre may still haunt our favourite...well, haunt, but the coherence of a Campbellian closed definition has been shattered. Where we might once have pinned the term *science fiction* to a generic form in which fantasia and futurology were partners, the term now applies to a discourse far better characterised by the conflicts of these two than by their alliance. And the dialectic of Romanticism and Rationalism is so engrained in the discourse, in fact, we sometimes talk as if no other aesthetics even exist, as if there is only this binary choice: the sword or the spectacles.

The reality is more gnarly though: while Romanticism and Rationalism square up against each other in mutual hostility, Passion against Reason, the hero's sword against the scribe's spectacles, there are aesthetics which refuse to play that game, twistier approaches, strategies that set Reason against *reason* as the aesthetic of the logical finds itself up against the aesthetic of the absurd, Passion against *passion* as the aesthetic of the sublime comes up against the aesthetic of the ephemeral.

The absurd and the ephemeral: the fifth columns of intellectualism and sensationalism respectively, out to rip them apart from the inside.

The aesthetic of the absurd we find in Kafka or Pinter is not the sensationalism of the wild Romantics. It is Rationalism turned against itself, in a cold-blooded murder/suicide pact of logic. No tawdry melodramas play in the operating theatre of cruelty; there are no frilly cuffs here, just surgical gloves. Where Romanticism wields the strange, the impossible, as a sword in a hero's hand, for the writer of the surreal it is a scalpel with which to vivisect the living psyche.	The aesthetic of the ephemeral we find in Joyce or Whittemore is not the intellectualism of the Rationalists. It is Romanticism turned against itself, an ecstatic dissolution of the sublime. No dreary social realist tomes are read under the Moorish wall; there is no critique here, only a kiss. Where Rationalism scries the mundane, the real, with a scribe's spectacles, for the writer of the moment, it is to be felt as the cigarette in your hand, lit by a friend at a funeral reception.

The enemy of my enemy is my friend, as they say, and it's no different here in the SF Café. Those dogfights can take an interesting turn when the sensational sword and the intellectual scalpel pair up against the spectacles of Rationalism, or when intellectual spectacles and sensational cigarette pair up against the sword of Romanticism. The two warring clans, the Campbells and MacDonalds of SCIENCE FICTION and FANTASY, can find strange bedfellows in the black sheep of each other's families. For those who want to fit everything into a neat dichotomy of Reason versus Passion, these twistier aesthetics fuck with that, often fighting on the wrong side, goddammit, ruining taxonomic purity. Though the cigarette stands for the potential *wonder* in an ephemeral moment of smoking, its rejection of the spectacular for the domestic can set it as hard against sensationalism as the most dogmatic Rationalist, locked to the mundane as source of the numinae that fire off affective epiphany. Meanwhile, the scalpel is wielded by writers who believe in Gödel, not gods, who adopt an inhuman dispassion in their scrutiny of unreason, but as they employ in their experiments quirks that breach not just the laws of nature but the strictures of logic, this sets them as hard against intellectualism as the most fervent Romantic.

So, the intellectualists may find themselves fighting side-by-side with writers of the moment who might hold little faith in Reason, who might have minimal real respect for all those mechanistic protocols of cold logic, but who despise the grand glamours of FANTASY for displacing passion onto projected follies.	So, the sensationalists may find themselves fighting back-to-back with writers of the surreal who might see little glory in Passion, who might have minimal real interest in the grand emotional dynamics of the sublime, but who disdain the totalising metanarratives of SCIENCE FICTION for wilful disregard of disorder.

But this is only the start of the recombination of aesthetics. If you look around the SF Café what you see is actually a whole host of writers and readers with a cigarette in one hand and a scalpel in the other. Thing is, *these* two aesthetics, the absurd and ephemeral, are not opposed to each other, do not cast themselves as opponents locked in mortal combat. They're almost as well paired as private narrative's common fusion of the logical and ephemeral in the mundane, the domestic—the observer/critic aesthetic at the heart of various modes of Realism and formulated into the Genre of Literary Fiction, with its slice-of-life character studies leading to epiphany as resolution.

So, with one writer, the ephemeral may become a key concern as they spurn the displaced passion of Romanticism, while with another the absurd might be employed to undermine the inflexible (un)reason of Rationalism; neither strategy entails a rejection of the other, though, so those two writers need not see each other as their hated foe. They may well be the same writer, the sort of obstinate, opinionated, downright thrawn motherfucker who looks at the aesthetic of the sublime and the aesthetic of the logical—and the whole tawdry turf war they've had going for two centuries or more—and sees them *both* as failing to do justice to the passion and the reason they idealise.

And that's where it gets really interesting, I think.

If I Bring Back the Ashtray…

It's those thrawn motherfuckers I see when I look at this field of strange fictions. Sure, there's the Campbellian closed definition, Science Fiction that was, in essence, a sort of Rationalist Romanticism. And now there's the schism between those two aesthetics that plays out in endless teacup tempests. But looking into that gaping rift reveals the true core of the field as pulp modernism, even from its earliest days. In many of the canonical novels or short stories of this field of strange fictions, what we see is not futurological fantasia, not an adventure with the sublime bound within a logical rationale, but rather writers striving to balance the sublime with the ephemeral and/or to violate the logical with the absurd.

For all my bias in that direction, I'm not talking about the New Wave here, mind—Ballard's catastrophes of the banal logical-ephemeral (i.e. mundane, domestic) world riven by the irrational or Moorcock's non-linear narratives of Jerry Cornelius degrading the Modern Pulp hero to a spotty adolescent in a London flat. Not yet, at least. I'm talking about Bradbury's "The Veldt," published in 1950, a tale as domestic as you can get and one where the irrational irrupts out of a viewscreen with all the scientific rigour of Freddy Krueger. It eats the main characters.

Yes, down in the SF Café, in the ghetto of Genre, there is, always has been, and probably always will be an audience looking for *more of the same*, where *the same* is basically a Campbellian Science Fiction. And there's nothing wrong with that. But in this so-called *literature of ideas*, born from the fusion of the intellectual and the sensational, futurology and fantasia, originality has been a counter-imperative to formulation from the start, novel or stories prized for having their own killer concept as a Unique Selling Point. And that means—has always meant—a sort of evolutionary pressure for novels or stories in this idiom to offer not *more of the same* but *something different*, a pressure that doesn't sit well with any closed definition.

For all the fiction designed to cosset the reader in conventions, that pressure within the field supported—indeed commercially *demanded*—a more exploratory fiction, one which sought to challenge the reader with subversions and outright breaches of those same conventions, which strove to serve as more (or simply other) than just consolatory fantasia and/or compelling futurology. The aesthetics of the ephemeral (as in Bradbury) and of the absurd (as in Vonnegut) are only to be expected as emergent features of a genre focused on the sublime and the logical where *transcends the genre* has been code for *what we want to read* since forever. I seem to recall hearing somewhere that the cover of an early edition of Bester's *The Demolished Man* sports that plaudit in its copy. Or possibly *The Stars My Destination*. Admittedly this is a titbit snatched from a faulty memory of a casual conversation that took place in the SF Café sometime…well, more than a minute ago. Anyway, over the decades, writers pushed the envelope continuously in a quest for novelty, carrying on into new territories, constantly challenging and overturning GENRE clichés, turning their tricks to satire (c.f. Frederik Pohl & Cyril Kornbluth or John Sladek), to semiotics (Samuel R. Delany), to whatever idiosyncratic interest they wanted to explore.

For a prime example of how orthodox this unorthodoxy is, how inadequate a simple closed definition in terms of fantasia and futurology is, we need only look at the fiction of Philip K. Dick, particularly the later works, where the ephemeral (c.f. *kipple*) and the absurd are often far more important than any sense of either the sublime *or* the logical. Asimov, Heinlein and Clarke may have been the Big Three who ruled the pantheon of pros back in the day. Hell, even for a kid coming to science fiction in the early '80s it was those three who benchmarked my entry-level experience of the field—Asimov's *I, Robot* the first proper SF book I read, Heinlein the first writer I obsessively collected, Clarke's *2061* the book that revealed to me the Law of Diminishing Returns. But Dick is the Dionysus to their Zeus, Poseidon and Hades, and it's his wild rites many are pointing to when they use that overloaded term *science fiction*. See *The Transmigration of Timothy Archer* or *VALIS* for so-called *science fiction* which is certainly not SCIENCE FICTION, neither Romanticist nor Rationalist at all, not remotely. On the back of my copy of *VALIS*, a simple quote from the book reads, "If I bring back the ashtray, can I have my prefrontal?" That's the cigarette and the scalpel in action right there.

If this fiction focuses on science at all, it is to use it as a metaphor, a mechanism through which to explore humanity and modernity. The questions that concerned Dick were not scientific but philosophical: what it is to be real; what it is to be human. Science, for Dick, is only one of the many forces which reshape the world into the strangeness of what might as well be a waking dream. Where Thomas Disch pointed accusingly at the fantasia of the futurology when he titled his book of essays *The Dreams Our Stuff Is Made Of*, he's talking pipe-dreams and daydreams. Dick is an emblem of the *actual* dreamstuff we might well find ourselves dealing with at times, in his 1960s suburban worldscapes ruptured by breakdowns of reality itself. This is the oneiric, the psychotic.

Dick's dreams aren't fantasias of the marvellous, but freaky visions of finding the kiosk you were buying a hot dog from replaced by a slip of paper with the word "kiosk" on it. Disch's own "Descending" is a similar blend of the domestic and the absurd (the absurd being potentially *far* from comic), as are many of Ellison's short stories, "'Repent, Harlequin!' Said the Ticktockman," for example. There's a whole *Twilight Zone*-style of fictions traceable back to (and through?) Bradbury, I'd say. For sure, a Science Fiction partisan dedicated to dreary taxonomies might dismiss most of those as being "really horror," but Dick's fiction is as often as not more strange than uncanny, not frightening so much as just plain nutso.

Dick's animatronic presidents and AI suitcases, ersatz realities and conspiracies are less about tapping into some logical/sublime novum-as-numina—speculation? sense-of-wonder? yeah, right, whatever—than they are about the paranoia and neurosis of being PKD in the late twentieth century, the era of McCarthy and Nixon, the Communist Witch-Hunt and the Sexual Revolution, Vietnam and Watergate…and serious drugs of course. *A Scanner Darkly* wears the thinnest scramble suit disguise of Science Fiction.

And Dick was far from alone, in the SF Café, in following the cultural shift from Rocket Age rapture through the Cuban Missile Crisis of the soul towards a Cold War détente of the banal and the bizarre. It was in this context, where the concerns were less the material aspects of technology and more the abstract potentials of modernity for good or ill—if not the strange actualities of modernity itself, the futureshock of living in the present—that the term *speculative fiction* began to be taken up.

Note the absence of capitals, by the way.

The Extremities of Unreason

Absurdity is not the only strangeness that gnaws at any pat boundary between the mundane and the strange, quite capable of worming its way into the private narrative with only the soft sutura of illogical behaviour, with events that don't rupture the epistemic modality (staying on the level of Holden Caulfield rather than Jett Rink, to use Lake's example). In looking at the Yorkshiremen sketch above, I noted a link to the old nursery rhyme "There Was an Old Woman Who Lived in a Shoe." To illustrate the true extent of the strange born from the clash of narrative modalities, far beyond the incredible and the marvellous/monstrous of so-called *genre fiction*, let's take that rhyme and rewrite it. First we'll excise the fanciful conceit and blatant impossibility (the quirk) of her living in a shoe, flensing the irrationality, to get a private narrative, a narrative of the mundane:

> *There was an old woman who lived in Peru.*
> *She had so many children she didn't know what to do.*
> *She gave them some broth without any bread.*
> *She whipped them all soundly and put them to bed.*

Not that poverty and child abuse are somehow so endemic in Peru that this narrative is vastly more probable set there than anywhere else. I'm just grabbing a random place-name that rhymes and scans. So, now let's add a little strangeness into the mix:

> *There was an old woman who lived in Peru.*
> *She had so many children she didn't know what to do.*
> *She gave them some broth without any bread.*
> *She drugged them all soundly and cut off their heads.*

The two versions each represent a different mode of private narrative, one remaining in the simple alethic modality of "could have happened," the other complexifying it with something similar to the comic "would not have happened," but with the opposite effect.

We can imagine the first rhyme fleshed to an actual story: set in a developing country with a high level of poverty (or a Scottish housing scheme, a US inner city, whatever), cleaving to the mundane in a grim series of events that are ultimately all too common, *too* everyday, it's a tale of the despair born of such poverty, the degradation of misery, the slow corrosion of a mother's spirit, her ultimate surrender to violence; driven by the *pathos* at heart of any kitchen-sink drama, any domestic narrative, in a formal sense we might say this narrative is *pathetic*.

The second narrative is, or we can imagine it as, another story: the events are not dissimilar, but this is a tale which pushes us beyond the realm of rational behaviour in that last line, confronting the extremities of unreason. It inspires not just pathos but something deeper and darker, transcending the merely miserable and becoming *terrible*. At the heart of this story is a profound transgression of the most basic laws of human behaviour: the monstrum of infanticide with its boulomaic modality: *must not happen*.

It's a quirk of desire/dread we're faced with rather than impossibility, "should not" rather than "could not." As far as rupturing reality goes, it all "could have happened." But as *should* becomes *must*, that *must* becomes hued with incredulity. The moral rupturing of murder is hardly the metaphysical rupturing of magic; there is a point however where some crimes are deemed so obscene as to be reckoned "against the laws of nature," not just wrong but *unnatural*, breaches of the natural order, the divine order even. We might well refuse to accept the very *possibility*: for all that an action is entirely possible, it does not change the sense of conviction, the alethic modality of "could not have happened…surely, *surely* could not have happened" that tints the monstrum in such a tale, inherited from the Greek concept of miasma, the stain of bloodshed, e.g., in infanticide, parricide or matricide. The very word *obscene* has its origin in such denial, in the monstra going unrendered in Greek drama, taking place *off-stage*.

There is more though. In such a story, we will surely see the monstrum coming. From early on, most likely, an epistemic modality will emerge: *will happen*. Where by all rights, we should expect no worse than the whipping of the pathetic narrative, say, in this story, we will sense the inevitable doom of the protagonist, be driven on through the narrative by the inexorability of their fate. The omens are likely to be liminal, diffuse, but I wonder if we can't also talk then of an epistemic quirk, a *prefigura*. However we parse it, though, this story is a quite other creature from the pathetic narrative, one powered by the monstrous.

To give it its formal name, of course, this narrative is *tragic*.

The comic and the tragic go hand-in-hand, the pity and terror of the latter what the absurd would inspire if we didn't laugh at these wildly outrageous events. Like the comic narrative, the tragic narrative is built from the irrational, the incredible, just not in the way that makes us break out into belly-laughs; in its use of the monstrum bound in pathos, tragedy offers us not the absurd but the *abject*.

The whole vocabulary of early tragedy—moira, hubris, ate, nemesis—defines a system (a social, natural, divine order), the activities that isolate and separate out an individual from that system, and the (automatic) response. The tragic hero is that member of society (that part of us) who becomes distinct from it, ceases to be a part of it and is denied, rejected, an object of revulsion. The tragic act is that action which is a potential human behaviour (again, part of us) but one forbidden as beyond all morality, rejected as an *inhuman* act.

So, the earliest Greek tragedy gives us the abject in the shape of Prometheus, divine rebel whose theft of fire is a crime against Olympus itself, an act that severs him from his community, renders him anathema. His punishment is an enaction of his abjection—an exile, a binding and a torture, a monstrum wrapped in pathos. Pentheus, in *The Bacchae*, similarly singles himself out, breaches the divine order by refusing to recognise Dionysus and is not simply destroyed for it but monstrously so, in abject shame.

Even in a more contemporary tragedy like *The Crucible* a similar theme emerges, with John Proctor already on the verge of abjection at the start of the play and Abigail Williams testing the boundaries, dabbling in the witchcraft (abjected paganism) of Tituba (member of an abjected race), out in the forest at night (two entire aspects of the natural world—the wilderness, the night—abjected as exteriorities, alterities). As Abigail and the girls become latter-day Furies, bringing their "pointy reckoning" to Salem, Proctor's stance against the hysteria is hubris just as his adultery is ate, calling down his own nemesis. At the end, like

Prometheus he is defiant even in his abjection, refusing to surrender his autonomy, his identity, by signing a false confession:

> PROCTOR [with a cry of his soul]: *Because it is my name! Because I cannot have another in my life! Because I lie and sign myself to lies! Because I am not worth the dust on the feet of them that hang! How may I live without my name? I have given you my soul; leave me my name!*
>
> **Arthur Miller, The Crucible**

This narrative of abjection is clearly relatable to the aesthetic of horror in its focus on the monstrum, albeit the monstrum of tragedy is seldom uncanny, as we might more often find in a work we classify as horror. From Aeschylus to Arthur Miller, *Prometheus Bound* to *The Crucible*, the structure of tragedy involves gradually ramping up the wrongness until we reach a crisis of abjection, the apotheosis of the hero's destruction. The tragic hero's heroism may in no small part be born of our recognition that the abject is in actuality a part of us, that our abhorrence of it is not entirely just—hence the pathos. There is a part of us—the part of us abjected in the tragic hero—that roars out with Prometheus against the gods, that stands with Proctor on the gallows and *will not submit*.

The tragic narrative of the rhyme above is a crude caricature of a tragedy, but in it we go from Mother Goose to Medea in four easy steps. The first line establishes the set-up of normality. The second introduces the monstrum in the disruption of social normality—the old woman has too many children to cope with—and in a fully fleshed-out tragedy we would expect more to be made of this. We might well see the children as a brood of bastards running wild, the community around responding with condemnation, the old woman trying and failing to control them. The third line sets up a conflict between the old woman's desire to support her children and her inability to do so; imagine this as the third act of a play and you can picture the slow build towards the character's tragic fall as her attempts to deal with this double-bind fail time and time again, if they do not, in fact, exacerbate the situation. And all the while, we can imagine, a village culture increasing the moral pressure on her, the pressure to *do something about it*. Finally, in the fourth we are given a climax worthy of Aeschylus, in a tragically irrational solution: infanticide. We can imagine a moment of Medean madness, a woman with her children's blood on her hands, screaming at the villagers who have driven her to this: *Done, done, done! Done and undone!*

That we know this kind of story could play out in the real world, that we know (e.g. female) infanticide is a very real problem in the world, does not mean that this private narrative remains mundane. The mundane has been shattered by the irrational, the abject, the monstrous, in the difference between a whipping and a decapitation. If the comic turns on a response of "No way!" the pathetic might turn on a similar sentiment, but it's one distinctly different in the affect invoked. We might say "No way," to the first narrative, but we're only voicing an empathic denial; we know all too well that the world is full of starvation and whippings. With the tragic however, this denial is forceful, powered by a sense that surely to God, surely to God, this could not have happened, *must* not have happened: No *fucking* way!

The Strange in the Mundane

If tragedy cuts a sharp silhouette with its apotheosis of misfortune, its distinct dynamics of modalities, this is not to say the pathetic narrative is an equally clear-cut mode. No fiction can entirely eschew the quirks of the strange if it wants to have any narrative drive whatsoever; the best it can do is exile the alethic quirks and confine itself to boulomaic quirks of more muted import, should and should not, rather than must and must not. And it is an aesthetic extreme to do so, one that cuts against the grain when the whole point of narrative is the dynamics. So, the utterly mundane being far from a default, we can discern dimmer examples of the strange in many of the private narratives that pass for realism, the mimetic weft of the mundane ruptured, by some quirk or other.

Between the tragic and the pathetic—in the fusion of the two—we find for example the mode of *melodrama*, deeply domestic whether set at the working-class kitchen-sink or in the middle-class drawing-room, but pushing the misery beyond starvation (even if it's just being starved of love), and whippings (even if it is just verbal whippings of dysfunctional relationships) and into decapitation (or emasculation, or incineration, even if these are purely of the psychological / metaphoric variety).

Melodrama will lower the scale of monstrosity so our state of shock is not quite so heightened, our suspension-of-disbelief not quite so tested, but even at the level of miserabilist British TV soap operas, we find the monstrum lurking. Abusive husbands end up as bodies under the patio. Blackmailers get beaten to death with pokers. Pathetic victims become tragic heroes, destroying their own innocence in attempts to overcome the villainy the fictive world throws at them. Domestic melodramas, even those which wear the respectable name of *drama* or *novel*, are rife with heroes, villains and Oliver-Twists-of-fate. American soaps have even gone as far as alien abduction and cursed jewels.

More respectable narratives can be scarce less strange. Thomas Hardy's work is full of impossible coincidences that assist in this or that poor character's destruction, c.f. *Tess of the d'Urbervilles*. Ibsen's *Ghosts* contains no real spectres but is steeped in the miasma of moral transgression (syphilis visited upon an innocent son; how much more miasmatic could this be?). These are borderline tragedy, powered by the same feeling of dread in places, pulling back from the ghosts and witches, omens and portents, poisoned blades and pokers up the arse, but still testing our credulity, not least with the bleakness of their vision.

We can see all of these modes emerging here and there through the history of the novel as private narrative, sometimes boldly, sometimes liminally. Looking to such works as Fielding's *Joseph Andrews* and Richardson's *Pamela* and most anything by Dickens, indeed, we might well trace the absurd, the tragic and the pathetic as three threads of a discourse through which the novel itself ultimately takes shape, not in an eschewal of the strange but in an ever more refined synthesis of its hues and flavours.

Pick a start point at Rabelais's *Gargantua*, say, as a prime example of the absurd at its broadest as literary device (compare the structure of the great "arse-wiping" scene to the "Yorkshiremen" sketch above). Leap to de Sade, who seized on the monstrous as the core of the moral melodrama which, in the novel form, tragedy had become. Skip back to *Don Quixote*; is it comedy or tragedy, or both? I don't know, but this is a discourse we're jumping around in, an interplay that ends up, perhaps, in *Catch-22*, where we are entirely unsure whether to laugh or cry in the face of the grotesque absurdity and abject horror of war.

In the twentieth century, out of this interplay, a cruel mode of the strange emerges that takes us back more properly to the question of possibility, to the alethic quirk rather than the monstrum so powerful it elicits denial of possibility. It's the other way around indeed, where the illogic is so disruptive, so unsettlingly surreal, that the absurd becomes monstrous. Part of the monstrosity though lies in a profound identification of the absurd *with* the mundane, in a sense that we're not so much seeing the mimetic weft of realism ruptured as we're seeing reality's true face, Burroughs's naked lunch, Blier's buffet froid, laid out before us.

There's a neat little serving of this in Lindsay Anderson's *If…*, where it's hard to tell at times whether the strangeness is simply the actual irrationality of life at a public school in the early '60s or whether it is…something more. Too wrong to be laughable, but too low-key an aspect of reality to be monstrous, tragic, the surreal is neither an irruption of the irrational into the rational world nor an encounter with that which has been expelled as irrational…not quite. It is less an exterior(ised) insanity which we laugh at or recoil from, and more a recombination of the rational world into dissonant juxtapositions.

The effect is unsettling but subtly so. When Malcolm McDowell and Christine Noonan begin their mock cat-fight in the café their behaviour strikes us as unusual but it is really just a combination of flirting and fighting. When the naked woman wanders through the boy's dormitory while they're out on their military exercise, it is unexplained but not inexplicable; what is strange is simply that combination of images, the suturing at odds with logic, the sense that this would not happen. We get a mounting sense of dissonance, that things are just a little bizarre. We can rationalise it as satire, as representation and exaggeration of all the *actual* absurdity to be fond in such a bastion of the English class system, but there's another wrongness here. And then McDowell uses a mixture of live ammunition and blanks during the exercise to make the reverend think he is going to be shot. And we cut to the headmaster's office, where the Crusaders have been summoned to apologise to the reverend. As the headmaster pontificates about their misbehaviour, he walks across the room to an over-sized writing bureau and pulls open a large drawer. The reverend, lying in that drawer like a corpse in a coffin, sits up to hear the apologies of the Crusaders. And in that one simple image, the mundane becomes the strange, and the satirical and becomes the surreal.

And now, if this sortie through the pathetic and the tragic has led us astray from the home turf of the alethic quirk as breach of possibility, we surely find ourselves once again in the realm of strange fiction, in the SF Café of the New Wave, in the strangeness of Bellona and Cornelius and Disch's "Descending."

The Solidity of the Stuff

Ask anyone in the SF Café what science is, and many will tell you it's a method, an approach, but just as many will, in all probability, describe it as products rather than process, as stuff. Maybe they'll describe it as a domain of knowledge, as the facts and principles accrued within that domain. Maybe they'll point to the theories and experiments, the sundry instances of the scientific method in action. Or maybe they'll just hold up some technological doohickey forged in the application of those theoretical principles and experimental procedures.

—Hey, man, check out my new iRobot! Now that's what I call science!

There's always been a tendency for the science in SCIENCE FICTION to focus on the latter, on the gadgetry and gimcracks, but this is not really surprising. The futurological fantasias that the label got slapped on were largely structured round conceits that this or that technical impossibility had been rendered possible in some fictive elsewhere and/or elsewhen, in Outer Space and/or the Future. The literary device that Darko Suvin terms the *novum*, the unit of *novelty* written into the narrative for the protagonist (and by proxy the reader) to confront, is essentially a fancy of a techne that does not exist (not yet, not quite). It is the imaginary technique which does what cannot actually be done, not here and now.

It's only natural for that mechanism to be figurated in the fiction as a mechanism in the concrete sense: the impetus to Romantic adventure creating a pressure for that conceit to function as a MacGuffin, a Maltese Falcon-style plot device…well, a physical object is much easier to fight over; and even where conceits are offered as more than just the basis of "let's pretend" fun, where there's an intellectual game of playing through the "what if" scenario in action, where working the conceit has become an end in and of itself, anchoring that conceit in an *object* offers the reader a focal point. The solidity of stuff is useful, and so writers of SCIENCE FICTION turned to robots and aliens the way another writer might turn to, say, cigarettes and scalpels.

Still, even where we're dealing firmly with imaginary artefacts of future science, the substitution of *speculative* for *science* is more accurate, since the novum is *not* known science, no more than the alethic quirk used in alternate history (or ALT HISTORY) is known history. If one is to claim any intellectual(ist) integrity in this enterprise, there's no place for pandering pretences that our conceits are actual possibilities; this is pure wish-fulfilment. The strange fictions I'm dealing with here are characterised by the *liberties* they take with the domains of knowledge they play in.

We can imagine a scientific fiction which does not employ the novum, one which instead utilises actual science the way war fiction utilises war, the way historical fiction uses history; but this just isn't what we point to when we say *science fiction*. A more accurate term, given the novum's kinship with the erratum of alternate history might be *alternate science*. We're not dealing with facts but with conceits. A cloned alien brain in a robotic body is not science but fancy, however arguable we consider its hypothetical possibility. It's a conjecture, a speculation that tickles our "Cool!" response precisely because it breaches the mundane reality of what is technically possible. And since the incorporation of erratum-based alternate history within the field is a given (c.f. *The Man in the High Castle*), calling it all *speculative fiction* to allow for that other flavour of quirk actually kinda makes more sense, no?

But the substitution of *speculative* for *science* also reflects a logical development of the novum itself, from the concrete to the abstract, from the mechanisms of unobtainium, handwavium and spuriotronic cogs, gears and circuits to the mechanisms of individuals and societies. The Campbellian closed definition of SCIENCE FICTION explicitly excluded "sociology, psychology, and parapsychology" as "not true sciences," but if the most instantly recognisable nova of the fictions were physical objects—Heinlein's dilating door, Bradbury's nursery with viewscreens for walls—the writers were often just as interested in the invented social structures that went with them. The group marriages of *The Moon Is a Harsh Mistress*, the "firemen" of *Fahrenheit 451*—ironically, if science fiction can be said to actually use real science, it is the soft sciences it employs more than anything, attempting to apply real principles of psychology and sociology to model the impact of a conceit on humanity, how we would respond to what could not actually happen.

To talk of *speculative fiction* rather than *science fiction* is to shift the focus from the solidity of the stuff to the impact of that stuff on humanity, from the mechanics of gadgets and gimcracks to the dynamics of psyches and societies. If we might tend to think of science in terms of its products, speculation is explicitly a process, and so the word serves as a banner of intent. This is about working the conceit, it says. And again, it seems a natural evolution for this approach to turn inwards.

Working the conceit had become a core concern of SCIENCE FICTION with its Rationalist hat on, and even with Campbell dismissing the soft sciences, the field was quite open to conceits wherein humanity was not just confronted with concrete nova but directly altered by them, not just biologically (Frederik Pohl's *Man Plus*), but also psychologically (Theodore Sturgeon's *More Than Human*), intellectually (Daniel Keyes's *Flowers for Algernon*), linguistically (Samuel R. Delany's *Babel-17*). Through conceits of biological evolution and chemical augmentation, writers side-stepped Campbell's strictures (which weren't exactly the Word of God anyway, not in a field where Horace Gold was publishing Bester's tales of ESPers and jaunting), and got their teeth into science as soft as the Sapir-Whorf hypothesis. The questions being asked in those four books—all sitting on my shelf in those Gollancz Classics editions from the 1980s as core members of the canon—are questions of identity, of the relationships of human beings to themselves, to each other, and to the world around them.

These are not "what if" stories but "what is" stories. What is reality? What is society? What is humanity?

And slowly but surely they approached the question, What is fiction?

Fusion Cuisine in the SF Café

Science fiction is the search for a definition of man and his status in the universe which will stand in our advanced but confused state of knowledge (science), and is characteristically cast in the Gothic or post-Gothic mould.

Brian Aldiss

In the SF Café, the beatniks had moved in, poncy artists and pretentious intellectuals, poets and (post)modernists, God bless 'em. The very sciences that Campbell excluded—sociology and psychology—were at the core of their interests. And when it came to literary aspirations, they saw no reason why science fiction should be any less innovative, any less rich than the mainstream in terms of style and form. It wasn't just that they wanted all-day breakfasts with eggs-over-easy instead of a burger and fries; they wanted Eggs Benedict. They didn't want a Diet Coke; they wanted an espresso so black and so strong it blew the roof of your head off. Screw the sugar rush and the fatty satiation of comfort food; they wanted you to feel the jitters of a caffeine overload along with the exquisite tang of a perfect Hollandaise sauce. They refused to recognise (or recognised as irrelevant) the territorial politics of rival aesthetics. The sublime, the logical, the ephemeral, the absurd—these were just the salt, sweet, sour and bitter flavours to be thrown into the mix, and fuck any purist's proscriptions and prescriptions that set one against another, forbidding miscegenations. If fiction is food, they wanted to be eating and cooking the finest fusion cuisine.

One could say that in their zeroing in on the desire for "something different," on novelty as a key ingredient, these writers were simply reinventing the Genre of Science Fiction each time they "transcended" it, keeping the conventions under constant revision. One could equally say that they were creating exemplary (rather than exceptional) works within an idiom *predicated on change* by manifesting that change in the idiom itself, in an act of recursion. Either way, in a subculture of writers looking for that "something different," it was only a matter of time before that search progressed to the next level, before those writers began to search for, find and offer difference in the very language and structure of the narrative itself.

So soon there was Delany's *Dhalgren*, Moorcock's *Cornelius Quartet*, Vonnegut's *Slaughterhouse-Five*. There was Aldiss and Ballard and Crowley and Disch and Ellison and Farmer and so on, some more experimental than others, but all of them bringing their own new twists to the form—looped and fractured narrative, metafictional and intertextual narrative. The fourth alethic quirk, that which ruptures the strictures of logic itself, packs the biggest punch of them—when the absurd goes beyond illogical human behaviour, at least, when it trumps even the chimera with a breach of physics that creates an inherent self-contradiction. (Hell, even when it doesn't, it can be a taste too rich for some.) Children's fiction and whimsical humour will play with words to take us over this threshold, e.g. where Alice, in Wonderland, has to run to stay in one place, such that her motion is not motion. But it's in the New Wave where we see a full-on explosion of this most confrontational of quirks, in disruptions of the very fabric of sense, continuity cut and spliced with hard suturae.

It is difficult to think of a more (post)modern project in any of the arts than that of speculative fiction where it turns its gaze upon itself in this way. Genre is inherently self-aware in its impulse towards formulation, its recognition of story as the unifying agency of a narrative; it is continually exploring its own boundaries, reifying or reshaping them. But this so-called *speculative fiction* was not simply self-aware but self-critical, analysing itself, reckoning the relationships between story and narrative, deconstructing and reconstructing its own nature from first principles.

The pastiche of Genre found in the work of Moorcock or Farmer is not simply referential play; it is speculation as to the nature of fiction itself. And without the cop-out of ironic distance, this (post)modernism spits on the High Art / Low Art distinction with a sincerity few in the ivory towers ever really had the balls to emulate. With Moorcock, or in Delany's *The Einstein Intersection*, we have a fiction (already a science of fiction) which takes fiction as its experimental subject, its focus of conjecture. How, it asks, *are we ourselves made* by the stories we make, by the language in which those stories are told, the semiotics and semantics? This was fiction tearing itself apart to understand how it worked, how all narrative worked, including those narratives of identity we call human beings. If it inhabited worlds and cities shattered by catastrophes—real or imagined, Dresdens or

Bellonas—no doubt much of this was a mark of the turbulent times the fiction was born in, but more than anything else this is, I think, a marker of…the alterior perspective at the heart of what was termed *speculative fiction*, a clearing away of artificed structures (which is to say strictures) in order to expose the dynamics of deeper connections.

In the SF Café, in the ghetto of Genre, in the City of New Sodom, a trap door had been discovered. In the cellar that it led to was a door, and beyond that door a system of secret tunnels—subways and sewers that led throughout the city and *beyond* it, across the nation, *around the entire world*. And everywhere they came up in the city of New Sodom.

Those who discovered those tunnels, who used them, realised that being part of a *subculture* did not simply mean being a member of some *component* culture within the system as a whole, a community sealed off by its boundaries of identity, walled-in within a ghetto. Rather a subculture was that which existed beneath the culture as a whole, permeating it as a mycelial network of interstices. That subculture might reflect the culture in negative (an oppositional *counter*-culture), as the sewers of Paris map precisely to the streets above, or it might be completely different (an entirely *alternative* culture), as the tube in London links the nodes of places in a pattern utterly unlike the streets above.

Either way, the underground discovered by speculative fiction linked all the important points in this world of New Sodom into one big city-system as ruptured in continuity as Dresden or Bellona, explored freely at this level

> —of the ghetto of Genre—meant fuck all—a writer could go anywhere they fucking wanted—did— fair game for the spelunkers of speculative fiction every corner of the city of New Sodom's tunnels—found the power cables gas pipes words images colourless green that linked it all—linguistic innards of a living thing— meant fuck all—kindred spirits in potholers from the uptown district of Literature—the Burroughses and the Burgesses exploring "our" terrain as we explored "theirs"—gourmet chefs check out the menu in the SF Café—going homeward to cook up fusion food in bistros—a buffet froid of a naked lunch—duck à la orange clockwork orange and colourless green—shook hands with them in the urban netherworld—ideas slept furiously and made sense—under the eldritch yellowy-blue glow of glow of glow of biophosphorescent slime seeped through the cracks in ancient brick walls—built mechanical minotaurs whose hollow roars echoed all through the underground—passer-by standing near a ventilation shaft the mushrooms that grew down there—audible even on the surface—a staple on the menu of the SF Café—fuck the territorial politics at street-level—now the walls—
>
> **Hal Duncan, *Rhapsody***

So they wandered far and wide, the Young Turks of speculative fiction; still, they did keep returning to the SF Café to tell their tales. It was their home. In the Bistro de Critique, in the uptown district of Literature, stuffed shirts still baulked at the unseemly strangeness offered by those (post)modern compatriots, reviled it as obscene pornography or revered it as intellectual play, declawing it with concepts like irony, or "irony," or even ""irony,"" rendering it safe by herding it off towards the Temple of Academia. In the ghetto of Genre, the writers lived free of the constraints of decency and decorum. In the ghetto of Genre, anything goes, man. When you live in the gutter it doesn't matter if you're filthy.

In theory anyway.

The Surrender to the Spectre

It is ironic that where Heinlein's coinage of the term speculative fiction was intended as a better specification of the form, a marker of the *extrapolative* rather than *technological* focus of the genre (i.e. requiring the *act* of extrapolation rather than the mere *presence* of science-based conceits and plot devices), it has been adopted largely as a descriptor for the field at its most inchoate, used as a default term for works defying easy categorisation within the tribalist rhetorics that stand in place of any coherent taxonomy. But in this explorative and experimental fiction-of-science, science-of-fiction, fiction-*as*-science, it seems apt as a reaction to the ossifying conflict of territorial nonsenses, as a rejection of the whole tired discourse of science fiction versus SCIENCE FICTION versus SCI-FI versus *science fiction* versus FANTASY versus fantasy. It's what the doohickey does that matters, not whether it comes under the heading of gadget or gimcrack. In the SF Café:

—Is it science fiction, fantasy or horror? you ask.

—Yes, answers the speculative fiction writer.

For all that this answer is apparently unacceptable to some turf war partisans in the SF Café, it is largely their insistence on closed definitions of these idioms as GENRES that makes it inevitable. Lurking in that label is a recognition that this fiction has, as far as many are concerned, stepped beyond the conventions of SCIENCE FICTION in a fundamental way. Aesthetically, the Young Turks of the New Wave were at odds with the most traditional aspects of the field and quite aware of it, as the title of Ellison's *Dangerous Visions* anthologies makes clear. But rather than argue with the reactionary writers and readers still seeking to bind their work to the closed definition of SCIENCE FICTION, the radicals of the New Wave in the USA simply adopted Heinlein's monicker and made it their own. And insofar as their chosen term has come to signify a broad aesthetic idiom of strange fictions—the superset of all the inextricably interpenetrating commercial GENRES of strangeness, and pretty much anything of comparable approach in its use of pataphor, regardless of rackspace label—they've largely succeeded in establishing a less restrictive model.

Still, when I look back for a branch-point, I see a long history of narratives that had ceased to be futurological fantasias even long before the New Wave. I see writers offering the novum as a source of futureshock rather than sense-of-wonder, conjecturing on the basis of angst rather than argument; I see writers for whom the aesthetics of the sublime and the logical are largely irrelevant as they work on projects quite at odds with Romanticist and Rationalist agendas—Delany's *Dhalgren*, Moorcock's *Cornelius Quartet*, Vonnegut's *Slaughterhouse-Five*, Zelazny's *Roadmarks*, Silverberg's *The Book of Skulls*. But when you're faced with those who predicate SCIENCE FICTION on the abjection of FANTASY and/or SCI-FI, to point to these sort of projects and their core qualities and say, this is science fiction, can be a fast route to a flamewar.

—No, that's really, properly fantasy.

—No, that's really, properly horror.

It seldom seems worth arguing.

As I see it? The estrangement effect of the alethic quirk (erratum, novum, chimera, sutura) is powerful, and the affective disruption that goes with it is not limited to the dread (monstrum) or desire (numina) that might slide a story over some imaginary border, "out of" *proper science fiction* and "into" HORROR or FANTASY. We're talking about conceits that can provide the foundations for tragedy or comedy as easily as for a Romantic adventure or a Rationalist thought-experiment—or for the sort of satire that is both tragedy and comedy, as where the dark absurd of Vonnegut's *Cat's Cradle* belongs with Heller's *Catch-22* more than with Heinlein's *Space Cadet* or Asimov's *Foundation*.

Where those quirks function pataphorically—as any conceit may—as the unbound vehicles of metaphor and metonym, we begin to deal, in fact, with the figuration of modernity in all its strangeness. Whatever label we apply to this fiction, I see in it a staggering range of narrative grammars and an openness to using all the various flavours of conceits. I *can* only be talking here about a fiction that plays not just with known science and known history, but with the laws of nature and the strictures of logic. I *am not fucking innarested* in limiting my scope, either in story or in study, in accordance with definitions closed to cordon off this territory from that, the fiction within my field of vision not being rigidly parametered and perimetered thus. So, if the flexibility I cleave to renders much of the stuff of which I speak improper in the eyes of a whole slew of label-arbitrators I can't be arsed arguing with, renders it illegitimate as SCIENCE FICTION, well, maybe another name is a good idea.

Down in the SF Café, of course, this is when the double-bind of the territorial rhetoric kicks in. To many, *speculative fiction* seems a coy and euphemistic evasion, a craven attempt to gain literary credibility by distancing one's work from GENRE…and hence a betrayal of one's ghetto comrades in favour of the dreaded literary elite. In all honesty, this may not be entirely unfair; many of the more literate writers who adopted the label made no bones about the taint of trash that they were trying to escape, their disdain of the generic product that defines the field not just to the outside world but even in the community of uncritical devotees. Through the act of abstraction denoted, *speculative fiction* signifies an intellect and intellectualism divorced from the dirty physicality of science, from any slack-jawed wonder at gadgets and gimcracks. It claims a cerebral rather than visceral effect, adopts an attitude of aloofness to the very GENRE it resides within. As much as it might denote the entire field of science fiction, fantasy and horror, it also connotes (or signals oneself to be a member of) a specific subset of that field—that which has "literary aspirations."

But I can't say this strikes me as a mortal sin. One thing to bear in mind: this is not an act of abjection as that meted out to FANTASY and SCI-FI. If there's a rejection of that which is a part of oneself, a recoiling from the generic, it is not a marginalisation of that formulaic product as alterity, as Other. On the contrary, this is a redefinition of *self* as alterity, as Other. Rather than fight a losing struggle against commercialism and conservatism, rather than battle for the broken banner of *science fiction*, for the right to carry an empty label and claim proudly, *we are it!* while expelling the Enemy as *something else*, it seems to me that many of the New Wave and their inheritors, to all intents and purposes, simply shrugged and walked away. As a marker more of literary intent than of aesthetic form, the term *speculative fiction* was and *is* a disavowal of the dross, but this renunciation was and is more surrender than betrayal.

If anything it is the desolate retreat of the defeated in the face of the intransigents' animosity, the abandonment of rhetorical ground to the reactionary. It's the slow dismal trudge of refugees down into the tunnels beneath the city, leaving the SF Café to its taxonomic turf wars, surrendering it to that hoary spectre of SCIENCE FICTION that haunts it still, rattling the shackles of its closed definition angrily as the dogfights rage on.

So it goes, as a wise man once said.

The Ghost and the Golem

SF as a Superset of SF

What SF writers write is SF.
Orson Scott Card

So SCIENCE FICTION is dead; but the death of SCIENCE FICTION is not the end of the story. Rather it's the beginning of it. Torn apart in the struggles of its factions, deserted by the blood and breath of its most explorative writers, the carcass of that old GENRE still sits in the SF Café, a leg here, an arm there, novitiates of this cult or that gnawing on its bones, sucking on what's left of the marrow. It's a grisly scene, but if these devotees only looked around them they'd see the ghost that dwells in every corner of the diner.

Everywhere in the SF Café you can still see the stains, still hear the echoes of that ghost—the closed definition reopened to a strange and subtle essence that defies all prescription. And for all that its blood was spilled out, the dying breath of SCIENCE FICTION was guttered into a golem. The spelunkers of speculative fiction mining phosphorescent filth from the bowels of the city of New Sodom, the SCI-FI freaks scraping kipple and kack from the bins of decades-old shit sandwiches out back, composting it to grow shrooms, we have built this thing to take its place.

This is the legacy of generations of writers who'd rather tackle adult themes than pander to puerile power-fantasies, whose interests lay with the soft sciences and humanities as much as with the hard sciences and technology, for whom the fiction was always more important than either the fantasia or the futurology. It is also the legacy of those who simply don't give a fuck about anything other than either fantasia or futurology. This is fiction in which the envelope has been pushed so far out, from ambition or expedience, that all descriptions and definitions—SCIENCE FICTION, SCIENCE FANTASY, SCI-FI, even speculative fiction—can only be, at best, nominal labels for it. It is the fiction that abandons those labels for a negation of description, an indefinition—the acronym *SF*, which might mean any or all of those things.

Arguably, where the term *speculative fiction* was, and still is, successful (to an extent) with readers, writers, editors, publishers, etc., for whom the intrinsic diversity of the field is a given and a glory, it is so in part because it abbreviates easily to *SF*. Hence it translates to the label of *science fiction* through that acronym, if and when required for the ease of communication; it is backwards compatible. Look at it from another angle and you see the power of *SF* as a nominal label.

That acronym reanimates the dead SCIENCE FICTION in the stains and echoes that pervade the SF Café. It binds it to the golem of speculative fiction and SCI-FI all mashed together, this clay-made, über-malleable monster of fictive clay. In it the dichotomy of SCIENCE FICTION and FANTASY is resolved into a unity utterly in contrast with the riven notion of SCIENCE FANTASY. We can even extend the *F*, echo it, to include both the closed-definition FANTASY and/or the openly-defined fantasy in *SF/F*, remove the dividing slash entirely in *SFF*, elide the one into the other as in *SFWA*, the Science Fiction *and Fantasy* Writers of America.

If we want to be all poncy and academic about it, we might even expand that acronym to *structural fabulation*. (Yeah, like that'll catch on.)

This is the beauty of the SF acronym, in fact, the beauty of the SF Café, that it offers a neutral zone where all the factions can communicate even if they do so in the most argumentative fashion. And as abbreviations go, where SCI-FI is cringe-inducingly cute and clever, SF is short and snappy, no nonsense, like the utilitarian acronyms of soldiers and businessmen.

That all the writers of a myriad subset SF methodologies are grouped together, SF as a superset of SF, is a mark of the indefinable nature of the field. Forget: the futurology; the Rationalist ideal of the logical; the Romantic wonders of the Rocket Age; the '60s and '70s fears of Future Catastrophe; the counterculture of acid visions and sexual revolution; every abandoned zeitgeist; the codified conventions of puerile pap; the cobbled combinatory systems of pulp plots, characters, settings, themes. Forget those illusions of SF as the innumerable permutations of an ever-changing set of tropes filched from deconstructed templates.

Or remember them, but remember them all.

This is a confusion of contradictions that can only be made sense of by cutting the Gordian Knot, by saying, like Spinrad, that SF is whatever is sold as SF, or like Knight, that it's what I point to when I use the term.

Paring the label down to these two little figurae, we make it stand for whatever narratives we throw at it; we use the fiction to define the model. It allows for any narrative to be written as SF, because we are applying the label after the fact, saying: this is SF because it can be sold as SF, because it can be bought as SF—not just literally but conceptually, *bought* not just in the *purchased* sense but in the sense of *admitted, swallowed, accepted*, as one buys an idea. In this vector of definition, in fact, in place of a model of SF, what we have is instead a method of reading a narrative, most *any* narrative, as SF.

REALISM, after all, the GENRE that cleaves to that which could have happened, which actually fits the subjunctivity level Delany ascribes to his *speculative-fiction*, is a relatively recent thing, an ideological aesthetic that sets itself apart from the bulk of strange fictions, under rackspace labels or otherwise, to use Clive Barker's metaphor in a BFS awards ceremony a few years back: an island versus the continent of literature.

To take one example, we might use this as a way of interpreting *The Epic of Gilgamesh*, look for a reading of the story as SF. This is a different thing altogether from laying claim to the work as an example of a genre; and it's entirely possible; we can understand this Sumerian poem of a hero's journey, in the context of its culture of origin, as embodying the cosmological conceits of his day, the speculations of the Bronze Age rather than the Rocket Age. John Gardner, as I recall, cites scholarly opinion that it was read as fiction; we should not presume naïve belief with our forebears, no more than with a fan of *Star Trek* or Joyce's *Ulysses*.

We can read Enkidu, Humbaba and the scorpion-men as cryptids, as *exotica*, as alethic quirks of geography rather than technology, of an era when the Great Beyond was spatial rather than temporal, the known world their analogue of our known science, the Cedar Forest and the imagined lands beyond the sunrise a terrestrial deep space. We can read the Deluge, the Plant of Immortality as hypothetical *arcana* of deep time, these metaphysical quirks in terms of the current workings of the world not requiring an alterior reality, only an earlier one. Adding this SFist reading methodology to the arsenal of Marxist and feminist readings has scope; insofar as SF is rooted in fantasia and futurology, an SF reading of a narrative constitutes an interrogation of its dynamics of passion and reason. Insofar as SF goes beyond this to unpack the full potential of its quirks, such a reading for the narrative modalities becomes an inquiry into the dynamics of narrative itself.

In the Fabric of History

In alternative narrative, as outlined in Lake's taxonomy, there is a different type of challenge to the alethic modality of "could have happened." Where in private narrative the events are on a personal level, a domestic level, remaining within the confines of a family or a group of friends whose lives would never impact on our own, in an alternative narrative the events are on a scale where we would surely notice. They may be mundane in terms of possibility but not in terms of scope. With Jett Rink, the James Dean character in the movie *Giant*, for example, we would know of his existence in the world, remember him as another Howard Hughes. This great industrialist would be written via reportage into known history.

We know for a fact that the events in this sort of fiction "could not have happened," because the world would be different than it is. So that conflicting alethic modality is introduced into the narrative, an erratum. With *Giant* we simply sustain Rink as a conceit, an elseworld analogue of Howard Hughes, as with every Hollywood movie or TV show set in the present with a POTUS who isn't the current incumbent. We barely notice. In the more pulp forms of strange fiction, another approach sets that conceit as its focus, makes a quirk of what "could not have happened *now*." That is to say, if we could rewind time to before the 1950s and replay history, this temporal impossibility might be undone. *Then* there could have been a Jett Rink. *Then* the events of *Giant* "could have happened." The resultant history would diverge from ours, branch off from it, continuing forward into an alternative reality we can envisage in a spatial metaphor, as a sideways step away through a second lateral dimension of time, the resultant present being another "now" where Jett Rink *is* remembered by the world as another Howard Hughes.

We're already playing the game of suspending disbelief, accepting these events as taking place in simulation, accepting for the sake of the story an ersatz world of ersatz people performing the drama represented in the sentences, so it is only a small step to tweak that ersatz world into another now, set apart from our own in some lateral dimension of unrealised potentialities. All worlds of fiction are alternative realities.

It should be noted, however, that both the degree of challenge and the degree of difference may be minimal. In this example, the counterfactual is no great stretch of the imagination and therefore no great challenge to the suspension-of-disbelief. We're not asked to accept *sweeping* historic changes with the story of *Giant*, and the simple fact that it is fiction is enough for us to swallow this minor revision in the fabric of history. Conversely, one might argue that the private narrative of a Peruvian multiple infanticide could be expected to impact on our lives were we, for instance, Peruvian; we would know of the old woman from news reports, remember her as a real-life Medea. The boundaries between private narrative and alternative narrative, by this reasoning, must be highly fluid and subjective. But in truth again we can see the old woman as simply an analogue of any infanticidal mother in reality, the ersatz murders a substitution for any number of real examples.

In the pulp form though, the conceit of difference becomes the point, as the narrative doesn't simply perform a *substitution* in known history, as when we switch in Rink for Hughes or an ersatz POTUS for the real one, but rather it posits *alterations* in the recorded events, breaches that conflict with known history just as the novum conflicts with known science or the chimera with the laws of nature. Remake *Giant* today but keep it set in its own time, portray Jett Rink using his oil money to run for President of the USA, and winning no less, and what we have is an alethic quirk. As the list of corrections to mistakes slipped in at the back of a book rewrite the text, so these counterfactual quirks, these errata, rewrite the mundane worldscape.

Now, let's introduce some errata into our nursery rhyme:

> *There was an old Nazi who ran the US.*
> *She had so many children to listen to her address.*
> *She gave them some TV without any truth.*
> *She whipped them up wildly, a new Hitler Youth.*

The Genre of Alternate History (which rather proves the emptiness of nominal labels in its misuse of *alternate* in place of *alternative*) can be positioned here as a form of alternative narrative which quite clearly *does* stretch suspension-of-disbelief in a way Jett Rink does not. If the Nazis had won WW2, if the South had won the American Civil War, if the Roman Empire had not fallen, and so on—these counterfactual conceits are revisions of known history, alterations that reshape the ersatz world of the narrative to something quite unfamiliar. All worlds of fiction are alternative worlds, but some are more alternative than others. Rewritten in the act of supposition, transfigured by the core quirk and any number of smaller quirks cast as ramifications, the ersatz worldscape comes to constitute what we might call an *elsewhen*.

There are narratives that use nova to storify the transfiguration itself; they render the alteration (as mistake, or correction, or both), within the narrative, via actual time-travel, presenting us with the jump back to change the course of history then the jump forward into the rewritten reality, e.g. Bradbury's "A Sound of Thunder," which changes the very basis of history—prehistory—with the death of a butterfly. Sometimes, however, the reader is simply thrust into the elsewhen and faced with the strange details that "could not have happened," individual errata from which they must reconstruct the core quirk, the underlying supposition, the counterfactual premise by which such fallout quirks might have come to pass (or *would have* come to pass, some Alternate History buffs are prone to argue, in their variant of the Contingency Slip Fallacy).

It's by no means certain, in fact, that even this will be offered. In the example offered above, there's little to indicate what small but significant change might have led to an old Nazi ruling the US. The focus is instead on developing the dystopian scenario of media control and the indoctrination of a generation born into fascist dictatorship.

Another Different Now

We find an equivalent approach in Lake's future narrative, where novum takes the place of erratum. Again we have the "could not have happened (now)" alethic modality introduced by quirks in the text, events we know for a fact to be impossible. The "could not have happened *yet*" alethic modality is simply another form of that: as errata breach known history, nova breach known science, expanding on it, extrapolating, speculating or simply fabricating in fancy; they breach temporal possibility simply by being hypothetical: by *definition*, any event set in the future could not *have* happened, the *have* indicating past tense. But that future setting, even if it's only twenty seconds into the future, makes for a get-out clause: where the alternative narrative can take a step to the side, the future narrative can take a step ahead, setting its quirks as artefacts of another different now, displaced frontally rather than laterally in the phasespace of potential realities.

Big Brother, humanoid robots, colonies on Mars—such hypothetical conceits are as temporally dislocating as the counterfactual conceits of ALTERNATE HISTORY, rendering the worldscape a different now, an ersatz reality as an elsewhen twenty seconds, twenty years or twenty centuries into the future, where things have changed enough that the impossible could have come to pass. Why, under the Paradigm Shift Caveat even the laws of nature may have been revised.

Where some ALTERNATE HISTORY stories will show their workings, so to speak, so there are SCIENCE FICTION stories which explicate their nova with infodump (the original intro to Bester's *Demolished Man*, for example, laying out a whole future history as a foundation before the story even begins). But as with ALTERNATE HISTORY, that elsewhen may be simply given as a *fait-accompli*, any underlying hypothetical premise left to the reader to reconstruct from the details, if indeed it is there to be reconstructed at all. We can illustrate this with another variant of the nursery rhyme, transforming its genre by changing a grand total of one noun and four pronouns:

> *There was an old robot who ran the US.*
> *It had so many children to listen to its address.*
> *It gave them some TV without any truth.*
> *It whipped them up wildly, a new Hitler Youth.*

The power of the alternative and future narratives resides in the way these errata and nova test suspension-of-disbelief: the alethic quirk is always already incredible. For some readers though, for these narratives to work they cannot simply be incredible. Here the "could not have happened" alethic modality is not allowed to *really* fuck with suspension-of-disbelief; the tension is not built up to a peak or crisis-point as it is with the absurd or the abject. In fact, where comic and tragic narratives exploit the tension between alethic modalities, the alternative / future narratives may well seek to resolve them as best they can.

Just Run With It

The Contingency Slip Fallacy and the Paradigm Shift Caveat go a long way to dewarping the alethic quirk, undoing the tension, but there's an extent to which these aren't even required. In the pulp tradition, the resolution of incredulity as a strain is partly inbuilt, where the conceits at their heart, counterfactual in one, hypothetical in the other, are so conventional as to be clichés—Nazis winning the Second World War, robots taking over the world.

We recognise these as tropes, idiomatic fancies that we accept for the sake of a good yarn—like those of NOIR, SWASHBUCKLER, WESTERN. We know the trench-coat-wearing detective is unrealistic. We know pirates were not actually like Captain Jack Sparrow. We know the portrayal of the Wild West on screen is mostly tosh. But we accept the popcorn quirks as tropes of idiomatic fantasias because it's more fun that way. Forget the history and futurology, the idea of rigour or even arguability. It's not really a matter of setting up a "what if," counterfactual or hypothetical, and extrapolating forward from that, finding a story in the ramifications. As often as not the story comes out of the tropes and those tropes are only bolstered with argument afterwards…if at all.

How did the Nazis win World War II? They just did. How do you get a robot that can think and act just like a human? You just do. They're tropes. Just run with it.

When it comes to known history and known science, if we're brutally honest, we need to accept that the alternative and future narratives of the pulp traditions posit, as often as not, counterfactuals and hypotheticals that are barely even subjectively *plausible*, never mind objectively *possible*. A subjective *perception* of greater possibility is not an objective *reality* of greater possibility, simply a matter of what the reader is willing to believe; and there are many strategies for persuading a reader, only one of which is to limit the strangeness to the temporal impossibilities of errata and nova, and only one of which is to argue plausibility. With the quirk of jaunting, for example, the reader is offered no theoretical basis. Bester walks roughshod over the laws of physics here, kicking thermodynamics to one side, pushing the dirt over it and saying, *Look, it's the Goodyear Blimp!* as he points in the other direction.

How does jaunting work in terms of conservation of energy? It just does. It's a trope in the idiomatic fantasia that our future elsewhens have become by Bester's time, with tropic features of asteroid mines, etc.; or it's a quirk offered as such, framed in an elsewhen constructed of tropes so that it's always already a legitimate move in the game of make-believe; it's a fresh entry into a shared mythos. If others have used the quirk before us then the conventionality it accrues as it becomes a *trope* situates it in its own ersatz nomology—hence the acceptance of FTL as a tradition of how the laws of nature work within Space Opera (versus in reality), and hence the popularity of quirks like wormholes, stargates and jump-points as the tropes of a more recent tradition of Space Opera.

Ultimately, there's a neat symbiosis: as quirks reused to cliché become tropes, they become tired, dewarped, no longer marvellous, but that very idiomatic familiarity makes the entire mythos a pre-accepted conceit, one we slip into as an idle play, with not a hint of credibility warp; meanwhile, fresh quirks that do actually test suspension-of-disbelief provide the crucial eyeball kick, the thrill of the marvellous that is the point of the game, with no more risk of the reader being kicked out of the story than there is of a soccer player suddenly thinking it's all just silly, so why not just pick up the ball and chuck it into the goal. The fantasia is idiomatic. Just run with it.

If some readers want more of a sugarcoating to make the alethic quirk easier to swallow, there are other strategies of excuse. With the general applicability of the Paradigm Shift

Caveat, a chimera may be masked as a novum simply by offering it as future reality, as Bester gives us jaunting in the future rather than the present. A bit of worldbuilding, and jaunting can be sold as another natural facet of an elsewhen of spaceships and asteroid mines. Working a little pseudo-scientific explication into that worldbuilding doesn't hurt, so Bester and a score of other writers present a magical power of ESP or jaunting as a "next stage in human evolution."

We can literalise the paradigm shift, present the quirk as a product of an entirely alien culture, with a conceit of visitors leaving behind technology beyond our understanding. That conceit may be a startpoint for the Strugatsky Brothers in *Roadside Picnic* to mine the strange for everything it's worth, but it can as easily be a way to sell one's snake-oil. Where we cast those aliens as ancient and extinct, I can't help but see an echo of the arcanum, as if the alethic quirk of Gilgamesh's era persists, a legacy of strange fictions past. From *Stargate* to *Prometheus*, we do seem drawn to mythic antiquity as an elsewhen strode by titans who claim novum status on the basis of pure grandiosity: they are too vast and ancient to be bound within our laws of nature.

None of these techniques make the chimerae any more rational as futurology—which is why proponents of Hard SF scorn them—but they do facilitate rationalisation, offering the get-out clauses, cyclic arguments and cover stories by which we construct and sustain an artificial sense of contingency, of a potential alternative nomology. They persuade us into a further spin on alethic modality, from "could not have happened *now*" to "could have happened *if...*" where what follows that "if" may amount to a wholesale revision of the rules of reality, validated more by self-delusion than speculation. So the quirk is dewarped, not wholly, but enough to gloss the boulomaic modality of the marvellous, the sense that the events presented "should have happened," with an illusion that they "could have happened." No torture of Sehnsucht here, the bolstering of plausibility may be a means to that end indeed: a deep immersion in fantasia.

For some, at least. The disparities between how far different readers are ready to rationalise the impossible, the differing effectiveness of different mechanisms for different readers, the multiple points of contention over where and how the nomological alterations become so wild as to be "just plain silly," where and how the sense of plausibility collapses—these go a long way to explaining the disagreements between readers as to what does and what doesn't constitute an SF narrative.

For some, the idiomatic elsewhen is just dull cliché, the Paradigm Shift Caveat is a cheat, and only reason will work to sell the impossible. The chimera is anathema, and even the unreality of the counterfactual or hypothetical quirk requires something more than handwaving, some argumentative counter-force to balance it. The "if" immediately produces a "but"—but *how*? In the comic or tragic narrative, to answer that question would dissipate the tension which these narratives seek to build, as is most obvious where the narrative forms blend, as in the tragicomedy of *Catch-22*, or the mundane and strange surreality of

If..., as in any such works which unsettle even as they entertain. But these readers are not interested in that tension created from the clash of modalities. They want explanations, explication. Which is fair enough.

Any turf war claim that the essence of SF lies in offering this is dubious to say the least, though. More than anything I'd hazard it's the idiomatic nature of the fantasias that has most import on the bulk of the audience, that we buy into the hokum as a game, because it is tropic, because it is generic, because this is Genre Fiction. With all that this entails.

The Form = Formulation Syllogism

Insofar as the excision of meaning from the nominal label *SF* is a refusal of strictures, it's an expedient gambit, but it also disacknowledges any distinction between genre as aesthetic idiom—"strange fiction as a mode comparable to poetry, tragedy or comedy"—and Genre as conventional template and/or marketing category, collapsing them all together into this empty symbol. It's little wonder then that others who look at that vacuity see only a signpost to the market where it's sold, see only the outer decor of the SF Café and its environs, the ghetto of Genre. In accepting that SF's nature is that of a discrete subdomain of Genre, in allowing SF to be treated as Genre, we invite a logical extrapolation from the common understanding of how marketing categories function, how Genres work, the syllogistic a priori reasoning by which SF is rejected as sub-literate scribbling. This Form=Formulation Syllogism, the argument that damns us, runs thus:

1) *Genre labels signal that a work conforms to a set of aesthetic criteria prescribed as Genre conventions;*
2) *these conventions are designed for producing works of a certain stereotypical Genre form;*
3) *due to their commercial imperatives and counter-literary value-systems, Genre forms have inherent flaws;*
4) *therefore: works conforming to those conventions will have those flaws;*
5) *therefore: works published with Genre labels will have those flaws.*

It should be clear to any SF reader that this is a gross misrepresentation, but judging by some of the talk you hear down in the SF Café, I'm not sure it is. So let's spell it out point by point. This is the essence of the distinction between aesthetic idiom, conventional template and marketing category:

1. *Genre labels signal that a work conforms to a set of aesthetic criteria prescribed as Genre conventions.*

No, there are works which get a GENRE label without conforming to the conventions. *The Transmigration of Timothy Archer* is hardly a "let's pretend" adventure nor a "what if" thought-experiment. It has little of Gernsback's "charming romance intermingled with scientific fact and prophetic vision" in it, not in the sense of futurology and fantasia. It is not Campbellian SCIENCE FICTION by a long shot. And this is not to say that it merely stretches the conventions by applying the Paradigm Shift Caveat to blur the border with fantasy, or by directing its speculation towards the soft sciences. Where it breaks with tradition in utilising religious conceits—transmigration, visions in the irrational revelatory rather than rational predictive sense, etc.—it establishes a new set of aesthetic criteria by integrating those conceits into what is other-wise a work of contemporary realism.

The publication and reading of this work as SF simply expands the zone of indefinition, asserts that however we conceive of this GENRE we must now allow for the incorporation of this type of novel. The GENRE label signals only this then: that something about the work has been deemed sufficient justification for any adjustments to aesthetic criteria required to accommodate it under that label. Personally, I take this work as proof that sufficient justification may entail no more than a smidgeon of strangeness and an author established within the field. (As far as the nominal label of FANTASY is concerned, it finds a parallel in Graham Joyce's *The Limits of Enchantment*.)

2. These conventions are designed for producing works of a certain stereotypical GENRE form.

No, for every reader there's a personal set of characteristics they see as sufficient justification to label a work SF. When that reader is also a writer, they may well set out to write a work that reads as SF to them, treating those characteristics as a set of aesthetic criteria. While some of these criteria are commercially standardised so that stereotypical GENRE forms can be produced to order, many are not. For some, criteria are no more than…the 2D outline of a work's base, with its greater structure entirely freeform. For others yet, characteristics are not criteria at all; they do little more than describe the general contours of the broad terrain on which the work is to be formed, a kernel of dynamics inherent in a mode.

Compare, in poetry: the conventions of the stereotypical LIMERICK as a GENRE, fun but formulaic; the strictures of the sonnet as a genre, based on a shape of fourteen lines and a volta but on any subject, in any tone; and the wildly notional characteristics of the poem, any work within that vast domain. Similarly, in SF, we have: the conventions of the stereotypical CYBERPUNK story, as it stood a decade or so ago; the much looser range of strictures back when the genre of cyberpunk was exemplified by the *Mirrorshades* anthology; and the wildly notional characteristics of any SF that doesn't fit such a template.

Delany's *Dhalgren* is not a product of conventions designed for producing works of a certain stereotypical POST-APOCALYPSE SF form. The ruined cityscape and social collapse of Bellona that lead us to label it post-apocalyptic fiction are at most the contours of its foundation and arguably no more than the gradient of the territory it inhabits, a kernel of dynamics inherent in the strange.

> *3) due to their commercial imperatives and counter-literary value-systems,* Genre *forms have inherent flaws;*

This means precisely nothing if the rackspace label maps to an aesthetic idiom rather than a conventional template. If a lack of thematic depth is inherent in the form of the Limerick, this is irrelevant as a critique of poetry. If a lack of thematic depth is inherent in the form of the stereotypical Cyberpunk, story this is irrelevant as a critique of SF. So the formulation of Genres under a rackspace label leads to works produced to fit standardised aesthetic criteria of e.g. character type, plot-structure, worldscape development and futurological novelty. So commercial imperatives may pressure for a neglect of non-required features such as depth of character and theme, may even embody a counter-literary value-system, preferencing crudely botched prose that "doesn't get in the way of the plot" over "style" that foregrounds its own craftedness. Applying only to the Genres contained within the genre's broad terrain, this is exactly as irrelevant as a critique of SF as a critique of poetry based on the flaws of the Limerick.

> *4) therefore: works conforming to those conventions will have those flaws;*

Again this now means exactly nothing. Works fitting the aesthetic criteria that define the sonnet as a genre need only fourteen lines and a volte. Formulation of a stereotypical Shakespearean Love Sonnet might lead to flaws of neglect (e.g. a lack of originality) and counter-literary value-systems (e.g. saccharine romantic sentiments), but the genre of the sonnet is distinguishable from this Genre precisely by its opposition to formulation, its literary imperatives to exceed minimum requirements, to build a multi-dimensional structure upon that outlined base. Formulation of a stereotypical Cyberpunk within SF may lead to flaws of neglect or counter-literary value-systems, but SF is distinguishable as a genre precisely by its opposition to formulation.

There are many Genres within SF, and many exhibit the sort of flaws that go with formulation: concerns with plot and worldscape built from futurology and fantasia overshadow concerns with character and theme; complexity and subtlety is deprecated as "pretension." An assertion that SF necessarily has these flaws because it is a Genre are like an assertion that poetry necessarily has the flaws of the stereotypical Shakespearean Love Sonnet, articulating only the ignorance and presumption of the speaker.

> *5) therefore: works published with* Genre *labels will have those flaws.*

The application of an ignorant and presumptuous judgement on the basis of rackspace label is not only false and misrepresentative; it's superficial, quite literally judging a book by its cover (the image, the imprint, the copy and blurbs, the label on the back), reducing a work to the brand image. Countless works within the genre of SF disprove that judgement by counter-example, works by writers such as Aldiss, Ballard, Bradbury, Bester, Butler, Cherryh, Clarke, Delany, Disch, Dick, Ellison, Farmer, Gibson, Harrison, Heinlein, Hopkinson, Jakubowski, Keyes, Le Guin, Lem, Moorcock, Niven, Norton, Orwell, Priest, Russ, Ryman, Spinrad, Sladek, Tiptree, Vinge, Willis, Zelazny.

Not that we really need to list these; the Form=Formulation Syllogism is demonstrably flawed on every count, failing to differentiate genres from Genres, assuming a universal process of formulation when the reality is the familial development we find as aesthetic criteria are simply adjusted to accommodate *The Transmigration of Timothy Archer* or whatever work is married into the clan, taking this nominal label as its name.

Transcending the Genre

Sadly, in our own conflations and confusions we invite these misperceptions by accepting the framework of logic in which genre means an aesthetic territory of formulation (as in *genre fiction*) rather than an aesthetic idiom (as in *the genre of a fiction*). This ghetto of Genre we ally ourselves with is defined precisely as the region where marketing categories and conventional forms collude to insist on formulation, in contrast to *non-genre* where they do not. *Genre* fiction versus *non-genre* fiction? All fiction is in a genre, even if that genre is only the novel or the short story.

When we talk of works as *transcending the genre*, position them as exceptional rather than exemplary, we tacitly accept: that the Genre label indicates some set of aesthetic criteria shared by Genre narratives, sought after by a certain target market; that the commercial impetus of those criteria constrain the form at a deeper level than the strictures of a sonnet, create a limitation of quality; that a narrative needs to circumvent those demands of form not by ignoring them (because then the narrative would cease to be Genre) but by some shift into a more elevated sphere of abstract action. We accept that the idiom we signify with the Genre label is a stereotypical Genre form that has to be transcended in this way.

If transcendence is our metaphor then truly SF is an incorporeal spectre, a ghost, slipped free of the flesh and bone forms long ago.

Of course, the fuzziness of the whole notion is expedient, allowing us to wave a hand towards the aesthetic idiom(s) we like, in the form of a shelf labelled SF, referring to this as *genre*, while simultaneously waving away the conventional templates we hate, happily referring to these as generic. When an outsider challenges us on this slapdash clumping of works, we might be able to articulate that SF as a rackspace label is bound to a set of aesthetic criteria too diverse to pin down with precision, diverse enough that they even allow for a *literary SF* with its definition lost somewhere among all the arguments. What we generally fail to articulate is that SF is not a Genre at all, but rather a mode of a myriad idioms and forms, a dynamic family of genres and Genres, the most ambitious and innovative craftsmanship wed to, and at war with, the most formulated and derivative crap.

Hey ho.

The ghost haunts the café, animates the lumbering golem of the field in its physical form. The name is sustained in our speech, the inchoate idea reiterated in every sibilant and fricative utterance of SF, because it offers a subtle strand of identity even in its indefinition; it is enough for us, as a community of fiction readers, writers, editors and critics to congregate around. In the spectral apparition and the material shape, there is enough rough semblance of Genre that these freaks might frighten the citizenry if they stepped out into the city at large; and both are bound to the SF Café by their shared history anyway, by their loyalty to a beloved heritage. And as long as the SF Café is sustainable as a commercial enterprise, as long as it keeps drawing in the punters with the promise of pulp thrills and spills, the promise of exciting entertainments, of Genre, the ghost and the golem have a home.

I feel the love, am loyal to that home myself—it's been fucking good to me—but I think it's worth being aware of the doublethinks we apply, as when we talk of transcending the genre. The relationship between genre and Genre is a weird balance of symbiosis and mutual parasitism, and it seems to me that our unadmitted recognition of that only leads to bitching about lack of respect on the one hand while, on the other, extolling works with a phrase that damns SF as derivative in its essence. The deal with the devil doesn't seem…well, that big a deal. Commercial pressures toward formulation have a corrosive effect on literary quality, sure; but the market for the most conventional forms subsidises the most literate and ambitious aesthetic idioms—works that might well be unpublishable outside the ghetto, without the security of a dedicated audience. The literary imperatives of the whole aesthetic idiom degrade the efficiency of formulaic products with their narrowly-defined utilitarian function as entertainment; but the continual influx of originality counteracts the Law of Diminishing Returns in a set of Genres where "more of the same" can paradoxically mean more novelty.

The ghost and the golem could not survive without the SF Café, but without them the SF Café would quickly become an empty shell.

The Model and the Machine

Ghosts, golems—these metaphysical quirks of fantasy are incongruous in an exploration of SF surely. Ah, well, let's just employ the Paradigm Shift Caveat here. Let's hypothesise that the parapsychologists are right, that in the future our empirical observations of some truly strange phenomena force a radical revision of our physics. No ectoplasm here though, no spiritualist mumbo-jumbo of the soul as some aetheric substance. We'll call it the Quantum Interconnectedness Principle then, say that reality is information and the universe a hologram, that every fragmentary particle of our cosmos contains an image of the whole implicate order, the urgrund.

In the SF Café every patron wears mayashades that reconstruct the urgrund from the fragment-forms immediately perceptible. In part a forensic analysis of reality, in part a data-mining of the urgrund, what is offered is, in essence, a heads-up display of information we could not otherwise have access to. Gaze into the eyes of another patron and the mayashades scroll their thoughts across your vision. Gaze out of the window and the mayashades flash glimpses of the future on the streets outside—a joyrider ploughing his car into a bus-stop queue you might be standing in five minutes from now. That sort of information is useful, after all; if we had not (hypothetically) developed the technology to access and utilise it we might even (hypothetically) have evolved a natural capacity, some sort of Externalised Simulatory Processing of the world we have to live in, some sort of...*ESP*.

Phil Dick sits in a corner, his mayashades on the blink, showing him the SF Café as a tavern in AD 70, a secret community of Christians hiding from the Roman Empire; his mayashades are communicating an analysis of society in figurative form, the ghetto of Genre as the Black Iron Prison of the Gnostics. They flash words in Koiné Greek across his vision, a language he cannot know but which these wondrous gadgets can use freely in their access to that urgrund. They offer him a reinterpretation of the world in which he is not Phil the SF writer but Thomas the early Christian. This is not a transmigration of souls, but rather reincarnation as retro-incarnation, as a downloading of the data that defined a long-dead psyche, a simulation of another's memories.

The ghost of SF is no supernatural spirit, just the simulacrum of an essence, the abstract agency we glimpse as we gaze round the SF Café with our mayashades scanning for hidden meaning, a wireframe model reconstructed in a virtual medium. As for the golem? Let's make the monster a machine, a robot made of muck instead of metal. We'll say its clay is carbon, the grey goo of nanotech devices, millions of minuscule mechanisms fused into one lumpen mass, given identity in the name projected onto it, SF as its logos and its logic.

Hey presto! Magic becomes science. Fantasy becomes SF.

For the benefit of those who care about that shit, you know.

Genre and the Generic

It's not that hard to see SF's relationship with Genre, I think, to critique it with clarity and objectivity, picking out juvenile tropes and themes from adult treatments—as Spinrad does, say, in his classic "Emperor Of Everything" article, showing Bester's smart and mature inversion of the heroic rags-to-riches power fantasy in *The Stars My Destination*. But resisting critical analyses that recognise the aesthetic idiom for what it is makes it easier to excuse generic twaddle such as *Independence Day* or *The Matrix*, to forget why these are twaddle because, well, they're enjoyable twaddle. Both are juvenile. Both are formulaic. Both are Genre in precisely the way that the Form = Formulation Syllogism damns it. We only need to compare them to, say, Gibson's *Neuromancer* or Stephenson's *Snow Crash*—to pick two works that are hardly lacking in the good old-fashioned plot-driven dynamics of the thriller or action / adventure genres they inhabit—to judge them pretty much derivative hokum. But if we like these two movies and hate another two—*Minority Report* or *War of the Worlds*—we can simply wave our hands, say that the former are *genre*, the latter *generic*.

This distinction is a wonderfully expedient sophistry. Both *genre fiction*, as we all too often use the term, and *generic fiction* are defined by the familiarity of their forms; more, they are fictions which exploit that familiarity. What they offer the reader, we say, what the reader requires of them, is a narrative composed of conventional template elements—plots and characters, settings and themes. There may be originality in the treatment, but too much originality, not enough familiarity, and that novel ceases to be generic; exchange even more familiarity for originality and it ceases to be of the genre at all. Or at least, this is the conventional wisdom—that it's all a matter of conventions. The marketing categories have become ghettoised as Genre because the Genres bound to them exist to be generic in this way, to provide the reader with *more of the same*, all gathered together in one place, under a certain branding.

But, of course, what we have then is *all this fiction gathered together under that branding*, the works that we love because they're genre-but-not-generic. And the ones we hate because they *are* generic and thereby *give the genre a bad name*, reviling them even to the extent sometimes of denying that they're really SF, refusing to recognise them as being valid examples of the genre on the basis that they're too generic. In contrast to the canon of definitive works that we describe as transcending the genre.

Run that by me again?

Personally, I'd like to see the word *genre* taken out back and shot, a bullet in the back of its head, if it's going to be so overloaded with meanings it's just gibberish skewed to self-serving doublethink. Even Campbellian Science Fiction might be best not considered a Genre if that's going to tangle us up in the morass of *genre versus the generic*. Its key stricture of futurology works more like the arbitrary constraint of an Oulipo writer than the conventions of form that mark out fiction as generic. Where Gernsback's definition sets out distinctly standardised aesthetic criteria in requiring the plot structures of Romantic adventure, Campbell's allows for entirely non-generic plot-structures as long as the fiction employs this strange Oulipo-style stricture of grounding fantasia in futurology.

And as for the ghost and the golem, the model and the machine, the stuff that's out there now? As for SF, or speculative fiction, or whatever you want to call it? Construct the narrative with MacGuffin devices and stock plots, and the SF novel or story may become generic, as much SF undeniably is. There is a mode of Epic SF which all too closely parallels Epic Fantasy with its exotic settings, noble heroes, quests as archetypal psychodrama, more Joseph Campbell than John W. Campbell. But SF as a whole, which delights in offering unfamiliar forms…is it really generic enough that we're happy to call it a genre, when to do so is inevitably to call it Genre—because it's not like the capitalisation I'm using here works in speech? Before you answer, bear in mind that every time we dismiss some formulaic dreck as generic or extoll the latest masterpiece with the rhetoric of transcendence we're reifying the notion of genre at the heart of the Form = Formulation Syllogism?

Fuck, if only "aesthetic idiom" didn't sound so damn poncy.

Thing is, if we examine other marketing categories—Crime, Western, Romance—it seems SF is not alone in being, essentially, an openly defined aesthetic idiom damned by the formulation that it's inextricably bound to. Crime, for one, is in a similar position to SF, with as much originality twisting and tearing at its orthodoxy of familiar tropes and tricks. (Or rather, as much originality emerging from its dynamics of quirks. What is a crime in fiction but the quirk of an event with a boulomaic and deontic modality of must not? What is a mystery in fiction but the quirk of an event left undetailed to introduce uncertainty, epistemic modalities of might/might not?)

All marketing categories have their deconstructions and subversions, parodies and pastiches, reinventions and restorations, non-generic works that might be better understood as Anti-Genre insofar as their categorical imperative is to bring something new into the family, to force the adjustment of aesthetic criteria required to accommodate them and thereby counteract the impulse to formulation. It's the paradox of the ghetto of Genre, that the canonical works are exemplary because they are exceptional, not just another iteration of *The MacGuffin Device*, but rather, like *The Transmigration of Timothy Archer*, freaks and sports.

A Fabulous Formless Starkness

But holding fast under a flag of pedantry in which *genre* means simply *family*, trying to unravel the conflations of aesthetic idiom, conventional templates and marketing categories that make the word, in a phrase like *genre fiction*, synonymous with *formulaic*, seems to be pissing in the wind. For all that the term genre might be applied to an aesthetic idiom as openly defined as the novel, for all that it may be applied, as a label slapped on a book shelf, to a marketing category that amounts to little more than "that stuff over there, that stuff I'm pointing to," I'm not sure we can redeem it from the abjection by which it is applied to that which is most commercially conventional and conventionally commercial, that which lives downtown in Genre rather than in Literature. So fuck it.

From here on in, in this book, when I talk of SF, I'm talking of a field and the various forces that comprise it. I'm talking of SF as a mode of fiction, an approach in fiction, a telling of tall tales with strange elements, where those elements are integral to the dynamics of the story, where the process of the story is generated from the strangeness of the idea, where the story is an event enacting strangeness. This is SF not as a singular form fitted to a template but as, at best, a loose federation of forms, a field so diverse that you can throw a hundred different definitions at it and none of them will stick.

All genre definitions will fail, I think, because they attempt to describe the field as this form or that, in templates of conventions, and all those forms may actually be, I'd argue—even the most conventional—better understood as forces, the illusion of delimitation (in terms of plot and character, setting and theme) ultimately a trick of perspective, these types and tropes of *genres* and *subgenres* mere snapshots of whorls in cigarette smoke, emergent from and embedded in a wider process: carving the fabulous in the reader's mind in an experience as sharply-defined as the so-called *genre* is inchoate. This is SF as a fabulous formless starkness of effect(s), bound only to an acronym that acknowledges its own emptiness of meaning in its rejection of specificity.

If the field is as definitionally circular as Spinrad's statement asserts it to be, this seems only right; the empty signifier of SF is far more apt as a label than science fiction. As Cheney said in the quote way back at the start, the genre of science fiction no longer exists. As we have declared right here, SCIENCE FICTION is dead.

SF, on the other hand, seems to be alive and well—for a ghost.

Or maybe it's not a ghost at all. Maybe that simulacrum of an essence we see as we gaze through our mayashades at the SF Café, that wireframe model of an abstract agency… maybe it really only wore the skin of SCIENCE FICTION the same way it now wears the golem's clay. Maybe it was there all the time, this field of forces, and simply took that form as a response to the time and place.

Part 2

RHAPSODY

The Combat Fiction Bar & Grill

The Wars My Destination

Gully Foyle is my name,
And combat is my nation.
Gunfire is my dwelling-place,
The wars my destination.

Alfred Bester, *The Wars My Destination*

The SF Café is a curious place. Take a wrong turn when you step inside the door, and you can find yourself not where you expected at all. Or rather, not *when* you expected to be. You walk into the SF Café, and mostly you're reckoning on seeing the shape of things to come—twenty minutes into the future, twenty years or twenty millennia—but there's a corner of the SF Café that's not the future at all. Take a step to the left, as the door swings shut behind you with a ting of the bell, and you may well find yourself in a today or yesterday where it's not the science that's strange but the history.

This is the SF not of Suvin's novum but of its compatriot errata, quirks of difference like the holes in your New Yorker's Swiss Cheese, points of divergence and the oddities of a world evolved from them. You look around the café, find the posters of 1950s Sci-Fi flicks are gone, replaced by images of Confederate victories and Nazi triumphs. Where the salt cellars on the Formica tables were once sleek chrome rocket-shapes, now they're khaki and bulbous…grenades. What the fuck?

You step back out the door, gaze around. The downtown ghetto of Genre seems unchanged, but now when you turn and look up, you see the proof of your shift sideways across the timestreams: where the sign above the door should read *The SF Café*, now you're standing before *The Combat Fiction Bar & Grill*. A parallel reality. An alternate history. And now, as you shrug and head inside, curious to explore this half-familiar elsewhen, the air shimmers around you; a jukebox comes alive with the sound of Swing. It's bang in the middle of the twentieth century, and the Combat Fiction Bar and Grill has just opened for business.

Out of the pulp fiction boom, a new GENRE has emerged, focused on warfare like that erupting in Europe even now. It comes from the industry of dime novels and magazines—*Nick Carter Stories, Flying Aces, Marvel Tales, Buffalo Bill Weekly*—draws on a 1920s/1930s recipe of hokey heroism, big explosions and valourous deaths as perfected in the Boy's

Own adventure. Without its American flavour it might not be so very different from the even earlier tales of Haggard and Buchan, except that in the hands of a few editors, in the magazines and publishing imprints that they run, a more solid shape has been given, with something of a novel twist to it.

Where it might be just one more in the stable of Street & Smith's pulp publications, under the editorship of John W. MacDonald, *Astounding Stories* in particular is bringing a level of Rationalism to this mode of Romance, reborn for the wars of the Industrial Age as MODERN PULP. Clear guidelines demand a sharp focus on plausibility: weaponry must work the way it works in reality; strategies must be authentic; the combat must be extrapolated with rigour. And so a whole new GENRE is born—inheriting from its romantic forebears but essentially Modern in its fusion of plot dynamics and intellectual mechanics.

MacDonald names it COMBAT FICTION.

As this GENRE matures, that rationalist bent takes its effect. As a new generation of writers enters the field, many turn a cold eye on the sensationalist fluff that is their roots. Oh, they devoured the pulps as kids and they retain a deep love of the boldness to be found there, the sheer vigour of stories driven by peril, driven by death and glory, the monstra and numinae of war; but as adults they now appreciate more mature themes. For them, the crass and pandering jingoism is something to be subverted. For them, warfare is not merely a backdrop for heroic adventure stories; rather it is an intrinsic element of plot and theme through which to explore the human condition. The twentieth century is a century of combat, after all. What other GENRE is better equipped to address the big philosophical questions of life and death, of what it is to be a human in this world of war? Writing in response to what has gone before, working with the accrued toolkit of tropes or simply with the substrate of war-as-metaphor or war-as-backdrop, this new generation begins to explore these ideas in greater depth, find new angles. Those who are conversant with the GENRE are increasingly aware of its potential, keen to exploit it. To exploit the dynamics of the quirks in ways unbound by conventional templates.

Certainly, the pulp roots show through. The commercial impetus of the GENRE is evident. Some COMBAT FICTION readers will buy any old shit as long as you slap a cigar-chomping sergeant on the cover—they want more of the same—and there are plenty ready to serve that up. But that dedicated readership offers a ready-made market for literate—even experimental—works dealing with war. Some readers have read all the permutations of the COMBAT FICTION novel, even the gritty realist ones, and they're bored now—they want something original, something novel, something different. So, publishers can take risks on unconventional works which might otherwise fail to reach an audience; the uncritical fans of GENRE supports the innovations of a non-generic aesthetic idiom—not COMBAT FICTION but simply combat fiction…the fiction of combat.

So, one writer called Alfred Bester, in his seminal novel *The Wars My Destination*, boldly flies his modernist colours in typographic trickery. In the opening pages of the book, he proclaims where he's coming from in no uncertain terms, with the rhyme quoted above, directly based on a similar rhyme from James Joyce's *A Portrait of the Artist as a Young Man*.

Verisimilitude/Authenticity

In one traditional pulp approach to alternative / future narratives, while the reader is thrown into an elsewhen for which they must reconstruct the underlying logic, there is a concerted effort to make that logic apparent, to explicate the elsewhen through the course of the narrative. The explication may be offered mainly in the form of rich pseudo-temporal detail—technological and historical worldbuilding—that is left to speak for itself in the internal consistency of its mimetic and pseudo-mimetic weft, to create a sense of *verisimilitude*. We can and should distinguish this verisimilitude from the sense of *authenticity* engendered in the narrative by ensuring that these details are also consistent with the theories of known science and known history if not the facts, the way we define the world and societies as working from our observations of how they've worked in the past. The difference is subtle, but it is that of appearance and actuality, many works achieving plausibility by a combination of excuse and verisimilitude rather than authenticity.

So, in those types of alternative / future narrative seeking a sense of authenticity over and above this, we find explication that attempts to provide a solid (or semisolid) base of theory and extrapolation on which these nova and errata can be grounded. In reconstructing the elsewhen, the reader may gradually unpack these quirks as the fallout of a basic suppositional premise: the assassination of Hitler leading to a more organised Third Reich, for example; or the advancements in AI required to create a properly intelligent robot.

For some, the rationalisations provided by a solid (i.e. arguable) suppositional premise, or rather by the acts of explication *indicating* such a premise, are essential as counterbalances to the "could not have happened" alethic modality, essential in order to sustain suspension-of-disbelief in the face of constant challenges. For each writer and each reader there are different thresholds at which the "could have happened" alethic modality can simply no longer be maintained, and for that set of writers and readers with the lowest threshold verisimilitude and authenticity may be critical. Without sufficient explication that threshold will be crossed, suspension-of-disbelief will collapse, the game of make-believe will be abandoned, and the reader will throw the book across the room in disgust. Speak to many hardcore fans of Hard SF or Alternate History, offer them a book where the counterfactual / hypothetical is treated as a fancy, no more, no less, around which to build a story. Watch them tear it to shreds with disdain for how "that couldn't happen."

From *The Naked and the Dead* to *Catch-22*

Unfortunately, there's a catch for these freeform stories exploring the monstra and numinae of war; their marketing as COMBAT FICTION places them below the radar of many middlebrow readers, who look at *Astounding Stories* and see only another Boys' Own pulp. Little wonder—it's *sold* as a Boys' Own pulp, with covers of All-American GIs socking Nazis, storming bunkers, stopping tanks in their tracks with a well-aimed grenade. And amongst its siblings, there might be a subtler title like *The Magazine of Espionage & Combat Fiction* here and there (espionage being a bedfellow of combat fiction from its earliest days), but it's mostly *Bloody Battle Tales* and *Glory!* and *Heroic War Stories*.

And more than anything, the public perception of COMBAT FICTION is shaped by John Wayne movies, where hokey heroism, big explosions and valourous deaths are still the order of the day. Not familiar with the written form, but seeing the lurid covers and sensational titles, they imagine all COMBAT FICTION to be written at that intellectual level; that's how it presents itself. They'd only have to read *The Naked and the Dead* to realise this perception was bollocks, but unfortunately, *The Naked and the Dead* is on sale from one of the most successful COMBAT FICTION imprints, with a brawny GI on the cover, cigar clenched in his gritted teeth. It's selling shitloads, but not to those who look at that cover and think "John Wayne movie."

(In another parallel reality, by the way, just another half-step to the left, Mailer's novel is sold without the label, and is as widely regarded as a twentieth-century classic as it is in our reality. It's not really regarded as COMBAT FICTION at all, in fact, much to the chagrin of the patrons of the Combat Fiction Bar and Grill. This is just literary snobbery, they say. *The Naked and the Dead* is clearly COMBAT FICTION, clearly of the same GENRE as *Biggles Defies the Swastika* and *300*—and *The Iliad*, no less! But that's another fold. In this one, those patrons need not worry; here, *The Naked and the Dead* is where it belongs, shelved in COMBAT FICTION.)

Mailer's novel is only the first of many to meet this fate. One day, a young writer called Joseph Heller sends his novel *Catch-22* to an editor, and the editor finds himself in a quandary. It's obvious from the first few pages of the manuscript that this is about warfare. But it's also obvious that this is a literary masterpiece. To a public who thinks COMBAT FICTION means "John Wayne movies," this non-linear, absurdist narrative might well be seen simply as what it is—a great work of fiction. To some reactionary fans of COMBAT FICTION, indeed, it might be too flagrant a breach of their expectations. But then again, to a public who thinks COMBAT FICTION means "John Wayne movies," the first hint of a WW2 setting might be enough to turn them off. And to the progressive fans of COMBAT FICTION, this will be exactly what they're clamouring for.

Marketed as GENERAL FICTION, it might stand a better chance of critical and commercial success. But its unconventional nature makes it a risky proposition. Maybe readers unfamiliar with Combat Fiction won't understand it. Maybe readers wary of Combat Fiction won't be open enough to understand it. Will they just see a confusion of conventions—brothels and bombing runs—and a silliness they can't make sense of, lacking the protocols of combat fiction? Will they simply be alienated by the strangeness of it all?

And there *is* this ready-made market for Combat Fiction. There *are* the fans who will buy it simply because there's an airstrip being blown up on the cover. There are a lot of them—and a whole lot of the others too, the ones crying out for innovation just like this. The non-linear absurdism is a Unique Selling-Point for them. This is an original take on the established tropes if ever there was one, a work which pushes the boundaries of Combat Fiction further than ever before. Within the genre, the editor is convinced, this will win instant renown. They'll say it transcends the genre.

And he's right. Whole generations of readers too young for it now, readers who haven't yet graduated to the mature works, readers who haven't yet been born, will one day buy *Catch-22* as part of the Combat Fiction Masterworks series.

If Only…

Quite different from the approaches of comic / tragic narratives which exploit the strangeness, the explications of Hard SF and a comparable style of Alternate History may be more akin to the implicit social models underpinning the plots of the pathetic narratives of the mundane. At their most extreme, like the domestic novel, these alternative / future narratives are seeking to *persuade* us that this really, honestly *could* happen elsewhen. They deny the absurd, the abject, the surreal. They deny the incredible, dewarp the quirk. They insist that the counterfactual / hypothetical is, was or will be a very real possibility. It *would happen* like that, they insist, if only…

That said, there is an element of excuse that remains even with works which remain firmly grounded in the mundane, where they utilise the character tropes of melodrama, the heroes and villains. It is the same heightened pathos, the same "operatic" quality, which gives its name to both Space Opera and Soap Opera, and even the most explicated narrative may retain that quality.

Unfortunately an obliviousness of the convention of explication may well contribute to why other readers are unable to connect with pulp at this level, even with works grounded firmly in the most reasonable counterfactuals and hypotheticals. Offer a solid work of Hard SF or Alternate History to a reader unfamiliar with those modes, and they may click to it. The technique works for many pulp readers, after all, so we can expect it to work, in some cases, even on those not attuned to it. If it *doesn't* work for them, however, it is liable to backfire completely.

From *The Sands of Iwo Jima* to *The Guns of Navarone*

It is the death knell for those paradoxically exemplary/exceptional works tagged as *combat fiction*, of course, in terms of wider recognition—to be shelved in a section of the bookstore that many readers simply will not think to browse. They don't particularly dislike John Wayne movies, those readers, but they're not fans of them, so why should they bother with that Combat Fiction section? If they want popcorn fiction, they'll go to the movies. If such a book gets reviewed, it's in the Combat Fiction magazines. It may be hailed as a classic by the patrons of the Combat Fiction Bar and Grill, but when they try to persuade the incognoscenti of its value they're met with arched eyebrows of doubt.

Today, in the Bistro de Critique, a sceptical friend lowers the copy of *Neuromancer* he happens to be reading.

(He sighs. He's only just finished arguing with a Crime Fiction fan that *Neuromancer* is not, as they were insisting, "really Crime Fiction" simply because it has criminals in it. In this fold, it should be noted, where the strange is a third mask between tragedy and comedy, where García-Márquezian *magical realism* has its mainstream bedfellow in Orwellian *speculative realism*, there is no question of a novum or chimera rendering a work "genre fiction." Still, those Crime Fiction fans will insist on laying claim to literature like *Neuromancer* that explores the noir idiom as part of its dystopian approach.)

He looks at the copy of *Catch-22* that's being waved in front of him.

—But that's Combat Fiction, he says. That's just formulaic dreck, isn't it? All hokey heroism, big explosions and valourous deaths.

The Combat Fiction fan tries; they really do. They list Combat Fiction works, detail their merits, insisting that the field is not intrinsically formulaic. Their incognoscenti friend is dubious that any Genre novel could really achieve the profundity of a Nobel prize winner, or stand the test of time, or satisfy a number of vague criteria of literary quality—that it could really be that good. The fan points to *The Naked and the Dead* as proof. But the title doesn't ring any bells to the incognoscenti. Eventually the Combat Fiction fan must point outside the Genre simply to find something the incognoscenti have read. So they point to Hemingway's *For Whom the Bell Tolls*, a recognised classic. This is dismissed as at most an influence on Combat Fiction, a taproot text, not an actual work of Combat Fiction.

Finally the sceptical friend is persuaded, against his will, to give *Catch-22* a go; he'll find it funny, honestly. He approaches the book with scepticism, expecting something like that John Wayne movie he caught on the TV the other day. It immediately becomes apparent that this is not *The Sands of Iwo Jima*, and by fuck, it turns out that he loves it. The blend of tragedy and comedy, the fragmented narrative, the dark humanism, the core conceit extrapolated not unlike the speculative realism that is his normal taste. An ambitious book like this is not really Combat Fiction at all. No, it belongs with *For Whom the Bell Tolls*, not *Where Eagles Dare*.

When he returns it to the fan, he happily confesses his appreciation, oblivious of the dark look flashing across the fan's face when he praises it as "not really Combat Fiction." The exasperated fan is just about to hit their clueless friend upside the head when another mate happens by. One of two things happens. Also a patron of the Combat Fiction Bar and Grill, but with more conventional tastes, Philadelphia Stein—Philly for short—can't help but clock the book he hated. It's "not really" Combat Fiction as far as he's concerned, not like Alistair MacLean's 1957 classic, *The Guns of Navarone*. Or Robert A. Heinlein's seminal work from just two years later, *Starship Troopers*. Now, those are proper Combat Fiction.

As the two fans argue over what is and what isn't Combat Fiction, the sceptical friend turns the copy of *Catch-22* over in his hands. On the back of it, a blurb proclaims how this work "transcends the genre." Well, he thinks, it certainly breaks the boundaries that stretch from *The Sands of Iwo Jima* all the way to *The Guns of Navarone*.

What We Ignore

For those who lack an interest in science and history, the explication will likely alienate them from the very things which make the book interesting for the pulp reader. They will be bored by the exposition, by diagrams and equations and dates and places laid out in tiresome detail. They don't give a fuck how richly detailed the elsewhen is. They don't give a fuck how well a flight of fancy is rationalised with solid extrapolations from an arguable premise. Indeed, the more acts of explication the work offers in an attempt to justify a "would have happened" alethic modality, the more bored they get with what reads to them as geekish obsession, a dubious mania for extraneous detail. In the end, regardless of this spurious explication, that whole suppositional premise simply strikes them as…a flight of fancy. We will likely see a scorn not just of the story in terms of plot, character and writing; rather it will be a scorn of the "ridiculous" idea, the "silliness" of the conceit, an inability to take the entire premise seriously. This is generally infuriating to the fan.

Ironically, offer these same readers a work which functions as a fanciful spectacle and they'll likely lap it up, because they are entirely familiar (and comfortable) with the Romantic technique of *excuse*. These are the people who will flock to the cinema to see Tom Cruise running from the Martians and have a great time, while SF readers will be screaming at the screens about why the fuck the Martians would wait underground a couple of thousand years, until humanity had developed the technology to fight them, before attacking. I'm sure most of us are familiar with this attitude, from friends and family who will happily sit and watch *Star Wars*, but who, when offered a serious work involving a counterfactual / hypothetical elsewhen extrapolated logically from a suppositional premise, will a) find it boring, b) dismiss it as nonsense, c) respond to any argument that, actually, if you think about it, it *is* quite plausible with a mixture of bafflement and disdain at the fact that you are geekish enough to "take this stuff seriously." After all, it's Sci-Fi; it's not *meant* to be taken seriously.

Sidelined by our own knee-jerk reaction against the attitude that "only a geek would take SF seriously," that "only a geek would expect rigourous science," pissed off by the implicit insult here (science is boring, so your interest is boring, so you are boring), we risk going off half-cocked in our response. What we ignore when we argue the case for SF as rational futurology, founded in theory and extrapolation, is that those alternative / future narratives which best serve as examples here are only a fraction of the field. Yes, explication is one of the tricks by which SF as a subset of SF prevents the quirks from overpowering the suspension-of-disbelief. But it is only *one* of the tricks.

From *Perilous Visions* to *War Stars*

What is and what isn't COMBAT FICTION? It's an argument that begins with *Catch-22*, if not before, and slowly comes to consume the discourse. With Vietnam and the sexual revolution as a backdrop, the '60s and '70s see a renaissance in COMBAT FICTION, much of it socio-political and experimental, treating the fractured world of war as a reflection of the confusing (post)modern condition. Dubbed the New Wave, some writers in this mode become uncomfortable with the very label COMBAT FICTION. Many works of COMBAT FICTION now deal with guerrilla warfare, terrorism, the Holocaust, the Cold War, civil unrest, psychological warfare, inner-city gang culture, drug wars, even disputes between neighbours or the "war of the sexes." Some of it is so abstract in its connection with war that a more accurate descriptor seems called for.

It's not combat that's makes this fiction what it is so much as it's the "confrontational element." It's *confrontational fiction*. Though coined by Heinlein, that term is taken up by writers like Ellison, like the cohort of Young Turks who appear in his seminal anthology *Perilous Visions*. Many fans of Golden Age COMBAT FICTION consider these writers of the New Wave to be "not really" COMBAT FICTION.

—Where is the solid grounding in actual warfare here? they say. Where is the rigour in weaponry and tactics? Hell, where's the damn story? Give me *Force 10 from Navarone* any day.

Meanwhile, the fan who sees this strange modern idiom as a battlefield of any and all literary techniques and tactics, a free-for-all where the rules of engagement have long since been lost, can hardly mention COMBAT FICTION to an intransigent member of the hardcore incognoscenti without facing a dismissive sneer and a reference to those *War Trek* fans who go to conventions dressed up as Spock, in their khaki *War Trek* uniforms, with their papier-mâché helmets, and toy rifles. It doesn't help that, in their uncritical love for all things Combat Fiction, those with the most devotion refer to the Genre by the cute and clever moniker of Com-Fi (pronounced "comfy" by those in the know these days.) It's hardly a damning indictment—a charge of enthusiasm to the point of silliness—but these strange subcultural shenanigans turn the brand image of Combat Fiction into a barricade.

The situation isn't helped when a young director named George Lucas, in homage to the *G.I. Joe* comics he loved as a kid, makes a puerile but rollicking piece of hokum called *War Stars*. John Wayne movies are out of fashion now, so Combat Fiction isn't a box-office draw any more, but *War Stars* is a surprise smash hit. Kids and adults around the world fall in love with it, and it changes the face of cinema, ushering in a new era of blockbusters, many of which have strong elements of Combat Fiction, but few of which have the depth of the written form. *Battle Beyond the Stars* is no *2001: A Space Iliad*. Most of the those who lap up this Com-Fi would not class themselves as fans. While arching their eyebrows at the fans, indeed, they feel no shame at enjoying this cinematic junk food, because they don't take it seriously, treat it on the level it essentially belongs, as a frippery. With disdain or disregard, they'll tell the proselytising fan: they don't mind spending a few hours on a flick like *War Stars*, but if they're going to read a book they prefer something substantial.

—But *War Stars*, some fans of the written form begin to declare, isn't really Combat Fiction. With its plot revolving around stolen plans, the infiltration of an enemy base, and the rescue of a captive agent of a resistance movement, it's clearly Espionage. Which is not a good thing, as far as they're concerned. The cult of Fleming has exploded by now, and the 1970s sees a glut of derivatives, often hugely successful; most follow such a rigid formula in their tales of James Bond clones on missions to uncover and foil the Evil Genius's plans for world domination that the term "espionage" becomes synonymous with sub-Fleming power-wank.

—Puerile wish-fulfilment, scorn the hardcore Combat Fiction devotees, hardly wrong but turning a blind eye to the subtleties of le Carré and Greene in the idiom they abject, and to the testosterone-fuelled power-tripping in their own backyard, in writers like Mac-Lean. No, Espionage is the enemy within. For some fans, *anything* from *Perilous Visions* to *War Stars* might be this enemy.

The incognoscenti, knowing nothing of this aesthetic turf war and seeing no sense in the distinctions being made…nod and smile.

Nod and smile.

Strategies of Resolution

It is possible to combine excuse *and* explication. Since both techniques work towards maintaining suspension-of-disbelief, one by widening the parameters of what's acceptable (android-as-conventional-trope), the other by arguing the acceptability (android-as-plausible-speculation) on a case-by-case basis, these two strategies of resolution can work in tandem, with the writer "spreading the load," so to speak, over both techniques. The fact that androids are a conventional trope (a given of the idiomatic fantasia) hardly negates the effect of a plausible scientific explanation based on A-Life and AI theories; it might make the work a bit more boring for the type of fan who'd rather you just got on with the story, but it might also make it more interesting for the type of fan who wants authenticity. Conversely, the use of scientific theory isn't going to *detract* from the conventionality of the trope, make it less excusable. You're not suddenly going to stop believing in the android because the author made it *more* plausible.

So you get the explanatory and excusatory techniques working together. You can offset less rigourous science with more vigourous (i.e. Romantic, adventurous, trope-bound) narrative, and vice versa. Early Heinlein like *Starship Troopers* is a good example. Giant bugs are kinda scientifically dodgy. Interstellar warfare without FTL is a bit unlikely to say the least, and FTL itself is hardly on a solid scientific basis. Heinlein's Cherenkov Drive is an Unobtainium Drive. In part, it's the form of Heinlein's book that makes it work, a bildungsroman in an idiomatic fantasia. Same with his juveniles where the science is even more handwavy. And this kind of stuff is at the core of what we label SF.

The two strategies can however be used pretty much independently, in more "purely" excusatory SF or in more "purely" explicatory SF, and just as readers will prefer one technique over the other, so too will writers. A deep commitment to one technique may even shade into an animosity towards the other. So, you end up with the HARD SF versus SCIENCE FANTASY schism within the genre.

There is, of course, a third option that is neither.

From *Slaughterhouse-Five* to Harry Potter

Time passes. Down in the ghetto, in the Combat Fiction Bar & Grill, there's unrest. One of the writers who's pushed the boundaries the most, Kurt Vonnegut, author of the classic COMBAT FICTION novel *Slaughterhouse-Five*, denies that his work is GENRE in an attempt to escape the inexorable taint of formulaic shit that goes with the label COMBAT FICTION. Regardless of the blatant and direct tackling of the subject matter of COMBAT FICTION, he rejects the confines of a GENRE dismissed by the general public as "John Wayne movies" and celebrated by many of its most ardent admirers on the basis of its "sense of glory." A large proportion of fans who now vehemently reject CoM-Fi as an implicitly derogatory term in favour of a less loaded *CF*—standing for combat fiction, confrontational fiction, or any number of alternatives—consider this a betrayal of the worst kind.

So it goes.

Time passes. Mainstream writers start turning their hand to combat fiction only to be regarded with extreme suspicion, if not outright hostility. Pat Barker's *Regeneration*, a novel set during World War One but taking place almost entirely in Craiglockhart War Hospital, is a point of controversy. For some fans, the problem is simply that Barker's book is old hat, done before. If Barker were familiar with the genre she'd know that the War Hospital story was a hoary old cliché, done to death. For others, the problem is that Barker leaves the trenches in the background, which is utterly at odds with the conventions of this Genre of hokey heroism, big explosions and valourous deaths. Barker, as a dabbling mainstream writer, doesn't really understand the way Combat Fiction works, and so her novel doesn't work as Combat Fiction. Barker compounds her crime by, in an interview, denying that she writes Combat Fiction, which she dismisses as "grunts with guns" stories. She accepts the label *confrontational fiction*, but few CF fans notice this.

So it goes.

Time passes. An Espionage series aimed at children and young adults—J.K. Rowling's Harry Potter books—takes hold in the public imagination. Adults who haven't read a novel in years are suddenly obsessed with Harry Potter, with its secret weapons to be sought after, intrigues to be uncovered, plots to be foiled. People like reading about machinations, it seems, and given the choice between middle-class, middlebrow, mid-life crisis novels and books in which a trainee secret agent thwarts the schemes of the Evil Genius Voldemort, they'll opt for the latter. Some of those writers who now treat *confrontational fiction* as an umbrella term for Combat Fiction and Espionage keep their fingers crossed that this will translate to an influx of new readers as fans of Harry Potter graduate to more mature works. Others simply see this as a mainstreaming of the confrontational genres in their most commercial and juvenile form, dubious that Rowling's fans will really move on to Heller and the like.

So it goes.

Peru or Mars

SF does not always excuse its quirks as conventions, or, like the pathetic narrative, explain how things are or might be, substituting the scientific for the psychological and socio-political, explicating the counterfactual / hypothetical until we're persuaded that, oh, well, of course this *could* have happened—not here, not now, but in the right circumstances, maybe, it *would* have happened. It doesn't always treat the quirk as an awkward untruth—a threat to suspension-of-disbelief that must be sugar-coated to be sold, with immersive artifice or reasoned argument.

To illustrate, let's try another alternative narrative:

> *There was an old woman in Peru, '52.*
> *She had so many children she didn't know what to do.*
> *She gave them some broth without any bread.*
> *She joined the revolt and replaced the State's Head.*

And another future narrative:

> *There was an old woman in Mars City 2.*
> *She had so many children she didn't know what to do.*
> *She gave them some broth and chips in the head.*
> *She ripped their meme-patterns, installed them in Teds.*

As you can see, the counterfactual premise of the alternative narrative is presented right up-front, and pretty much composes the entirety of the story, but it's hardly a product of extensive research into the socio-political situation in Peru in the 1950s, possible revolutionary factions, and events and actions which might have led to the deposing of the government of the day. And the future narrative is hardly notable for the less-than-rigourous science underpinning speculations on the viability of Martian colonies, robotics as toys, and the potential translation of human thought-patterns into other media so they can be made to persist outside the human flesh. Neither of these narratives seeks to establish its authenticity.

In those two examples, the disjunction should be obvious between, on the one hand, alternative narrative and ALTERNATE HISTORY, and on the other hand, future narrative and HARD SF. The sort of alternative narrative which simply changes the past and tells a story in that altered setting (*The Man in the High Castle*? *The Plot Against America*?) is quite distinct from the type of ALTERNATE HISTORY which pivots on theory and speculation regarding (often military) courses of particular events. The same holds for future narratives and HARD SF. In the latter example there's not even the slightest effort at justifying the quirks as solid supposition.

But given that it's essentially a four-line story, why would we want to bloat the poem up with the infodump of explication anyway? Is it any less functional as a future narrative? And, hell, in the first example, rather than leaving out all the specificity of dates, peoples and places necessary to rationalise a counterfactual coup, I could have (with a few problems of rhyme and scansion) simply substituted Ruritania for Peru and still had what is fundamentally an alternative narrative. In *The Prisoner of Zenda* there is not even the remotest attempt to explicate the scenario as premised.

From *The Iliad* to *War and Peace*

In the uptown district of Literature, in the Bistro de Critique, where LITERARY FICTION is the order of the day and the discourse of propriety is always on the menu, a discussion kicks off about this trend in reader tastes. A bookshop assistant who hangs out down in the Combat Fiction Bar & Grill from time to time tries to explain. She describes the simple desire of readers for something more heroic, and the expectations readers have of GENRE FICTION fulfilling that desire. She begins to speak of the thwarting of those expectations by fiction which does not, in fact, fulfil this desire—but this last point is lost amid the horrified cries of the middle-class and middlebrow regulars of the bistro, busy bewailing the debased taste of adult readers who would lower themselves to reading GENRE FICTION, denying point blank that any work of COMBAT FICTION could be more than formulaic dreck. To the bookshop assistant they seem driven by some bourgeois neurosis about genre cooties eating away at the foundations of civilisation.

The bookshop assistant, as a reader of CF—a marker of mode rather than identity to her, not a brand label but a shorthand for an aesthetic idiom—is all too familiar with this prejudice, knows that argument is futile. She might point to everything from the *Iliad* to *War and Peace* as examples of CF, but the very idea will be dismissed as ludicrous; these aren't COM-FI. She knows that *For Whom the Bell Tolls* will likewise be disregarded along with any work that wasn't published in the actual marketing category. She knows that *Slaughterhouse-Five* will be classed as satire or postmodernism. And there's no point even mentioning *The Naked and the Dead*; this will be entirely unfamiliar, having been published under a COMBAT FICTION imprint, consigned to the ghetto of Genre. Why should anyone take her word that there are CF novels of the very highest calibre? With a mind already made up about COM-FI and its freakish fans, why should anyone sift through the shit of that section in their local bookstore for the gems these crazies claim are hidden in the muck?

As a last resort, the bookshop assistant draws a wild comparison to fiction which focuses on, for example, science as a metaphor or backdrop rather than combat. Imagine, she says, a hypothetical and absurd new genre label…call it SCIENCE FICTION. And then she traces out a strange counterfactual scenario where such recognised modern classics as Delany's *Dhalgren*, Lem's *Solaris*, Ballard's *The Drowned World*, a whole host of landmark novels, are all lumped together under an arbitrary rackspace label. She conjures a pseudo-history of the world, a parallel timestream where—crazy as it may sound—these sort of books are considered *genre fiction*.

—If the course of events only played out a little differently, she says, you can see how a disjunct could exist between the reality of this field and the popular perception of it. Just as it does, she argues, for combat fiction. Or confrontational fiction, or CF, as she prefers to call it. Surely, she says, you can't fail to see the absurdity of a prejudice dismissing these works simply because they're *genre fiction*, where this *genre fiction* contains a novel like *Dhalgren*.

(She doesn't stop to think before picking *Dhalgren* as an example. It's so familiar in its renown that the very name of its apocalyptic city-setting, Bellona, has passed into common usage as a term for any catastrophic collapse from civilisation to senselessness. Bosnia was "a real Bellona." Rwanda was "a real Bellona." New Orleans in the aftermath of Hurricane Katrina was "a real Bellona.")

Trust me, she says. *Catch-22* is at least as good as that, maybe even better. The only reason it's not considered a modern classic is because it's seen as COM-FI, and COM-FI is seen as hokey heroism, big explosions and valourous deaths—all that John Wayne movie shit. But the real CF that's out there is about as far away from that as you can get. It's not all plot-driven Boys' Own adventures. It's not all about weaponry and strategies. The characters and themes and prose can be way more important than any of that—and are in *Catch-22*. If it wasn't for the misperceptions surrounding that COMBAT FICTION label, *Catch-22* might be as much of a household name as *Dhalgren* is today.

The incognoscenti remain unconvinced. The sort of breadth of definition she's talking about would cover everything from the *Iliad* to *War and Peace*, and that's not a GENRE just a gesture at such.

To Exploit the Estrangement

The Peru and Mars limerick examples are boiled down to a ridiculous simplicity, but the future narrative is a good example of what's actually going on in a lot of SF; it's a little microcosmic picture of how at least one type of SF story may be constructed and, in its blithe disregard for any real honest-to-god theory and explication, it begs the question: why the fuck *should* we take this kind of crazy shit seriously? Mars colonies…chips in the head…identities stored as "meme-patterns"…downloaded into "Teds"…Hmmm. You don't think that sounds a bit…fanciful?

We can and do take it seriously, but not because it's possible. This is fiction containing elements which utterly contradict our knowledge of how the world is; those elements aren't possible but at most have the possibility of one day becoming possible. Right now we don't have Mars colonies. The only people with chips in their heads are a few loons at MIT who read one too many issues of *Mondo 2000*. Identities cannot be stored as meme-patterns. And what the fuck is a Ted, anyway? (It's a robotic teddy-bear, dude. Isn't it obvious?) Half of that story is telling us "this could not have happened," and none of it is functioning as explication to counter that.

So, of course your average reader with only a passing familiarity with pulp, recognising the dependence on conventionality, recognising the strategies of Romantic adventure stories—the heroic cowboys and the evil monsters and the gosh-wow rocket-ships and so on—is going to wonder why on Earth we take this cock-fluffing fiction of the marvellous seriously. As long as we continue to justify SF by reference to the plausibility of the science, they'll continue to counter with the references to the innumerable works where no such plausibility is evidenced, the countless cases that work, that we immerse ourselves in, suspend our disbelief in, regardless of their fanciful content…simply because the tropes that they're constructed from are accepted as "harmless fun."

Of course they too are wrong. Yes, one technique for dealing with the disruptive artificiality of the counterfactual / hypothetical is to explicate it. Yes, another technique is just to excuse it as an idiomatic whimsy. But an equally valid technique is to *exploit* the estrangement, as a surrealist might. Like the comic and tragic narrative, this type of (alternative / future) narrative functions by making the irrationality of the quirk an integral component of the story, a structural feature. It treats the import of the quirk—and the tension towards disbelief that it generates—as a strength to be utilised. As the comic and tragic narratives are built around the absurd and the monstrous, so this narrative is built around the implausibility which it capitalises on.

From *The Guns of the South* to *The Plot Against America*

> *That's some catch, that Catch-22.*
> **Joseph Heller, Catch-22**

So our bookstore assistant heads back to the Combat Fiction Bar and Grill. She begins to wonder, on her way, how events might have played out for the field of CF if that *combat fiction* label had never been coined, if they just had "war novels"—like modernity novels, but focusing on combat rather than progress as their background and theme. She imagines a world where *Kelly's Heroes* isn't blithely lumped in with *Schindler's List*, or *Life Is Beautiful* with *Where Eagles Dare*; where fans of John Wayne movies, *Commando* comics, Alistair MacLean novels and other such COMBAT FICTION don't kvetch about some latter-day *Catch-22* not playing by the rules; where there's no need to argue the validity of *Slaughterhouse-Five* with the granfalloon of a tradition stretching back through Faulkner and Tolstoy and Shakespeare to the *Iliad* itself; where there's no bitter resentment of the lack of respect for *genre fiction* like *The Naked and the Dead* or *Starship Troopers*; no bitching about mainstream writers who deny their work is COMBAT FICTION when it's set in a war hospital; no teacup tempests over how COMBAT FICTION is polluted by INTRIGUE; no cringing at the self-coined nickname of COM-FI because that's *really just* the movies and TV shows, which *really just* give CF a bad rep.

It's natural for her to think this way. ALT HISTORY is part of the GENRE, after all, with all its counterfactuals of Confederate victories and Nazi triumphs. She's not that big on the whole *Guns of the South* approach herself, but the subgenre's been a corner of CF from way back. She's imagining a world where there's no argument over whether or not Philip Roth's *The Plot Against America* is "really combat fiction," just at the point where she pushes open the door of the Combat Fiction Bar and Grill. As she walks inside, takes a step to the left, she's imagining a world where the lack of classifications means *Catch-22* isn't "not really" COMBAT FICTION to either fan or incognoscenti.

Because in her fold, there's a double-bind of double-binds. As much as the incognoscenti apply that notorious axiom—If it's COMBAT FICTION, it can't be good; if it's good, it can't be COMBAT FICTION—the fans have their own, it sometimes seems, those who're looking for "more of the same" at least: if it's "not really" COMBAT FICTION, it can't be good, if it's good, it can't "not really" be COMBAT FICTION. That fan axiom is written into the very nature of GENRE itself, the demand of readers for something that coheres as a GENRE.

If it's exceptional, it can't be exemplary; if it's exemplary, it can't be exceptional.

It's a real Catch-22, she thinks.

The Booker and the Bistro de Critique

Those Rocket Age Rhapsodies

No SF novel ever won the Booker.
Somebody, Somewhere, Somewhen

Hang out long enough down in the ghetto of Genre, in the SF Café, and eventually you'll hear this axiom, or an axiom like it, muttered with a certain tone of harrumph, a petulance in proportion to the wounded pride. Maybe you'll say it yourself, sullen in your sense of injustice, disregard; I know I have. And whenever it's spoken, that truism will likely spark a little to-and-fro on the exclusion of SF from the modern canon. There is, after all, an absenting in the absence, an *active* excision; the ghetto of Genre is a territory of the abject, an enclosure for the refused, that paraliterary pulp exiled from Literature—despite the fact that literature means only that which has been written—delimited as Genre—despite the fact that every work of literature sits within some genre or other.

But the question is: What are we going to point to as the stuff that *should* have won the Booker, the works of SF that prove to the outside world how good SF can be? Looking at our heritage of Asimov, Bester, Clarke and so on, would any of it actually rate that laurel if the prize had existed back in the day? Of the writers working since 1969, the year the Booker was born, how many of them can we imagine on the shortlist? Dick? Ellison? Farmer? Gibson? Heinlein? I love the work of Philip K. Dick—great ideas—but maybe the pills and booze had an impact on his prose because it just ain't that sparkly. Ellison's power was always as a short-story writer. Farmer, Gibson, Heinlein…we can go through the alphabet, and here and there a few names might jump out, but even with my own nomination, as a disciple at the altar of Delany, I'd actually be pointing at works like *Dhalgren* or the Nevèrÿon books—works which will only invite the old "Yes, but that's not really SF" from insiders and outsiders alike.

The questions is: Once we scrap the crap of badly-written adventure stories, technothrillers, thought-experiments—the sensationalist or intellectualist lettuce for the genre bunnies, all too often potboiled to pabulum—just what novels do we have that deserve the Booker, what writers of the required level of literary merit that inarguably classify as SF?

The responses range from the blinkered to the blind, from the faith of those who'd argue Heinlein was as good as Hemingway to the heresy of those who'd argue William S. Burroughs was as much SF as Edgar Rice Burroughs. So the boundary debates begin.

When we say SF do we mean SCIENCE FICTION, SCIENCE FANTASY, SCI-FI or what? Do we mean any weird-ass, experimentalist, non-mimetic mind-fuck novel which was sold as SF? If that mind-fuck novel wasn't sold as SF but *might* have been, does it prove SF can cut it with the big boys if it wants to, or is it just proof that the label damns us to the literati, that SF won't get the kudos if it doesn't disclaim its nature, cough a phrase like *speculative fiction* up its sleeve? These are the questions that genre bunnies obsess over. (Clearly I'm included in that category.)

And from the boundary disputes come the land-grabs, the fingers pointed to claim everything from Orwell back to Wells and beyond, through Shelley and Swift to Shakespeare. From Huxley to Homer. Casting the net so wide is understandable, right enough, when SF fans feel they're expected to provide examples of SF with literary chops, works up to the quality of the "classics from the history of literature," an all-encompassing taxonomic level that includes everything from *The Epic of Gilgamesh* onwards. When you're working on that scale, putting the David of a few decades of SF up against the Goliath of all acknowledged literary masterworks ever, well, David's going to reach for a big-ass stone, even if he has to stretch pretty far. But this strategy only brings the argument down at the first hurdle, if one is facing some straw literati to whom these embryonic SF works are, at best, precursors to or influences upon the GENRE of SCIENCE FICTION. Such finger-pointing says nothing for the works born in the modern era's ghetto of Genre, those Rocket Age rhapsodies, those Information Era operas of futurology and fantasia.

And it's all about them and a very contemporary action of canonisation by award. It's all about the Booker and the Bistro de Critique where that's something of a big deal.

From Huxley to Homer

We need to focus in then. What we forget in these debates driven by defensiveness is that the period from Huxley back to Homer is out of bounds anyway: if it's a valid comparison we want, and precursors and influences are to be excluded for SF, since SF didn't exist before Day Zero, we have to scratch all the classics from before Day Zero also; these are inadmissible as non-SF by the same logic; the taxonomic distinction didn't exist. Where *literary fiction* is set against *genre fiction* both have burned their bridges to the past, set themselves as things of that so twentieth-century dichotomy. Like the genre bunnies of LITERARY FICTION have any more claim to Shelley, Swift or Shakespeare than us? Get real, realistas.

It is as if a GENRE of FANTASY DRAMA had come into existence over the last decade or so—with *Angels in America*, say, as its precursor, its prime influence. It would be absurd to ask fans of this idiom to provide examples measuring up to a millennia-long heritage of "literary drama" classics like *Prometheus Bound*. To expect them not to simply point at *Prometheus Bound*…or *Angels in America* indeed. Still, in ten years of that commercial Genre maybe nothing would have won the Pulitzer. The bright lights, big bucks, Broadway productions might have garnered Tonys as they sold shitloads of tickets to punters looking for a little extra sparkle in their spectacle, but of course we're talking largely commercial drama here, more *Cats* than *The Crucible*. So no FD play ever won the Pulitzer, genre bunnies might mutter.

—No shit, the straw literati might say in return.

In the SF Café, as we kvetch about the latest longlist or laurel-winner, at some point, eventually, the underlying assumption that empowers our sense of grievance will surface: the certainty of SF's unwarranted marginalisation. This lack of respect has nothing to do with merit, we're sure, and everything to do with the prejudices of the prize-givers, the elitism of the literary establishment, those to whom *literary fiction* and *genre fiction* are entirely different entities…and never the twain shall meet. The ones who'd say, in that elsewhen, that neither *Angels in America* nor *Prometheus Bound* should really be considered works of Fantasy Drama.

Weirdly, we buy into the idea that it's all about the realism and unrealism; we buy into the bootstrapping rhetoric that sets mimetic Literary Fiction as the paragon of the literary, imagining that the non-mimetic is what the straw literati hate. We bemoan the dearth of imagination in this dreary stuff, the way the dreaded literary establishment reviles our strange fictions for the strangeness. Pah! Those mundanes think only Kitchen-Sink Realism and its siblings deserve respect! If an SF novel ever did win the Booker, we're sure, those bastards at the Bistro de Critique would just say, well, that's not SF. Poor us. Poor little genre bunnies.

—Ah, but wait, someone might say. That was then and this is now. If from Huxley back to Homer is of no consequence here, the mere fifty or so years since then is hardly more than…a parochial school prize-giving. An end of term assembly at which—oh noes!—the emo kid never gets to give a speech as dux. So fuck?

A paltry half-century of realism being the bees' knees? All that proves is that the chic clique kids of the Bistro de Critique do actually change their tastes over time. So a certain label is out this season. That only makes it more likely that the flightiness of fashion will return us to that vast heritage stretching back from Huxley to Homer—to homunculi, to Hamlet's spectral sire, to Yahoos and Houyhnhnm.

A Bastion of Intellectualism

Let's take a step outside the ghetto of Genre entirely, take the underground a few dozen streets uptown and a score or so years into the future.

The Bistro de Critique sits in the uptown district of Literature, just round the corner from the Temple of Academia with its ivory towers and quiet cloisters. It's been there for a long time, centuries rather than decades, a bastion of intellectualism. The arguments and affectations of its patrons down the years have formed the discourse through which the notion of a canon has been defined—this pantheon of recognised classics—amid the cocktail party chatter of book launches and literary festivals, the bluster and bile of snipewanking reviews and scuttlebutt.

Fashions have come and gone in the Bistro de Critique. Rationalist and Romanticist aesthetics have been adopted and abandoned, replaced by (post)modernist flavours of the month. In the twentieth century the Bistro de Critique was the stomping ground where philosophers of fiction formulated the systematic approaches of NEW CRITICISM, STRUCTURALISM, DECONSTRUCTION, et al., these GENRES of thought constituting the literary establishment that's always been the bugbear of the SF Café genre bunnies.

There is no conspiracy of malice, of course, and never has been, most of the slights and injustices we suffer born of ignorance more than intention. In our talk of literary elites we fabricate coteries of sophisticates, sneering and scheming, working magics over the middlebrow to sustain their power; but this is not how establishments work. The privilege and prejudice permeates the systems of articulation, the ideologies and the institutions, the GENRES of thought. There are no individual enemies to point to as the Templars of this literary establishment, no secret sect of scornful power mongers, but there is nonetheless an organisation in the system itself, an emergent enterprise with principles, strategies and tactics that include the negation and marginalisation of a certain class of fiction, the proletariat of pulp. This is a discourse born of Europe's colonial imperialist period; if you don't, can't, won't see classism, misogyny and racism as institutionalised, Literature as an institution reifying those prejudices, Cock help you. It is not a matter of an elite sneering at us scum, but of an enterprise with privilege as its end and means to that end.

Or at least that used to be the case. This is the future, after all.

This is twenty years into tomorrow, and the Bistro de Critique has changed. A new critique has swept aside the Old Guard, declared an end to the Culture Wars, a critique we'll call, in the spirit of futurological fancy, DYNAMISM. To sum it up in the crudest way possible, DYNAMISM is a critique focused on the suspension-of-disbelief as a base-line of balance in the reading experience, and on the disruption of that equilibrium as the fundamental and formative force within narrative. When we read, our suspension-of-disbelief is a pretence that the events recounted did happen, but what makes that reading an experience of narrative is when an event is introduced that fucks with this base-line modality, an event that should not, would not, maybe even could not happen. Taking its lead from Todorov's theory of narrative equilibrium, expanding the notion of subjunctivity level advanced by Delany in his essay "About Five Thousand Seven Hundred and Fifty Words," describing the protocols of narrative in terms of quirks of epistemic, alethic, deontic, and boulomaic modalities, DYNAMISM roots the very essence of fiction in the onward impetus born of the tensions such modalities constitute.

Comedy and tragedy can be understood as playing with—no, driven by—the boulomaic modalities of *should* and *must*, intersecting with the deontic (i.e. of duty) modalities that bear the same labels, dancing into the alethic modalities of *could* and *would* that the strange fiction genres are all about, working also with the epistemic modality of *will*, the *impending* part of *impending doom*. Crime and mystery fictions play with epistemic modalities like *might*, with quirks of uncertainty.

Only the REALIST genres predicate themselves on the absence of such strangeness—a denial that renders them inherently flattened in these dimensions, incapable of the deep dynamics generated by such disruptions of credibility and certainty. More fool them. For sure, such flat fictions can be affectively engaging, supremely so where they retain the quirks of desire/dread and duty, but like poetry stripped of metaphor, like a rock band playing unplugged, it has essentially limited itself. All it takes is an understanding of how narrative really works in terms of these modalities, and the straw literati's scorn of the strange becomes a risible pretension, an intellectualism that is not at all as savvy as it postures.

Elsewhen in this sortie through New Sodom, you might be seeing glimpses of how that hypothetical critique might look, as we delve into the details of this so-called DYNAMISM, but for now let's just take it as an imaginative conceit: that over the next twenty or so years, criticism actually comes to focus on the buttons pushed in narrative, on how a fiction is more than just some thick mimetic weft we trudge through, how it is powered by the warp of should not, would not, could not. Imagine that as this DYNAMISM repostulates narrative as a visceral rather than cerebral experience, it reinstates the sensational at the heart of reading, rejects the anodyne model of fiction as mere observation regurgitated and recombined. It overthrows the middle-class and middlebrow valuations and valorisations of an obsolete twentieth-century aesthetic that privileges faux reportage over honest figuration.

When this hypothetical DYNAMISM hit the Bistro de Critique, we must imagine, it shattered any illusion of a divide between Genre and Literature. One can only dream.

Exploitation and Estrangement

> *A work belongs in the genre of science fiction if its narrative world is at least somewhat different from our own, and if that difference is apparent against the background of an organized body of knowledge.*
> **Eric S. Rabkin**

Let's look at that future narrative nursery rhyme in a bit more detail to try and trace exactly how it's working.

There was an old woman in Mars City 2.

The first sentence dislocates us from the here and now, introducing the new subjunctivity of "could not have happened *now*" by positioning the events in an obviously invented place—Mars City 2—a simple combination of known terms which do not belong together in our world. There's a cognitive dissonance here, an estrangement, but it's mitigated by conventionality. On one level the convention is from the real world, the name-structure of the settlement being in a recognisable, traditional format—Kansas City, Sun City, Mexico City…Mars City.

On another level, we also recognise a fictive convention, the SF tradition of naming otherworldly colonies in that format. Given that there's a Sun City in the real-world, there's a vague possibility that we could read this as an alternate narrative rather than a future narrative, assuming that this invented Mars City is still located on Earth…but this reading is pretty unlikely. Even if you've never read an SF book in your life, you're more likely to map the relationship thus: Mars City is to Mars as Kansas City is to Kansas, as Mexico City is to Mexico. And just to seal the deal the extra SF convention of the numbered colony is thrown in—it's not just Mars City, it's Mars City 2. And again this maps to a real-world convention—the numbering of military bases, scientific stations, rocket ships, and so on.

The result is that the sense of dislocation is balanced with a sense of *relocation*. A synthetic elsewhen which eases the estrangement can be easily constructed by the reader out of the very words that create the estrangement in the first place.

Normality Within the Strange

An aside: Compare how the original nursery rhyme sets up a similar estrangement with the word "shoe," but does not offer a counter-balance of interpretability. Compare also the parseable structure of "Mars City 2" with a name designed to signal a style of fantasy other than SF—where there might be clues in the linguistic roots of the name to the "location" of the city in a sort of conceptual space (e.g. "Katambuktu," "Saint Beaucoup") or not as the case may be (e.g. "Rakkasneru").

In both we are offered a relocation to a synthetic elsewhere, but the elsewhen of this other style of fantasy is positioned in a landscape of culture and language rather than an imagined future, the pataphor creating its own context. With such fantasy the dislocation might even be offered with no relocation whatsoever, or with a relocation to a synthetic elsewhere that lacks even the conventional signal of place which we're offered in the capital

R of Rakkasneru. I could easily imagine a writer like Jeffrey Ford, for example, beginning a surreal little fable with the first line of the nursery rhyme exactly as it stands: *There was an old woman who lived in a shoe.* This is why I referred to the "nascent fantasy" of the nursery rhyme. But I'm getting ahead of myself here. Back to the future narrative:

She had so many children she didn't know what to do.

If the first sentence dislocates (and relocates) us, creating a sense of estrangement, the mimetic weft of the second sentence reassures us that, regardless of this estrangement, the story *does* still relate to our own experience, by focusing on the comprehensible relationship between a mother and her children; it sets up a completely recognisable situation and a completely recognisable problem. One might say that the writer is distracting the reader from the dissonance, forestalling any collapse of the suspension-of-disbelief by saying: don't worry; this is about human beings just like you. But "distract" is the wrong word. Rather I think the writer is establishing a sense of normality *within* the strange, establishing the relationship between the elsewhen which is strange to us and the here-and-now we know. This is the sense in which SF is often said to be about the present rather than the future. Think of the sort of classic PKD novel where the elsewhen is a Mars colony in the future, but is portrayed by Dick with the mimetic weft of 1950s suburban America.

If estrangement is cognitive dissonance, we might call this quality of the mimetic weft *cognitive consonance*.

The Coalescence, The Collapse

She gave them some broth and chips in the head.

Moving on, the third sentence fuses the mundane and the strange, the old and the new, balancing the quirky novelty of "chips in the head" against the traditionality of "broth"; but it also, in following on from the first two, develops the narrative. Attuned to the try/fail cycle of plot, understanding that the broth is an attempt to solve the narrative problem, we understand also that the chips in the head are to be read as a part of this story. Our interest is piqued. Are the chips in the head connected to the broth? Are they another attempt at a solution? Will they work? If so how?

She ripped their meme-patterns, installed them in Teds.

In the fourth sentence we're given the solution in a double-whammy of quirks. We can discern an instantly recognisable feature of SF here in the worldbuilding effect of language, whether it's actual technological jargon ("ripped," "installed"), pseudo-scientific portmanteau ("meme-pattern"), or a known word recontextualised as the signifier of an invention ("Teds"). Again we see situational estrangement, in the idea of a "meme-pattern" and in the implication that these can be recorded.

The important thing, however, is that the linguistic innovation is not just situationally estranging; it is *structurally integral*. The resolution of the problem and the fusion, the coalescence, the *collapse*, of these…estrangements into the singular supposition of "chips in the head which allow us to rip a person's meme-patterns and install it elsewhere" are inseparable. At the point where we grasp just what those chips in the head can do—when we realise that a mind, having been recorded, can be downloaded into a robotic teddy-bear so that the mother no longer has all these hungry kiddiewinks' flesh-mouths to feed—we are being given not just a (novel, strange) suppositional premise but a solution of the problem, a resolution of the plot.

The Novel Novel

So we can see here an example of the cognitive estrangement Suvin sets as characteristic of the novum. What we're looking at is an overload of linguistic strangeness, coinages piled on top of one another, heaped around the core idea of "chips in the head" until the conceptual mass is sufficient for that accumulation of suggestions of innovation to collapse into a singular idea. This novum is not the same thing as a trope, not at all—though most nova will eventually be recycled by later writers, and a trove of tropes derived from the process of conventionalisation, symbolic formulation. Even when a novum is constructed in a fiction which plays with existing tropes, familiarity is of less import than the estrangement, the peculiar novelty it capitalises on.

Suvin's novum is a "genre device" if ever there was one, but what constructs his SF as a subset of SF, a genre of cognitive estrangement, is less the quirk per se than a specific approach to it, an approach of exploitation. If the comic narrative exploits the absurd *sutura* and the tragic narrative exploits the *monstrum*, this particularly conceptual type of future narrative exploits the novum. Strictly speaking, rather than *future*, the term *novel* would sit better beside *absurd* and *monstrous*, but it would be rather confusing to talk of novel narratives or novels that exploit the novel, so we'll have to live with it.

These nova work, and make the story work, make us take it seriously, because they function as conceits that are both original and meaningful. The reader enters the story with a willing suspension-of-disbelief. The writer deliberately fucks with that, introducing a quirk. But that quirk is neither mere thought-experiment (which may lack meaning) nor mere fancy (which may lack originality). Rather it integrates plot *and* theme, glues the story together around it, its power resting in the peculiar relationship of literal untruth and non-literal veracity—albeit that the veracity is multiplicitous and reader-generated, pataphoric rather than metaphoric, if the narrative is truly exploiting the quirk rather than co-opting it to crude allegory.

Okay, the writer says, if you're happy to believe my plausible lies, let me give you an *implausible* lie. Let me give you the absurd, the abject, the surreal—or the novum. Let me give you a strange conceit, a quirk. Yes, it's patently unreal. Yes, it's going to throw you out of that cosy alethic modality of "this could happen." But it's an integral part of the story without which the story would not function, would not be a story at all. And if you just keep your disbelief suspended, with that lie I'm going to try and tell you something true. Or rather, I'm going to give you a figuration you can apply to whatever facets of the world you will, and hopefully find, in seeing those facets defamiliarised, their truths.

Those Old Equations

There is a conflict that emerges here between the first two strategies of explication and excuse and the third strategy of exploitation, since the latter is geared towards *challenging* that suspension-of-disbelief. If the strangeness is excused or explicated doesn't that make it less strange? This is especially problematic with the novum. If the android is an utterly familiar trope, or rationalised to the most rigourous degree, or both, surely it can't continue to function as a *novum*, surely that dissipates its *novelty*. Doesn't it just become another tired variable in those old equations?

Well, yes…but…

The trope trove of SF has been constantly replenished over the decades by writers generating new nova in their work precisely because novelty is essential to the novum. The power of the old nova is dissipated as they are conventionalised into tropes, but as we exhaust the strangeness of the spaceships, aliens and robots, we add cyberspace, singularities and posthumans. There is a disenchantment with the Rocket Age, to be sure. Scientific advance now feels more commonplace and our world is so techno-whizzy anyway that the sense-of-wonder which drives SF may well be less intense for many. We're harder to futureshock too. But we haven't yet, to my mind, entirely run out of strange new scientific ideas—strange enough to test our suspension-of-disbelief, and new enough not to be conventional.

Also, over and above the replenishment of the trope trove with new nova, there is a constant détournement of those tropes in order to defamiliarise them. So you have the robot as genre convention—a mechanical worker, occasionally treated as sentient but more usually a mindless drone—and in order to make a good SF story you have to add your own twist. Asimov gives us (the logical permutations of) his Three Laws of Robotics in *I, Robot*. Bester gives us the AI psychosis of "Fondly Fahrenheit." Sladek gives us the put-upon child robot of *Roderick*. Each is, in his own way, using the conventionality of the trope as something to kick against, to confound expectations. A genre using conventions to excuse implausibility creates expectations around those conventions. A writer can either meet those expectations or go out of their way to fuck with them.

As a Grenade

Does that reimagined trope then become a novum itself, or is the novum within those stories located in the twist—the Three Laws, the psychosis, the childhood? I don't know. We should not cling too hard to the articulation of a shift in narrative modality as an object in the text; the notion of the quirk it is a useful encapsulation but let's not be too literalist about it; sometimes the novum will be better seen as a more abstract effect that is generated by the work rather than an item of content, a thing which the work contains. Rather than a noun, the novum of an SF narrative, as a form of quirk, as a matter of modalities, is a narrative itself, boiling down to a noun-verb statement with a modal auxiliary hue (if you can even reduce it that far); that's what distinguishes it from a trope.

In its deliberate inversions and subversions, this type of SF can read as parody, pastiche or satire, or it can read as something more serious, more pointed, a sort of fictive critique of conventions, a sort of anti-genre. As should be obvious from the examples of Asimov and Bester, this has been going on in SF from *way* back. If there is a danger that even the new twists will be exhausted, the trove is not yet all played out. Every so often you see even the hoariest old cliché transfigured by some cunning subversion. Writers take this as a challenge.

And if explication can declaw the strange, this is not the whole story. A writer may build the most rationally explicated world through the details and then throw a novum right into the heart of it as a grenade. Indeed, in something like *2001* you have the futurology of the human spaceship (no artificial gravity, no hyperdrive, and it takes a long time to get to Jupiter) but with the monolith as a huge big novum at the core of the story. The remake of *Solaris* might be another example where you have a backdrop that's not wildly weird, that's made acceptable by its visual extrapolation from our time (in terms of technology, style, culture, etc.), and then the novum in the middle of that, the utterly inexplicable alien consciousness of the planet. In some senses, you could say, the verisimilitude and authenticity of the human culture only heightens the strangeness of the alien other in both of those fictions.

So, if you can then, theoretically, put these all together you end up with…what? Maybe Bester's *The Stars My Destination*. There you have some of the classic tropic conventions—space travel, asteroid miners. These are treated with some level of scientific theory and extrapolation (though I'd have to say, not much). The story itself, as we all know, is straight from *The Count of Monte Cristo*. How Romantic do you want to get? But Bester fucks with the conventions, makes Foyle an anti-hero, an Everyman. He treats jaunting and PyrE as nova, weaves all these elements together into something that combines the best of all three approaches to SF.

Their Unrealised Potentialities

Bringing it all back to the idea of suspension-of-disbelief, the game SF plays, more often than not, is to play the alethic modality of "could have happened" off against the alethic modality of "could not have happened." It's rare for an SF work to simply collapse back into the pathetic narrative by explaining *everything*, and rare (though maybe less rare—and quite common in the visual media) for it to excuse itself as formulaic Romanticism where *anything* goes. But it's also rare, I'd say, for an SF work to not utilise excuse or explanation at all, to remain purely conceptual. Rather, those excuses and explanations become mechanisms for sustaining the tension, for offering little releases here and there, little placations which mitigate the sense of incredibility enough that the reader gets drawn into a more intense state without suffering incredibility-overload and getting kicked out of the story.

If you look at some of the most novum-saturated SF—like *Neuromancer*, say—the denseness of the environment is mitigated heavily by borrowings from the noir idiom, by constantly reminding the reader that this is a thriller, so it's okay, 'cause this sorta wild adventurous hokum is acceptable in a thriller. And by reigning the time scale in to a very near-future, extrapolating low-level computing and information technology rather than space travel and immortality and other such Grand Science, Gibson achieves a hard edge, an illusion of plausibility. This is perhaps one of the reasons why cyberpunk took off so well; it was able to utilise all three techniques of dealing with the incredible—to excuse, to explicate and to exploit—with incendiary results. Hell, look at that opening line about the sky being the colour of a TV set tuned to a dead channel. Its voice is noir (excuse,) its description is bleak naturalism (explication,) and it's simultaneously the opening statement of the conceit that permeates the novel, artificial reality (exploitation.)

We could break the field down into subsets of SF narrative which *only* explicate, *only* excuse, or *only* exploit, but in truth all three techniques may be present in any one narrative. More importantly though, if the hypothetical novum is only a particular type of quirk that can be exploited in a certain way this raises the question of its comparison with other types of quirk exploited the same way. What about the complementary counterfactual and metaphysical quirks which offer us deviations other than innovation? If these errata and chimerae lack novelty they have their own power in the resonance of their unrealised potentialities. We can expect to find them explicated and excused too, and we can expect to find them, like the novum, thoroughly and gorgeously exploited.

And unrealised, I'd note, is not the same as unrecognised. Whether it's a matter of explication, excuse or exploitation, tapping the trope-trove or adding to it, reinventing or replenishing, the power of the quirk is such that for all the gulf of propriety between the uptown district of Literature and the downtown district of Genre, the estrangement I'm dealing with here is far from being the sole province of the latter.

A List of the Most Laudable

It had to happen, that turning of the tables in the Bistro de Critique. For years, the distinctly literary approach of many writers in the ghetto wasn't just inviting comparisons with their forebears and contemporaries in the uptown district of Literature; it was demanding it. A critic could hardly help but see the influence of Vladimir Nabokov in the work of Jeff VanderMeer, say, or of Franz Kafka in the work of Jeffrey Ford. The walls of the ghetto slowly weakened as writers like Michael Chabon and Jonathan Lethem tunnelled under them to pass freely back and forth; and eventually those walls came crashing down, a brave new world emerging from the ruins, a world foreshadowed by the placement of Kelly Link's *Magic for Beginners* at #3 in *Time* magazine's Top Five Books of 2005, alongside Kazuo Ishiguro, Salman Rushdie, Ian McEwan and E.L. Doctorow. In this new day and age, it was inevitable that deserving works of SF would finally catch the eyes of the literary establishment.

As far back as 2008, in fact, an article in the *Times Online* set out the fifty greatest British writers since 1945. It was the sort of utterly subjective list which says more about the people who put it together than anything else, but kind of interesting for that reason. If the *Times* doesn't count as literary establishment, after all, what does? Whether we agree or disagree personally with the names on it, this is a list of the most laudable, not in the sense of the most objectively worthy, but in the sense of the most feasibly lauded, of those who the compilers feel secure in placing on their little pedestals.

In the Bistro de Critique that list might have passed without much notice, but I remember laying it out on the counter of the SF Café, and grinning to myself. Looking at this list, you see, you have a handful of poets:

1. *Philip Larkin*
4. *Ted Hughes*
23. *Penelope Fitzgerald*
31. *Derek Walcott*
36. *Geoffrey Hill*
39. *George Mackay Brown*
47. *Alice Oswald*
48. *Benjamin Zephaniah*

You also have a couple of non-fiction writers:

40. *A. J. P. Taylor*

41. *Isaiah Berlin*

You have a grand total of ten writers who have worked solely within the genre(s) of realism, contemporary or otherwise:

7. *V. S. Naipaul*

12. *Iris Murdoch*

20. *Anthony Powell*

21. *Alan Sillitoe*

25. *Barbara Pym*

30. *John Fowles*

33. *Anita Brookner*

37. *Hanif Kureishi*

45. *Colin Thubron*

46. *Bruce Chatwin*

You have two writers who've worked in the popular genre of the spy novel:

14. *Ian Fleming*

22. *John le Carré*

Of the rest, well, we'll separate out the writers who've played around with historical and prehistorical fiction, because while these could be seen as artificially constructed elsewhens comparable to those of fantasy or alternate history, they're more exotic than fantastic in its common usage (the incredible with implications of the chimeric and/or the marvellous), and we wouldn't want to push a point. So:

3. *William Golding*

26. *Beryl Bainbridge*

49. *Rosemary Sutcliff*

Then, however, you have a whole bunch of fiction writers, all of whom have, at some point in their career, written works which utilise the strange in its strangest mode—nova or chimerae, disruptions of credibility, the alethic modality of could not happen. Some writers have worked with a sort of slipstream blend of naturalism and the unreal, some have only written one or two works utilising a strange conceit of some description, and some are best described as magic realists (or even Magic Realists, if we want to consider the approach a closely definable, marketable category.) But more than a few have written what we'd call *science fiction*, *fantasy* or *horror*—and in the outright Genre usages of those terms):

2. *George Orwell*

5. *Doris Lessing*

6. *J.R.R. Tolkien*

8. *Muriel Spark*

9. Kingsley Amis
10. Angela Carter
11. C. S. Lewis
13. Salman Rushdie
15. Jan Morris
16. Roald Dahl
17. Anthony Burgess
18. Mervyn Peake
19. Martin Amis
24. Philippa Pearce
27. J. G. Ballard
28. Alan Garner
29. Alasdair Gray
32. Kazuo Ishiguro
34. A. S. Byatt
35. Ian McEwan
38. Iain Banks
42. J. K. Rowling
43. Philip Pullman
44. Julian Barnes
50. Michael Moorcock

That's twenty-five of the *Times Online*'s fifty greatest British writers since 1945. Which is to say fifty percent. As opposed to ten dyed-in-the-wool realists. Which is to say twenty percent, over that last half-century and a bit—where of all time periods we should expect to see the mimeticists privileged over purveyors of the strange, of the incredible and marvellous.

Ah, yes. I still remember thinking wryly of how this was at odds with the ghetto mentality of us genre kids: yeah, that damned mainstream with its literary establishment, always pissing on our genre cause they're, like, mundanes, so boring, so banal. All they'll ever take seriously is that dreary, dull, depressing REALISM stuff... Yeah!

Even as far back as 2008 the writing was on the wall, the names of twenty-five bona fide writers of strange fiction scribbled in black ink graffiti on a stall in the toilets of the Bistro de Critique. This was the shape of things to come.

The Last Realist

—No SF novel ever won the Booker, they say in the SF Café, damn near every year, when that season comes around. In the SF Café, every year when that plaudit is about to be announced, we can expect more of the same old same old, mutterings about the absence of *genre fiction* from the shortlist. But this is what's happening right now in the Bistro de Critique:

In the Bistro de Critique, the Last Realist comes staggering out of that toilet stall, dishevelled and haggard, eyes wild with visions of the future he's a fugitive from, visions of geeks and freaks lauded for writing tales of singularities and superheroes, visions of the *Untermenschen* pouring out of the ghetto of Genre, storming the Bistro de Critique.

—There's a Reign of Terror coming! he cries. Well, a Reign of HORROR, strictly speaking…and FANTASY, and that sodding freaking SCIENCE FICTION too. An Unholy Trinity of the Unreal. Oh, they don't always call it that—they're fucking sneaky that way—but it's…it's…*genre fiction!*

He collapses into a chair, slumps forward, head in hands.

—We just didn't see it coming, he moans. I mean, no SF novel ever won the Booker.

He looks down, kicks his heels.

—I mean, okay, sure, Rushdie got the Booker of Bookers with *Midnight's Children*, and but that's not SF, albeit you could maybe argue it's a work of fantasy, I guess. And, okay, sure, we teach Spenser and Milton, Shakespeare and Blake in the Temple of Academia. And, okay, sure, we always had a lot of time for Kathy Acker, Mikhail Bulgakov, Angela Carter, and…well, too many to mention, really.

He coughs nervously.

—But that's not the point. Thing is, the question was never whether any SF novel deserved to win the Booker, as much as it was whether any novel that deserved the Booker was really SF. Like, *Midnight's Children* may be a work of fantasy, but it ain't FANTASY, see? You and I know that; it's LITERARY FICTION. Hell, even the genre bunnies got that; why else would they talk about *literary fantasy* or *literary SF*? As if those weren't oxymorons!

He slumps further forward till his head rests on the table, buried in his arms, his words (and sobs) muffled.

—It used to be so simple. We had them in their place with the whole *literary/genre* thing. Spenser, Milton, Shakespeare, Blake—when they tried to co-opt the canon to their cause we just laughed, said they were appropriating ancestors for a spurious validation. And as for Acker, Bulgakov and Carter, they aren't *genre* writers, we said. If they aren't generic, how can they be *genre*?

—But everything changes, he tells the gathered literati.

In the Bistro de Critique of twenty years into tomorrow, he's now the only one left still scorning the grand claims of all the genre kids, insisting that it was the realism in the magic realism that made these works great, that *Midnight's Children* may be *fantastical* but it's not really *fantasy*; that no SF novel will ever win the Booker, and for good reason; that *The Road* winning the Pulitzer doesn't count. Oh, but he should have seen it coming.

—Am I too late? he says. What year is it? Have they given the fucking Nobel to Doris Lessing yet?

The Librarian's Sad Smile

In a corner of the Bistro de Critique sits a spy—one of us. In another timestream just a step to the left, she might be a bookshop assistant arguing the merits of a counterfactual category of COMBAT FICTION. Here in this elsewhen, she's a librarian with a taste for good SF, listening to the time traveller's tale with wry interest, with a sad smile.

Oh, yeah, baby, she thinks. You should have known. Didn't Moorcock get the Guardian Prize for one of the Cornelius books? And can't we geeks and freaks happily claim *The Cornelius Quartet* as bona-fide, honest-to-God SF? Moorcock is ours, a Grand Master of the SFWA, no less. He's written New Wave SF and SWORDS & SORCERY, and even CONTEMPORARY REALIST novels like *Mother London* that put your shit to shame, motherfucker. He's a one-man goddamn emporium of literary experiments, but one thing we know for sure: he's one of us, a genre kid. And while Moorcock and others like him have published straight-up balls-to-the-wall pulp fiction, Moorcock and others like him have also created masterpieces that—to use the fucking tired old fucking phrase—*transcend the genre*.

To the librarian that phrase is articulated with an irony that inverts the implicit admission of limitations, revealing a deeper truth: that over forty years ago we realised it wasn't about rising above the boundaries but about tunnelling under them, burrowing down through the bowels of the city, wiring ourselves into its nervous system. In this era of SF defined in negative space, redefined by every act of indefinition that comes when we slap that nominal label on whatever we can sell as SF, to transcend the GENRE means to expand the idiom.

Not that you'd know this from the talk in the ghetto, where those deep tunnels under the SF Café have become a haven from the incognoscenti, a safe and cosy *Watership Down* warren for genre kids become genre bunnies. We poke our noses out, sniff the air and the merest scent of fox or farmer in the air sends us scurrying back to safety. We peer out of the rabbit hole, peek between the blades of grass, but we're blinded by this myxomatosis rife within our warren, spread by our living in such close proximity, a disease of timidity that leaves us sightless and frothing at the mouth, twitching in delirium, whimpering about the lack of respect given to SF, how those howwible elitists at the Bistwo de Cwitique don't wike us.

The librarian has the same sad smile whenever she sits in the SF Café, listening to that kvetching. Mostly, she'd rather be there than in the Bistro de Critique, but whenever award season comes around, man, the genre bunnies do tend to get agitated. Like, they're out to get us, all those straw literati, the farmers and the foxes of the self-defeating fantasies that keep us cosily in our little burrow. It's a cold, hard world out there. And we don't deserve it, you see. We've shown them how good SF can be, how cute and fluffy and eminently likeable we are, and they still don't wike widdle us. They must be nasty, cruel, vicious. Oh, yes. Foxes and farmers bad, rabbits good. SF community good, literary establishment BAD.

Lemme just load up my flamethrower here, and put it in the hands of our librarian. Don't worry; we're torching the Bistro de Critique as well. Let the whole sorry shithouse go up in flames, I say.

Of Kudos and Catches

So no SF novel ever won the Booker. So fuck? Screw the Booker; awards don't mean shit. What we're really talking about here is kudos, the currency passed back and forth in every conversation at the Bistro de Critique. That's what we really want, the kudos that we feel our favoured works are due. Bookers and Nobels are only indexes of that literary credit. Strip away the talk of canons. Focus on valid comparisons within the timescale of SF—the last fifty years or so. For a measure of the modern classic then, let's turn again to a little work of absurdist comedy offering a depth of character and theme that makes most SF books look like the teenage wank-fantasy of a Hollywood schlockbuster charlatan…and that makes most mainstream books look like the mid-life crisis of an under-aspiring MFA tutor. Let's take Heller's *Catch-22* as an example.

We don't want the Booker. We want the due respect that would be given freely to our equivalent of *Catch-22*, if our GENRE of SCIENCE FICTION was as counterfactual as COMBAT FICTION, our exemplary works of SF published without the damning label. Or at least, that's what my figurative librarian wants. She happens to think *Dhalgren* is one of the seminal works of the twentieth century, period, that if it wasn't for the stigma of GENRE that goes with the SF label it would be recognised as such. That if *Catch-22* had been sold as COMBAT FICTION it might easily have suffered the same disregard.

The comparison is more than apt. The central idea of Heller's novel is, after all, a sort of speculative fiction, an invention of bureaucracy rather than technology, but a "what if" scenario nonetheless and, like an SF speculation, a structural element of plot and theme. What if there was an absurd regulation that put all soldiers in the double-bind of a no-win situation, a rule that any soldier seeking exemption from combat on the grounds of insanity must be, by definition, sane and therefore not exemptible?

With this crystal concept at its core *Catch-22* throws its main protagonist, Yossarian, into the horrific fantasia of World War II, the dystopia of humanity's inhumanity extrapolated from that rule. The rule changes throughout the book, becomes more general, a pataphor creating its own context. Eventually we come face to face with it in its most sinister form, when the US army closes down a brothel, taking the prostitutes away and validating all of this by reference to Catch-22. What law justifies their action? Catch-22. Don't they have to show this law, to prove it exists? No, the law says they don't have to. And which law is that? Why, Catch-22, of course. The core concept here is as incredible as a fair whack of Kafka.

For all its non-linear construction, *Catch-22* is an utterly accessible book, using humour the way SF uses strangeness, to give the reader a pleasure they wouldn't find in many dreary realist tomes. It dances, it plays, it gives the reader a ludic inroad to its thematic kernel, all the while developing it to intrigue us, horrify us, point us back at the reality being satirised, re-presented in an imaginative transformation. It shows us the unreal so that we see the real within it. Not unlike SF.

A work which is both a commercial and a critical success, garnering as much cash as kudos. A popular work but not a populist one. A book which has achieved some degree of cult status and which should therefore, if we genre bunnies are right in our myopia of incipient myxomatosis, be excluded from the canon because of that cult status. The literary establishment don't like cult books, we think, because they are their own cult, worshipping at the kitchen sink, allowing no other gods before them but the One True God of REALISM. So why does *Catch-22* stand as one of the twentieth century greats when so many of our great works lie neglected at the bottom of the rabbit warren under the SF Café? Because it's not lumbered with the label COMBAT FICTION?

The prize-givings and prattle in the Bistro de Critique don't matter a fuck if that's the way it is. So a few fucktarded phonies there—those straw literati who may or may not be the big dealio we make them out to be—bind our strange fictions in our very own Catch-22: if it's SF, it can't be good; if it's good, it can't be SF. Feh.

Dude, these motherfuckers can be torched with the flick of a finger.

A Fancified, Fanciful Fancy

The Catch-22 that gives Heller's novel its name is a conceit. Not in the Petrarchan / John Donne / Metaphysical poet sense, but analogous to such, a suppositional fancy adopted for the sake of its figurative import. What exactly do I mean by conceit? Here's one definition:

> *An extended metaphor. Popular during the Renaissance and typical of John Donne or John Milton. Unlike allegory, which tends to have one-to-one correspondences, a conceit typically takes one subject and explores the metaphoric possibilities in the qualities associated with that subject.*
>
> **Silva Rhetoricae**

But this definition doesn't quite tell the whole story in its characterisation of the conceit as metaphor-writ-large. Looking at the definition of the word outside the realms of rhetoric, gives us a richer picture of its webwork of associations. So, from *Dictionary.com* we get a wider-ranging set of meanings, in which we find:

conceit:
- *a favorable and especially unduly high opinion of one's own abilities or worth;*
- *an ingenious or witty turn of phrase or thought;*
- *a fanciful poetic image, especially an elaborate or exaggerated comparison;*
- *a poem or passage consisting of such an image;*
- *the result of intellectual activity;*
- *a thought or an opinion;*
- *a fanciful thought or idea;*
- *a fancy article;*
- *a knickknack;*
- *an extravagant, fanciful, and elaborate construction or structure.*

Discarding the primary meaning of pride, paring away the redundancies, and splicing and dicing the attributes into a semblance of order, what we arrive at is the idea of a conceit as: an elaborate (*fancy, extravagant, exaggerated*) and fanciful (*intellectual, ingenious, witty*) construction or structure (*turn-of-phrase, passage, poem*) based on an idea (*poetic image, thought, opinion, comparison*). It all sounds rather fluffed-up, rather flouncy. Lurking somewhere in the connotations of those terms there's hints of flippancy, of being too clever for one's own good, of needless complexity. A conceit is an idea with an inflated ego, whimsy masquerading as the grandiose.

A fancified, fanciful fancy.

The futurological and cosmological suppositions which underpin SF (e.g. Bester's PyrE) are conceits adopted for the sake of a good story (i.e. as MacGuffins) and/or to make a point by concretising and extending a metaphor or metonym (as Bester's PyrE concretises what it signifies—power,) unleashing it to pataphor and representing its impact on characters and worldscapes, rendering it both plot device and locus of theme. For many, the use of an incredible conceit is sufficient to render a work fantasy. For many, the use of an incredible conceit based on arguable supposition is sufficient to render a work SF.

If we accept the absurd regulation at the heart of it as an arguable supposition, *Catch-22* is not just a good comparison to SF. It is SF. The conceit may be legal rather than technological, but so fuck? How many dystopias are based more on hypotheticals born of sociology and psychology than anything else? It's not a question of whether there are SF novels that measure up to *Catch-22*. The works of Ballard, Burroughs, Vonnegut—surely there's a list as long as my arm of books with power and insight and ambition to match

Heller's. Hell, there's *Catch-22* itself, if we want to look at it that way. Of course, if you have a problem seeing *Catch-22* as a work of sociological SF, maybe you feel the same with Ballard, Burroughs, Vonnegut. No matter. I'm always happy to point to pulp modernists like Bester who used their conceits in a more populist way. With only the odd James Joyce reference and typographical experimentalism.

The point? Twenty years from now, I hazard, the Bistro de Critique will have been rebuilt on the charred ruins of a discourse razed by the recognition that conceits are, you know, an effective tool for a writer, duh. Twenty years from now, I hazard, what's been going on in SF for the last fifty years will be blindingly obvious. Forget all those labels we use to obscure the emptiness of that signifier, *SF*, in an illusion of diverse "subgenres"—ALT HISTORY, SPACE OPERA, CYBERPUNK, STEAMPUNK. These are scribbles on sticky labels patched together with Sellotape to cover up the fragmentation of a field of countless forms, a confusion of comedies, tragedies, satires, adventures, parables, even allegories (though I think of allegory as rather a simpleton second cousin; if you're going to use the figurative as a means to the end of polemic, just write the damn polemic).

So, over the last half-century and a bit we've gathered together the good, the bad and the ugly of this…strange fiction into a cosy warren called SF, into a construction so complicated, so many tunnels burrowing this way and that, the cellar of the SF Café long since collapsed into one big hole in the ground, an empty space where meaning used to be. The ghost of SF howls in that abyss. The golem of speculative fiction stands on the edge, looking down into it, giggling insanely at the senselessness. At this…conglomeration of disparate works lumped together on the spurious basis that, well, there's something about them all we like. It has these "speculative elements." Like poetry using metaphors instead of eschewing them. Like a rock band using amps rather than deliberately going acoustic.

So that field is characterised by the use of these fancified, fanciful fancies—these conceits. These quirks. Twenty years from now, I reckon, scorning it for that will seem like cocking a snoot at a rock band for using amps.

Reverse the Polarities

The truth is, there's already plenty of strange fiction out there getting the kudos—like Rushdie's *Midnight's Children* winning the Booker of Bookers. McCarthy's *The Road* winning the Pulitzer. It's just that the absence of the label means these works aren't punted down into that rabbit hole of pulp, hidden in the darks of paraliterature. It's just they don't languish in our little warren of a marketing niche. It's just that a writer has to eschew the stigma of category fiction if they want a shot at the dicky-bow ceremony with champagne and hors d'oeuvres; they gotta ditch the emo makeup if they want to be made dux. No shit. Does it matter? If that *Times Online* list is anything to go by, they can just do whatever the fuck they want, and when the dust has settled, like as not, they'll be valued for what they are anyway.

In the meantime…?

In the SF Café, the day after the time traveller's arrival at the Bistro de Critique, our librarian sits with her comrades, playing devil's advocate, as they bitch about not getting invites to the uptown cocktail parties. What do they expect, after all? There's a whole lot of dross in the darks of the warren that is Genre.

—Hell, she says, we recognise the formulaic product for what it is, every time we segregate it out in an argument with an outsider, every time they dismiss the whole field with a reference to some heinous example of Hollywood wank and we shake our heads. No, we say, that's not proper science fiction. That's Sci-Fi. Do you seriously think they're ever going to get that?

We can't ignore the gaping disjunction between the formulaic product with its cardboard characters and prefab plots, between the potboiled pulp and the solid SF, the works that take Genre by the balls, squeeze hard and say, "We play by my rules." We talk proudly of our *genre fiction*, but where we diss the formula fare as *generic*, we're tacitly acknowledging that the good stuff is good because it treats Genre as its bitch. It takes a sledgehammer to the formulae, tears pulp into bits, chews it up, spews it out in huge spitballs to be sculpted into extraordinary forms. And we're acknowledging that the bad stuff doesn't. Then we're surprised that shilling shit with our shinola gives us a bad rep.

We live in the ghetto of pulp fiction, but disown it even as we do, playing the same game as our highbrow, high-society nemeses of the Bistro de Critique, with our very own version of their Catch-22, an irrational "We-like-it-so-it-must-be-SF" rule. They say, if it's SF, it must be bad; if it's good, it's not SF. We say the same of Sci-Fi; it's just that where it meets our standards of quality control we use the phrase *proper science fiction* instead of *proper literature*. Every movie or TV show we dismiss as Sci-Fi—is that really so different from some straw literatus insisting that William Burroughs was a Beatnik writing experimental fiction rather than some SF scribbler? We can bitch about Atwood denying that she writes science fiction, but is this really that different from an SF writer insisting that what they write isn't Sci-Fi?

—So no SF novel has ever won the Booker, says the librarian. So innumerable works of SF that stand on a par with *Catch-22* fail to garner the kudos they deserve because they're tainted by the stigma of Genre. So maybe it's time for us to reverse the polarities, think the unthinkable, speak the unspeakable, say: They're right, you know. Genre equals generic equals formulation. So maybe we shouldn't call it genre. Maybe we shouldn't call it SF. If the label is empty, do we need it?

If the great works of SF are lumped in with crud that shares, at most, some superficial features with it, in the same way that a John Wayne flick shares superficial features with *Catch-22*, it's no surprise it doesn't get the plaudits. Maybe it's time we stopped burrowing down to hide the best of SF in the bunny warren of tunnels under the SF Café. Maybe the day's coming when those strange fictions can just stand upright, walk out across the field and be met with dropped jaws and awed silence. Foxes turn tail and run. Farmers piss their pants in fear: My God, that book walks on its hind legs; that ain't like no bunny I've ever seen!

I mean, we can bitch about the Booker and the Bistro de Critique, but it don't mean squat if we're doing it from our hidey-holes, safe and sound in the delusion that we are and will ever be this little paraliterary thing called *genre fiction*. A *genre fiction* marked out by the fact it uses one particular tool—the quirk—marked out by the fact that it doesn't limit itself by excluding that tool, the way the genres of REALISM do. I gotta say, I'm not seeing that strange-fictional approach as in the weaker position here, binding itself with injunctions that narrow its scope with every strategy rejected. Far as I can see, the SF I'm talking about doesn't essentially reject any strategy. Like a lot of those works in the period stretching back from Huxley to Homer, I reckon, it doesn't see any fucking reason to.

Which seems a fairly natural approach to me, I gotta say. I mean, how exactly does using every fucking tool in the box not constitute the default condition of fiction? So we've had some fifty-odd years in which the realistas kept their shell game going, more or less, doing their best to sell the absence of the strange in their fiction as a marker of their serious chops. Meh. Give it a few decades and we'll see how the kitchen sink holds up against a fiction as fucked-up as our reality.

—Bollocks to the bunny warren, says our librarian. The ghetto is our past, but the whole fucking city is our future.

The Kipple Foodstuff Factory

The Leopardskin Print of Thrift Shop Drag

> *Good news for you, good sirs, that I am no longer Don Quixote of La Mancha, but Alonso Quixano, whose way of life won for him the name of Good. Now am I the enemy of Amadis of Gaul and of the whole countless troop of his descendants; odious to me now are all the profane stories of knight-errantry; now I perceive my folly, and the peril into which reading them brought me; now, by God's mercy schooled into my right senses, I loathe them.*
>
> **Miguel de Cervantes,** *Don Quixote*

So here I find myself, a ghetto kid in the city of New Sodom, sitting in the SF Café, drinking my black coffee as I scribble and scratch, slice and stitch, trying to make some sense of the turf wars and textual tricks. Here I find myself, somewhere after Delany and Disch, seeing a power in the very language of this stuff I call strange fiction, but seeing no small reason why that power might be damned to ignominy, saying:

—F'r sure, no SF novel has ever won the Booker. Yeah? And? So? What? Has any Crime novel ever won the Booker? Has any Romance? Has any Western? Let's simplify it: Has any work in any Genre of extruded formulaic pabulum you care to name ever won the Booker? Has any work in any Genre born of the fricking pulps, in any commercial marketing category specifically designed to target a niche with a promise of generic factory-line junk fiction ever won the Booker?

This is fuck all to do with an antipathy to strange fiction—that fiction born in the breaches of reality, be it fantasia or futurology (or both, or neither, for that matter). *Midnight's Children*. Booker of Bookers. Join the fucking dots. No, this is about junk fiction, about pulp fiction. So no novel with the tramp stamp of a Genre on its back ever won the Booker?

No shit.

The middlebrow, middle-class literati of the Bistro de Critique aren't about to invite a bunch of crack-addled whores and hustlers in red leather miniskirts or denim cut-offs to their cocktail parties. Just 'cause we all know the ghetto chic stylings and those who wear them well enough to tell the bohos from the hobos, don't expect the incognoscenti to. We see Tiptree-winning transvestite performance artists; they see tramp-stamped tarts in the leopardskin print of thrift shop drag. They see the bad rep that the ghetto has for a reason—because business is done on the street corners, johns passing through in their cars, pulling over at a painted face—pancake makeup gaucher than a 1970s cover illustration of Gully Foyle's tattoos. You have to be a regular down here to know that the guy or gal leaning in the driver's window, batting long black eyelashes as they barter, isn't promising the sort of good time that a stranger might expect them to be.

—Best mindfuck you'll ever have, baby, they're saying.

In truth, as we know, they're touting tickets for some whacked-out warehouse ninja gig with Warhol on the light show, Dallesandro dancing, Old Bill Burroughs croaking his crazed junkie rap over the beats. They're selling the address of a secret spectacle designed to blow your mind, but there's no way to know that unless you hang down here by habit. If you're just passing through, baby, all you see is another hustler climbing into some kerb-crawler's car, being driven off towards a sordid handjob in an alley somewhere out of sight.

Another book with a spaceship or a dragon on the cover, bought and sold, a few bucks for a shallow buzz.

—Hey, big boy, the next streetwalker says to yer passing member of the incognoscenti. I'll show you a good time.

—No thanks, says they with a discernible disdain and a wave of the hand. I don't really like Sci-Fi.

Cut to a lecture in the SF Café:

The Metaphysical and the Mythic

If we turn to the fourth narrative mode in Lake's taxonomy, the fiction of nomological quirks, we get to the root of idea that there's a qualitative difference between SF, which deals with science (the possible), and fantasy, which deals with magic (the impossible). In this model, fantasy is equated totally with a *mythic* narrative distinct from alternative / future narratives as that which involves nomological rather than temporal impossibilities, not erratum or novum but chimera.

In alternative / future narratives there is a synthetic elsewhen offered to resolve the "could not have happened" subjunctivity level by displacement forward or sideways in time ("could not have happened *now*"), but with the mythic narrative there seems, at first sight, to be no such get-out clause. Where the nova or errata are largely temporal impossibilities, the quirks of mythic narrative are *nomological* impossibilities, events which entirely contradict the laws of nature. In Delany's theory of genre he describes the subjunctivity level of fantasy as "could never happen" (his naming of the city of Nevèrÿon, indeed, seems quite significant in this context), and this seems to be an apt description of the mythic narrative as Lake outlines it.

However, we have already noted the fact that many of SF's quirks are also metaphysical aka nomological impossibilities, events that breach the laws of nature; they are chimerae masked as nova. We've also noted (albeit implicitly) that the quirks of works classed as fantasy may be far subtler than a crescent sun, hell, may be even subtler than jaunting or FTL, as with the example of Peake's *Titus Groan* where the nomological impossibility is so subtle as to be almost not-there. The castle of Gormenghast is big. It is *incredibly* big, so big that it may well evoke a sense of incredulity, the alethic modality of "could not have happened," so big that one has to wonder if it could actually support its own weight against gravity. But this chimera of an edifice is the nearest that this fantasy novel comes to "magic," in the quirk of the castle, in the conceit of a reality which can support such marvellous/monstrous scales of construction.

Still the distinction is there. The elsewhen of *Titus Groan* isn't a parallel reality, based on a counterfactual where one upper-class family isolated themselves in a mansion, which just grew bigger and more self-contained over centuries. Nor is it a future reality based on a hypothetical where the class system has been extrapolated to a post-technological environment of grandiose decay. It's more of a metaphysical dislocation we get with the novel, a sense that this world is somehow run on a less complex set of rules than our own. This world is simpler, more basic. The nomology it exhibits is more crudely functional, one that has abandoned the limitations and equations of engineering that would rule out a castle of such immense size. If we can step forward or sideways to elsewhen, we can also—

Cut:

In the Closet

We rile at the response of the incognoscenti, but that handwave of dismissal—I don't really like Sci-Fi—that unconsidered condescension that sends many a genre kid into waves of apoplexy is not hard to figure, really. What they're saying is, *I'm just not looking for a handjob.* Skeezy strip joints, clip joints, lurid neon signs of dragons wrapped round dancing girls, cock rockets firing for the skies, the streets of Genre are a gauntlet of gaudy promises—CHEAP THRILLS! CHEAP THRILLS! CHEAP THRILLS! Come and get it, baby, every corner of the ghetto proclaims.

—No thanks, they say. I don't really like Sci-Fi. I'm not looking for cheap thrills. And a penicillin shot.

Our faces burn, our fists clench, when those hoity-toity literati cock their snoots and roll their eyes at our protests that this is arrant prejudice. Cheap thrills? Fuck you, asswipe. But you know, we're really sorta standing there, in our red leather miniskirt or our denim cut-offs, saying, Hey! I'm not a whore. I'm not a hustler. I'm a professional masseuse! We're wearing our mother's hip-hugging skirt, baby, our big brother's butt-snuggling cut-offs, and most of the time we *are* promising thrills, the sensationalism of sense-of-wonder, a fiction driven not just by the incredible but by the marvellous, the *shoulda* in that *coulda shoulda woulda been*, whether it's dragons or Dyson spheres. We are the slatternly faggot sons and legs-akimbo slut daughters of a whore mother and the patchwork monstrosity that is Frankenstein's mob, hookers and hustlers just like Momma was and every bit as insatiable as our innumerable dollar-dishing daddies. And it's time we made our peace with that.

Sure, if we do pick up some incognoscenti on some metaphoric corner, if we get them back to our ghetto crib and that MODERN PULP heritage all too suddenly rears its heads—SCI-FI, you say?—well, we can shove the parents in the closet, slam the door behind us, and shout over our hidden horror's thumps and protests: "It's not SCI-FI! It's science fiction! It's SF! It's speculative fiction! We can be literary too, damn it! Don't you oppress me with your elitism!" They're just gonna blink uncomfortably at our sudden irrational hostility, at our strange unfathomable defensiveness. At the really loud cry of "I am SCI-FI! Hear me roar!" coming from that closet behind us.

—So what's with the crack-whore pimp-daddy beast of a thousand cocks in the closet? they say.

—Not us, we say. We're with Mary Shelley and Jules Verne, H.G. Wells and George Orwell. We're a class act, baby. And it's only ten bucks to go around the block with us. Just give us a try and you'll see!

—A warehouse ninja gig thing, you say? A rave with performance art on the dance floor and a salon of literary discourse in the chill room?

—Totally! We just give our tickets to the guy in the sex shop, and he'll let us round back, past the toilets and the back-room poker game, downstairs to the basement S&M dungeon and...why are you looking at me like that? Like I'm trying to finagle you into a clip joint?

And they back away slowly...baaaack away slowly.

—Maybe we could just go for a burger? you shout after them. I know this great little joint called the SF Café.

Not that we can persuade them there either.

Cut:

A White Whale Which is God

An even more subtle metaphysical conceit might or might not be found in *Moby-Dick*, depending on how far we read the White Whale as a metaphor of the divine—God or Leviathan, God-*as*-Leviathan—a theme bolstered by the naming of Ahab and Ishmael, and the heightened Biblical quality to much of the prose. There is a deep sense of strangeness to Melville's novel, a sense that the events are incredible, that the whale is not just metaphorically but literally Ahab's divinely-ordained nemesis, a chimera. But does that conceit require a displacement to a fictive elsewhen? Such a displacement is possible but not necessary. It's possible to read the White Whale as a metaphysical force, not just a real-world whale but an actual representative of Fortune, Providence, God. But at the same time, it's not required. The crucial question is whether the symbolic feel does or does not sever us from a subjunctivity of "could have happened."

For me the answer is "not quite." It reminds me of Thomas Hardy's use of Providence or Fortune, or of the Greek idea of hubris and nemesis, but this seems quite in keeping with the Providentialist metaphysics of the time Melville was writing. Coming to it from outside that Providentialist context you could argue that it *now* reads as taking place in a different metaphysical elsewhen (which raises all sorts of issues about whose metaphysics we're using as the starting point), one where the divine manifests itself through actions and synchronicities. The level of synchronicity and manifest meaning Melville offers us, however, is within the parameters of his idiom. Which is to say, Melville doesn't breach the suspension-of-disbelief any more radically than Hardy, Dickens or any number of contemporaries. This may only be to say that the mythic, even for these "realist" writers, is not entirely disallowed in favour of the mundane, that it bleeds into their work just as the absurd and the monstrous do (together, for example, in the form of Dickens's grotesques).

The distinction I'm trying to draw here is between works which simply utilise a different metaphysics and those which knowingly and deliberately breach suspension-of-disbelief with a chimera—i.e. with a quirk that is accepted as contrary to the metaphysics of the writer (and, the writer presumes, the reader) but which is entertained for its significance. It is a slim distinction, but there is a point where literary techniques of coincidence, synchronicity, foreshadowing, etc. (which can be quite over-the-top in novelists of that Providentialist period but were, to all intents and purposes, par for the course) become substantive and integrated, crystallised and emboldened into the metaphysical conceits which give us the mythic narrative.

Here's the thing: Ultimately, if *Moby-Dick* pushes us to the limits of suspension-of-disbelief, it does so in a way that is as tragic as it is mythic. The White Whale is as terrible as it is incredible, more so, and Ahab himself a figure of terror and pity. The whole novel is more the story of Ahab's self-destruction than it's an exploration of a chimera, the metaphysical conceit of a White Whale Which is God. But it's interesting that a lot of strange fiction readers and writers connect with Melville's book, sense a kindred spirit in it, and I'd suggest that this connection is because it does something we recognise. What it is doing, or what we are reading it as doing, if we see the White Whale as an actual avatar of divine nemesis, is offering us a build-up of these quirks—Queequeg in his coffin like the reverend of *If…*, Ahab's summoning of St Elmo's fire, the sea itself as a strange realm of what Farah Mendlesohn terms the portal-quest—to an eventual crisis of strangeness that reads as mythic.

Cut:

The Kipple Foodstuff Factory

The Kipple Foodstuff Factory sits at the heart of the ghetto of Genre, spewing out noxious fumes from its blackened brick chimneys, spewing out poisonous effluvia into the river from its rusted iron waste-pipes, spewing out lorry-loads of processed and packaged foodstuffs to be delivered to every café, bar and diner in the ghetto. Built in the first half of the twentieth century, it introduced the city to the very idea of junk food. Burgers, fried chicken, fish-n-chips, kebabs, you name it, the KFF created an entire industry in its boom; and it's still churning out its own brand of schlock, though it's been in competition now for over half a century with the countless cooks (and capitalists) who, as employees, tweaked its recipes (and recipes for success) until the shoddiness was just too much and they just had to strike out on their own.

You can get a far better burger than a KFF schlockburger these days, from any number of soul food entrepreneurs. It's hard to get worse. The Kipple Foodstuff Factory gets its raw resources from the city dump and the sewers, essentially reconstituting shit into schlock, a sort of pseudo-meat one step away from Soylent Green. (And the right colour for it, if undercooked, to the extent that KFF Burgers were affectionately dubbed "boogers" at the gastronaut conventions of the 1950s, a moniker that spread to burgers in general and has persisted to this very day in public parlance.) But the Mob seems to have a thing for KFF products, rich as they are in crack cocaine, and nobody in the restaurant business wants to piss off the Mob, so the owners of eateries across the city serve those KFF schlock products, regardless of the fact that they have zero nutritional value and highly variable toxicity levels; hey, if it keeps the Mob happy…

As loath as we might be to admit it, they serve those boogers in the SF Café, and people buy them by the shitload, the glopping gruel of extruded pulp, thickened to solidity with gosh-wow technotoys and adolescent geekwank, pure formula fare. That's not all that's on the menu, of course, not by any means. The fry cooks down here in the ghetto of Genre are every bit as skilled as many a master chef in the uptown bistros of Literature. From the basic ingredients through to the methods of preparation, their cuisine has little in common with the dreck of mass-extruded KFF products even though it shares a menu. You won't find those production-line values here, no design-by-committee-and-focus-group, no franchise bullshit. The best and the brightest—even the middling and mediocre—are often working without a recipe, or at very least playing fast and loose with various recipes, getting creative with the classics.

There are real burgers here too, then, burgers that are made by hand—made to a recipe as old as the hills, for sure, and hardly haute cuisine, but an honest kind of junk food that puts the extruded KFF shit to shame even when we're talking patties of the crudest kind, adventures in space shaped by subtexts of neo-fascist wish-fulfilment, cleverly-crafted thought experiments revealing only some poor scribbler's utter incomprehension of human behaviour. Asimov's cardboard characters. Heinlein's descent into didactic drivel. We're not talking Michelin stars, baby. But at its best, this is our soul food. It's seldom just a burger, really. It's a cheese'n'bacon-burger or a chiliburger. Pepper and onions ground in with the beef. Big chunks of jalapeño in the chilli. Refried beans on the side. It's a burger with an extra kick, an extra tang that grabs you by the taste buds, tells you someone actually put a bit of effort into making this hit the spot.

There's even some crazy fusion going on in the SF Café kitchen, real cordon bleu cuisine that in a different context might be labelled "culinary cooking" (like, yanno, "literary fiction"). In the SF Café you'll find quirks filched from Fantasy, Horror, Western, Noir, you name it, all cooked up daily, just as fresh and just as spicy as the Pomo Chilli of the Bistro de Critique. The chefs in both kitchens apply the same grab-bag approach to writing, where anything and everything might be thrown into the mix. Hell, the ingredients of that Pomo Chilli—nanotech, spaceships, remote viewing, future dystopias, Lovecraftian gods, Sumerian mythology, climate change, robots, aliens, hard-bitten detectives, historical characters, and so on—they learned that shit from us. We cannibalise the bona fide pulp fiction of every fucking Genre around. SF as it stands now is a crazy cuisine of countless forms and flavours.

Down at the greasy spoon SF Café there's lots of tasty fast food on the menu. Soul food or Savoury Food or speculative fusion—it has a lot of names. The KFF boogers are sold as take-out from a little window in the front, but walk inside the door and you'll be hard-pushed to find a single patron actually eating that crap. We all know better. You'll find a whole fucking lot of them eating burgers rather than steak tartare, but that's hardly surprising. And the tournedos Rossini can hardly be called unpopular. That's the stuff we really rate, of course, not junk food at all, but fine fare that we know the literati of the Bistro de Critique would be jealous of…if they would ever deign to taste it.

Still, it's little wonder those incognoscenti are resistant when we try to coax them down to the SF Café, tempt them with the treats in store; cause there's a motherfucking massive KFF franchise sign in neon outside, lit up night and day. And it's little wonder our insistence on the glories of the menu doesn't shatter the shackles of prejudice and lead naysayers into the light; 'cause in our insistence that there's Sci-Fi and there's proper SF, that there's boogers and proper burgers, somewhere along the way, somehow, it seems we've become…a little over-zealous in abjuring the soul food with the schlockburgers. 'Cause God forbid anyone confuse what we call SF, what we call burgers, with the junk it was born from and still shares a menu with.

Cut:

To Be Written as a Palimpsest

Science fiction represents the modern heresy and the cutting edge of speculative imagination as it grapples with Mysterious Time—linear or non-linear time.
Frank Herbert

How then do we reconcile this mythic narrative with alternative and future narratives, the chimerae with the errata and nova?

The mythic narratives of the past, written in worlds where geography was as undeveloped as history and science, generally apply a comparable technique of spatial dislocation rather than temporal dislocation; the laws of nature need not apply everywhere, so travel far enough from home and one might well find chimeric inhabitants of chimeric realms. So, in Sumer, we get the Heaven of Anu visited by Adapa, situated in the sky, and we get the Kur of Ereshkigal visited by Inanna, situated in the earth; we get the underground source of all fresh-water springs in the Abzu of Enki, we get Dilmun as the same deity's Edenic island (possibly modern-day Bahrain), and we get the remote lands visited by Gilgamesh, the sacred Cedar Forest of the giant Humbaba, and the valley of the sunrise where Atrahasis lives, guarded by scorpion-men. In Greece we get the underground netherworlds of Hades and Tartarus, Hyperborea in the farthest North, the Hesperides in the farthest West. And so on.

In the context of the times, whether we understand them as literal or symbolic theories, these alterior landscapes can be considered hypothetical conceits of geography rather than technology, foreign elsewheres rather than future elsewhens, beyond the known world just as the future narrative is beyond known science. In the cosmology Christianity inherits from Jewish apocrypha, we find this notion of metaphysical elsewheres systematised and abstracted into seven heavens above, seven hells below and seven earths between them, a multiverse of alterior realms. The idea that these realms constitute afterlives, and the disjunctions from our temporal world that this creates (to eat the food in most is to be bound there forever), is abstracted to the Eternity of a God beyond time itself (and yet existing in his own linear process of time—thinking, acting). In its purest articulation the spatial dislocation becomes that of *inside* and *outside*, the Great Below and the Great Above of Inanna reformulated as the Deep Within and the Great Beyond, the immanent and the transcendent. The Outer Space of these narratives is Outer Time.

These geographical elsewheres, then, converge with ideas of temporal cycles, such as the Greek idea of the Golden Age, the Hopi and Maya ideas of the "Fifth World," or the Ragnarök of Norse myth which implicitly positions the world of the Aesir before ours via the survival of the Völsungar as ancestors of humanity. With the mythic narratives of many cultures, built from the errata that are yet to become known history in the hands of Herodotus and suchlike, there is often a sense of a discrete Age of Myth, an age of gods and demigods and giants walking the earth. The very beginning of the world, in cosmogonies such as that of Hesiod, is posited as a process of generational development—Ocean and Chaos begetting Day and Night, Earth and Sky, and so on, the ordering of reality as the laying down of strata of (meta)physical principles. In these cosmogonies creation is evolution, the accretion of complexity as the (meta)physical features of the world develop from the basics of darkness and light to the intricacy of living beings. Each day is an utterance, an iteration of the cycle, laying down a sedimental strata of form upon the cosmos.

The Deluge is perhaps the most significant symbol in this context, an emblem of the cleaning of the slate that separates a primal era (emergent from chaos and therefore containing the chimera *of* that chaos) from the latter-day known world, this world with its strangeness expunged in the transition from prototype to product. The Deluge is a scouring of the vellum upon which reality has been sketched out in rough forms, from first principles, in preparation for the narrative of our world to be written as a palimpsest over that which came before, cleanly delineated in bold ink, consistent and complete. Here, in this positing of a before-time, we see something akin to the common conceptualisation of fantasy realms as set in a cycle of time before our own, a history before history.

Compare Delany's portrayal of and proposed translations for the name of his pre-historical fantasy realm, *Nevèrÿon*—"across never," "across when," "a distant once," "across the river," "far never," or "far when"—the way they point not just to distance in time but to a partitioning of time (and by water). Parse the term *metaphysical* itself into its root morphemes—the Greek root *meta-* originally meaning "with" or "after," but now often used to mean "beyond" or "above," to convey a sense of a *higher order*. Compare our notions of *higher planes* of existence, the *super*natural, the *profound* (from the Latin *fundus*, meaning "the bottom," "the deep"), the *urgrund* (ur-ground) as a base substratum.

Bring together these fragmentary articulations of a root metaphor from a modern context in which the world is a ball in space and our orientation defined by gravity, and the interior/exterior relationship of one model becomes equivalent to the up/down relationship of the other. I am not suggesting that this is how the ancients actually conceived of the metaphysical relationship between their known world and the alterior sphere(s) of divine order, but I am suggesting this as a logical extension of the proposed model: that in the face of chimerae, we re-orient ourselves, parse our estrangement as a conceptual dislocation in what we might think of as a third temporal dimension—an *up-down* axis of time orthogonal to the *forward-back* and *side-to-side* axes of the dislocations associated with the novum and the erratum; that we can conceptualise the metaphysically alterior world as an elsewhen with no more difficulty than that involved in imagining the elsewhen of a future or parallel world.

Cut:

A Conversation at Cross-Purposes

—Come on in, baby, we tell the incognoscenti. This is a proper burger joint, the real deal.

—No, thanks, they say. I don't really like boogers.

—Don't call them boogers, we bristle. They're burgers.

—Sorry, they say. I know you take your boogers really seriously, but—

—Burgers! Boogers and burgers are totally different things.

—Whatever. Look, I don't really eat junk food at all. I like culinary cooking.

—But proper burgers aren't junk food. They're nothing like that shit the Mob goes for. Hell, they're real food, unlike that hoity-toity culinary cooking. Fucking vegetarian tosh. I mean, come on, look at that. Doesn't it look tasty?

—Uh, sure, but that's steak tartare. I thought you said this was a burger joint?

—Steak tartare's just a fancy way of pretending what you like isn't really burger! But it is. See the red meat? See? Burger!

—It's raw. Boogers are cooked.

—Burgers! And they don't have to be cooked. The chefs in the SF Café long since moved on from that fry cook junk food stuff. That's, like, Trad burger, Golden Age burger. The New Wave did away with all that; and we're still finding new ways to make burgers. Look at this! Appetising, right?

—Yes, but that's pâté.

—And this.

—That's tournedos Rossini. Looks nice.

—And this.

—That's chilli con carne. Sure, I like a good chilli, but that's just…cooking. It's not a burger.

—But it's all red meat! So it's all burgers! Or what are you trying to say: if it's a burger, it can't be good; if it's good, it can't be a burger?

—No, I'm saying it's crazy to call a bowl of chilli a booger.

—Burger!

—Whatever! Look, culinary cooking isn't limited to that cheap ketchup and fries approach, but a burger is a patty in a bun. With ketchup and fries. That's basically all there is to them. Like those.

—Oh, for fuck's sake! Those aren't proper burgers at all. Dude, those are boogers. Typical! You think that's what all burgers are like cause that's what fricking Planet Hollywood sells as burgers. But that patty-in-a-bun junk food bullshit has nothing to do with actual burgers. Planet Hollywood is, like, decades behind the SF Café. Our burgers aren't limited to—what?

—The fuck are you on? Look, *that* is steak tartare. *Those* are burgers.

—No, they're boogers. *That's* a burger. You just won't accept that burgers can be every bit as good as culinary cooking.

—Bollocks to this. You're nuts. I'm out of here.

—Go on then. But you can't dismiss all burgers as boogers if you're not even going to try a proper burger.

But they're already backing away slowly, looking past us at the chimneys of the Kipple Foodstuff Factory that tower over the skyline of the ghetto, wondering what crazy-inducing chemicals they spew into the air here.

Cut:

The Discourse of Argument

The result is three forms of narrative—alternative, future and mythic—based on three forms of quirk—counterfactual errata, hypothetical nova and metaphysical chimerae. All three types of quirk perform in equivalent manners: each breaches the "could have happened" alethic modality, presenting a challenge to suspension-of-disbelief; but each can be and is rationalised as a sort of temporal displacement; with each the reader transforms the disruptive sense that this "could not have happened" into a sense that this "could not have happened *now*." Even where the quirks are metaphysical chimerae, this does not prevent the reader from constructing a synthetic elsewhen in which they *could* have happened. The conceptual relocation in the mythic narrative is simply in a different direction, so to speak, to that of the parallel or future narrative.

Crucially, this renders that elsewhen *arguable*. It is not arguable within the discourse of *science*, but then neither is the counterfactual elsewhen, which is arguable instead within the discourse of *history*. Rather than posit the metaphysical elsewhen as a qualitatively different type of construct, I would suggest that it is entirely arguable in the discourse of *philosophy*. Despite what their names might suggest, Nevèrÿon, Neverwhere or Never-Neverland do not throw the reader into realms of absolute impossibility; they assert themselves as outside the sphere of temporal (technical / historical) possibility, but even as they do so they remain open to, and may even invite, explication as suppositional approaches to nomological possibility, explorations of the potentials of nature rather than of history or science. We can understand these quirks in precisely those terms, as figurative signals of the discourse of argument—history, science or philosophy; where the counterfactual argues with known history and the hypothetical argues with known science, the metaphysical argues with known nature.

Cut:

Of Burgers and Boogers

Of course, not all burgers are schlockburgers. We know that all too well in the SF Café. We've moved on from the days when the clientele and the cooks lacked a sophisticated palate, when it was ketchup and fries with everything, because that's what you do when you're cooking for kids. But the whole burger/booger distinction is just kinda cracked. All those "It's not Sci-Fi! It's SF!" remonstrations just sound sorta nuts, all the more so when we're disowning the soul food with the junk food, all of it, as ersatz boogers, in flagrant denial of the fact our Golden Age SF was born from exactly that. Or when blind loyalty to the tribe has us proclaiming steak tartare a type of burger, scorning the incognoscenti whose rampant elitism must be what leads them to deny the true nature of raw mince, veil it with some fancy-ass name.

Truth is, you will find burgers on the menu in a lot of uptown restaurants, not seen, in that context, as junk food, but still basically burgers. Down in the SF Café, we discuss examples of uptown's "culinary cooking"—dishes by Atwood or Roth, say. We bitch of how these are blatantly burgers, just like ours—but not so good, we say often, as attempts to reinvent the wheel, hamstrung by ignorance of our conventions, the proper way to make a burger. Sometimes we make sense, sometimes not: that dystopian dish *The Handmaid's Tale*, for sure, that's ground beef in a patty, flame-grilled and served on a bun; the beef stew of *The Plot Against America* is not a burger by any stretch of the imagining, though, except in the wacky zeal of true believers who've seen stew served as burger over and over again in the SF Café, yeah? And besides it has red meat in it, so it must be so. Even if the meat is actually venison.

Not that this makes Atwood or Roth SF writers, mind. In the SF café they're seen as outsiders, part-timers. Up in the Bistro de Critique, meanwhile, the very suggestion would be laughed off as a blatant attempt to appropriate the cream of culinary cooking for the sake of prestige. As another grab by those ghetto-born geeks with hard-ons for the future, pointing at Wells or Verne, Shelley or Orwell, say. As if you could call Orwell's dystopia a burger when he's tackling the twentieth century head-on, reimagining Stalinism and fascism from his direct experience of it during the Spanish Civil War, not telling some Boy's Own Adventure of battling squids in space. These are sophisticated chefs, not fry cooks of junk fiction, dishing out burger novels full of fat and sugar and salt and artificial flavourings, all crafted in absolute obeisance to a traditional recipe! What next? Is Kafka a Horror writer just like H.P. Lovecraft, just exactly like H.P. Lovecraft, because *The Trial* is dripping with fear and paranoia, its main character pitted against profoundly disturbing irrational forces?

It's hard enough to get the incognoscenti to see past the absence of ketchup and fries with something like Atwood's work, the fact that it's not handed to you by a spotty adolescent who needs to learn some hard truths about personal hygiene—to persuade them that actually this isn't how most burgers are served in the SF Café. It's hard enough to sell them on the truth that extra ingredients of good prose and characterisation can render a work "culinary cooking" by their standards and not stop it being a fucking burger. It's not going to get any easier if we ourselves shroud the whole discourse in an artificed dichotomy of burgers and boogers.

Especially not when we're pointing at steak tartare as an example of good burger. Or when we ourselves are ignoring the cheese, the bacon, the chilli, the jalapeños, the refried beans, etc., on the patties of ground beef that remind us just a little too much of our pulp roots, when we're so desperate to highlight the steak tartare we'll happily find some spurious rationale to sweep aside all the pulp, all the junk—the soul fiction with the schlock fiction—in a distinction between burgers and boogers that defies all logic.

—It's not Sci-Fi, we insist, It's SF.

Every time you say that a Venusian Slime Boy dies, you know.

Cut:

The Dimensions of Estrangement

One thing to make clear: While the metaphysically dislocated elsewhen of the mythic narrative as I'm outlining it is clearly suggestive of the secondary world of fantasy, this model is at odds with many definitions of those elsewhens as essentially inarguable (alterior rather than alternative realities), and of fantasy as a whole as distinct from SF precisely by its alethic modality of "could never happen." In this model, even if secondary worlds and fantasy are distinct in other respects, that differentiation is questioned.

Taken solely as a model of the mythic narrative, this is not a substantial contradiction of the model of fantasy predicated by John Clute in *The Encyclopedia of Fantasy*. One key distinction emerges however, where Clute considers fantasy not just a matter of stories understood by their authors and readers to concern the impossible, but as a *project* in and of itself, one which requires the scientific worldview of the Enlightenment to set the boundaries of what is and isn't possible—the laws of reality—in order that realism can come into existence first. *Fantasy* and *the fantastic* are defined by their negation of the realistic, as a "counter-statement to a dominant worldview."

In this model, that scientific worldview is not required, with the quirk defined in broad terms as any disruption of the suspension-of-disbelief by a response of incredulity—the sense that an event "could not have happened"—here in conflict not with laws of reality as defined by science, but rather with the reader's individual nomology, their concept of the laws of nature. As a theory of the techniques rather than the genres of fiction, for now I'm more interested in trying to identify its relationship to various projects in literature (e.g. tragedy or comedy) than identifying it as a project in its own right. This narrative form based on metaphysical quirks can and should therefore be considered in a far wider context than the Enlightenment, anywhere we can expect to see such a nomology. If it's tempting to equate the chimeric with the fantastic we might want to bear that in mind; there may be project here, but if so, it is no more post-Enlightenment than tragedy and comedy are.

There is more to Lake's mythic narrative than metaphysics however; in his description, these fictions deal with "things which never actually happened, or could have happened in a *literal reading*, but *encapsulate important truths* for the tellers of the tale." There is a specificity in the italicised phrases that we should be wary of, an implication that we are to understand the mythic narrative as intrinsically metaphoric, the chimera as symbolic rather than just strange. This adds an additional requirement that is not applied to alternative / future narratives; and the assumption it suggests is reinforced by the sense of archetypal symbolism associated with the term *mythic*. It should be stressed that this model implies no such assumption.

For this reason, the alternative / future / mythic narrative nomenclature is going to be discarded from here on in, in favour of a taxonomy of the nature of the conceit itself—i.e. counterfactual / hypothetical / metaphysical—or the quirk—i.e. erratum / novum / chimera. What we arrive at with this model is not a taxonomy of texts anyway, not a system of genres (e.g. ALTERNATE HISTORY, SCIENCE FICTION and FANTASY) so much as a system of the *dimensions of estrangement* from which we *construct* genre (or at least begin to). It is this estrangement, in whichever direction or combination of directions, that is at the heart of all strange fiction, and it is the basic equivalence of the act of dislocation, regardless of direction, that underlies the historic and aesthetic unity of the field, whichever label we apply to whichever of its myriad permutations.

Cut:

The True Face of SF

We've had our backs to the closet door too long, running that bullshit mantra over and over in our minds: Oh, that's not proper science fiction; that's the schlock of SCI-FI; that's half FANTASY, half Hollywood, half whatever—half something else that any fool can see is not the True Face of our valid literary form, said True Face being all serious and shit, all furrowed brows and bearded pondering. If it's not good, it's not SF, we say. What kind of sneering elitist are you, disdaining our genre on account of all this schlock that doesn't count, no sir, not one bit?

Man, that's a killer strategy, that is, an awesome way to persuade the incognoscenti that we're not crazed hokum junkies, high on hackwork, trying to pimp our addled euphoria to anyone who passes. Yeah, vehement denial that we've got anything to do with the crack-whore pimp-daddy beast of a thousand cocks locked in the closet. Bitter accusations of snootcocking snipewankery when they *point out* that crack-whore pimp-daddy beast of a thousand cocks in the closet. Offended outrage when they assume the mindfuck we're touting is a cheap handjob, just because we're, like, standing on a street corner dressed to sell our arses. And because our first words to a prospective customer just happen to be "Hey, big boy."

Some of that good old-fashioned ghetto attitude—yeah, that'll totally persuade them that not every honking big sign for a massage parlour means what they think it does in this part of town.

Fuck that shit. Let's open up the closet, let the beast out. Let's all of us go on *The Jerry Springer Show*—My Parents Are Trash and So Am I. We'll throw a few chairs around, get weepy and maudlin, and have done with it once and for all. There's nothing wrong with pulp as pulp, no *proper* way to do fiction in this postmodernity, no need to scorn sweet GENRE's entertainments just because they might be dodgy art by some uptight arsewipe's Victorian value system. So they might be hokum at the best, hackwork at worst? Escapist pandering? So fuck? What are we, Puritans, disdaining pleasure for its own sake? Bollocks to that. Screw the sentiments of Cervantes's Quixote. I love the junk fiction I grew up on, pornography of wonder that it was. I love my slutty slapper of a harlot mother, 'cause, ya know, she does give real good head; a million teenage boys will testify to that. I love her monstrous bestial mate of a million base appetites, the pimp-daddy dragon to her Babylon, 'cause he's nothing if not generous, and a boy's gotta eat. And in another world, elsewhen, they'd both be seen without the filter of petit-bourgeois propriety and prejudice that paints them as trash because Cock forbid fiction actually be dynamic, visceral, *sensational*.

But let's not bullshit the bullshitters.

When the incognoscenti back away, saying they don't like SCI-FI, it's the formulaic junk of MODERN PULP that they're rejecting. And if the acronym *SF* always expands, for them, to *schlock fiction*, if they don't get the wacky way that we abjure the strange tautology (to them) of *formulaic genre fiction*, the way we point them at an utterly implausible oxymoron (to them) of *literary genre fiction*, if we lose them in our rookery of overloaded terms, it is in part because we're shrouding sense in daft denials, disacknowledgements of where we came from, where we are now, what is and always will be going on down in the ghetto.

We wouldn't be here without pulp, without the schlock we're all too keen to point away from when it comes to lineage. If the True Face of SF is all furrowed brows and bearded pondering, it also has a rather lurid shade of lipstick, and metallic eye shadow that makes early Bowie look subtle. Why shouldn't it? Strange fiction is queer fiction, kids.

Cut:

A Sort of Metaphysical Equilibrium

If we are to see the metaphysical narrative as utilising a third vector of dislocation in a 3D timespace, a Z-axis to the X and Y of counterfactuals and hypotheticals, then the logical question is whether these chimerae are treated in the same way. In other words, do writers use the same techniques we have identified to validate these metaphysical unrealities, to prevent the collapse of suspension-of-disbelief? Do they explain them, excuse them, exploit them?

The simple answer is *yes*. Here's another nursery rhyme as illustration:

> *There was an old woman who lived back in Mu.*
> *She had so many children she didn't know what to do.*
> *She gave them some broth and marked all their heads.*
> *She cursed them to die, but was killed by the dead.*

In the elsewhen of this variation—the mythical land of Mu—causality works in a whole other way to the world we know. A word, a will, a "mark" can act magically on the world. Dark magic, however, may well come back and bite you on the ass. There's still a sense of cause and effect, a sense of logic, and people still clearly need to eat to survive, but the rules of the game are different. The metaphysics is different.

But there is a level of (albeit implicit) theory and extrapolation here which aligns this rather folkloric metaphysical fiction with those ALTERNATE HISTORY or HARD SF forms of fiction which seek to explicate the how and the why of the implausibility. We should recognise in this story an idea of reciprocity in magic. In many metaphysical fictions the systematic nature of magic will be spelled out. We'll be told that there are underlying principles—*As above, so below*; *Like affects like*. We'll be told that magic utilises elemental forces—fire, earth, water, air. We'll be told that there is black magic, white magic, sex magic, death magic, that a spell aimed with evil intent will lead to ill effects on the user. And so on. This type of explanatory approach seems so persuasive, indeed, that there's a whole New Age industry of neo-pagan craziness aimed at those who seriously believe this stuff.

The point is simply that there is a form of (explicatory, pathetic) narrative which utilises the chimera but seeks to return the reader to a subjunctivity of "could have happened" just as the (explicatory, pathetic) narratives which utilise counterfactual and hypothetical conceits do.

The folkloric vibe of this variation of the rhyme, it strikes me, is related to a *moral* component to that explication. The metaphysics of this world is one in which good and evil are active forces. To act wrongly, using magic to kill, disrupts a sort of metaphysical equilibrium. In response, the metaphysical order seeks to restabilise itself. Action leads to reaction. The dead return to revenge their murder. This is the moral logic of the fairy-tale, where the wicked will meet their comeuppance and the good live happily ever after, the moral logic of the generic Romanticism we find published as Fantasy. (It is, of course, also the moral logic of the generic Romanticism we find published as Alternate History and Science Fiction. It is, of course, also the moral logic of tragedy.)

As another example, here's that rhyme rewritten into the fantastic idiom by its most closed definition (chimeric and marvellous), in its most generic form, the Fantasy of elves and dwarves, heroes and maidens:

> *There was an old dragon who lived in Caer Dhu.*
> *She had so many hatchlings she didn't know what to do.*
> *She gave them some maids to eat as their bread.*
> *A knight came and killed her and cut off their heads.*

Imagine this narrative expanded into a ten-volume saga of several-hundred-page volumes heavily detailed with pseudo-historical worldbuilding; it's not hard to see that we have narratives which use the same mix of explication and excuse we find in Alternate History and Science Fiction. There are clear traditions in Fantasy that tend to explicate or excuse, for example, a conceit such as the "Big House" of *Titus Groan*. In one tradition, it might be explicated with some sort of theoretical Stone Magic, explaining how these towers upon towers don't collapse under their own weight; if the "hardness" of SF lies in the explication, maybe we should be talking also of *Hard Fantasy*. In another tradition, it could simply have been built by giants, elves or angels, excusing the implausibility with conventionality; if this works in SF, with the grandiose structures left behind by ancient alien races, maybe we should also be talking of *Epic SF*.

In *Titus Groan* however that implausibility becomes part of the pataphoric resonance, part of the meaning of the conceit. One obvious tenor for this Big House is the country estate of Edwardian society (often dubbed, indeed, the "big house" by locals), which itself can be read as metonym of that entire society—overbuilt to the point of incredibility. It is redolent with the potential of its own collapse. The architectural conceit, the societal structure of the characters, the style of the prose, and the plot all play off one another. Both SF and fantasy have their Hard and Epic varieties, utilising excuse and explication in different measures, exploiting the incredible, building it to a crisis of spectacle, but both have their more Conceptual flavours, to steal a term from the field of visual arts.

Cut:

That Pornography of Wonder

So, yes, our slut mother, MODERN PULP, is a crack whore who gives blowjobs for ten dollars a pop. Or maybe MODERN PULP is the pimp as our Old Man, the patriarchal ponce of pleasure selling the Muse's pretty mouth. Or he's a raddled junky gigolo. Or she's a molly-house madam. That's what GENRE is, what it does. It gets down on its knees, unzips your fly and uses all the sensual skills of its slick tongue to give you a few minutes of loveless but ecstatic pleasure. And there's a lot of that in us, MODERN PULP's brood of similarly hopped-up hustlers and hookers. Oh, there's also a whole lot more, another sire or dam—a Frankenstein's monster of another mother or father in the *modernism* part of *pulp modernism*—but our cribs are here in the ghetto of Genre.

So the literati of the Bistro de Critique dismiss the fiction of that whole domain, that *genre fiction*, out of hand, can't see all the shinola for the shit. So when you show those self-same literati some shinola ripped out of that context, then they'll laud it to the heavens. So they'll blithely then dismiss all claims that it belongs with junk as junk, because, well, it's not junk but genius. That's not prejudice; it's just that half the time the discourse is completely fucked by our sophistic double-thinks, our schizoid denials of the stark reality.

Generic fiction sucks as art by most standards. Pulp fiction, junk fiction, sucks as art. It may not suck at all as what it is. Rather than mere extruded product it might be fine handicraft, simple but solid, substantial in its own way. It might be soul fiction that's full of fat and salt and stuff that just ain't good for you but that tastes fucking delicious. But as literature designed to give us a quick fix of formulaic figuration, nothing more, it sucks as art. Fiction that does *not* suck as art, does not suck as art because no matter what tropes and techniques it shares with that pulp fiction, it does not gain its primary power from their familiarity; we might well get a similar high from similar ingredients, but we'll also get fucked up in a whole other way, from a deeper weirdness than wonder. It is not just a derivative retread of hoary conventions made to fill a hole. It is not recycled pabulum, commercial dross designed to satisfy an appetite for escape. It's not just that pornography of wonder, that loveless pleasuring. Hey baby, me show you good time! Ten dollah, suckee suckee.

Zzzzzzzzzzip.

—Oh, baby. You make me feel so good.

But that reality makes it a little awkward when you're living deep in the ghetto of Genre, when you've grown up loving soul fiction but the whole discourse says that pulp is—and can only be—a schlock fiction every artist should abjure in shame; so our distinctions between "literary" and "generic" GENRE FICTION, between SF and SCI-FI, emerge as a desperate misdirection from the overwhelming predominance of that sensationalist hokum:

—Don't look at the slut behind the curtain fellating the fourteen-year-old boy. Ignore the junky gigolo on the nod in the toilet, blissed out on his fix of fascist power-fantasy! Look over here, look! Look at the dancing fingers!

Fuck that shit. The only distinction worth making is between the grifters who play the shell game of formula fiction, taking cash from the punters for a moment's thrill without even a hint of handicraft in their hackwork, and the grafters whose writing actually has an ounce of creative effort, even if it's all put into the purest and most pandering pulp. The grafters may not be making great art by most standards, the handjob of hokum they're offering may be shallow and loveless, but it's only the formulaic pap that's truly without substance, not just loveless but gutless, spineless, soulless. Fuck that Kipple Foodstuff Factory schlock. But when it comes to pulp fiction in general…fuck any bullshit preciousness that would lead us to abjure its lusty excesses. So it's got a bad rep, and for some damn good reasons. Deal with it.

Respect is for schoolmarms and church ministers. This is New Sodom, not New Sunday School.

Cut, with a switchblade, with a quirk, rusty or razor-sharp:

The Ground Ever-Shifting

Here's another rhyme:

> *There was an old goddess who lived with Anu.*
> *She had so many children she didn't know what to do.*
> *She made them some humans to cook them some bread.*
> *But Marduk got angry and cut off their heads.*

Here there's no explication, no attempt at explication, and indeed there's a certain illogic to the whole sequence. Why make humans to make bread if you're a goddess and could just skip the middle man, make the bread yourself with your awesome goddess powers? Why does Marduk just get angry all of a sudden? What the fuck is this story trying to tell us? For the modern reader, the use of the Sumerian template here—rather than, say, a more familiar Greek or Christian or Judaic set of tropes—may render the story entirely incomprehensible. The fantasia is not idiomatic.

If you know your Sumerian myth you can probably fill in the gaps. Marduk, see, he's a young and dynamic warrior god who supplanted Anu round about the time Babylon became the big power in Mesopotamia. The old goddess who made humans is clearly an example of the Middle Eastern mother goddess, probably associated with grain (the bread), and probably usurped along with Anu. Her children, who got their heads cut off by Marduk—that's clearly a reference to the Sumerian equivalent of the Titans, Tiamat's monstrous brood who were defeated by Marduk. Because there was a shitload of them stirring up trouble. Compare the apocryphal giants, the Anakim, wiped out in the Flood of Genesis. Cross-reference to the Annunaki, the underworld gods usurped by the younger Igigi. And so on.

If one is familiar with the traditions of character, background and story-structure this is based on, then the narrative is not entirely senseless. It's a bit short for a proper epic poem, but expand it into a few hundred lines with the right conventional epithets and repetitions ("There was an old goddess who lived with Anu. There was an old goddess who lived with the God of Heaven. There was an old goddess who lived with the Father of the Gods"), and it might seem you end up with the metaphysical equivalent of those narratives which excuse their implausibility as Romantic adventures where anything goes in the name of a good story. But not all conventions are Romantic, and the conventions in which this narrative is rooted are anything but pulp tropes. A Sumerian audience would certainly take that rhyme a whole lot more seriously than your average Space Opera fan takes his interplanetary romance. Ultimately, if we were expanding that narrative to the length of a modern novel, the writer would probably have to introduce both explication (of the Sumerian context) and excuse (by casting the struggle in a contemporary Romance idiom) in order to make it comprehensible.

Or alternatively they could just run with it as is, exploit that very strangeness, the sense of disorientation caused by the rules working in some unfamiliar or wrong-feeling way. Ultimately, there are narratives which keep the ground ever-shifting beneath the reader's feet by sending constantly conflicting signals, shifts in alethic modality that play off against each other, maintaining the tension, building it to the outcome, and doing so with little concern for any differentiation between counterfactual, hypothetical and metaphysical quirks.

We need another term for all these narratives considered as a whole. We need a term which captures that breach of subjunctivity level while making no assumptions about its nature (singular or composite—a step sidewise, forward, down, or in multiple directions at once) or what will be done with it (whether it will be explained, excused, exploited or some mixture of the three). We need a term which doesn't assume inviolable boundaries between this here, that there and whatever elsewhen.

That term, I'd suggest, is *strange fiction*.

There is a fourth dimension too, born of logical impossibility, the quirk of the sutura.

Cut, and stitch:

THE SECRET CUISINE

Miso Soup at Midnight

Night in the city of New Sodom. A librarian sits in the SF Café, looking out on the ghetto of Genre. The whole place has become a little chi-chi over the years, beatnik artists moving in above the brothels and the crack dens. Might almost forget it's the ghetto, if that avant-garde street theatre troupe out on Mass Market Square didn't blend in with the hookers and hustlers, make it all look like just one big sensual experience for sale. And whenever she swings by the Bistro de Critique, friends shudder at where she hangs: *That dive?* The librarian takes this in her stride. There's no point whining about your area being badmouthed when your next door neighbour runs a crack house and, well, you do like a bit of a puff on the old hash pipe now and then.

A status update scrolls across the lenses of her mayashades: epistemic modality detected—*is not happening*. Curious. This is meant to be non-fiction, she knows, reportage. She can suspend her disbelief, pretend an epistemic modality of *is happening* is at play here—just as she would with any fictive narrative in present tense—but it's unsettling to realise she's just a figurative device. But hey ho.

Hey ho indeed. Fact is, Genre is a dirty and disreputable part of town but it's that way for a reason, and at the end of the day, the librarian kinda likes it. This is a place where freaks and weirdos feel at home. The bars here are more fun. The rent is cheap. And Mass Market Square is way more dynamic, exciting, and relevant than the uptown galleries full of middle-class bores clinking champagne glasses and droning on about how jejune the latest wunderkind is really, darling, just so trite, really, overhyped. There's a trade-off between the social stigma and squalid trappings of the Genre ghetto and the freedom that it gives to work outside the tight-ass strictures of "proper literature" which until recently also meant the tight-ass strictures of CONTEMPORARY REALISM.

Until recently. A change is in the air.

She looks out at the Kipple Foodstuff Factory that dominates the skyline, but sees also, through her mayashades, hints of a future screamed of by a time-traveller in the Bistro de Critique—the fallen walls of the ghetto, gourmet guerrillas from the slums pouring out into the city. And beyond maybe.

As a traveller once, she remembers walking into a Japanese restaurant in a little town in North Carolina. Cool, she thought. Japanese: miso soup; tempura; ramen; noodles hot and spicy; tang-rich food to make your taste buds tingle. But no. No miso soup on the menu here. Swear to Cunt what you had was:

Beef in soy sauce with rice.
Prawns in soy sauce with rice.
Chicken in soy sauce with rice.
Beef & Chicken in soy sauce with rice.
Prawns & Beef in soy sauce with rice.
Chicken & Prawns in soy sauce with rice.

Or, hey, wow, the Special…

Beef & Chicken & Prawns in soy sauce with rice.

Fucking awesome.

Here now, in a booth of the SF Café, she sips the miso soup she couldn't get that day. The exact miso soup she couldn't get that day. It's a quirk, you see, a little rupture in the mimetic weft of her mundane narrative, the stream of stuff that she's pretending is happening. This now…this is an event that could not be happening. Fuck the epistemic modality; this is alethic modality we're talking now, not factuality but possibility.

She could be sitting in a booth, looking out a window, but to be sipping the actual miso soup she couldn't get that day, here now at midnight in the SF Café…that's an impossibility of level…what? She's not sure if it's known history, known science, the laws of nature, or the strictures of logic itself that have been ripped apart to drag that miso soup out from the nowhere to the here now.

Frankly, she doesn't give a fuck what level impossibility it is though. She's got miso soup at midnight and it's fucking tasty.

The librarian jaunts.

Figurae Generated and Combined

In this 3D-time model of counterfactual, hypothetical and metaphysical conceits, the inclusion of one type of conceit does not preclude the inclusion of one or both of the others; any potential combination is available. Stephen Fry's *Making History* offers us the classic combo of novum and erratum in the invention of a time-machine that allows the prevention of Hitler's birth. Philip K. Dick's *The Man in the High Castle* skips the novum, simply positing a counterfactual reality in which the Nazis won WW2; the introduction of the *I Ching* as a tool for divination, however, presents the reader with a metaphysical quirk, a chimera. In Bester's *The Stars My Destination*, the jaunting is another such chimera, a magical ability to wish oneself elsewhere presented alongside the hypotheticals of space travel, asteroid mining and so on. Where proponents of HARD SF argue that the inclusion of magic in a narrative renders it fantasy rather than SF, this is a prescriptive application of the label that does not map to the field, many of the most respected works in the canon, in truth, being profligate in their mixing of quirks.

In this model, it is not that certain tropes (dragons, FTL, etc.) function as ingredients that suddenly transform the genre of a narrative (to FANTASY or SF) just by being dropped into it. Nor, for that matter, do we suddenly transform the genre of the narrative again (to SF or FANTASY) if we only add or subtract another ingredient of plausibility. Essentially, in the model of strange fiction based on shifts in narrative modality, we are reversing the polarity, treating those "contents" (errata, nova and chimerae) as the end results of a literary technique of estrangement, the *effects* of strangeness rather than the *cause*. These quirks—dragons, spaceships, magic, FTL—are not things which, in and of themselves, make fiction strange. Rather they are the epiphenomena of an underlying process of semiosis, figurae generated and combined to create meaning, gaining their symbolic power by their application. Genre is not a question of which trove of tropes one uses, of a characteristic set of quirks; rather it is a quality emergent from the underlying dynamics of modalities, the nature of the impossibilities and our affective responses to them—the uncertainties and ethical imperatives too, if we include epistemic and deontic quirks in our scope along with the alethic and boulomaic.

A simple analogy would be to map this 3D time idea to the trinity of primary colours—red, yellow and blue—not simply as shades in their own right, in their purest forms, but as the dimensional qualities which define the shades we encounter on a painter's palette. The private narrative sticks to the muted tones of charcoal-and-chalk, painting its picture of "things as they are" in subtle shades of grey. The strange narrative may splatter glaringly gaudy primary colours in the centre of the canvas—counterfactual red, hypotheticals yellow, metaphysical blue—but it may also work in combinatory mixtures of those primary colours—oranges and greens and purples. Most shades of strange fiction might even be "natural" colours—ochres and umbers and ambers rather than the bold primary pigments of a child's paint pots. Or coppers and golds and silvers as much distinct for their *sheen* as for their *shade*. The division between SF and fantasy is about as sensible at times as a division in an art gallery between "Orange" landscapes (*Sunset in the Desert IV*) and "Blue" landscapes (*Winter Ocean at Night, Moonlit VII*), the science/magic distinction between SF and fantasy as superficial as the colour of the foil in which the writer's name is embossed on the cover of a tatty paperback sat on a table by a bowl of miso soup.

On Adamantium Pinions

We imagine genres as delimited by formal strictures—like the sonnet's fourteen lines and volta. This need not equate to formulation any more than Oulipo constraints do, but we can't deny it does. As the librarian looks out on the Kipple Foodstuff Factory, she's looking at the impact of mass-production in the twentieth century, the pulp boom that was built on formulation. All of the genres boxed and shipped as category fiction did become codified with strictures of form by which more of the same could be churned out, schlockburgers made to recipe from Soylent Brown.

(Soylent Brown? It ain't people, but it comes from them.)

Still, from the start there was an insatiable demand for ongoing détournement, soon even the bricolage of tropes stolen from WESTERN, NOIR, ROMANCE, and who knows what else, the result a hydra-headed hybrid of formulae—the collage, homage, pastiche and parody cooked up by the likes of Farmer and Moorcock, yes? We imagine this to be what makes the menu in the SF Café so peachy keen: New Wave Chilli; Cyberpunk Pad Thai; New Weird Rogan Josh; New Space Opera Bolognese. We imagine it's the ceaseless recombination of recipes.

The librarian glances at the menu on the window that don't have none of them fancy foreign words. All it says is:

1) *SF Special Hamburger (However You Want It)*
2) *Fantasy Special Fried Chicken (Just How You Ask)*

The librarian can't remember if she ordered the miso soup she couldn't get that day in North Carolina as a Number One or a Number Two. It doesn't really matter to her, not half as much as the local rag's food critic at the next booth over, who just described his coq au vin as "transcending the genre."

Every time we use the phrase "transcends the genre," she knows, we surrender to the corollary of positing genre on formal strictures—that our fiction essentially made to formulae must become other than itself to become good. We invite the literati of the Bistro de Critique to sneer, as if we were poets touting our sonnets as "genre poetry," trite doggerel made to the fourteen lines and one volta formula unless—aha!—one sonnet throws off its shackles, transcends those strictures, becomes great. It is a vacuous valorisation of novelty over substance to imagine a missing line or an extra volta is what makes a sonnet great. It's also wrong, an insult to the genre that fails to understand—to write a sonnet should be to eschew formulation anyway.

This is how *genre* becomes a dirty word, indeed, how it comes to carry the stench of puked up schlockburgers, overflowing the gutters, filthing the sidewalks, trodden underfoot and carried everywhere we walk. How can we bitch about the snootcockers of the Bistro de Critique when we ourselves laud our exemplary works as rising on adamantium pinions, unchained from the Augean mire we've made. Behold the dark horse, loosed from stables of writers shitting!

For the love of Cock, she thinks, we hail the works of Aeschylus and Euripides as Greek Tragedy. We don't extol them as transcending genre, as if to write a Greek Tragedy back in the day would obviously have been derivative hackwork.

A Glint of Hypothetical Gold

It is possible to apply broad taxonomies based on the tonal qualities imparted by an artist's palette: This artist does not just use red and yellow, we might find; they use counterfactuals of copper leaf, hypotheticals of gold foil, seeking to suggest the sun and all its solar symbolism of day, of the noon world shown crisp in the shining light of reason. This other artist does not just use blue, we might find; they use metaphysicals of silver, seeking to suggest the moon and all its lunar symbolism of night, of a dark world picked out in the low light of mystery. We have a whole culture of cross-wired metaphors to tell us how these aesthetics are so deeply distinct. SF is golden, solar, masculine, scientific. FANTASY is silver, lunar, feminine, magical.

How does an artist like Bradbury fit into this dichotomy though? Where do we place "The Veldt"? At first glance, this seems a simple work of Golden Age SF, our eye catching a glint of hypothetical gold in the holodeck playroom of the children; but as we are drawn into Bradbury's painting we see hints of metaphysical silver slowly building until, as we step back to look at the whole picture properly, we realise that the playroom is far more of a chimera than a novum. As the lions come to life, devour the parents (the playroom a monstrum now as well as a chimera), we realise that if we have been taken one step "forward" into the future we have also had the floor drop out from under us, fallen one step "down" into a different type of elsewhen.

Ultimately, the shared dislocatory effect which underpins these narratives unifies all the disparate forms into a single field of strange fictions, the quirk that creates that effect the nearest thing we'll find to the sonnet's "fourteen lines and a volta." There are negotiated (and renegotiable) conventions as to how that dislocatory effect is dealt with, whether we explicate, excuse or exploit the quirk, but even these bridge the genres as often as they divide them. There are different forms of strange fiction, just as the sonnet has its Spenserian or Shakespearean structures, but in many respects these are marked out more by how we parse the incredibility of the quirk in terms of affect than anything else. This is self-evident with horror, the genre defined simply by our emotional response. It is far from clear however, with SF and fantasy, where the binding of sense-of-wonder to one and the severing of appetence from the other has created the irresolvable clash of definitions and aesthetic territories I've referred to as the Great Debate.

That continuous conflagration is something I keep returning to here, partly because in all of this there's a part that keeps on asking, dude, isn't all this strange fiction you're talking about basically just fantasy by another name? And if so, why the fuck rename something that's already got a perfectly good label?

The Secret Cuisine

To understand what's actually going on in any idiom, any genre, we need to turn this model inside out. Forget the notion of genres as delimited by formal strictures. The strictures are techniques. With a volta this is obvious, but even the number of lines is not a limitation; it is a technique of economy and of structural patternings—two sevens, two sixes and a two, three fours and a two, four threes and a two. Those techniques are core components, conceits around which individual works develop an entirely original articulation, not boundaries on what that articulation can be.

You can make anything with the core components used in the SF Café—those alethic quirks. They are no more than a breach of the ongoing possibility of the narrative, after all, the injection of an alethic modality of *could not happen*. That is the technique at play in the SF Café's cooking, the secret ingredient that could be anything that could not be—by history, science, laws of nature, rules of logic.

No, there are no strictures on what you can do with the alethic quirk, only tribes of taste—look, see them now, as the librarian turns her head—raging for burgers only in the booths, fried chicken only at the tables, tribes of taste raging for proper burgers, proper fried chicken, tribes of taste raging against each other and against the chefs, with the insufferable petulance of the entitled. We do have our favourite recipes and the right, we think, to expunge all else from our café. We are a plethora of follies, not least in the fervour with which we howl injustice that the sating of our demands for "more of the same" should lead to derision.

Still, as the turf wars of the clans carry on, the librarian wouldn't give it up for the world. She has the miso soup she couldn't get that day. She might wonder why the chef doesn't head uptown to the district of Literature, but she asked him fifteen minutes ago and he simply smiled.

—The secret cuisine, he said.

So she'd ordered a Number One or a Number Two. It doesn't really matter because she didn't even specify how she wanted it, just gave a shrug: surprise me. And so, five minutes ago, he came out with the miso soup.

Truth is, the ghetto of Genre, every dive bar and greasy spoon in the neighbourhood itself, is a substrate that nurtures truly refusenik writers too. Sure there are those who sneer at miso soup. What the fuck, they say, is miso anyway? Some kind of animal? But they do buy a lot of burgers. So publishers piggyback off the sales of formula fare to support the secret cuisine that is the true heart of every genre. They know the demand for works which treat a technique as core component, as mere conceit around which the articulation is developed, prized precisely for its originality.

To deny this is simply ignorance of the historical reality and of the underlying mechanisms by which literature evolves. It's an ignorance born of blind desire among the tribes of taste. Among the literati it's born of the fact that when they do come slumming in the ghetto and end up in the SF Café, they see a menu of hamburger and fried chicken, and a host of culinary clansmen fighting over it, wordspittle flying at how the enemy's recipes are all schlock. And maybe while they're there, they'll turn to see the chef bring out a bowl of miso soup to the woman sat looking out the window at the Kipple Foodstuff Factory, and a plate of coq au vin to the man with the notebook at the table.

—This transcends the genre, they'll hear him say.

This is why the cuisine is secret.

That menu promising SF Special Hamburger (However You Want It) doesn't help. Miso soup is not hamburger whether it's served in a fancy uptown Japanese restaurant or in the SF Café. It's not HAMBURGER, HAMBURGER/FRANKFURTER, NEW GRILL, BURGERPUNK, HAMFURTER or FLIPGREASE. It's fucking miso soup. And the literati slumming it in the SF Café, watching the librarian sip her miso soup, they've seen it served as miso soup in that fancy new Japanese joint, Pomo, in the uptown district of Literature. They know it ain't a fucking burger. Must be a little quality cuisine slipped in, or some sly sleight-of-hand disguising of the dreck. They speak of miso soup served by some uptown chef, food critics raving of Ishiguro's *Never Let Me Go*. Which definitely isn't burger, they say a little too loud.

The atmosphere in the SF Café flips in an instant. It irks that they deny this is a burger. It irks that Ishiguro must have tasted the miso soup here, reconstructed the recipe. It irks that he failed to properly follow the formal strictures. It irks that Ishiguro gets kudos where our chefs don't. It irks that he didn't come from the ghetto of Genre, didn't sprout from the cracks in the literary sidewalk, struggle up out of gutters thick with filth. It irks that he didn't learn his craft in Mass Market Square, hasn't paid his dues. And now he's out there making miso soup just like our boys, denying that it's hamburger and getting lauded by the critics. How come he gets the kudos and our chefs don't?

The simple answer: because he didn't call it fucking hamburger.

The complex answer: this is not about burgers and recipes, constraints and kudos, struggles and dues; or it is in a way, but at the heart of it, where it matters, it's really about the secret cuisine, about the quirks that you can do anything with, that anyone, anywhere, anywhen can do anything with.

At the Heart of Sehnsucht and Saudade

When it comes to *fantasy* and *the fantastic*, the discourse that has developed over the decades with regards to this field of quirk-driven narratives is fraught with problems of indefinition and over-definition. For many, both terms are interchangeable and used in a wide sense, to signify the underlying aesthetic or approach of any work utilising quirks. The quirks might be the chimerae of Benjamin Rosenbaum's "The House Beyond Your Sky," or of Jorge Luis Borges's "The Book of Sand," but they might equally be the errata or nova of works that others would class as ALTERNATE HISTORY or HARD SF. More significantly, while there's a deep allure of the marvellous in Borges's idea of a book with infinite pages, that allure is not the driving affect of the story, and Rosenbaum's story is perhaps even more ambiguous, the world it presents more strange than most of us would wish for. If the terms *fantasy* and *the fantastic* are applied to work such as these it is not to be read as implying that we *yearn* for these conceits to be made real.

As the definition of fantasy is closed however we tend to see not just a focusing in on the chimera, but also on specific affects conventionally associated with it. There are those for whom fantasy is indelibly coupled with a sense of daydreams and reveries, defined by that yearning, by the boulomaic modality of *should*. Some disdain the genre as wish-fulfilment on that basis, but others see this as a deeper feature. The numina is at the heart of Sehnsucht and saudade, and to conflate these with the sort of cosy consolatory cock-fluffing Moorcock skewers in his "Epic Pooh" essay is shallow to say the least.

There is an aesthetic of the idyll we find in Ray Bradbury's "The Scythe," for example, even as it enters into the terrain of horror. There are stories like Jeffrey Ford's "The Annals of Eelin-Ok," a tale largely powered by a sense of loss in direct proportion to the quirky charm of its conceit. With stories like these in mind, it would not be a criticism to call fantasy the literature of desire. As much as a partisan of the open definition might seek to distance the form from any suggestion of consolatory purpose, the term itself does have its roots in the Greek *phantos* and its sense of making visible. To create a fantasy is, by one definition, to *fantasise*.

So. On the one hand we may have an open definition equivalent to John Clute's superset of *fantastika*, defined in his "Fantastika in the World Storm" essay as that fiction characterised by "contents" that are "understood to be fantastic," a definition that encompasses all sorts of (post)modernism and magic realist works, never mind SF, fantasy and horror. On the other hand we may have a closed definition roughly equivalent to Clute's subset of FANTASY, defined in the same essay in terms of a specific narrative grammar highly suggestive of yearning in its stages of Wrongness, Thinning, Recognition and Return/Healing.

The problem with the open definition is its denial of the sheer force of convention, the inseverable association of fantasy with yearning. One can dismiss as ignorance the apparent inability of the incognoscenti to get to grips with the notion that fantasy does *not* necessarily equate to wish-fulfilment nonsenses of magic, elves and dragons. But even Clute's narrative grammar is articulated figuratively in the imagery of FANTASY's conventional chimerae—heroes, wounded lands and happy endings. And given the symmetries of the grammars identified in Clute's model, and their clear application to the field, it is difficult to argue against the logical pairing of HORROR as a literature of dread with FANTASY as a literature of desire.

The problem with a closed definition such as Clute's, on the other hand, is that the model it applies to the genre as a whole is couched in the stereotypical iconography of EPIC FANTASY and sufficiently restrictive that works many would consider as within the genre simply due to their incredible content are excluded, redefined as fantastika. The application of a stereotype to a genre, X, and the subsequent relabelling of every non-stereotypical work as *not really X* should be all too familiar to SF readers, the same strategy of redefinition by which SF has been and still is dismissed as Romantic adventures about robots, aliens and spaceships…or lauded as *not really SF*.

Given the commercial mass of the field, it is hard to blame SF readers for buying into that stereotype (as hard as it is to blame those who have the same attitude to SF). Given the literary diversity of the field however, it is hard to deny fantasy writers the right to reject it (as hard as it was to deny those who had the same defiance with respect to SF). Unfortunately, the result is a babble of incompatible terminologies in which one man's *fantastika* is another man's *fantasy*, and one man's *fantasy* is another man's FANTASY. It is the exact deadlock of conflicting definitions we find in the Great Debate.

The Great Eggs Benedict Scandal

The librarian remembers the Great Eggs Benedict Scandal which made the truth of the secret cuisine clear to her—Bradbury's *Fahrenheit 451* versus Huxley's *Brave New World*. Back while the New Wave writers were learning to read, never mind write, Bradbury was chef at the SF Café, serving up his own secret cuisine while the place was still as greasy spoon as they come. So one day a customer comes in and takes a seat at one of the tables. She's in her usual booth, not far away, can't help but hear when he asks for a burger…maybe sort of like that eggs-over-easy malarkey but…not quite…something different.

—Surprise me, he says.

So out comes Bradbury with Eggs Benedict to put the fancy bistros uptown to shame, beats Huxley's hands-down, everyone agrees, as they all come to try it over the next few weeks. But does he get kudos for it in the *Writing City Journal*'s food column? Does the SF Café get kudos for this dazzling dish of dystopia? Or do those bastards at the Bistro de Critique just ignore this instant classic, keep blathering on about Huxley, even denying that when he does Burger à la Eggs Benedict, it's actually burger. In the Temple of Academia, rituals are enacted in celebration of Saint Huxley, but Bradbury…?

The architect François Truffaut just built a motherfucking monument to his dish, the librarian remembers reading in the paper one day, as she sat in the SF Café, listening to the kvetching. A skyscraper in midtown.

Still, around her the culinary clansmen raged of the literati's unjust hatred of all burgers…and raged of the literati's love for this Huxley's burger. They raged that the twisted literati turned a blind eye to the bacon and relish of Huxley's burger, had no idea of the greater glory of the bacon and relish in Bradbury's.

One slumming literatus frowned, perplexed. Bradbury's dish is great, for sure, but it's Eggs Benedict, not burger. Burgers have ground beef in them.

The clansmen howled! The bistro bastard was insisting it's all formulation. Every clansman knew you could have eggburger! Couldn't he see the bacon and relish that prove there's more to burger than mere formulae! See?! See the Hollandaise relish?!

But the librarian, she knew. This Burger à la Eggs Benedict, this dystopic dish, it wasn't ground beef. It was eggs, and not just any old eggs—the eggs of a cockatrice from the next century. Like Huxley's were the eggs of a harpy from a next century two steps to the right. And it was that special ingredient that really mattered, the thing that could not be, not here and now.

And should not be, she realised.

She looked down at the Eggs Benedict on her plate. Her mayashades scrolled instant analyses, coded in glyphs of light, across the lenses: detected modalities: negative boulomaic: should not be; negative deontic: should not be; positive alethic: would be if…; analysis: impossibility + contingency > possibility; and this:

is dystopia, she realised, in the quirk of a monstrous egg that could not be unpacked to contingencies that meant it could be if, if, if…not here and now, but one day. Wireframe edge detection traced the substructure of narrative logic, the dynamics blossoming from a single conceit. No recipe, no formulae, just…a core component around which articulation unfolded by the deep drive of narrative itself, in an articulation original and unconstrained.

She saw the quirk at the heart of it, the egg wireframed to abstraction: flense specificity; abstract to base form. Neither cockatrice nor harpy egg, origin unknown, nature unknown, the ovoid collapsed to sphere, the sphere collapsed to singularity, a point of pure potential from which anything impossible could hatch. It hatched.

—You see the secret cuisine? said the chef at her side as the true form of the alethic quirk filled her vision—novum, erratum, chimera, sutura.

—Why the fuck do we call this burger? she said.

—Eggs Benedict?! some clansmen snarled. Who the fuck is called Benedict anyway? Faggot intellectuals, that's who! Ben maybe, but fucking Benedict? That's a name for traitors and Catholics. It's just a fuckin' hamburger.

—Ah, said the librarian.

Nomology Is Nomology

There's an additional consideration of scope, as mentioned earlier with regards to *The Encyclopedia of Fantasy* definition of fantasy and the fantastic as a project. The idea is: that we must consider fantastika and/or fantasy as a product of the Enlightenment; that while texts like *The Epic of Gilgamesh* can be and are claimed as fantasy by many, this is casting the net far too wide; it's impossible to be sure to what extent writers or readers would have distinguished the incredible (implicitly chimeric, implicitly marvellous) as a distinct quality before the separation out of mimetic literature from non-mimetic; there certainly wasn't an identifiable project to be distinguished out from that mimetic literature as fantasy.

There is an extension of this that could be articulated. This is not Clute's point but it's a related one, not uncommon in discussions of the boundaries of fantasy: that it's impossible to be sure how far readers would have reacted with disbelief at narratives portraying events we now consider utterly incredible; that we don't know whether they would have considered them fantastic as we do; that only with the advent of the scientific worldview with its sense of the laws of reality can we really assume a reader will be judging a work by those laws.

I'm deeply dubious of this aspect of the argument. In the pre-Enlightenment world there were still geography, philosophy, religion, a whole host of disciplines devoted to detailing the laws of nature as they were understood at the time. Nomology is nomology, whether it is scientific, religious or simply philosophical. There seems little question to me that narrative was capable of breaching nomology as an aesthetic purpose long before the scientific worldview came along. The scientific worldview did not imbue us with a sense of nomology, simply redefined the *terms* of that nomology and the basis of how we construct it. The argument confuses the absence of *our* consensus nomology (and the methods underlying it) with the absence of *any* nomology at all.

We need only remember the importance of the ancient concept of "miasma" in Greek Tragedy to be faced with a clear example of pre-Enlightenment literature exploiting a breach of entirely non-scientific nomology. For the ancients there may have been no idea of thermodynamics, but there was a widespread notion of a natural, social and divine order, the laws of nature as the laws of God. While we need to reconstruct these sorts of beliefs from the non-narrative literature of historical cultures, which may be difficult for a culture like that of Sumer, this is hardly an impossible task when it comes to, say, Classical Greece.

Further, one might well challenge the extent to which the nomology applied by a modern reader will in practice be more rational(ist) than that of an post-Enlightenment reader; one might well suggest that any number of factors (e.g. religious faith) will render the modern reader's nomology just as much an acquired set of laws of nature rather than a systematic set of laws of reality. Given that nomological beliefs—religious, philosophical or scientific—are a fairly fundamental aspect of any culture, the argument comes dangerously close to implying an absence of basic cultural features in the absence of those post-Enlightenment values. We, of course, the assumption seems to be, from our Western "civilised" perspective, have a distinction between the fantastic and the realistic; we cannot be sure that the same is true of more "primitive" cultures. This is what the Greeks called hubris.

The League of Fusion Fry-Cooks

The librarian gazes out the window. The shadow of the Kipple Foodstuff Factory still hangs over us, but at least we know it's there. Truth is, the junk fiction is everywhere. The Mob makes every eatery in the city carry those KFF schlockburgers. Truth is, the Bistro de Critique carries them too. Hey ho.

We call it all burger, wonder why it gets no respect, when even before the New Wave broke the "boundaries of genre," chefs like Bradbury were cooking whatever the fuck they wanted to. Still, the Mob sends goons round every other day to strong arm our boys into hackwork. We're just lucky some goons love them Eggs Benedict, shrug as we serve them up: guess we all like a little something different now and then; just…keep it on the QT, call it burger, don't make out that you ain't scum like us. Besides, the Boss Man hangs in the Bistro de Critique, and it's important to him that he's got "class."

But the secret cuisine can't help but evolve. The more the tribes of taste try to impose their formulae, the more the result is simply dialectics—thesis, antithesis, synthesis. Change. So food fads come and go in the SF Café—New Wave, Cyberpunk, New Weird—the menu changing with the times, each new fry-cook doing brave new things with a million variants of burger and fried chicken, crafting bizarre creations of fusion cuisine, adding a signature dish wholly original, unique, exquisitely crafted from raw conceit. Détournement. Bricolage. Quirks.

At some time in the past—nobody knows when—a secret society was formed, a League of Fusion Fry-Cooks, dedicated to the art of fast food haute cuisine, sharing recipes and raw ingredients, tricks and techniques, their motto: *Miso Soup for the Soul.* They have plans to storm the Bistro de Critique, it's said, schemes the librarian knows will one day come to fruition…if the tales of a traveller in time are true. The project is graffitied across the ghetto of Genre, written in invisible ink right here, if you only read between the lines. Yes, they walk amongst us in the streets, meet in the back-alleys. They wear harlequin masks and dance to disguise themselves as street performers. Maybe you're one of them. Maybe I am.

Out on the streets of the ghetto, a masked harlequin (maybe you, maybe me) walks by, in their hand a Molotov cocktail of mixed metaphors—fry-cooks and fusion cuisine, schlockburgers and cafés, ghosts and golems. This is the strategy of our strange fictions, quirk upon quirk, conceit upon conceit, extended and involuted till they all shear off from a simple coherent sense, the vehicle of metaphor unmoored from its tenor, defying reduction to mere allegory. This is how we see the world through our mayashades: a quirk with a cosmos of chaos inside, all that could not be.

The librarian takes another scan of her surroundings, orients herself from another angle of vision. She's out on the street now. This could not be, but if you can sip the miso soup you couldn't get that day in North Carolina, you can do anything.

With Faces in Their Bellies

The counter-argument born of the open definition would be that the fantastic is a technique in the text itself, and that the Greek term for that technique, *phantasia*, is perfectly applicable now as it was then. Plato, Aristotle, the Stoics, all distinguished out those phenomena of imagination, dreams and visions in which perception somehow blends with judgement (is, we might say, recombined by it, Hume's "missing shade of blue" constructed in the colourspace between other directly experienced shades). So, elsewhere in *The Encyclopedia of Fantasy* we read that "in the Graeco-Roman world […] *phantasia* was a technical term in the study of poetic techniques for representing these stories, and ancient literary criticism for the first time drew a clear distinction between the possible and the 'mythic' or 'fabulous.'"

If we now utilise a sort of conceptual temporal dislocation as a rationalisation for the impossibilities, the examples offered earlier with regards to metaphysical dislocations clearly suggest that those pre-Enlightenment writers were utilising *spatial* dislocation in exactly the same manner, displacing the impossible events to an else*where* rather than an else*when*, some remote land beyond the known world (rather than known history or known science) where things might work differently—where people might be gigantic or minuscule, might even have their faces in their bellies. From Herodotus and Apollonius on, through Marco Polo, the legends of Prester John and suchlike, we can see phantasia in the traveller's tale. Exploiting the incredible in the shape of the *exotic*, these are unquestionably strange fiction.

Pornographia dell'Arte

The librarian taps a smoke off Kid Pulp, offers a light.

Kid Pulp is working the same corner as per usual, busking and hustling, offering wild songs and ten-dollar blowjobs, dancing in a red leather miniskirt or denim cut-offs, selling limber feats as pole dance peep shows improvised with lampposts and blindfolds. The strumpet stripling slinks round a pimp, a bookstore buyer in fur coat and gold rings, diamonds in his grin bought with monies made by mining star dreck. Prissy passers-by who took a wrong turn from uptown gasp as punters splash out cash for the harlequin's masque, a Pornographia dell'Arte that might well end in blood and tears instead of spunk these days.

This is the vision through the librarian's mayashades, of course, filtered through the figurative, view skewed towards the sordid. It's how society sees the sensational, painted lurid by the streetlight's glow, painted lurid with boulomaic and deontic modalities, quirks of desire and duty. We seldom see what is, too busy projecting onto it what should or should not be.

Kid Pulp, fully paid-up member of the League of Fusion Fry-Cooks, will have none of that *should not be*. Kid Pulp was suckled at the cock/paps of a dam/sire known as Romance, does not deny the Babylon that spawned not just Kid Pulp but all of New Sodom. No defensive twitch when this harlot/hustler's heritage is thrown back in Kid Pulp's face by those brought up on the right side of the tracks. No shame, no sham of fierce certainty that Kid Pulp is not that kind of girl. Or boy. No shoving that parental shame into a closet, starving it to a skeleton for the sake of prim decorum. A whirl, a twirl, and the sparkly logo on Kid Pulp's crop top comes clear, the brand name of SF.

Dressed in such gaudy duds of glossy packaging, Kid Pulp figures, why get your knickers in a twist when the literati sneer? The sideshow sells well when it's painted pretty colours and comes cheap on the street-corners, so we shill ourselves as Sci-Fi, wear the label in a wild and willing deal with the devil. Through the single-setting mayashades that most don't even know they're wearing, it sure looks like we're just following the family trade (rough trade, that is,) as we stand out there beneath the streetlight, touting cheap thrills to sad johns.

—Show you a good time, if ya want it, honey. A tasty treat. Fresh, juicy meat.

It all began, you know, with self-righteous prigs reviling whores and faggots, proles and primitives, as slave to base sensation. With Romance as an unmarried mother, ill-gotten with child by the entire mob of the mass market, whore with a bastard in her hysterical womb, kicked out by the bushy-bearded patriarchs, no mercy but the workhouse or the madhouse. (It would be nice if a less sexist figuration of Romance could be found here, but it would be a denial of the semiotics at play, which is sexist; the discourse of the sensational is inextricable from the discourse of the hysterical.) Her recent history is starvation and desperation, the brothel trucks and army whorehouses of the Culture Wars. Kid Pulp was born of the Joy Division of fiction, and I don't mean the fucking band.

Kid Pulp is not a hooker/hustler because of some moral degeneracy, is not fallen, just a fall guy. Bastard offspring of ROMANCE and Frankenstein's mob, Kid Pulp grew up hustling that sweet ass, knows it's hard to scrape a living any other way, knows other ways are more degrading in the end. The propriety of polite company finds quirks a little uncouth, see, the cocks and cunts of narrative. The sensational is the sensual, and the sensual is the sexual, shockingly gauche. The secret cuisine is a naked lunch to the petit-bourgeoisie: genre fiction; pulp fiction; penny dreadfuls; dime novels; sensation novels; Gothic; Romance. The Pornographia dell'Arte is a pandering Grand Guignol of all emotions.

So Kid Pulp got real, faced the facts. You made your bed, says Kid Pulp, now you've got to spread your legs on it, bite the pillow and think of England. Kid Pulp is New Sodom out of Babylon, our Woman of the Ghetto, our Boy for Sale. Elsewhen, Kid Pulp would have been a faggot whore priestess prince black madonna in scarlet and purple drag, offering entry into sacred mysteries of flesh and spirit, eros and logos. Elsewhen, Kid Pulp would have been none of this, more than the idealised and demonised metaphors emergent from a history of abstraction and abjection. So those snooty literati see a slapper in these Bacchic revels? So fuck? Deal with it.

Kudos comes at a price, Kid Pulp knows: ditch the miniskirt and cut-offs, move uptown; or join the fucking revolution.

A Strange Fiction of Antiquity

There are other techniques we could identify, and other genres which might be made explicable in terms of quirks or analogues thereof. One might well look at the occult-history novel in these terms. Like comic, tragic or strange fiction, *The Da Vinci Code* or *The Name of the Rose* exploit a sense of the incredible which challenges our suspension-of-disbelief. Where these other modes utilise the absurd, the abject, the surreal or the quirk, the occult-history uses the *arcane*. Like tragedy and comedy there is no dislocation to a non-existent elsewhen; rather it is the links between historic events that are used to weave large scale patterns of conspiracy, to build these up to a point of collapse, at critical mass, into a sense of (incredible) lost (hidden, ancient) truths beyond imagining. The *arcanum* of occult-history bears a remarkable resemblance to the errata, nova and chimerae already detailed. A novum, indeed, which gains its novelty from its being previously unknown, may even *be* an arcanum, which gains its mystery from the fact it is a pointer to further and greater unknowns. The monolith in *2001*, for example, is both.

One might even look at the occult-history's relative, the mystery novel, where the events are not strictly speaking incredible at all—they do not challenge our subjunctivity level—but *are* intriguing. Like a mundane tragedy we have at least one event, a crime, that "should not have happened" and, while the mystery novel remains on one level a pathetic narrative, in the "could have happened" subjunctivity level, rather than going full-steam for terror and destruction, offence to the laws of God and Man, how often are the clues it throws at the reader quirks, things which don't fit, which "should not have happened" (the enigma of the object-out-place) or which in combination "could not have happened" (the contradiction of different versions of events)?

And how much of the very purpose of the book is to reconcile those clues into the solution of just how this "*could* have happened," just how it "*did* happen"? If epistemic modalities are unresolved until that point, perhaps we can speak of driving quirks in the absentings and obfuscations: the *lacunae* of "what did and/or did not happen"; the *limina* of "what might and/or might not have happened." The quirk of a corpse in a locked room as an alethic irresolution: the *cryptica* of "what could and/or could not have happened."

The cryptic is modern perhaps, but the monstrum and numina, the absurd, the arcane, the exotic—these are "genre devices" of a strange fiction of antiquity, one that existed long before the Enlightenment, albeit one that was reshaped radically in that era. If the strange fiction we know now (by whatever name) emerged out of a reconfiguration substantial enough that we might wish to retain a distinction between *phantasia* and *fantasy*, I'm not convinced we should be looking at the texts of one as the "taproots" of the other. A better visual metaphor, I think, might be to understand that pre-Enlightenment period in which realism and fantasy were allied as the "trunk" and what came afterwards as a splitting into two great branches, the mimetic and the semiotic.

The Idiom of the Ascetic

In the Bistro de Critique, Orwell and Huxley serve dystopia, a taster of the secret cuisine that remains unseen. They're spared the sneers, suited up in pinstripes—no red leather miniskirts or denim cut-offs here. No turning tricks each night, sating sense-of-wonder-lust, ten dollars a pop. No formulae here for churning out pot-boilers by the pound. No pimps hawking hackwork product in Mass Market Square. They are members of the League of Fusion Fry-Cooks—they and others like them; but these chefs of the quirk were spared that whole grotesque and glittering scene, the garish spectacle of sensation that turned Sci-Fi into a slight.

Brooding in the ghetto for nigh on half a century, bitter at the literati, clansmen stalk the dark. Beware, the unwitting wanderer from uptown who says the wrong thing in the ghetto. The tribes of taste are seasoned warriors of the flame, and they know insult when they hear it.

They howl at midnight on the streets of Genre. The works they love are reviled while worthy (wearisome) "mainstream" fiction garners all accolades, as if the idiom of the ascetic were the only way to tell the truth. Worse, much of it is no longer "mainstream," not mundane but strange, miso soup for the soul. Still, the literati laud Ishiguro's dish by its supposed distinction from SF, constructing the root cause of failure ultimately, in any novel, as not eschewing the essential nature of one's genre. As if to work in an idiom other than the ascetic could only mean to be bound by formal strictures. As if they are still working in the idiom of the ascetic simply by not being trite. The writers themselves speak in these terms. The secret cuisine is so secret even some of its greatest chefs don't know they're practising it, don't know it exists, how it works. And so they buy into that same grand folly, abjuring the very idioms their best works are in. With this, they win the kudos of the literati, lose out on all the infamy and fun.

—No SF novel ever won the Booker, growls a prowling clansman on his way into the SF Café.

The librarian swings a shotgun from inside her longcoat, blasts the bullshit axiom from the air. Screw the Booker, she thinks. She'd rather have a hookah.

She stands in the doorway of the SF Café, past and future glimmering in her mayashades. She sees Kid Pulp working uptown in the theatres, other harlot/hustler harlequins crashing gallery openings and cocktail parties, noising up the regulars at the Bistro de Critique, hustling a little ass now and then to pay the rent, or dancing—prancing, entrancing maniacs blowing flutes instead of johns. For all the abjurations, every Ishiguro is another sleeper agent of the League of Fusion Fry-Cooks slipped in to open up the bistro's back door, let the slumdogs in, slavering and savage.

But that's tomorrow. She looks round, sees them here now, more and more by the day, her fellow agents, talking the Pornographia dell'Arte in the SF Café or on some corner of Mass Market Square. They talk of the kudos and cash success stories of twentieth-century literature, the canon of writers that includes Joyce alongside Hemingway, Faulkner alongside Steinbeck, writers such as Rushdie, Bulgakov, Carter, Calvino, García Márquez, Pynchon, Vonnegut, and so on. They talk of modern classics that don't sit any better in the contemporary realist's tower block than in the SF flophouse. They talk of that scene, the flavours of the month, the lists and prizes, the slow assimilation of contemporary realism, its descent into formulation. They know formulation when they see it, living in the ghetto. They talk of a spotlight wearing thin for the idiom of the ascetic. Kelly Link was in *Time* magazine a whiles back, they say, Top Five Books of the Year.

Change is in the air. There are always choices, chances.

The secret cuisine cannot be contained.

Breaking the Deadlock

Ultimately, as sympathetic as I am to the open definition of fantasy, the tendency of this definition towards an argument that "it's all fantasy" and the inevitable misreading of that assertion as "it's all FANTASY" makes it about as useful as a taxonomy that classes every colour on the palette as a shade of blue. The similarities in the way chimerae, nova and errata are utilised does not mean the latter two are "really just" instances of the former, no more than all fiction is fantasy simply because it's fabricated, no more than all *writing* is *fiction* because it's fabricated. Follow this path and we end up saying that mathematics, physics, chemistry, language itself, are all subsets of fantasy—they're just complex artifices of the human imagination, after all, representing reality in the form of abstracted symbolic patterns. This is a blurring of the term *fantasy* which renders it so vague as to be useless.

It's for this reason above all others that I prefer to replace this overloaded terminology of *fantasy* and *the fantastic* as applied to the open definition with that of *strange fiction*, to strip away the accreted associations and start from first principles, try and model the field as a fiction of quirks, examine how these work, how the acts of mimesis, those sentences which present themselves as representations of an ersatz actuality, are interrupted by acts of semiosis, sentences that remind us that the representation is an artifice, that the events described "could not have happened." And that would be the closed definition, focusing in on the alethic. In the open definition, all flavours of modality are in the field of vision.

I'm less concerned with fighting a side in that debate than I am with breaking the deadlock by identifying the exact point(s) of contention, so for me the term *strange* offers a fresh slate and a territorial neutrality. It nixes those associations. It carries no further proposition, explicit or implicit, about the nature of the quirks it is founded on, the semiotic "contents" by which we can characterise this type of work. Or rather, to be more accurate, it carries no implications as to how we *respond* to these quirks. It simply says that they breach our expectations that the narrative will function as a representation of an ersatz reality modelled closely on our own. A vocabulary of *strange fiction* and *quirks* offers a distance from those conflicting connotations that are introduced whenever we talk of the content of the field in terms of SF and fantasy.

(There is, of course, the old tried and tested *weird*, but in its origin in ideas of fate, in its application to the uncanny and supernatural rather than just the queer or unusual, and in its associations with the religious and fictional conventions of certain chimerae—e.g. ghosts and vampires—we risk narrowing the focus to the excused metaphysical, rendering it no better a fit than *fantasy*. The history of this word within the commercial genre also establishes it as a sub-generic term, calling up associations with particular pulp writers like Lovecraft or magazines like *Weird Tales*. This is one reason why I'm wary of the term *New Weird*, over and above the fact of that *New* tacitly acknowledging that the label is sub-generic and commercial, placing this fiction in relation to the New Wave as another Movement within the genre.)

We need a term which can be applied beyond the commercial strictures of genres and movements, one we can apply analytically to those works published before or outside the marketing labels, such that the application is not political and subjective but rather critical and objective. With its etymological roots in the Latin *extraneous*, meaning "of external origin," and its modern application to the foreign, the alien, the queer, the other, *strange* is an eminently suitable term, with much less conceptual baggage, as much a description of the set of narratives to be examined—strange fictions, fictions which are strange—as a naming of an aesthetic form.

And, of course, it abbreviates neatly to the old familiar SF.

A Water Feature in the Gardens of Literature

The librarian heads out across Mass Market Square, towards the subway, checking in with the League of Fusion Fry-Cooks over her aether uplink, telling them all about the Bistro de Critique's strange visitor from twenty years into tomorrow, how he told of a Dynamism sweeping in to overturn the tables. Her contact listens with great interest.

Here is a secret of the secret cuisine. The "mainstream" of literature is only what is in the main stream, and this is not the contemporary realism of the kitchen sink. That idiom had a brief boom in the 1960s, as angry young men roared for realism in the name of relevance, no frills, no nonsense. It was an egalitarian agenda, born in a backlash against elitist artifices of the modernists, eschewing the strange and sensationalist quirks, seeing deceit in all conceit—but in an honest and passionate dream of telling stories *of* the common man *for* the common man. They saw the unreal as irrelevant, the incredible as mere fancy; they could not parse the strange to its meaning.

(Their attitude is not entirely unfamiliar. We have our own realists, our own Rationalists, down in the ghetto of Genre, in the SF Café, dug into their little corner, behind a barricade of tables, muttering darkly about the death of Science Fiction.)

It had a brief boom in the 1960s, this idiom of the ascetic, this genre, but it never made the mainstream, which is and always will be populist, commercial…Genre. The League of Fusion Fry-Cooks have more than a little sympathy for those angry young men, and a smart of sadness that they failed to see the Molotov cocktail in the quirk…more so that their battleground could only be lost to the bourgeois. Because they had walked away from the mainstream in the abrogation of quirks, diverted into the sidestream of "proper literature" where taste becomes a class marker, where appreciation serves to signify status, where that sidestream is therefore reduced to a water feature in the Gardens of Literature.

It was never about the mainstream, but about the manners of the Bistro de Critique, what was à la mode today, what was "proper." Three hundred years ago or so, two oppositional aesthetics were well-matched in their struggle for legitimacy as they clashed head-to-head. Romantic and Realist genres were the tribes of taste among the middle-class and middlebrow, back in the day, constructing modernity in a dialectic not unlike that to be found today in the SF Café. Oh, but one aesthetic was that of the vulgar proles and of "women's fiction."

It was infantile, unsophisticated, this aesthetic of mere storytelling, fanciful as folklore and fable, primitive as the superstitions of the savages. It was then—and remains now—the mainstream that feeds the bulk of water fountains across the city of New Sodom, but this very fact was enough to damn it in the end. A true gentleman—not a vulgar prole, not a hysterical woman, not a primitive savage, not a child—surely knew that these gushing fountains of quirk were…unseemly. Only in the Gardens of Literature might one find that shallow birdbath with a china cup from which to sip the refined liquidity of edifying art. Why, one could see just how refined it was, absent those quirks!

It was inevitable that the petit-bourgeois would latch on to the legitimacy of egalitarianism to justify what is really a scorn of the popular. Mass Market Square. The Pornographia dell'Arte. This is what they really hate, the impropriety of it all. The bourgeois were only too happy to co-opt contemporary realism, formulate and commercialise it with formal strictures on the acceptable use of quirks. Transform it to the faux reportage of the social observer, enlightened, educated, edified and edifying. So it became about the impropriety of the sensational, what art must not be if it was to be serious, worthy, intellectual. Some literati may be held accountable, but many were—and are—as much casualties of the Culture Wars as anyone; when one is raised within the rhetoric of abjection, it is often invisible, not least to those most privileged by it.

The abjection is unsustainable though; the impetus of art is always against propriety, and so the reactionaries will always be revealed, by their own words, as antagonists to art. They say the china cup is necessary, but every now and then a writer comes along to smash it with contempt, show it up for the genteel nonsense it is. And some literati nod appreciatively even as others slip a fresh cup back in place. They say the liquid in the birdbath must be pure, but every now and then a writer comes along to piss just a hint of quirk into it, maybe more than a hint. And after decades of art refined to bland banality, melodrama watered-down to mundane crises, trite epiphanies, some literati hail the tang of strange conceits even as others grumble at the taint. They say the flow of it all must be kept subtle, slow and delicate, never a spectacle. But writers who see how this is all in the name of etiquette and the status it affords will feel the heft of a sledgehammer in hand, and grin as they smash that decorative folly, let the fiction come fountaining forth in a great geyser. And if some literati flap their hands in outrage, others will dance barefoot in the mud.

And the League of Fusion Fry-Cooks will move among them, handing out hors d'oeuvres of pure quirk, peachy keen articulations conjured out of raw conceit, rich delicacies one cannot help acquire a taste for. Scotch eggs of a basilisk from a yesterday that never was. Whether they call it burger or fried chicken is irrelevant; it is the secret cuisine.

It may not remain secret for much longer.

The Order of the Blue Flower

Hal Duncan

The Rapture of Unreason

I grew up around Christians who believed in a seven day creation, preached the reality of Hell and Judgement, and railed against the lie that was evolution. They were also, for the most part, racists and homophobes... And the only difference between them and me was that I had a father who shoved a science fiction paperback into my pre-teen hands and ordered me to read it. After all, it's pretty hard to be prejudiced against blacks and gays when you're a-okay with Klingons and the Green Men of Mars.

Lou Anders

So the 21st of May, 2011, came and went without a whiff of the Rapture, nary a hint of Moby Douche, the Great White Fail, breaching the firmament above. No star called Wormwood fallen from the sky, turning a third of the waters to tasty absinthe. No angels treading the wine gums of the wrath of the Lord. Not a peep of New Jerusalem on the early warning radar. Instead, the next day came in New Sodom, with Benny the Rat still in the Vatican, Fred Phelps still on the streets, and Harold Camping still on the radio, still selling his shtick. The Rapture was postponed apparently, till the 21st October.

And did it come then?

I was too busy having one fuck of a fortieth birthday party to notice.

Yes, I'm cynical. Deal with it. Dawkins, Hitchens and Pullman are a little po-faced in their harrumphery for my liking, but colour me sceptical and run me up the "oh really?" flagpole, because when it comes to religion, you can keep your gestalt schizophrenia; I am not innarested in your condition. It's that whole Enlightenment thing; I favour a worldview that's less inclined to burn me at the fucking stake. It's not a problem with religion per se, you understand, just bugfuck nutjobbery in general. The rapture of unreason.

I came to New Sodom from a small town in Central Scotland, see, a queer kid in exile from a childhood I can't help glimpsing in the picture Lou Anders paints of his own upbringing—albeit backwards in a different way, a New Town housing scheme, built in the 1970s to take Glasgow's overspill, to punt the plebs out to the suburbs, greener pastures, bluer skies and flowers. The razor-gang culture of Glasgow's inner city, the small town mentality of an Ayrshire village, crossbred to perfection with anti-Catholic bigotry in place of racism, it was *swellegant!*

There wasn't a whole lot of creationist evangelism, but racists and homophobes? My formative years were the era of the National Front, Nazi punk bands like Skrewdriver, the "Gay Plague" of AIDS, Clause 28. Good old Clause 28, outlawing the "promotion of homosexuality" in the public sector. I proposed it as a topic for our school debating society, I recall, but the teacher had to sadly veto it. A debate on Clause 28 might be construed as "promoting homosexuality," you see; to allow pupils to argue Clause 28 could be a breach of Clause 28, a sacking offence.

(That's some clause, that Clause 28, thought this homo Yossarian.)

Point is, religion wasn't the driving force, but the reactionary bollocks sprang from the same source, the abrogation of ethical judgement to received moral wisdom, the bugfuck nutjobbery of the righteous. All prejudice presents itself as piety, propriety. And if today I proudly wear the title "THE.... Sodomite Hal Duncan!!" gifted to me by homophobic hatemail, I don't know that it's just being a bugger that makes me bolshie. It's not just the background of bigotry as resonates with me in that opening quote from Anders. A geek and a gawk in specs, with elbow patches on my blazer, I was a teenage Spock even before sexuality kicked in, booted me out of any dream of normativity, into the evermade estranged reality of the queer.

I could almost imagine, then, that it wasn't the day my teacher vetoed that Clause 28 debate that set me on the path to New Sodom, a blue flower pinned in my lapel, but rather the moment a mate shoved a copy of Asimov's *I, Robot* into my hand. I could almost imagine it was the logic of the Three Laws, reason and the scientific worldview, that set me against the bugfuck nutjobbery, the hysteria and hate, the rapture of unreason. I could almost imagine it was the experience of alterity accepted in Klingons and Green Men of Mars that served as antidote to the conditioning of my culture.

Almost.

The Forgotten Sibling of Comedy and Tragedy

> *You have literally as many forms as Proteus; and now you go all manner of ways, twisting and turning, and, like Proteus, become all manner of people at once, and at last slip away from me in the disguise of a general, in order that you may escape exhibiting your Homeric lore.*
>
> **Plato, Ion**

If this substitution of *strange fiction* and *the quirk* solves the problem of overload by abandoning the open definition of *fantasy* and *the fantastic*, does this mean that those terms are now free to be applied solely in the context of a closed definition? Might we now focus in on one particular type of strange fiction which utilises its alethic quirks in a specific way, calling this and only this fantasy? It is a temptation. We might now simply accept, as subsets of these strange fictions, a pair of narrative grammars driven by the numina on one hand, the monstrum on the other, the marvellous here, the monstrous there, setting *fantasy* up in partnership with *horror*.

But there is, I think, another identifiable discourse of narratives that might legitimately compete for a label of *fantasy* (as one can label works of Aeschylus, Shakespeare and Miller *tragedy*, as one can label works of Aristophanes, Shakespeare and Orton *comedy*), a mode of narrative that exploits the sort of quirks we think of as the fantastic, which is to say, the alethic, the incredible (as tragedy exploits the abject, as comedy exploits the absurd), but which walks the line between Clute's Thinning and Thickening, between the marvellous and the monstrous.

If I would argue against some of the narrowly focused views of what fantasy does (e.g. Clute's narrative grammar of fantasy), seeing these as overly restrictive (as if one were to describe all tragedy in terms JACOBEAN REVENGE TRAGEDY, as if one were to describe all comedy according to a model based on BEDROOM FARCE), it is because I see works touted under that label navigating a middle ground we might call Twisting, applied to the novum in Clute's schema but equally applicable to the chimera, or indeed to the erratum or sutura.

This particular mode of fiction would be that in which the incredulity engendered by any flavour of quirk is not just significant and structural but is *escalated*, the tension of alethic modalities developed to a crisis-point comparable with those we find in tragedy or comedy. It would be the narrative of incredulity in the same way that tragedy is the narrative of pity and terror, comedy the narrative of humour. It would underlie Clute's grammars of horror and fantasy as, in large part, the dynamics that makes them *not* tragedy and comedy.

It is not difficult to discern this form of narrative in works we class as fantasy, to point to the spectaculism and sensationalism of contemporary EPIC FANTASY as evidence for a narrative of incredulity. But with the term *fantasy* in play, the associations of that term lead us to a selection bias, an over-specification of the quirk as chimeric, bind the incredulity to metaphysicality when we might as easily be dealing with hypothetical or counterfactual conceits. This is all the more probable given the clear lineage of this mode of strange fiction, the general focus on chimeric conceits all the way back through Tolkien and Lewis, MacDonald and Morris, through the Gothic novel to the texts of chivalric romance and fairy tales (trunk texts or taproot texts). And that lineage is skewed to the marvellous.

Formally speaking, the base narrative mode should be considered a structural approach to the alethic quirk in general rather than to any one flavour of quirk. Scatological humour is not the essence of all comic narrative. Metaphysical impossibility is not the essence of all strange narratives. The incredibility I'm interested in here *might* be the chimera of a magic sword but it might as easily be the exotica of men with their faces in their bellies, the cryptic arcanum of a lost city of legend, the novum of a chess-playing automaton. And it might not be so simply marvellous, might not follow that path off to one side.

If we trim away the gold fruit and red leaves and blue flowers of all these different modern flavours of strangeness, trace the twigs that bear them back past their branch-points, there is a heritage for all these fictions in a form that goes back far beyond the Romantic period, one that places it on a direct par with tragedy and comedy, with a contemporaneous origin. Peake might well be a better analogue of Miller and Orton here, in a middle path for this strange fiction which would border chivalric romances but side more with Cervantes, and carry on back through Shakespeare (*The Tempest*) to Apuleius (*The Golden Ass*) as analogue of Aeschylus and Aristophanes. The picaresque of pre-Enlightenment Europe is as much a part of the discourse of this mode as the chivalric romance and the fairy tale, and in its Classical analogue of the Milesian tale we find, I would argue, an ideal figure of strange fiction in its own right, a fiction founded on the exploitation of the quirk.

Given that the term *fantasy* is highly arguable when we cast the net so wide, will inevitably slide sideways to stand as flipside of horror, given that I'm really talking of a mode which takes those two grammars as extremes as it tends more wholly toward the marvellous or the monstrous, I'm going to surrender the label of fantasy as I surrender the label of science fiction. Apply it as you will. To leave the whole sorry mess of turf wars behind us, as a name for this central and fundamental mode of strange fiction, I will appropriate a term with roots in the same Classical culture as tragedy and comedy, one that's not too obscure—that's quite familiar in the fields of poetry and music, in fact—but largely out-of-use now as regards narrative. As the forgotten sibling of comedy and tragedy then, I'm going to talk of *rhapsody*.

Camp Consolation

> *When I say "missing the point" what I mean is that (so it seems to me) Benford's real concern is that scientific rationalism—or simply rationalism, full stop—is under constant attack from base superstition and base prejudice...When Benford disses the rise of fantasy, it seems to me his real concern is the loss of science fiction's core message: that it can introduce the reader—particularly the young reader—to one of the core values of rationality: questioning the accepted order of things.*
>
> **Gary Gibson**

That quote from Anders comes from a few years back, from another cycle of the Great Debate. Picture a blogosphere of heads hitting desks as Gregory Benford testifies, brother, against a rising tide of unreason in the shape of FANTASY. Fantasy being Harry Potter, rotting the rational faculties. Anders, like Gary Gibson, stepped in to defend Benford, to cut through the turf war rhetoric, highlight a crucial point—the import of reason as antidote to prejudice. Anders presents it as impartiality towards alterity, Gibson as dubiety towards normativity, but both speak to the core of the critical nous: that it abjures the feedback loop of faith, purges the valorisation of credulity, the belief that questioning belief is wrong.

The rapture of unreason sustains the rapture of unreason. This is what makes it unreason, the inverse and inhibition of the discursive, the self-correcting.

Those core values Gibson refers to are dear to me then—analytic intellect against the onslaught of folly. When push comes to shove, that teenage Spock still stalks my little noggin, raising an eyebrow at the rapture of unreason whenever it appears—at the fervour for the End of the Enlightenment you hear, for example, in the crazytalk of those who believe Obama is a Kenyan Muslim. For all that I've argued in this book against tribalist Rationalism, I come to the strange fiction genres as one who identified first and foremost as a reader of SF. As a child, I loved Michael de Larrabeiti, Susan Cooper, Alan Garner, but that's like saying I watched *The Box of Delights* on the BBC, hardly a true fandom. No Frodo or Fafhrd for me, no Conan or Elric, only John Carter got by my no-swords policy at one point. (He was nekkid.) Instead, Asimov led to Bradbury, Clarke, Dick, Ellison, Farmer, Gibson, Heinlein and so on.

Did it teach me acceptance of alterity, that SF? A little, maybes. From the Mule of the Foundation series to the Martians of Bradbury's "Dark They Were, and Golden Eyed," there's much that might resonate with a kid queered by desire, finding solace in the local library, turning from Sarek on the screen to Simak and Sladek on the page. I remember how Heinlein unlocked the closet door for me with his sexual libertarianism, how Delany kicked that door wide open. It makes sense. The fiction of the strange is, by definition, the fiction of the alterior; surely it must then, by definition, render the alterior familiar.

And yet…every boy's own adventure needs its savage enemies. We'd do well not to forget that what we're dealing with here is category fiction born of the pulps, barefoot summer games of heroes and villains. For all we might point at what it is now, or at the deeper, wider heritage of strange fictions outwith the commercial field, from Gilgamesh on, talking of science fictions and fantasies unbound by the imperatives of juvenilia, our taproots are in the Street & Smith that published *Nick Carter Weekly* and *Buffalo Bill Adventures* alongside *Astounding*. It's out of that soil this cultivar of a strange blue flower has sprung.

There's an aesthetic inherited from that pulp, one that idealises individualism as will-to-power, appeals to emotion over reason, discards the restraint of realism to glory in the wonder of the incredible made manifest, the sublime. It's an aesthetic which looks to the past for imagos of virtue in the cowboy or the knight, even where it renders them as spacemen. It's the aesthetic which gives us fascism wherever its self-infatuation extends to the culture at large, the folk as hero, wherever it demonises or fetishises alterior cultures—as it so often does. It's the aesthetic of Romanticism, and if we've one thing to learn from the twentieth century it's how badly that aesthetic can go wrong.

So, to use Anders's examples, the Klingons and the Green Men of Mars are savages of Romance, their warlike characters determined by ethnicity much as we find in Tolkien's orcs, in all those races of FANTASY whose "swarthy" skin is evermade a signifier of inhumanity, alterity as wrongness. The same sources offer races we are far less a-okay with: the Ferengi of Star Trek; the Black Men of Burroughs's Barsoom. Essentialised grotesques, their greed or violence (or moral degeneracy, one might say) suggests we're more a-okay with biological determinism than anything. Sadly, it seems, the fiction of the strange can just as easily render the alterior foreign, an exotic Other readily made monstrum when the story calls for a sensational foe.

My scepticism kicks in then, I confess, at heroic fantasies of SF freeing children from their shackles of conditioning. Would it were so. The reality of the escapes we've found, may still find, from the bugfuck nutjobbery of our immediate environs—whether that bugfuck nutjobbery be Creationism or Clause 28—is that these are holidays as often organised to rapture us in moral bromides as to teach us to challenge them. As space cadets in brown shirts, we have learned songs of the sublime along with science and survival skills. In wild campfire tales of adventures elsewhen, told at Camp Consolation by counsellors who were themselves taught by such tales, for a fiction of scientific Rationalism, SF can be terribly Romantic.

Stitchings of Songs

rhapsody:
- Music. *an instrumental composition irregular in form and suggestive of improvisation.*
- *an ecstatic expression of feeling or enthusiasm.*
- *an epic poem, or a part of such a poem, as a book of the* Iliad, *suitable for recitation at one time.*
- *a similar piece of modern literature.*
- *an unusually intense or irregular poem or piece of prose.*
- Archaic. *a miscellaneous collection; jumble.*

Dictionary.com

So what do I mean when I talk of *The Golden Ass*, *The Tempest* and even *The Lord of the Rings* as rhapsody rather than fantasy? If the exploitation of the absurd or the abject result in comedy or tragedy, and the limitation of that use leads to the private and pathetic narratives of drama and melodrama, what do I mean when I say that the exploitation of the quirk results in rhapsody?

Well, the term is exapted from its origins in the rhapsodes of Classical Greece. Literally, *rhapsody* means "stitchings of songs," referring to the repertoire of mythic, comedic and otherwise episodic tales that the rhapsode would weave into the frame of the *epos* or epic, the framing structure remaining constant but the selection of songs varying with each performance according to the rhapsode's judgement of his audience's tastes. In a superficial sense all three narratives named above share a certain stitchedness, their framing narratives containing tales told and songs sung, performances within performances and shifts in register to match the changing content's mode. There is myth and mystery in these texts but also comic escapades, episodes of light relief. This is what the fairy-tale and chivalric romances share with picaresque and the Milesian tale. It is the freedom of form they inherit from comedy where the escalation of absurdity is repeatedly released, in contrast to tragedy's continual building of tension. Comedies are allowed to sprawl; they defy the grip of tragedy's (moral, social, natural, divine) order.

Where comedy may be as wildly inchoate as a Monty Python movie however, rhapsody always returns to the framing structure even if, as in the modern rhapsody, that structure is disassembled, integrated into the episodes, buried in the episodes as the framing narrative of *Catch-22* (the story of the horrors of the war, the epos and tragedy in which Yossarian is Achilles and Snowden Patroclus) is buried in the absurdist chapters each devoted to the individual narrative of one of the characters. The irregularity and improvisational quality associated with rhapsody in its contemporary application in music and poetry is not absent in our application of this term to prose narratives, but neither is the quality of intensity, of ecstasy; rhapsody is held together by this intensity, the profundity of affect, the *gravitas* it inherits from tragedy.

What I am suggesting is essentially this rhapsody as a conceptual frame for those tap-root/trunk fictions that are neither comedy nor tragedy but share features of them both in their dynamics of incredulity etc., the disruption of modalities as a driving power in the history of Western literature. Rather than accept the model of fantastic fiction as a product of the Enlightenment's scientific worldview, an unrealist irrationalist fiction abjected by the newly invented Rationalist realist literature, and rather than ignoring this aesthetic struggle entirely so as to apply the genre labels of fantasy or science fiction willy-nilly to everything from *Gulliver's Travels* all the way back to *Gilgamesh*, I'm suggesting we turn this model inside-out: imagine comedy and tragedy as the pillars of a gateway, a portal through which the rhapsode entered the city of New Sodom millennia ago; imagine the history of rhapsody as the long road to the heart of the city in the present day, marked out between the absurd and the monstrous, through Milesian tales and Latin novels, through the chivalric romance and the picaresque, through dramas of Calibans and Ariels, through travellers' tales, through anecdotes and allegories, through narratives cognisant of their own strangeness long before the Enlightenment brought a scientific worldview to bear. We don't need science to tell us what defies the laws of nature; we have our tears and laughter to tell us that; we have our open jaws and wide eyes.

This is rhapsody as the narrative form that employs the full range of quirks, as the narrative that is, through Chaucer and Cervantes, Defoe and Richardson, Fielding and Sterne, the root of the private and pathetic narratives which will eventually eschew those quirks entirely. This is rhapsody as that mode of strange fiction driven by the deep dynamics of incredulity, a mode that has carried on in the ghetto of Genre all through the era of mimetic fiction's dominance of Literature, the rhapsody that is re-emerging in that domain right now.

The Echoes of Faith

> *A world remains of which man is the sole master. What bound him was the illusion of another world. The outcome of his thought, ceasing to be renunciatory, flowers in images. It frolics–in myths, to be sure, but myths with no other depth than that of human suffering and like it inexhaustible. Not the divine fable that amuses and blinds, but the terrestrial face, gesture, and drama in which are summed up a difficult wisdom and an ephemeral passion.*
> **Albert Camus, *The Myth of Sisyphus***

SF has always had a love/hate relationship with Romanticism, happy to utilise its aesthetic of the sublime, but uneasy with the suspension of critical nous such rapture entails. Sense-of-wonder is a sense of incredulity tinged positive, created in the breach of possibility—the technical or historical, physical or logical alethic quirk—so to appreciate the incredible in SF is paradoxically to fancy reason capable of that which it is not—not yet. Where even critics claim for SF an alethic modality of "could have happened," untrue because this would require technical possibility, the rapture is revealed: we fancy the fancy practicable. The denial is endemic. Our (in)credulity always already a betrayal of a wholly rationalist aesthetic—pretending the practicality of a quirk—it seems the less easy we are with the game of suspended disbelief as a game, the more we must gloss the impossible as possible, the implausible as plausible.

The rigour required to cleave to what's *actually* plausible is the province of a rare few, not the core of the genre. An SF that eschews all mumbo-jumbo—a truly scientific fiction working only on the novum, with no place in it for errata, chimerae or suturae—this is a fantasia of the genre's future, a HARD SF or MUNDANE SF ideal, not an accurate model of our roots. This is not to criticise it *as* an ideal, simply to say it's not the picture as it stands, as it has ever stood. The wildest technical impossibilities are seldom adequate, let alone the tamer ones which have real plausibility.

Instead, freely employing the Paradigm Shift Caveat to excuse all manner of impossibilities, SF blithely accepts into its canon works which breach not just known science but the laws of nature, works where the conceit is ultimately metaphysical. If a wormhole or FTL drive or an ability to jaunte is not glossed as magic, it remains a chimera, no more possible—or even plausible—than a teleportation spell. It requires a spurious physics in place of the established one. The difference in the text, like that between a mentalist and a magician, is only the shtick that sells the trick. The difference in the reading may be an actual plausibility we afford the chimera sold as novum, faith furtively sneaking in the back door as we swallow the pseudoscientific spiel of the illusionist. It's a fun twist on the game, to suspend the disbelief that would remind us we are suspending disbelief, but where it is afforded more weight, a fancy of hyperspace is more credulous than that of an astral plane; this is a tautology.

An SF that applies the Paradigm Shift Caveat or some other flimflam to legitimise those wilder quirks, but scorns them when (but only when) rendered as magic, is a fantasia of the genre's present, glossing the illusion as a feasible marvel because it pulls the bouquet of blue flowers from the sleeve of a lab coat rather than a robe. It is a divine fable, and the higher the snoot is cocked at the frolics of those who don't buy the shtick, projecting one's own doubly-suspended disbelief into their gameplay, the more it reveals itself as grandiose conceit, its imagined tether of possibility mere credulity. The deeper the scorn of a magic carpet as against an *Analog* story of teleporting sun whales, say, the more we must arch a Spocklike eyebrow at the judgement lending such credence to the latter whimsy, so requiring it that it damns the former for not accommodating this doubly-suspended disbelief.

The more a straight man identifies as homophobic, experiments show, the more likely he's aroused by gay porn, as if that hate is a song of fierce denial roared to drown out dread desire. I can't help wondering what scorn of magic carpets comes from a similar doublethink of denial, angst at the echoes of faith that scorn reveals when not directed at teleporting whales of the sun, whether that doubly-suspended disbelief simply isn't a game for some, but rather an actual belief, shorn of all doubt so as to disacknowledge that it is belief—not truth—that all those marvels now impossible are nonetheless more fundamentally possible, made so by the power of unknown science, even breaches of the laws of nature admissible, so limitless that capacity is in this credo.

Like Beads on a Bracelet

We do not always reconstruct elsewhens from these quirks. Narratives characterised by such quirks do not always invite us to parse them as indexes of a coherent worldscape. The alethic quirk, incredible because it is a motif misplaced (a man in space, jaunting) or a recombination of forms (a crescent and a sun fused), may invite no such rational interpretation. Thrown into a mimetic narrative without any sense of coherent structuring, they might suggest to us only that what we're reading is an oneiric narrative, with no worldscape to reconstruct—only a dreamscape. This is the only fictive setting offered by the movie *The Science of Sleep*. In its mimetic detail it points to a story taking place in the real world, but the environment it offers us is a dreamscape in which the day's events are recombined with fancy and unreason. The instability of these types of narrative is often alienating precisely because of its illogic, regarded as "experimental" (i.e. an experiment that failed.)

In narratives better classed as ludic than oneiric, we begin to see, in the relationships of those quirks, the arbitrary rules of play, the logic of a game. So Lewis Carroll's *Alice in Wonderland* offers us logic-puzzles and syllogisms made flesh; but if there is more order here than in a dreamscape there's still no coherent worldscape. The same is true of most allegory, where the rules applied are those of analogy (e.g. *Pilgrim's Progress*). Here the quirks function as vehicles of metaphor (often crude, blatant), their behaviour bound by the proposition they exist to act out in vehicle-form in order that it can be translated into tenor-form by the reader, parsed into a moral. In parable, where the quirks are played down or removed so that the text can also be read as straight mimesis (a prodigal son rather than a Vanity Fair), or in fable, where the imagery is more directly rooted in mundane reality (a talking fox, say, rather than a Slough of Despond), we start to see the beginnings of worldscape. Still, there is little of the elsewhen here, our suspension-of-disbelief requiring an acceptance of whimsical make-believe or of worthy figurative sermonising. It is not entirely surprising that allegory is not the most popular mode of contemporary narrative.

Satiric narrative takes the strategies of fable a step further though. As it attaches its moral message to a specific real-world target rather than offering it as a general axiom of righteousness, it becomes an act of mimesis in its own right, a representation of the target of its derision. The Cloud Cuckoo Lands of satire may still be rendered incoherent and fanciful by their comic exaggerations, their absurdities, but the more accurate their representation of the target underneath that absurdity, the more acute the critique they offer. It is still largely the rules of analogy around which the fictive environments of satire cohere, but as the motifs and milieus are fleshed-out as fabricated forms, the edifices of absurdity begin to slip free. Somewhere between Swift's Lilliput and Kafka's Castle, perhaps, satire becomes story.

Where satire lets the story take over, where the rules of analogy are replaced by the rules of narrative logic, a change takes place. Here in the diegetic narrative—the story as a told-tale, an autotelic artefact—the behaviours of the quirks and their environment must be integrated into the story as a whole. They must be coherently and comprehensively understandable as elements of the unfolding dynamics, even if this means unmooring them from the rules of direct analogy. Diegetic narrative, it should be made clear, does not necessarily involve quirks. (Not all fiction is strange.) Its motifs may be purely mundane even if they carry the symbolic meaning of theme. Where they *are* strange however, story's demand for suspension of disbelief drives writer and reader toward the creation of worldscape. The strange must be excused as within a conventional framework (worldscape as mythos in its contemporary sense) or explicated as an original creation—or better still both. So we may even find, to borrow a phrase from film theory in a bad pun, the "extra"-diegetic elements of infodump and backstory.

Other strategies are evident in this fiction which some might call fantasy, others fantastika or phantasia, but which I'm referring to as rhapsody, and it's largely these other strategies that are my reason for this naming. From the earliest tellings of tales in written history, long before the metafiction of the (post)modernists, the stitching-of-stories has been a strategy for maintaining suspension-of-disbelief by drawing the reader into the story. As Gilgamesh sits listening to Atrahasis's embedded story of the Deluge, the reader sits at his side. As Lucius, transformed into an ass, listens to the tale of Cupid and Psyche, only one of many strung through his own story like beads on a bracelet, our awareness of the artifice of story is focused on that inner tale; we are for that moment in an exactly corresponding situation with the protagonist because we, like him, are listening to this embedded tale. These metafictional structurings—like the epistolic form of *Dracula* or the found-text claim of *Manuscript Found in Saragossa*—are not designed to distance us but rather to immerse us, to offer us sleight-of-hand subterfuges by which we might just continue to imagine this story real. As the character—Gilgamesh, Lucius, Miranda or Frodo—sits listening to a story within their story, or watching a play within their play, we are being offered a subtle mimesis: their worldscape as one which is *like ours* because stories are told in it, a worldscape which is, we are being told, more real because of that.

This is the fiction that I'm referring to as rhapsody, this stitching of mimetic representation, oneiric imagery, ludic rules, allegoric morals, satiric critique and diegetic story into complex quiltings of narrative. And it is in this fiction that, as those quirks become unmoored from direct relationships of meaning, the diegesis, or the layering of diegesis, becomes a syntax in which these symbols articulate new meanings. Story becomes a language with the sort of narrative grammars that John Clute discusses in his "Fantastika in the World Storm" essay, and with these quirks as motifs, semes coined in the process of narrative, we end up with a fiction that is not just mimetic, oneiric, ludic, allegoric, satiric or diegetic, but *semiotic*. It bears a remarkable resemblance to (post)modernism in some respects, but this may only be because if the project of Modernism was to fuse Romanticism and Rationalism, the end of that project may mean, in the end, a return to the freedom of form that existed before the ideological schisming of that original Great Debate.

A Romance with Reason

There is nothing whatsoever in science—and this should be shouted from the rooftops of every scientific institution—that makes it immune from such abuses... Some scientists will dispute this, claiming that the values of open, objective enquiry, mutual criticism and protection of learning in the accumulated wisdom of science amount to an ethical system which, if applied to the world, would make it a better place, potentially protected from future horrors. This is not wrong, just fantastically utopian. Such values are not exclusive to science; they preceded it. Science sprang from philosophy, theology and even magic. The reason it became science at all was because of the direction these disciplines took in the course of the Renaissance.
New Scientist

It should be clear where I stand on the belief that reality cannot be ultimately amenable to reason simply because Old Nobodaddy in the sky slipped the ineffable into his crock pot of creation—dude, I am not innarested in your condition—but as the article on scientism in the special fundamentalism issue of *New Scientist* quoted above makes clear, the belief that the world is "accessible to and ultimately controllable by human reason" is also "a profoundly unscientific idea…neither provable nor refutable." Likewise the notion of science as a universal panacea for all human folly. The author points to Hitler's use of the biology of Ernst Haeckel, the roots of Stalinism in Marx's conviction that a science of history had been discovered, to illustrate the dangers of this scientism, this fiction of science as hero. It would be bully to believe that everything is and must be explicable and that explication will and must lead to ethical improvement—it's certainly a good operating assumption, I'd say, tried and tested—but to take that stance as a conviction is an act of faith.

My scepticism calls shenanigans then at the zeal of loyalists like Benford, at the overturned tables of the SF Café, the volleys of blanks fired at brothers-in-arms, accusations of intellectual cowardice, cultural treason. Where a writer takes umbrage at the Hugo win for Harry Potter as fandom's betrayal of science in favour of superstition, I see Rationalism that has ceased to be rational, goaded to pious outrage at the folly of the faithless. A fantasist writes of a blue flower's petals stewed to a tea that, with one sip, transports the drinker to another world, a nightmarish détournement of biological determinist pulp, say, and they are the enemy because this unmoored metaphor of estrangement is not…a sun whale using paradigm-shifted science…in a story that casts religion as the source of ethics, science as a straw man of relativism that—quick, push the button!—excuses rape?

My scepticism asks whether SF is engaging with the rapture of unreason here or surrendering to it. Is it analysing the semiotics of reactionary agitprop to defuse it, dissecting the madness of societies, or retreating into the secure self-certainties of ghetto guttersniping?

Is it applying Kohlberg's studies of the stages of moral development in children to critique the conventional worldview as not historically but psychologically immature, or being raptured in a fancy of holding the fort against the savage hordes, of the infrastructure of fandom infiltrated by a treacherous Fifth Column of fantasists—which we must imagine uttered with the emphasis of a sibilant hiss?

Anders and Gibson offer conciliatory perspectives—the former focusing on "narrative complexity and whether the speculative material you read (whether SF or F) serves to turn your brain on or turn it off," the latter refraining from imposing a definition on fantasy which, "like sf and every other form of literature, is a tool to be used in whichever way a particular author chooses to use it"—but moderates seldom set the tone in the Great Debate. The rapture of unreason won't stand for such nuanced opinions.

Instead, characterisation collapses into caricature: the hawk-eyed, square-jawed, intellectual brilliance of SCIENCE FICTION in the red corner; the slack-jawed, blinkered, credulous nonsense of FANTASY in the blue corner. Science versus Superstition. Or vice versa—the noble poet versus the dreary pedant, the artistic versus the autistic. Dynamism versus mechanism. To close the definitions of science fiction and fantasy to a Rationalist SCIENCE FICTION on the one hand, a Romantic FANTASY on the other is tiresome whichever corner is claimed. But those who would do so will seldom be swayed, caught up in their self-heroising narrative.

One expects such from the Romantic, such refusal to countenance the contrary, but reason is discursive or it is not reason. Where that conviction of the limitless efficacy of science turns to condemn the absence of conviction—refusing as inadequate commitment belief held as an operating assumption, as if only absolute conviction were truly conviction—this is not Rationalism but a romance with Reason, blinded by love. Where it collapses the complex discourse to the faithless and the faithful, eliding in one all possibility of truth, eliding in the other all possibility of error, it is not just unsound in principle but in practice, calls us to question the functionality of its dysfunction.

A Substrate of Rhapsodies

Fitting all this theory of strange fiction into the original three-axes-of-story idea, what we have now is Lake's third axis, the axis of what he calls *genre devices* analysed in terms of quirks which actively challenge suspension-of-disbelief, playing with subjunctivity level, invoking incredulity by breaching known history (errata), known science (novum), the laws of nature (chimera) and the strictures of logic (sutura). Understanding subjunctivity as alethic modality, however, invites an expansion to encompass not just alethic modality, but boulomaic, deontic and epistemic modalities too; it's only logical to look for quirks in these areas, and not difficult to identify immediately the numina and monstrum as artefacts of boulomaic modality, the generation of a *should/must happen* or *should/must not happen* tension driving the narrative. There is a full framework waiting to be developed here, a toolkit of quirks by which we can decompose a text to the constituent elements a reader will use to parse it as being of this and/or that particular genre(s), elements that are clearly driving forces in the dynamics of narrative.

With this theoretical basis, we can now look at a type of fiction which some aren't even sure exists, but which is constantly labelled and relabelled by writers and critics who have at least a vague sense that there is something to point to here, even if they can only point in the general direction: that inter-slip-cross-genre-stitial-stream stuff, the type of strange fiction that intransigently refuses to be fitted into any genre; the type of strange fiction that gets published under this label or that and argued over by SF fans; the type of strange fiction Bruce Sterling labelled "slipstream" in his *Catscan* essay, but that some of us prefer to call *infernokrusher*.

Burroughs's *The Naked Lunch* is on the list of works Bruce Sterling identified as "slipstream" in his essay—works that aren't necessarily seen as SF but which manifest some quality SF readers pick up on and identify with—because it is essentially strange fiction. It's a book which I consider as much of a predecessor for my own work as many of the strange fictions published in the commercial genres. It is a rhapsody. Peter Ackroyd, J.G. Ballard, Angela Carter, Guy Davenport…we could go through Sterling's list from A to Z and pick out, or add to it, authors that spark a sense of recognition, a feeling that, yes, they are doing something similar, something *specifically* similar. This is simply, I think, a recognition of their *strangeness*. This does not, however, distinguish Sterling's slipstream, my infernokrusher, from any other brand of strange fiction.

There is at once a recognition and an oversight, I think, in the notion of slipstream, cross-genre, interstitial or infernokrusher fiction, of the underlying unity of strange fiction. Simultaneously, we are pointing at the cohesive identity of an idiom in its own right, as and when we label it, but in the labels we choose, we seem invariably to position it as a liminal, marginal construct of leftovers and left-outs, as a border, a transgression of borders, an activity in the seams. I see it rather as a substrate, a substrate of rhapsodies, within and upon which the dialectic of Rationalism and Romanticism has played out to create a multiplicity of genres at odds with each other, obscuring a unity as multi-faceted, yes, but as cohesive as that of tragedy or comedy. Slipstream or infernokrusher, strange fiction as rhapsody, this is not (or not just) some itinerant mongrel of the interzones.

It is the third mask of drama, its gaze not mirth or grief but shock, as on the face of Caravaggio's decapitated Medusa.

This Improper Conjuring

They said, "You have a blue guitar,
You do not play things as they are."
Wallace Stevens, "The Man with the Blue Guitar"

Any rational view of the field should not blind us to the countless writers of strange fiction set on blowing up the walls of Camp Consolation by means other than the novum of science fiction. The erratum that contradicts known history rather than known science, the chimera that contradicts the laws of nature, the sutura that contradicts the strictures of logic—all of these quirks may be grenades thrown at the accepted order of things. It is simplistic to imagine those most outré quirks, the chimera and sutura, always indices of base superstition.

As an eyeball-kick born of Romanticism, a metaphysical quirk is likely no more (or less) than literary SFX, no more (or less) powerful and perilous than a novum used the same way; that the thrill of incredulity is the quirk's purpose in being is all we need know to know the nature of the game. If the marvel is to be taken seriously at all, it is as a pataphor, a figurative vehicle of metaphor unmoored from its tenor and rendered concrete; which is to say, it exists to be read for its non-literal meaning. To project belief is silly-kittens; if I write about a Styx-water swilling cynic collecting an unbaptised infant's soul for the Nursery of Limbo, dude, this is not evidence of faith but a critique of it.

Where fantasy is FANTASY, its definition closed tight to the monomythic mode—to the magically-gifted darlings of destiny, black-and-white struggles of Good and Evil, Dark Lords threatening the bucolic idyll—a supreme wariness *is* called for. Where the wonder button is being pushed, there may well be Romanticism at play, and of the most reactionary sort. Alternatively though, the text may be articulating a modernist agenda, seeking to resolve the agon of passion and reason, emotion and intellect. It may even be the product of a rationalist's Absurdism—because the absurd is the modern rationalist's work even in its apparent illogic, clinical as an autopsy, dissecting a system to expose its disorder(s). Pinter is never more coldly analytic than where exchanges are filleted to a series of non sequiturs.

But the notion of magic as a foreign element is expedient. All problems of structural clichés—of character and setting, plot and theme—all the trite formulae for escapist pabulum developed in the pulps of category product as generic junk food…all of this improper conjuring can be circumscribed as wish-fulfilment and encapsulated in that one word. Every fault in SF can be nailed to this romantic irrationalism. It is never SF that is of pandering purpose, puerile import; if it seems to be, this is because it is not pure SF. It is contaminated, seduced by the exotic colour of the blue flower, intoxicated by its soporific fragrance, polluted by its narcotising essence—magic, which is to say faith.

A contemptuous snort at a bugbear fantasy of fantasy dismisses the imperative of improper conjuring upon all category fiction. It is the first trick taught at Camp Consolation: to ignore a morass of hackwork and focus on the kernel of quality in one's beloved genre; to ignore the kernel of quality and focus on the morass of hackwork in another; to treat the superior work as exemplary here but exceptional there; to take one mode as essentially good but swamped with dross, the other as essentially bad but scattered with the odd diamond. Such doublethink is a self-reinforcing view. As prejudice presents as piety, so it renders its faults as products of influence, scapegoats the reviled enemy as a blight creating wrongness by a process of corruption. The deflection strengthens conviction, certainty of worth rewarded with certainty of worth.

In the rapture of unreason, history itself may be rewritten.

A Smeared Zone of Detritus

The problem is partly that we continue to think and talk in terms of genre. Take a work which uses, say, the counterfactual conceit of a twentieth-century ideology called Futurism (on a par with Fascism or Stalinism), the novum of nanotech, and the chimera of a magical language. Splice in a pathetic narrative that focuses on WW1, the Red Clyde and the Spanish Civil War. Do you end up with something that sits across genres, in a gap between genres, or in a zone between genre and mainstream? Or is it just the same strange fiction that writers such as Bester and Bradbury were writing back before these terms were invented, before SF and Fantasy had been separated out as marketing labels, before the whole rift between literary Realism and pulp Romance was opened up and stabilised by the processes of commerce and academia into the dichotomy of "mainstream" and "genre," a nomenclature defined more in terms of commercial and critical marginalisation than in terms of literary form, a dichotomy more economic than aesthetic? Couldn't we just say that it's strange fiction, fiction distinguished by the use of the quirk? Alternatively, couldn't we just say that it's rhapsody?

Or maybe we might say, No, this is *infernokrusher*!

I'm not a huge fan of subgenres or movements, but infernokrusher is a movement that revels in its own de(con)struction. It's about romping wildly across all territorial boundaries rather than defining a niche, carving out a territory within or between existing genres. Slipstream? That would require we recognise a boundary between Genre and Literature, positioning ourselves in a smeared zone of detritus caught between. Cross-genre? That would require we recognise the same boundaries, characterising ourselves as magpie-style gatherers, sourcing one element of our work *here*, another *there*. Interstitial? That *still* requires we recognise those boundaries but positions us in the truly marginal territory of the cracks between, like weeds between paving-stones. Infernokrusher is not about being situated across genres, between genres, or between genre and mainstream. Infernokrusher doesn't give a fuck about genres, not in *that* way.

Kessel and Kelly, in their anthology *Feeling Very Strange*, quote from a discussion on slipstream that ran on David Moles's blog, in which the term "infernokrusher" was coined by Meghan McCarron, and in which a whole host of contemporary writers try to pin down what they mean by the term. Kessel and Kelly ultimately follow Sterling in their view of slipstream as a literature of the postmodern condition, of cognitive dissonance, the estrangement that comes simply of living in the twentieth / twenty-first century. But how then does this differ from that common-or-garden SF which, according to Suvin, is *all* about cognitive dissonance? What's the difference? What is it that these works *do*?

A Terrain of the Strange

> *[Benford] talks about SF's infrastructure being invaded by fantasy writers and fans, implying that there was a time when the two genres WERE separate. In fact, if you look at British Fandom's infrastructure you see evidence of this...you have the BSFA and you have the BFA, and the BSFA, I get the impression, clearly favours SF over fantasy. So unless the BSFA was an attempt by SF purists to split the genre off, I think that your historical model has problems.*
>
> **Jonathan McCalmont**

Only in a short time frame that skips the formative period of SF entirely, skips everything before the 1970s, can we really sustain this notion of fantasy infiltrating SF from outside; and McCalmont's example of British fandom backs this up. The British Fantasy Society began in 1971 as the British Weird Fantasy Society, an offshoot from the British Science Fiction Association set up in 1958. Which is to say, the infrastructure of fantasy writers and fans was created by an act of separation out from SF, and in the same year the category of FANTASY began separating out from SCIENCE FICTION with the establishment of Ballantine Adult Fantasy Books.

Before this first true FANTASY imprint, diversity was the rule in the SCIENCE FICTION imprints. The focus may have been on the latter-day E.E. "Doc" Smiths of science fiction in Campbell's *Astounding*, but most of the seminal magazines of the strange fiction genres—*Weird Tales*, *The Magazine of Fantasy & Science Fiction*, *Galaxy*—were publishing the Leibers and Lovecrafts of fantasy and horror alongside such fare, the three genres intimate bedfellows from the start, right up through the Golden Age. No writer better encapsulates the fusion of forms at play than Bradbury, sliding effortlessly between the modes, from SF to fantasy to horror, in a story like "The Veldt."

Bradbury himself claims *Fahrenheit 451* as his only real work of SF, yet his fantasies took the default label of the day—like Silverberg's *The Book of Skulls*, Zelazny's *Roadmarks*—pointing us at the real seam of alterity running through SF. His legacy is not just popular TV shows like *The Twilight Zone*, *The Outer Limits*, *The X-Files*. It is New Wave stories like Disch's "Descending", Ellison's "'Repent, Harlequin!' Said the Ticktockman." It is *Interzone* in the '80s, *The Third Alternative*, all that slipstream blending of the mundane and the strange that characterises the UK and US indie press. It is Jeffrey Ford and Kelly Link. It extends beyond the fantasy of the magical, even beyond the fantasy of the weird, old and new—a terrain of the strange that encompasses the liminality of Todorov's fantastique, Freud's uncanny, Pinter's absurd, Jarry's pataphysical along with the broadest of bizarro pulp. Looking to the history, it was there from the get-go.

But then…BOOM! The meteor of Tolkien hits the city of New Sodom, his impact shaking the SF Café to its foundation, shockwave travelling far beyond it, opening the age-old crack that splits our beloved haunt in two. In the ghetto of Genre, in the SF Café, the recognition of a wider market than the regulars leads to whole new imprints, a whole new commercial category, and formulation. The informal term fantasy gets formalised into a label for this new category—and that new category is populated with Tolkien's peers and predecessors at first, but then…let's see. Is that category characterised by works like Bradbury's *Something Wicked This Way Comes*, Silverberg's *The Book of Skulls*, Zelazny's *Roadmarks*? Hell, no. It's dominated by the rotting corpse of Tolkien—the high heroism of "Epic Pooh," as Moorcock scathingly calls it—and the noxious vapours of its decay, the umpteen volumes of *The Chronicles of the Objects of Power*. Those fantasists of the weird who gag on the stench of Tolkien's fetid cadaver find there's little welcome for them at the tables of adventurers on steroids.

The pap propagates, filling the tables, spilling out through the café. The rationalists in the booths react in horror. Suddenly McCaffrey's Pern books and Herbert's *Dune* look suspect; their symbolic and structural tropes (dragons in one, epic in the other) reek of this unreconstructed Romanticism, this…*fantasy*, the term ceasing to signify any old incredible conceit of the marvellous, the uncanny or the monstrous—a carousel that can reverse ageing, a man turning into a beetle, a wheeling-dealing devil—come to signify instead specific formulae of story, structures of Romanticism—e.g. the monomyth at the heart of *Star Wars*. No matter that SF has been selling snake-oil chimerae with a veneer of science for the last fifty years, from Buck Rogers onwards, now the shoddiest pulp charlatanry has a name by which it can be abjured. It is not SF, but fantasy. The Force is magic and jaunting is science.

Magic and monomyth, those fantasists of the weird say, is not what fantasy really is. That, they might say, is only market forces at their most heinous. Those market forces are all too persuasive though. At the booths of SF, they're regarded with suspicion by those most devout in their idealism, most repulsed by the atavistic nonsenses of wizards and knights.

And that suspicion has an impact. Fast-forward through the social pseudo-realisms of feminist SF, through the constant paranoia about "the death of science fiction"—as if it was not already the spectre of SF, that emptied signifier—through the boom of cyberpunk, the burst of New Space Opera, the blast of the Singularity, in which it is reborn in new flesh, new forms. The result? Science Fiction is risen from the grave. The definitions may contradict, requiring fuzzy set systems of subjective models, but there is certainty now in opposition to indefinition.

The ghost of SF as an empty signifier is exorcised, must whisper itself into the nanotech grey goo golem of speculative fiction to survive. Adrift in the SF Café, it stands in the corners or at the counter, wanders the gaps between the tables, lurks at the margins, in the indie presses of the UK and the US, small press magazines and webzines, anthology series. As the corpse of Tolkien rots down to its skeletal frame, the golem talks of slipstream and cross-genre, interstitial fictions, interzones and third alternatives, the weird. Clute's fantastika as a faction inherently estranged from the SF Café's main agon of aesthetics, as a fiction of estrangement. Those who would once have shrugged and said their work was SF simply because it could be sold as such now shrug that fantasy has become the default label. The SF Café echoes with Knight's and Spinrad's indefinitions transferred to another signifier:

—Fantasy is what we mean when we point to it, they say, a rosebud wristlet of blue flowers made obvious as they do just that, raising their hand to point at everything and anything. Any strange rhapsodies.

Strange in the Strangest Way

If we rearticulate Sterling's thesis, we might, I hope, get to the heart of a type of fiction which is not just strange but strange in the strangest way. If I fall into the use of dichotomies like *genre* versus *mainstream* here, bear in mind that these are only informal approximations in the schema of strange fiction proposed. Ultimately, in the infernokrusher spirit, we need to put a bullet through every instance of those terms, blast them the fuck out of the discourse. We need to give the whole debate a lead injection of the strange—the absurd, the abject and the incredible most of all—take a flamethrower to it and burn away all that pertains to strange fiction in its general sense, all the commonalities that are simply the product of their being strange fiction, whether sold as genre or as mainstream. Explode the very terms *conventions* and *strictures*.

If we characterise this type of fiction as Sterling does, by features of attitude, composition and style, there is little that infernokrusher does, attitudinally, that other types of strange fiction don't. Likewise, compositionally, many of Sterling's characteristics are simply those of strange fiction which exploits rather than explains or excuses, characteristics of rhapsody. And his focus on irrationality, "darker elements" which refuse to be made sense of, simply point towards an overlap between the strange and the monstrous, the natural co-occurrence of the alethic modality of "could not happen" and the boulomaic modalities of "should not happen" or "must not happen," the unease that these engender.

Stylistically, however, Sterling identifies additional techniques of estrangement we have only touched on—collage narrative (think Burroughs), metafiction (think Borges), typographical layout (think Bester). These are the techniques of the modernists and postmodernists, of course, so perhaps all we are talking about here is a subset of (post)modernist strange fiction. But Sterling's characterisation of the elsewhens of this type of story as *not* "clearcut departures from the known world," as "integral to the author's worldview," as "in the nature of an inherent dementia" point us to something other—or something more—than the dislocations we have posited for strange narratives.

This is an explicit rejection of the idea that the reader's way out is to reposition the narrative in an elsewhen in which they "could have happened." Does this type of fiction simply not perform these dislocations then? One way to put it might be to say that the reader is indeed dislocated but left hanging in the subjunctivity level of "could not have happened" because they are refused the *stability* of an artificial elsewhen under their feet. Or we could look at another way. We could say that it does dislocate the reader to an elsewhen, it's just that it does something extra. It does indeed rip the reader sideways and forward and up, to a hypothetical, counterfactual, metaphysical elsewhen.

It's just that it brings the whole fucking reality we live in with it.

The Impossible Blue

Art is not difficult because it wishes to be difficult, but because it wishes to be art. However much the writer might long to be, in his work, simple, honest, and straightforward, these virtues are no longer available to him. He discovers that in being simple, honest, and straightforward, nothing much happens: he speaks the speakable, whereas what we are looking for is the as-yet unspeakable, the as-yet unspoken.
Donald Barthelme

In the SF Café, if one looks out of the corner of one's eye at the lapels of this patron or that, one might notice a blue flower as a buttonhole, a sweet-scented and asymmetrically-petalled orchid of a shade somewhere near azure and indigo, across from cerulean and cyan. Take a walk outside, squinting your eyes against the sunlight and you might notice these flowers growing from every crack in the sidewalks of the ghetto of Genre. They sprout in the crack that runs right across the floor of the SF Café. It is a strange blue, the blue of the blue flower—enigma and exotica, artifice or anomaly.

For one SF loyalist—let's call him Strawman—those blue flowers on the lapels of the SF Café's irregular regulars are a vile sight. Often you'll hear him mutter that the blue flower is a weed to be eradicated, a sign of all that's wrong with the ghetto of Genre, the lotus of the lotus-eaters. Those who wear it, he's convinced, do so as sign of their allegiance to some mystic cult, some latter-day Golden Dawn or Theosophical Society…an Order of the Blue Flower. He does not trust such an enigma; all enigma is the ineffable to Strawman, and the ineffable is the irrational. It is fantasy. He recoils in revulsion from the heady hallucinogenic Blue Flower Tea served in the SF Café…which is an entirely natural response of disgust to blue-coloured food, of course…not reasoned, not rational, but natural.

His suspicion is not entirely misplaced. The blue flower was once a symbol of Romanticism: the blue flower of Novalis's *Heinrich von Ofterdingen*; of Joseph Freiherr von Eichendorff's "Die blaue Blume"; the flower that Adelbert von Chamisso saw as the symbol of our striving for love and eternity; the flower Goethe searched for in the countryside of Italy; the flower C.S. Lewis declared himself a votary of, associated with the yearning of Sehnsucht. Strawman hears tell of it in George R.R. Martin's *A Song of Ice and Fire* series. He hears it in the talk of latter-day Romantics, their boasts of the grand lineage of their cult—MacDonald, Tennyson, Macpherson, Spenser, Malory, Geoffrey of Monmouth. But if Strawman looked closer, he might see that the emblems of an imaginary lost idyll those dreamers cradle in their cupped palms are paper copies. Closer still and he might see the real blue flower they don't even know they're wearing on their lapels. He might see the blue flower he's wearing on his own.

The blue flower is not fantasy but rhapsody, the strange. If it might be supernatural, some magical blossom sprouting and blooming through rifts in reality itself, it might as easily be extraterrestrial, an alien life-form carried to the planet by a meteorite. Marvellous or monstrous, uncanny or weird, all we can say for sure is that it has no place in our experience of the world. To glimpse the blue flower is to see something with no place in all known history, known science. It might even be beyond the laws of nature or the strictures of logic. Or not.

If Strawman studied his own blue flower, he'd find that its blue is Hume's hypothetical "missing shade of blue," a shade unknown in nature, never seen, but imaginable in the mind's eye…perhaps. This was Hume's thought experiment: if conception is a recombination of perception, he asked, could we then imagine a colour we have never sensed? Hume was unsure, but given that blue and yellow, green and red, black and white, we now know, are only the symbolic dimensions in which our sense of colour is constructed as an abstract modelling of light frequencies by opponent processes, to take this literally rather than figuratively, the positive answer is obvious. It's like asking if we can imagine a number between fifty-four and fifty-six without ever seeing a group of fifty-five things; the possibility is self-evident, our mind a palette made to mix shades of colours which are always already imaginary.

To push the question beyond the literal though, towards a deeper interrogation, is to make the blue of the blue flower a figuration of the figurative itself. It is to imagine that blue only our symbol of another missing shade, a blue that lies not between two shades we've seen but beyond them all—a bluer-than-blue. The blue of the blue flower is a colour out of colourspace imagined in place of a colour from beyond it, a surrogate we conjure in order to visualise the strange flower right in front of us. It is our rendering of the as-yet-unspoken, which was once Romantic, once purely a locus of the sensational, but which became, with the advent of modernity, too dangerous to leave unspoken. It is the impossible blue by which we articulate what others claim ineffable, do so figuratively in defiant experiments of unmoored metaphor, success uncertain. It's the entirely new yellowish-blue seen by the subjects of Billock, Gleason and Tsou's experiments in suppressing the mutual inhibition of opponent processes that otherwise prevents such a sensation.

The blue flower is that from which Philip K. Dick's fictitious Substance D is derived in *A Scanner Darkly*. It's the strangeness in that fiction that's not Romantic awe but existential angst, in which metaphysical questions of the nature of reality are bound to questions of the nature of humanity, in which scientific rationalism is far from the point but in which the core value of secular humanism is—empathy. It's the blue flower worn by Lil the Dancer in David Lynch's *Twin Peaks: Fire Walk with Me*, an oneiric enigma of signifier divorced from signified, the irrational perhaps, but the unreason masked by mundane shams of order, the faux reality of the suburbs; it seeks to render the as-yet-unspoken of the bugfuck nutjobbery that lurks beneath. It is not the ineffable but the touchstones by which we demarcate it, begin to make it effable. It's the blue flower that might have been described in the meticulous botanical detail of a Guy Davenport story, "The Meadow," say…though it so happens that it wasn't.

Bradbury, Silverberg, Zelazny—all wear the blue flower as a buttonhole. All strange fiction writers wear the blue flower, whether they call it supernatural or extraterrestrial, both words parsing to the same relational meaning, different only in the subtle shading: super- or extra- denoting from above, outside, beyond; natural or terrestrial denoting of or pertaining to the condition we were born into, the soil that we live on, the world as our material environment. The blue flower is the quirk, and the quirk is alterity. Wherever strange fictions serve as a force against base prejudice, it is because of how they treat that alterity—not credulous in a conviction that we will be saved or slaughtered by the extraterrestrial or supernatural but sceptical of all Camp Consolation's tales that cast the Other as enemy. It is all too easy to be prejudiced against blacks and gays when your SF is telling you that the invading aliens and the mutants in the wastelands are just plain dangerous.

Where this is our heroic fantasy—that the blue flowers are poisonous weeds to be stamped out—we are not tackling the rapture of unreason but surrendering to it. We will be until we are able to see the flower on every lapel, our own included, until we can see that we are all of us of the Order of the Blue Flower.

The Tower of Mimeticists' Bicuspids

Every Crack in the Sidewalk

Living in the ghetto, the stranglehold that contemporary realism has exerted over the literature of the last half century or so seems self-evident, with all that is unreal, weird, *strange*—the novum, the erratum, the chimera—largely relegated to the margins, magical realism pretty much alone in being afforded recognition as LITERARY FICTION rather than GENRE FICTION. The patrons of the Bistro de Critique do have a tendency to see those fields of fiction schismed off as Genre rather than Literature in terms of the dominant formulation—as more interested in plot than character, more concerned with worldbuilding than prose.

Is the perception wholly unfair? Plot is deeply important in that GENRE fiction which requires not just *narrative* but *story*, and the conceit is an integral aspect of these strange fictions, extrapolated out through the text, the reimagining of reality at the core of what the work is saying and how it says it, from the worldbuilding of Tolkien or Peake to most any work by Ballard. This is why "mainstream" writers who use the strange (Franz Kafka, Italo Calvino, Jorge Luis Borges, William Burroughs, Gabriel García Márquez, Angela Carter, Edward Whittemore and so on) appeal deeply and widely to the SF market, why SF readers are drawn to them, why SF writers very often cite them as influences and write similar works that they can then sell as SF. We recognise the blue flower on their lapels.

Beat writers, (post)modernists, magic realists, all manner of fantasists, fabulists and plain old weird-ass experimentalists have been popular amongst SF readers so long that a market for their work is well and truly established within the ghetto of Genre, a more dynamic and cohesive market possibly than anything the district of Literature has to offer. There are whole magazines, anthologies and imprints which focus primarily on this type of fiction and form a significant facet of the field. More conventional magazines, anthologies and imprints continually publish fiction of this type, reflecting that facet. Result: there are writers like Kelly Link and Jeffrey Ford, who reside largely in the ghetto of Genre but who clearly belong in the same aesthetic territory as those writers above, in terms of both approach and quality. The idea that these writers are unconcerned with characterisation and prose is risible at best. The Blue Flower Tea of the SF Café does not dull the palate but stimulates it.

Truth is, we've had delicatessens in the ghetto of Genre for decades now, and gastro pubs selling gourmet cuisine to the hipsters. The SF Café isn't even the only place to go.

Hell, we've got opium dens dealing prose that will get you *truly* whacked out. Head down to the Paraliterary Diner and try out some of the Delany. Or some fresh Lucius Shepard might be more to your taste. Ask Matt Cheney at The Mumpsimus Tourist Centre what's good and tell him I sent you. You may have walked a few blocks in, seen a few of the most popular tourist spots—Gaiman's Café, Le Guin's Bar and Grill—and a few of the old run-down greasy spoons (man, I wouldn't let my dog eat at Tolkien's Trattoria)…but you have to check out the centre and the side-streets around it, not be spooked into flight by the wildlife, weird as we may seem at times. Remember to take some time to smell the flowers that sprout from every crack in the sidewalk.

It is unfortunate that, for those writers of Literary Fiction who have little concern with the pataphor, the concrete metaphor or conceit, a passing awareness of this technique shades into a sweeping dismissal, an assumption that Genre Fiction focuses on this element to the detriment of the prose—but more for them than for us. The ramification of the prejudice that results from this is that there's a whole literary technique which their fiction excludes, and a readership, it seems, who care little about the vast potential squandered, but do care about: well-turned and well-heeled sentences; well-observed and insightful characterisation; a pat epiphany at the end.

The Raw and Visceral Drive

Uptown in the Bistro de Critique, they talk of prose concerns in terms of a work's "level of engagement with its medium." Downtown in the SF Café, we scorn this as an interest in style over substance. Ultimately, the disjunction here is structural: they're talking about engaging with the low-level structure of *prose* as craft (sentential structure, semantic sets, syntax, rhythm, etc.), while we're talking about engaging with the high-level structure of *narrative* as craft (scene structure, character dynamics, plot, pacing, etc.). In reality, prose or narrative, it is all structure, and recognising this opens up a line of defence…and of attack. Down in the SF Café we might talk of (superficial) surface execution and (substantial) internal content, but if we want to argue in the Bistro de Critique, it will be much easier if we talk their language, talk of engagement with the medium, with the craft of fiction, with *narrative*.

The failures of low-level craft in pulp fiction are undeniable. The countless examples of appalling prose may well be contrasted with the importance placed on plot, idea and world. Characterisation is liable to be shallow where the narrative grammar of horror / thriller / mystery / adventure / epic calls for engagement with a largely external conflict. And this is hardly the place to look for epiphanies of the ephemeral. But conversely, prose that is not well-heeled may nonetheless be well-turned, characters that are backgrounded rather than made psychological studies of are demonstrably *not the point* of the narrative, and the absence of a trite epiphany, more sophomoric wank than true satori, is no bad thing.

To say that even the purest pulp is not engaging with the medium in its focus on narrative over these features is like saying that a punk band are not engaging with the medium when, with a simple line-up of singer, guitar, bass and drums, they deliberately set out to make rock songs in the classic three-minute format of verse, chorus, verse, chorus, middle-eight, verse, chorus. They may well be less concerned with intricate guitar licks, syncopation in the drum beats, the melodic skills or clever lyrics of the singer. That doesn't mean they're not concerned with the craft of the rock song. Actually, they're deeply concerned. The purity of structure, the raw and visceral drive achieved by disregarding executional polish and focusing on simple, tight *songs*—that's what they're concerned with.

Here's a thought experiment. Take a short story outline and get two different writers to flesh it out, a Literary Fiction writer and a Genre Fiction writer. What you *might* end up with is two different piles of words, yet the same plot and characters. But another scenario is equally likely

The Literary Fiction writer works straight from your outline, focusing on the polish of the prose, the social and domestic documentary detail, the effects of voice in creating plausible character(s), the reflexive comment, the tone; they end it with a moment of profound melancholy as the protagonist gazes at a blue flower crushed underfoot on the sidewalk.

The Genre Fiction writer says that your plot is thin, your setting is irrelevant, your first quarter is throat-clearing, your characters are dull, their interactions are uninvolving, your structure of action is saggy in the middle, there's no narrative drive and no sense of climax and resolution. In their story, that blue flower sparks a thought leading the protagonist to solve a problem.

In the end, the changes each writer makes so that this outline works as a story for them, by their aesthetics, are so substantial that even the plot and characters in those two piles of words are radically different. Assuming those two writers are entirely unconcerned with the other's views, they are nevertheless equally engaged with the medium.

The priorities of each may lead them to neglect the qualities prioritised by the other, and where readers subscribe to one aesthetic and reject another they will be responsive to one version and dismissive of the other. This dichotomy was historically and culturally self-evident in English literature's divide into Novel and Romance, and there are still remnants of it in the divide between Literature and Genre.

But that divide between Literary Fiction and Genre Fiction is born of a sleight-of-hand redefinition of both terms—a conflation of markets and modes. *Genre* means a specific aesthetic form of fiction (of whatever quality), but it has also come to mean any fiction aimed at a particular set of markets. *Literary* means high-quality fiction (of whatever aesthetic form), but it has also come to mean any fiction *not* aimed at that particular set of markets. We only have to smear the two meanings of each term and—*voilà!*—by definition LITERARY FICTION and GENRE FICTION are a mutually exclusive taxonomy and any particular work must be considered one or the other. This is really just a circular definition of any fiction aimed at a particular set of markets as of a lower quality than fiction not so aimed.

Strip it down to the underlying politics of these aesthetic territories and we find a flat assertion, a judgemental privileging of the values underpinning one set of fictions over those underpinning another: the valorisation of Story by GENRE FICTION is *wrong* because it leads to "non-literary" fiction, while the valorisation of Style by LITERARY FICTION is *right* because it leads to "literary" fiction; to value Story is *bad* taste because those are the standards of GENRE FICTION, while to value Style is *good* taste because those are the standards of LITERARY FICTION.

This is no more and no less than a petit-bourgeois exercise of privilege in order to reinforce privilege, the application of literary aesthetics *to* literary aesthetics as a self-validating signal of social status, a demonstration of the power to judge, in which the judgement is itself an assertion of its own legitimacy.

Fuck that shit.

A Semiotic Approach

Scouring away this High Art / Low Art Culture Wars crap, the question of Style versus Story remains, the question of to what extent these generalisations might be fair and to what extent each type of fiction, GENRE FICTION or LITERARY FICTION, might neglect the values of the other. Answer: both Style and Story are masks for the reality that words are the only substance: prose is narrative is prose is narrative; the only difference is structural focus, on the concrete or abstract levels of effect, on internal and/or external action.

If GENRE FICTION focuses on Story at the expense of Style, does LITERARY FICTION focus on Style at the expense of Story? The dichotomy is meaningless. A pulp narrative of shoddy prose conjures a shoddy narrative, only succeeds because the skimreader bounces from benchmark to benchmark, constructing the story for themself. Meanwhile, a well-heeled sentence that is slick but shallow is as bad as prose as it is as narrative, for all that a good grasp of tone allows the writer to craft a passable sense of inner conflict and resolution, a similitude of plot in the shifting of emotional tensions, all wrapped up neatly with the faux-resolution of a moment of epiphany.

A plague, I say, on both these houses, but *doubled* on the mediocrity of the middlebrow. Cock save us from the skimwritten formulaic trash but, by the Good Lord Cock Almighty, *damn* the banality of well-crafted but insipid prose delving deep, but without drive or direction, into a conjuring of the tedious, neurotic, facile angsts of the straight white middle-class male, reaching for some slightest scrap of inspiration to end it on with a limp and maundering pseudo-apophenia. Have we lived and fucked in vain that our wild literature of the aeons, from the first furry faggot giantkiller through to the wounding of an autumnal city and beyond, should be spin-doctored as such an anodyne creation as the *literary*?

Even if living in the ghetto of Genre did mean being lost among the *Untermenschen* of narrative junkies and subsisting only on the hackwork prose handed out in the soup kitchens, having not a single eatery serving more than kippleburgers, the alternative might well be seen as a cocktail party of self-styled *Übermenschen*, snorting prose and nibbling on the flimsy narrative hors d'oeuvres handed out by obsequious serving staff, the sort of fiction Michael Chabon refers to as "the contemporary, quotidian, plotless, moment-of-truth revelatory story."

To return to the music metaphor, preferring prose over narrative the LITERARY FICTION fan extolls the literary equivalent of prog-rock epics, bloated and pompous, albeit expertly played by skilled musicians. They praise twiddly guitar wank and widdly synth shite, recoiling from the three-chord, three-minute blasts of energy that are GENRE FICTION because some of the more popular musicians can't play their instruments for peanuts—have good songs but lack polish. At least The Stooges are not sterile.

And to recoil from GENRE FICTION, of course, is to miss out on those who *can* play, and to fancy one's ignorance an actual absence. At its extreme, these musos become advocates of an idea that this lack of polish is systemic, that the best punk band could *never* be as good as a prog band, because punk (with a few rare exceptions) will always be hamstrung by its intrinsic faults, whereas prog, being the standard against which all rock should be measured, is a higher art form.

Not only is this nonsense, but the impoverishment of LITERARY FICTION will be far more extreme than any lack of prosaic polish in GENRE as long as this is ultimately what is meant by *literary* as opposed to *genre*: where the former insists upon a purely mimetic approach, a fiction of *representation*, the latter is identified by a distinctly semiotic approach, a fiction of *figuration*. Where the realists inherit from Rationalism a focus on observation and articulation, a focus on the low-level structuring of language (Style) as a medium through which an insightful study of some situation in the world may be developed and offered to a reader, writers of the category fiction abjected depart from this precisely in the dynamics they inherit from Romanticism, their supposed focus on the high-level structures of language (Story) unpacking to a low-level vitality of pataphoric prose, a medium in which the semiocosm is re-engineered directly.

On a superficial level, it should not be difficult to understand the trope-sets of character, plot and worldscape that are found in SPACE OPERA, EPIC FANTASY, CRIME, WESTERN or ROMANCE as symbols within a supersystem of semiotic systems, a lexis of spaceships, dragons, detectives or bodice-ripped heroines for which the narrative is syntax. It should not be hard to see in these metaphors with their iconic vehicle unmoored from tenor, the capacity of a conceit like Heller's Catch-22, the infinite capacity of the sum of every and any potential such conceit.

Ultimately, all generic tropes can be analysed as quirks, not as copied conventions but as disruptions of suspension-of-disbelief, or of affective equilibrium; as objects and individuals, events and settings charged with wonder, awe, horror, desire, *whatever*; as fictive elements that are sensationalist, a strain on credibility or whatever, precisely because that power is their purpose, and that purpose at the heart of art.

Insofar as *any* fictive element can be so invested, made a quirk by context, it is not simply that these genres utilise these semiotic systems as trope-sets. It is not simply that the genres create meaning by combining these tropes into a narrative. It is that they *generate* quirks through the dynamics of narrative and in so doing reconstruct the semiocosm that lives in us and in which we live, our filter on reality, our language for making sense of it.

It is in this respect that Genre Fiction takes a semiotic approach anathema to the realists of Literary Fiction, in this respect that it exhibits semiosis as a process, in the same way that realist fiction exhibits mimesis. We can only ask then: if the semiotic fiction of Genre allows the mimesis associated with Literature, while the mimetic fiction of Literature *absolutely* rejects the semiosis associated with Genre, which is the more aesthetically limited and limiting form?

Incisors, Canines or Molars

But it is not so simple; it never is. There are Genre Fiction writers who are deeply concerned with Style, just as there are Literary Fiction writers who are deeply concerned with Story. The same goes for readers. Just as there are Genre Fiction readers who find it hard to read a work without at least serviceable prose, there are Literary Fiction readers who find it hard to read a work without at least serviceable narrative. The big difference is that where one subset of self-identifying genre kids who don't much care for prose are largely notable by their over-zealous positivity as regards their own tastes (and a vacuous inverse snobbery about "style over substance"), that small subset of incognoscenti who don't much care for narrative are made notable by their over-zealous negativity as regards the tastes of others and by the privileging of their position.

If the former are harmful, their patronage allowing mediocre prose to survive and flourish in the ghetto of Genre, the latter are worse, their patronage allowing mediocre narrative to survive and flourish in the district of Literature *and* consistently devaluing narrative as they devalue the semiotic approach so as to inflate the value of mimesis. In their abjection of these fundamental aspects of writing they do more harm to themselves than anyone else though.

A grand ivory tower dominates the uptown district of Literature, the Tower of Mimeticists' Bicuspids, built of teeth pliered out of the mouths of LITERARY FICTION writers by their own hands. Originally, as the name suggests, the teeth were only meant to be bicuspids—those sort of *in-between* teeth, the ones that aren't incisors, canines or molars, that aren't particularly good at cutting, penetrating or grinding, that seem, in fact, to lack any real purpose of their own—but once the LITERARY FICTION writers started ridding themselves of those seemingly pointless outgrowths of enamel, well, it seems they found it hard to stop.

—The tooth is not the truth, they muttered sagely. We need to strip the mouth of all this meaningless decoration, the glamorous artifice of the lying smile, the deceit of dental gleaming. So they stripped themselves down to the bare essentials needed to mumble the nasalised bilabial *mmm* and the sibilant hissing *sss* of *mimesis*.

The tower has risen over the decades till it's fifty years tall or more now, but it's looking increasingly unstable. In the Bistro de Critique this instability is sometimes viewed as a corrosion of the foundations, blamed on the proles of Genre naturally, on the dumbing-down of culture, every YA book bought by an adult, every GENRE FICTION novel sold for airplane reading, every comic book and DVD another brilliant-white brick of lost bite kicked from the bottom of the structure. In truth, that ivory tower is mainly crumbling under the weight of the egos sat at the top, spitting at the peasants down below who want hard ground more than hot air. Well…I *say* "spitting"; it's more the inevitable drooling slabber of those with only gums and lips between their saliva and the outside world.

This is why some LITERARY FICTION writers of actual ambition, like David Mitchell or Glen David Gold, have adopted the methods and modes of GENRE FICTION, why GENRE FICTION writers like Michael Chabon or Jonathan Lethem have broken out of the ghetto and become mainstream, why all manner of works with their aesthetic homeland in the ghetto of Genre (the SF of *The Time Traveler's Wife*, the YA of Harry Potter) are ignoring that ghetto for the much wider market of the city of New Sodom as a whole. There's a demand for something, something that is not being supplied by LITERARY fiction, something that these types of writing do supply.

It is not happy endings they want; it is simply *endings*, period, rather than the pseudo-ending of epiphany. Beginnings, middles and endings, and maybe not in that order, but at least discernible as *structure*. They want narrative, the sort of tight, focused, dynamic *drive* you get in genre, and not at the expense of polished, interesting prose, but *with* it. Where the aesthetic of the ephemeral once gave us a breathless *yes* whispered under a Moorish wall, now the epiphany is formulated. And as with any such formulation, "more of the same" only goes so far, and there comes a time people start looking for "something different."

When the audience is turning to GENRE FICTION for more dynamic narrative, what does this say of its availability outside these sections? When kids are suddenly reading again because of series like Harry Potter, what does this say about keeping the reader's attention? When adults are picking up these books after not having read a novel in years, what does that say about the dismal state of a Literature that's been driving readers away in boredom over the last few decades? When new writers are increasingly bringing Genre Fiction qualities over into works sold as general fiction, and finding an eager market, what does this tell you about the vacuum they're filling? In the Bistro de Critique (and even, in truth, in the more gentrified corners of the SF Café), some see this as a dumbing-down, but what's happening is not a lowering of the bar, rather a *heightening*, an increased demand for greater craft in terms of narrative.

And if there's anything to be learned in the Tower of Mimeticists' Bicuspids, fuck it, we've got no qualms about dropping by now and then just to see what's new. Hell, we're thieving gypos and uppity niggers, cheap whores and predatory faggots, scum who like to ramraid the kitchens of that ivory tower at every opportunity. We gate-crash the parties, steal the hors-d'oeuvres narratives, snort more than our fair share of prose, check out what's hot and what's not, noise up the nobs when they start sounding off about the yobs, and head back home with new recipes for the SF Café. Some of us do anyway. Many are happy just to flip their patties and serve up the same old burger plots and beery sentences, but there's a vibrant subculture devoted to the druggy delights of prose and the gastronomic glories of narrative, and those of us in that scene, we've tasted the best fixes and food of both worlds, learned from it, and set out to better it.

If the toothless mimeticists don't know the best the ghetto has to offer—either because they never thought to look, or because a few bum steers led to a hasty retreat and a firm distrust—fuck 'em. Let them hang and let them fall. It'll be peachy keen to see what blue flowers bloom in the rubble and what weird new forms are built out of the wreckage of the Tower of Mimeticists' Bicuspids by the generation of mutants who've been hanging in the ghetto of Genre for the last fifty years, partying and watching that structure sway in the breeze.

Okay, okay, let's be honest. We do kind of like to take a kick at that edifice whenever we're passing. Our librarian is there right now, in fact, chipping away at its base, planting some C-4 charges in the holes. All she has to do to set them off, as a librarian, is recommend the right work of the right genre to the right person, open up their eyes to the power of semiosis.

—*The Yiddish Policeman's Union*?

BOOM!

—*The Time Traveler's Wife*?

BOOM!

—*The Borribles*!

BOOM!

Steel Dreams of a New Daedalus

In the Bistro de Critique, an old orthodoxy of "mundane good, outré bad" is already crumbling, with writers like Chabon and Lethem making their mark while pointedly refusing to forsake their roots, the seats they still occupy in the SF Café. Despite our best efforts to shirk respectability and maintain our freakish status as outsiders, the literati are starting to nose around the ghetto, interest piqued in what's happening down here, where the harlots and harlequins hang out. The cocktail parties are getting stale now, maybe, and, *darling*, I hear Miéville's monster shows actually have *ideas* in them. How quaint! And this VanderMeer chap's apparently dancing the *Nabokov* of all things. What are they calling this stuff? The New Weird? New Wave Fabulism?

Call it the League of Fusion Fry-Cooks. Call it the Order of the Blue Flower. Call it the fucking New Modern Army.

In the early decades of the twentieth century, in the era of mass-production, in the apotheosis of the Enlightenment, it seemed the strata of humanity and history were peeled away by new ways of understanding—psychoanalysis, evolutionary theory, archaeology. In an increasingly interconnected world, the strange realities of other cultures were being brought home to us. As were the horrors of mechanised warfare. A new form of fiction, some thought, was required to represent a world as savage as it was civilised, as driven by passion as by reason. So an audacious project began, to wire together the best bits of both Romanticism and Rationalism, create a Frankenstein's fiction which was more virile and imaginative than the middle-class melodrama of the Realists but more relevant and subtle than the florid self-delusions of the Romantics. The result was modernism.

Like the mimetic fiction of Literature this fiction had the drive to document the details of reality, offering no easy ride, no penny-dreadful diversion, but like the semiotic fiction of Genre it freely utilised the mythic, the oneiric, the psychotic, the strange, accepted dreams and delusions as a part of that reality. Across the arts they sought to reinvest the modern era with something of the archaic—as in Picasso, influenced by cave paintings, painting the Minotaur-like bull in his *Guernica*, as in Joyce's use of the Ulysses myth, of Daedalus, of the giant Finn McCool. Perhaps this came from the nature of the project, constructing its representations out of fragments of perspective scaled up to experience scaled up to knowledge. Through cubism and collage, Modernism attempted to tackle the chaos of our world, to deconstruct and reconstruct it into a semblance of order. Where the Romantics and the Realists failed to fully face this unfathomable world, revelling in the unreason or rationalising it away, modernism took the absence of meaning as a challenge.

Modernism heard Nietzsche's dread pronouncement on the death of God and rolled its sleeves up: time to get to work. Nihilist, existentialist, postmodernist from the start—because postmodernism is only the strain of modernism that takes the end of metanarrative as its metanarrative—it was a project so grand that the whole of history had to be material, including that history that hadn't happened yet—the future. That future is history now, with the sculptures of the Futurists as its memorials, the mechanical landscape of the Machine Age remembered, fetishised in the dynamics of steel forms fragmented to show movement, *change*. SF is the annals of that historical future, the chronicles of the twentieth century's kinetic potentials as they emerged—fascists on the moon and communist aliens, feminist and capitalist dystopias and utopias—typewritten on a counter-top of shining Formica in the SF Café, amid the accreting kipple of broken Bakelite and plastic dreams—kipple accreting into a truth coded in trash.

The psychological landscape, to the Surrealists, was as much grist for the mill, a similar terrain of fragments thrown together out of context, mundane images juxtaposed to create cognitive dissonance and, perhaps, new meaning: a man in a bowler hat with an apple where his face should be; a man in a bowler hat with one false eyelash; fish people; mushroom people. The best of what we call SF is a similar cut-up-and-fold-in of the imagery of reality, of the structures of history and myth, the future and the psyche, steel dreams of a new Daedalus. Take a little bit of this culture, a little bit of that, splice and dice, fold and unfold. The best of what we call SF is engaged on the same project, using the same techniques and tools as the most highbrow of the highbrow modernists, every imagistic phrase another petal on a blue flower.

The modernist monster rampaged through literature, roaring in the cloisters of the Temple of Academia, tearing up the Bistro de Critique, pissing on conventions, gobbling up GENRES and spewing them out in pastiche, searching for meaning everywhere, anywhere, in the Fourth Dimension or in the lint stuck in a belly-button; and, in the absence of any absolute certainty, it was left howling its emptiness, or simply laughing madly at the futility of it all. In the end, it was such a damn *freak* that the backlash of horror and incomprehension left it out on the frozen wastes. A black hole always already at the heart of the beast, what put the *post* in (post)modernism (and the reason that *post* is bracketed) was not the failure of that project, only the recognition that the one metanarrative worth shit was a blank page in a nihilist's notebook.

The modernist experiment and its fall-out left most outside the Temple of Academia, and many inside, utterly aghast.

—What the fuck is this madness, they cried, this gibberish, this self-absorbed, self-referential, stream-of-unconsciousness fiction-which-ate-itself? Take your crazy-ass *Finnegans Wake* and get the hell away from me, ya goddamn loon.

So the uptown mimeticists stepped in, offering a nice and safe *Literary Fiction* for readers and critics averse to the outré excesses of semiosis. And the downtown semioticists stepped in, offering a nice and safe GENRE FICTION for readers and critics averse to the mundane banalities of mimesis. But on either side of the barricades, uptown with the bores at the cocktail party or downtown with the whores in the ghetto, a few writers furtively carried on the tradition. They had to play the game in each environ, but at the end of the day there *were* at least havens for the hobo pomos and the homo bohos in the Bistro de Critique and the SF Café.

In the Bistro de Critique they still have the bones of that modernist monster, holy relics wired-together and made to play-act in the puppet-show of (post)modern archness, the semiosis couched in intellectual irony for the uptown crowd. In the SF Café, the mimesis had to be similarly couched in sensational rapture for the downtown crowd, but we have the heart of that big old Frankenstein's fiction, that lumbering patchwork creature obsessed with all the grandiose tales of creation, muttering with mad eloquence about Prometheus and God, Adam and the Devil, but deep down craving only empathy, membership in the human race. We have the heart of modernism, with all its insane ambition, wired into the golem that is clawing its way up out of the cellar even now.

This Cannibal Creation

The sociography of SF is a sociography of abjection after abjection, of denial upon denial. The Tower of Mimeticists' Bicuspids hasn't fallen yet. There are still those among us who think the Order of the Blue Flower is a nefarious sect bent on perverting SF with fantasy. The League of Fusion Fry-Cooks still have to sell their haute cuisine as hamburger. The Kipple Foodstuff Factory is still a blight on the cityscape of the ghetto of Genre. We bitch about the Bistro de Critique even as the Last Realist bewails our victory over it. We still deny—*abject*—most everything there is in SF that makes it great.

We're not Fantasy. We're not Sci-Fi. We're not Literary Fiction.

We deny our Pulp bitch-dam's streetwise *nous*, deny that we've been hustling our asses because we chose to, because life in the ghetto means freedom. We deny everything we've learned suckling on our dear old momma's plentiful paps, deny that we've learned how to turn tricks like real pros, paint ourselves up in pretty colours to hawk our wares on the street corner. Yet each day, each night, we straighten up the red leather miniskirt or guddle the bulge of our denim cut-offs, and stare at our face in the mirror as we put a fake eyelash on.

Even as we do so we glimpse this strange thing looking back at us, the part of ourselves inherited from this cannibal creation, ugly and miserable and awful to look at, what with both eyes on the same side of the face and all—our golem and our doppelgänger. It's not gonna win any popularity contests. It's not gonna have the punters oohing and aahing with that old sense-of-wonder satisfaction. But there's something intriguing about the images reflected in its eyes, about the echoes in its voice as it whispers in the back of our head, the voice of the ghost that possesses both it and us.

We deny this too.

That's not us, we tell ourselves. No, we're weird but not *that* weird. We're outré but not *that* outré. The ghetto is accepting of freaks but not *that* accepting. That old monster's just too damn *out there* for most folks. We're not pulp, but by God, we're not modernist. No. Let's just call ourselves SF, because then no one can ever accuse us of being, God forbid, "pretentious".

So we fix our dress and head out into the street, a harlequin and a hustler.

Slipstream or Infernokrusher

> *Category is a marketing term, denoting rackspace. Genre is a spectrum of work united by an inner identity, a coherent esthetic, a set of conceptual guidelines, an ideology if you will...*
>
> *...what seems to me to be a new, emergent genre, which has not yet become a category...*
>
> *...is a contemporary kind of writing which has set its face against consensus reality [...] fantastic, surreal sometimes, speculative on occasion, but not rigorously so. It does not aim to provoke a "sense-of-wonder" or to systematically extrapolate...*
>
> *...simply makes you feel very strange; the way that living in the late twentieth century makes you feel, if you are a person of a certain sensibility. We could call this kind of fiction Novels of Postmodern Sensibility...*
>
> **Bruce Sterling**

Or we could call it…**INFERNOKRUSHER!!!**

Of Loose Threads, Shreds, Scraps

> *Slipstream, ultimately, is just a wussy term. We should be drawing names less from wishy-washy words (slip, stream) and more from monster trucks (krusher, inferno.)*
>
> **Meghan McCarron**

At the heart of this term *slipstream* is an image of a zone of turbulence, where *mainstream* and *genre fiction* mix. It is an image of a sleek chrome bullet-train of GENRE dragging up dead leaves and detritus from the mainstream tracks as it rockets relentlessly forward. It is an image of that Gernsback-Campbell Express already gone, past in the blink of an eye, the sonic boom of the New Wave still echoing, but the most noticeable mark of its passing simply the way our hair still whips across our faces, the cloud of dust still whirling around us, the air sucked from in front of our mouths, the tug we feel to follow in its path…the effect of its passing…the slipstream. It is an image of the perturbation of mainstream by GENRE, of ragged edges where modernity has torn through an otherwise tranquil and reflective fictive mode, of loose threads, shreds, scraps sucked up and tumbling in the wake of rocket-powered pulp prose. At the same time it is an image of genre as the pocket of air which is doing the disruption, an atmosphere of fiction that sort of travels with the genre but is not genre, which sloughs and swirls off to settle in the mainstream, like a piece of litter dropped from the window of that train.

Monster trucks, bullet trains or rocket ships—SF likes its technotoys. The Golden Age sent rockets into the deep space of '50s and '60s imaginations. The New Wave watched them plummet down to apocalypse. Slipstream—or infernokrusher, to give it its correct name—puts a warp drive on a Winnebago and then fires it at a black hole. Or drops a burning angel on an Airstream trailer in the middle of the Mojave. Or doesn't.

A Cold Inferno

> *It is important to note that an infernokrusher sensibility does not require literal infernos or crushing.*
> **David Moles**

An image that crops up time and time again in my writing is, I have realised, the image of hot air shimmering over tarmac on a summer day. I suppose it represents a tremulous, tenuous quality to perceived reality, the idea that mirages and distortions are essential parts of this world, entirely natural if illusory products of sweltering heat. I wonder if that image doesn't suggest that somewhere down that road, at that point in the distance where the tarmac and the blue sky meld into rippling artifice, reality itself is warping, coming apart in the heat of the summer sun, such that the road, if one could reach that tissue-thin but always distant portal of illusion, might lead us into worlds of utter strangeness. I'm sure it suggests the haze of summer days, the dreamy daze of memories of childhood, because summer is, of course, the cyclic childhood of the soul. Ray Bradbury, that great pre-proto-infernokrusher writer, blowing up genre conventions left, right and centre with his speculative, horrific, marvellous, domestic, rhapsodic fictions, knew how important summer is symbolically and sentimentally. He knew that it also represents the shattering of those dreams, the end of innocence, the tearing of that numinous idyll's very fabric in the last day. All summer in a day, and if that day ends, and you miss it…

Hot summer days always make me think of death, by the way. It's fucking gorgeous today, so of course my thoughts turn towards sorrow, a less literal form of crushing, a cold inferno.

In That Same Interzone

The only native in Interzone who is neither queer nor available is Andrew Keif's chauffeur.

William Burroughs, The Naked Lunch

The first ever issue of *Interzone* I bought, at the tender age of Xteen years old, was the one that had Ian Watson's "Jingling Geordie's Hole" in it, a fucked-up little tale that might well be called horror but which reads, in parts, like one of those contemporary realist tales of English childhood, of imagination at play in bleak post-war reality, of innocence lost. Two boys lark about in a cave associated in local legend with a mythical worm. Flirting, facilitating stranger games with readings from Marlowe's *Edward II*, one of them seduces the other into sexual experimentation and, following the blood and the semen of their tawdry encounter, there's a dark, impossible and increasingly disturbing pregnancy. As I say, it's a fucked-up little story.

As a queer, of course, I found the story fascinating, even more unsettling, perhaps, because of its—for me—erotic charge. But as turbulent as the tension between lust and revulsion in that story was, and as much as that turbulence reflected my own adolescent confusion of desire and fear, the real tension at the heart of the story, the key source of the strange, strained, estranged feeling of the story is, for me, the tension between the mundane and the monstrous. Like many of the plays of Dennis Potter, I think, "Jingling Geordie's Hole" positions itself between these things we call *genre* and *mainstream*. Devils and frozen heads and noir detectives and musical numbers shear off the pulp world and are turned into the stuff of Potter's plays. I remember discussing Potter's last plays, *Cold Lazarus* and *Karaoke*, with fellow members of the Glasgow SF Writer' Circle when they were shown on TV shortly after (or was it just before?) his death. Fans of the rackspaced strange recognise a kindred spirit in his essential weirdness, and they scoop it up into their big net of like-SF-but-not-SF as the bullet train of Genre whips it up into their reach, into that *slipstream* zone. Potter ripped up reality time and time again in his work, but often in subtle ways. Middle-aged adults playing children in summery idyll of *Blue Remembered Hills* transforms the meaning of the play in a fundamentally strange-fictional way, a conceit that gives it the faintly creepy quality of something not quite natural.

Watson's story, born in that same interzone of the mundane and the strange, snatches scraps of reality to integrate into its horror—grammar schools and cruel childhood games, skinned knees and scraped elbows—enough to give it not just the superficial mimetic quality of a plausible backdrop for a speculative thought experiment or a marvellous adventure, but to make that mimesis a purposeful component in its own right. Horror might be said to involve, more often than not, the irruption of the monstrous into the mundane; here, it can be argued, I think, there is an irruption of the mundane into the monstrous, in terms of the mode of storytelling, the purpose, the whole approach. As I say, it's a fucked-up little story.

Given that *Interzone* took its name from Burroughs's city, while "Jingling Geordie's Hole" lies, as I recall, at the extreme end of its output at that time, I think it's fair to say that a certain "fucked-up" aesthetic was at play in those early days of the magazine, before Cyberpunk, before the New Space Opera, before the New Weird, or Mundane-SF, or even Infernokrusher. Me, I always thought of it as a logical follow-on from the New Wave that gave us Ballard with his classic apocalyptic novel, *The Krushed World*, and Moorcock with his Infernal Champion series.

Oh, okay, yes. I made those up. So fuck? When you're driving a monster truck at literary conventions, reality is just another genre.

Impact Zone

So are we as much reacting to the horror and absurdity of the post-9/11 world as we are being ironic and silly?
David Schwartz

Imagine that bullet-train of slipstream derailed and crashing through brick walls of factory yards, ploughing its way across allotments, carriages whiplashing and shearing, sideswipes shattering garden sheds and greenhouses, bursting gas mains so they spout and blossom in great blooms of flame where the sunflowers should be; and imagine passengers or parcels scattered from their appointed places—numbered, lettered seats or shelves—thrown through the windows and French doors of inner-city flats or suburban semi-detacheds, to land in broken, bloody bits in the kitchen sinks and drawing rooms of Little Britain. (There's a decapitated head in the fruit bowl, Harold. That's nice, Marjorie.) Fuck that smeared zone of sliding, slithering meanings, of insubstantial streaming whirls of involuted definitions. Fuck that shit. Slipstream? The slipstream is an impact zone, not the confusion, not the area of collusion of separate forms of storytelling—of strange and mundane genres—but the *collision*.

Fire is Your Friend

I blew up the plums
that were in the icebox
and which you were probably saving for breakfast
forgive me
I like fire

Theodora Goss

I like fire. I used to play with matches as a kid, as kids often do. Me and my best mate would buy a pack of matches from the newsagents in the housing scheme where we grew up; then we'd gather litter, and light little fires, down by the train lines in the scrub of dirt beneath the footbridge where the glue-sniffers left their crisp pokes and tins of Bostik empty of all but the stink.

Later, as an adolescent, me and a different best mate would have lots of fun burning my collection of Christmas aftershaves, turning cans of hairspray into flamethrowers (like in that Bond movie, you know), even trying to burn the word FUCK into a football pitch during the World Cup. I much prefer fire to football, you see.

I made up stories as a kid, to get myself to sleep, about a hero known as Flash. (I was a big fan of those old Flash Gordon serials.) As an adult I somehow ended up resurrecting him in my fiction, in a bomb-throwing anarchist called Jack Flash. In his first appearance, he was blowing up an orgone-powered airship. He has a Zippo.

—Peachy keen, says Jack.

And the Very Soil Sown With Salt

Demolition is the new deconstruction.
Benjamin Rosenbaum

After a number of years attending the Glasgow SF Writer's Circle, in my early twenties perhaps, having had a number of short stories critiqued and having built up over the years a full shoe box of bits and bobs of background and plot ideas, chunks of paragraph and solitary sentences, novel synopses and poems and adolescent journals railing in petulant wrath against the injustice of the world, and notes, and more notes, and more and more and more notes, I found myself increasingly frustrated with my inability to bring it all into focus. The fragments refused to join up into stories. Or worse they latched onto each other, stuck and clumped together in ludicrous, jarring, clashing tales, misbegotten and misshapen by my inability to abandon what needed to be abandoned. I was a bit of a loon in those days, maybe—compulsively, almost schizophrenically syncretist, trying to "put it all together," find the grand, unifying story that all of it could be fitted into. It's still a tendency I have, to cross-wire, to combine, to cut-up-and-fold-in, smashing multiple stories into bits and splicing the smithereens back together as a single multi-threaded narrative. Krushing is fun. The point is that back then, no matter how I knew the theory—that old idea of painting out the bit you most like in the canvas, in order to let the picture work as a whole—I couldn't seem to put it into practice. Sometimes a favourite character has to be taken out into the desert and have his head caved in with a lead pipe. Sometimes an elaborate city you escape to in your juvenile dreams has to be burned to the ground and the very soil sown with salt. If you want to control what you write, have conscious control over it, rather than let it just be a vessel for your most self-serving fantasies, I reckon, sometimes you have to show it who's fucking boss. So one day I took my shoe box of scraps out to the same football pitch where I'd tried to burn the word FUCK all those years back, and I set fire to it, everything I'd ever written up to that day, every piece of fiction and non-fiction, all the sophomoric philosophy and puerile poetry, even the odd treasured tale that felt actually almost accomplished; I reckoned it had to be all or nothing. So I burned the whole fucking lot of it, and it felt fucking good.

However you take the whole wonderfully ludic and ludicrous idea of labelling a literary approach *infernokrusher*, I can honestly say, hand on my heart: fire is pretty. I much prefer fire to streams, whether they be mainstream, slipstream or a stream of yellow piss with which you write your name in snow.

The Answer is Yes

How far is the distance between infernos and krushing?
Theodora Goss

How far is the distance between *genre* and *mainstream*? Are they distant enough to get to terminal velocity as you put the pedal to the metal and accelerate from one towards the other? Or are they so close that they're already pressing in on one another, krushing what lies between them, in the interzone?

The Area of Turmoil

It didn't take long to realise what was on those shelves. It wasn't quite SF and it wasn't quite mainstream either. It was all stuff that wasn't one or the other, or books by mainstream writers that were marketed as mainstream but which, to the discern-

ing SF fan were actually distant relations of SF; or books by SF writers which might be acceptable to people who didn't think they liked SF; or mainstream novels written by SF authors, Iain Banks being a prime example... So it was obvious; slipstream was a catch-all for anything that [Forbidden Planet] thought they could sell, but which couldn't strictly be marketed as SF.

Erich Zann

I shared a flat for a while with Gary Gibson in the early '90s, while he and Erich were working on their slipstream magazine (even stood in for Erich at a convention once, in a Prisoner of Zenda ruse I probably owe apologies for), and in conversations with them and with the other writers of the Circle or mates who were fans of SF, it was interesting to see the division between those who just shrugged and pointed, able to say instinctively "this is slipstream," and those who were just utterly baffled by the term.

"Slipstream is just the area of turmoil where any two genres meet (in my opinion)," Erich wrote in his first editorial.

Many people complain about the vagueness of the term "slipstream," but I think a more precise definition for slipstream could conceivably be constructed from Sterling's article. Yes, slipstream is a grouping of fiction which largely consists of: a) mainstream works picked up by the genre; b) genre works splintered off into the mainstream. But what Sterling says is:

> ...Slipstream might seem to be an artificial construct, a mere grab-bag of mainstream books that happen to hold some interest for SF readers. I happen to believe that slipstream books have at least as much genre identity as the variegated stock that passes for science fiction these days...

Bruce Sterling

What these works have in common, I think, may be that they fuse the mimetic impetus of "mainstream" (i.e. REALIST) works with the semiotic approach of "genre" (i.e. ROMANTIC) works, while rejecting the formal strictures of both modes. Slipstream is, because of this, partly defined by the purists who identify these works by the absence of conventional strictures (and therefore reject them from the traditional canon, as not-quite-proper-SF or, conversely, not-quite-proper-mimetic-realism), and partly defined by the eclectics who identify these works by the presence of features of strangeness shared with SF (and therefore conscript them into the new canon).

Infernokrusher is more interested in cannons than canons. We have no conscripts, only kill-crazy berserkers.

T-Birds and Splatter-Patterns

Core infernokrusher fiction would never forget to fill up the tank.
Karen Meisner

One of the stories that went up in smoke when I burned everything was an adolescently "hilarious" balls-to-the-wall splatterpunk piece of nonsense called "Janet and John Go Shopping" or "T-Birds And Splatter-Patterns." I never could decide. It still survives in a critique copy or two somewhere out there, I suspect; there are members of the Circle who are inveterate hoarders. Craig Marnock is virtually our bloody archivist, in fact; I'm sure the bastard still has one hidden somewhere.

In its comic-book violence, the story wasn't exactly what you'd call realistic. Most of the action centred around a psychotic android (of sorts) and an equally psychotic Thunderbird-driving heroine. And most of it involved wanton destruction in a shopping mall. I believe I may have just discovered Hunter S. Thompson at the time. Or K.W. Jeter's *Dr. Adder*. Or *Alligator Alley*, by (allegedly) Dr Adder himself. Gonzo journalism, gonzo fiction, whichever it was, it rubbed off on me. I was never particularly interested in futurology. I just wanted to blow stuff up. But then, as David Moles's fragmentary (or is it fragged?) "Notes Toward an Infernokrusher Manifesto" tell us, so does Nature, so does God.

Well, yes. Blowing stuff up is fun, after all. Things go boom.

Peachy keen.

An Inner Identity

We only want Humour if it has fought like Tragedy... We only want Tragedy if it can clench its side-muscles like hands on its belly, and bring to the surface a laugh like a bomb.
The Vorticist Manifesto

Sterling, in his essay, identifies a range of characteristic qualities to slipstream. If he doesn't quite give a satisfactory definition he does at least give a description of slipstream's basis in "an inner identity, a coherent esthetic, a set of conceptual guidelines, an ideology if you will."

As Sterling characterises it, in terms of attitude, slipstream
    sarcastically tears at the structure of "everyday life"
    has an attitude of peculiar aggression against "reality"
    has, towards its material, a cavalier attitude

> opposed to the hard-SF "respect for scientific fact"
> violating the historical record of, for example
>> history
>> journalism
>> official statements
>> advertising copy
> treating these:
>> as raw material for collage work.
>> not as real-life facts

In other words…Fuck that shit. Fuck the laws of nature. Fuck known history and known science. Fuck the strictures of logic. This is strange fiction as the fiction of the stranger, the fiction which deliberately sets out to challenge even the epistemic modality of reportage, those texts which claim that the events they describe "*did* happen." At best these texts, in truth, manifest an alethic modality of "could have happened".

I've always been suspicious of everyday life, of the mundane world of newspapers and those who believe everything they read in them. When you're a sixteen-year-old queer and the papers are telling you all homosexuals are child-molesters, so the children must be safe-guarded, so this law must be passed preventing teachers from "promoting homosexuality," when you can't even debate this fucking Clause 28 in the school debating society because the law says you can't, well that makes for a pretty cavalier attitude towards the discourses out of which the "everyday" is constructed.

I've said elsewhen that I saw Clause 28 as some sort of absurdly, horrifically real Catch-22. Felt like I'd slipped right into another stream of time, you might say, a parallel world designed by Heller with a little hand from Kafka. I was never one to cry myself to sleep at night though in a—you know—girly kinda way.

Hell, no. When the world's fucked up like that it's time to reach for the flamethrower and the laughing gas.

That Little Posturing Puerile Ego

> *Are we just watching the repressed aggression of people who were bullied in elementary school, or is something else going on here?*
> **Matt Cheney, *The Mumpsimus***

It seems almost banal for me to say—as if it's news to anyone—that there's something of a tendency for put-upon geeks to revel in revenge fantasies of intricate detail, imagining sublime immolations and sledgehammers upon skulls. When you're a scrawny geek faggot growing up in small-town Ayrshire, it's quite easy to reach a peak of suicidal, homicidal fury and frustration that's almost ecstatic in its breathless height. You crank up the volume on the heavy metal, you pull on your black leather Gothgear and you re-imagine yourself as the very avatar of the Jungian shadow, righteous in your narcissistic rage. It's all bullshit, of course, pipe dreams of pipe bombs…until the day you actually walk into your high school with a shotgun.

What I'll say then, is: that's not infernokrusher; infernokrusher doesn't give a shit about such petty rationales as revenge. Infernokrusher takes that little posturing puerile ego out behind the bike sheds, gives him a cigarette and says, settle down. It's no fun blowing stuff up if you do it out of anger. Infernokrusher finds that sorta psychological self-abusing and self-excusing wish-fulfilment just plain dull. Infernokrusher is, as Benjamin Rosenbaum has quite rightly pointed out, as much about being krushed as it is about doing the krushing. The mere presence of monster trucks does not make art infernokrusher; it's what you do with them that counts.

Deconstruction/Demolition

Fuck Art. Gimme a goddamn knife.
Dr Adder, Alligator Alley

As Sterling characterises it, in terms of composition, slipstream
    contains non-realistic literary fictions
        which avoid or ignore genre SF conventions
            not using fantastic elements which are
                clearcut departures from known reality
                    futuristic
                beyond the fields we know.
            neat-o ideas to kick around for fun's sake
        but using fantastic elements which are
            ontologically part of the whole mess
            integral to the author's worldview
            in the nature of an inherent dementia
        tending to:
        not create new worlds
        but to quote them
        chop them up out of context
        turn them against themselves.
    has unique darker elements which often

>   don't make a lot of common sense
>   imply that:
>   nothing we know makes a lot of sense
> perhaps nothing ever could

Slipstream—sorry, *infernokrusher*—takes a cut-throat razor to the hackneyed clichés of both strange and mundane genres. It cannibalises them, retrofits them, treats them the way Godzilla treats Tokyo, the way Burroughs treats Interzone. Smash and grab. Cut up and fold in. Chuck a Molotov in behind you as you leg it. With a swaggering disregard for both the extrapolative thought-experiments of Rationalists and the escapist worldbuilding of Romantics, this approach to fiction is often, it seems, one that dissects pre-existing realms, drives an idea right through the heart of them, smashing them down to their constituent parts and then crushing those parts against each other to see what gives.

To me, that's as much a method or mode of writing as a genre, and maybe it *is* all down to what Sterling calls a postmodern sensibility. The mix of intellectualism and archness that I always think of, and that always makes me cringe, when I hear the word *postmodern* is maybe just my illusion, an occluded view of a process that's really part aesthetic reckoning (rather than dry, intellectual analysis) and part innocent, playful demolition job (rather than arch and knowing deconstruction).

Much of what we call science fiction rationalises the irrational, the fanciful, the fantastic, with its futurologies and extrapolations, while in much of what we call fantasy and horror those irrational elements are already rationalised, made sense of in their associations with desire and fear, the sense-of-wonder and the sense of the uncanny, rationalisations which may well play no small part in the subtextual psychodramas underlying even some of the hardest of HARD SF novels. Perhaps infernokrusher is confused with domestic realism because it takes an approach at once more playful and more serious. What if we allow the irrational to remain irrational? What if we reject the Romantic and Rationalist worldviews and say maybe there are no easy answers? What if we neither explicate nor excuse? What if we do not even allow the reader to compartmentalise the strange, to exile the incredible to a constructed elsewhen?

What if we just rev up the engine of the monster truck, lean forward over the steering wheel with a mad glint in our snickety-sharp grin, pull the hand-brake off and floor it? Destination immolation.

The Nature of the Catastrophe

> *HE WAS ON THE BRAWLING SPANISH STAIRS. HE WAS ON THE BRAWLING SPANISH STAIRS. HE WAS ON THE BRAWLING SPANISH STAIRS. HE WAS ON THE BRAWLING SPANISH STAIRS. HE WAS ON THE BRAWLING SPANISH STAIRS. HE WAS ON THE BRAWLING SPANISH STAIRS. HE WAS ON THE BRAWLING SPANISH STAIRS. HE WAS ON THE BRAWLING SPANISH STAIRS.*
>
> The Burning Man jaunted.
>
> **Alfred Bester, *The Stars My Destination***

On a hot summer day, about a thousand years ago, it seems, when I was sixteen years old, my brother stepped out into the path of a Ford Capri.

Death is full of surprises.

Fire up the inferno of a star with enough fuel and it'll go nova. Take it as far as it'll go and that star collapses under its own weight crushing itself into the singularity at the centre of a black hole, where the laws of physics themselves break down. That's a good metaphor for sorrow, I think, that great catastrophe of emotion, which hits us not unlike a big motherfucking monster truck.

We believe we know what "could have happened" and "what could not have happened." We're full of shit. Strange fiction, in its exploitation of the incredible, has always reminded us of that uncertainty, of the potential catastrophes awaiting us.

A Burning Box of Text

> *Infernokrusher is always intense.*
> **Karen Meisner**

As Sterling characterises it, in terms of style, slipstream
    may be conventional in narrative structure
    may screw with representational conventions, pulling stunts that
        get all over the reader's feet
        suggest that the picture is leaking from the frame
        such techniques as
            infinite regress

    trompe-l'oeil effects
    metalepsis
    sharp violations of viewpoint limits
    bizarrely blasé reactions to horrifically unnatural events
    concrete poetry
    deliberate use of gibberish.

If strange fiction manifests the alethic modality of "could not have happened," the strangest of the strange is that which does so with the sutura, shattering the very coherence of the narrative, the representation of an event as a process that runs from A to B to C, from beginning to middle to end. Acknowledging its own nature as fiction, this (post)modernism tears up its own structure, fucks with linearity, plays fast and loose with point-of-view, and generally challenges all aspects of mimesis in order to force the reader to recognise the process of semiosis at play. It breaks the fourth wall not to distance the reader from the narrative but to engage them with it directly, to drag the reader *into* it by rendering the experience of reading an aspect of the drama, to make the act of reading a dramatic encounter in its own right.

What this strange fiction is doing is upping the ante in terms of impossibility. Here we are offered not simply temporal impossibilities, not simply nomological impossibilities, but logical impossibilities, outright self-contradictions. The events shown contradict not just that set of contingent truths we hold to as known history and known science, the laws of nature; they contradict each other, contradict themselves, contradict reason itself. Beyond the counterfactual, hypothetical and metaphysical conceits of strange fiction, these quirks of narrative are best described as *pataphysical*.

Call it slipstream or infernokrusher, this is the strange fiction I found when, having stumbled into the SF Café, sitting down at the counter with my hand-made map of the ghetto of Genre in front of me, the ghost of a dead brother haunting me with visions of countless counterfactual worlds where history recorded no blood on the tarmac and innumerable hypothetical futures as yet unrealised, I turned from a burning box of text to look out from this entirely fictional scenario, through the shattered wall of a greasy spoon, at the reality of myself, sitting on a leather sofa, tapping out this sentence on my laptop: *As I look out my window now, through the curtains that close the room off from the night, I see that:*

- the crescent sun is high, the moon low;
- life is not for the faint-hearted;
   so why the fuck should art be?

Scottish author HAL DUNCAN's debut novel, *Vellum,* garnered nominations for the Crawford, Locus, BFS and World Fantasy awards, and won the Gaylactic Spectrum, Kurd Lasswitz and Tähtivaeltaja awards. He's since published the sequel, *Ink,* the novella *Escape from Hell!,* various short stories, a poetry collection, *Songs for the Devil and Death,* and two chapbooks, *The A-Z of the Fantastic City* from Small Beer Press and the self-published *Errata.*

www.ingramcontent.com/pod-product-compliance
Lightning Source LLC
Chambersburg PA
CBHW081207170426
43198CB00018B/2881